1916

A Global History

Keith Jeffery

BLOOMSBURY

NEW YORK · LONDON · OXFORD · NEW DELHI · SYDNEY

Bloomsbury USA
An imprint of Bloomsbury Publishing Plc

1385 Broadway	50 Bedford Square
New York	London
NY 10018	WC1B 3DP
USA	UK

www.bloomsbury.com

BLOOMSBURY and the Diana logo are trademarks of Bloomsbury Publishing Plc

First published in Great Britain 2015
First U.S. edition 2016

© Keith Jeffery, 2015
Map by John Gilkes

Endpaper image credits:
Left column (from top to bottom): The German battleship Schleswig-Holstein fires broadside
during the Battle of the Skagerrak © Mary Evans/Sueddeutsche Zeitung Photo; Senegalese troops
on the march at St Raphael on the French front June 1916 © Mary Evans/Robert Hunt
Collection/Imperial War Museum; Flora Sandes © Library of Congress.
Centre column: Verdun (France), Military cemetery of the armoured fort of Douaumont © akg-images;
Battle of Verdun 1916, a French infantryman on watch duty wearing a gasmask, 26 July 1916
© akg-images; Russian troops practicing bayonet drill, the Eastern Front, 1916 © Pictures from
History/Bridgeman Images; Waiting in line in Germany during 1916 © Mary Evans/Sueddeutsche
Zeitung Photo; British entering Dar-es-Salaam, East Africa © Mary Evans/Pharcide.
Right column: French colonial troops, Salonika Front © Imperial War Museum/Robert Hunt Library/
Mary Evans; Indian troops in East Africa © Illustrated London News Ltd/Mary Evans; A line of Italian
Alpine troops marches on Adamello © Mary Evans/Alinari Archives.

ISBN: HB: 978-1-62040-269-6
ePub: 978-1-62040-271-9

Library of Congress Cataloging-in-Publication Data has been applied for.

2 4 6 8 10 9 7 5 3

Typeset by Newgen Knowledge Works (P) Ltd., Chennai, India
Printed and bound in USA by Berryville Graphics Inc., Berryville, Virginia

To find out more about our authors and books visit www.bloomsbury.com.
Here you will find extracts, author interviews, details of forthcoming events and
the option to sign up for our newsletters.

Bloomsbury books may be purchased for business or promotional use.
For information on bulk purchases please contact Macmillan Corporate and
Premium Sales Department at specialmarkets@macmillan.com.

In memory of Peggy Visick, 30 May 1916 to 5 September 2009.
A reminder that good, as well as bad, came out of 1916.

Contents

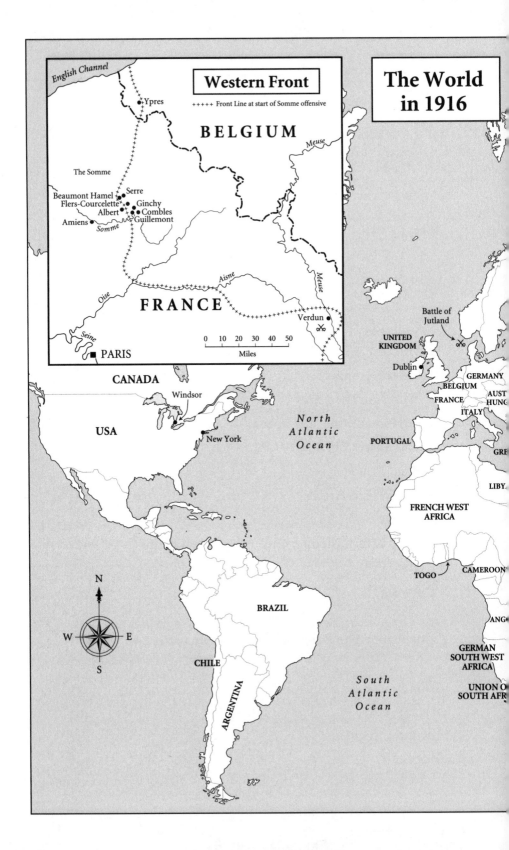

Western Front

+++++ Front Line at start of Somme offensive

English Channel

• Ypres

BELGIUM

Meuse

The Somme

Beaumont Hamel • Serre
Flers-Courcelette • • Ginchy
Albert • • Combles
Amiens • • Guillemont
Somme

Aisne

Oise

FRANCE

Meuse

Verdun •

Seine

■ PARIS

0 10 20 30 40 50
Miles

The World in 1916

Battle of Jutland

UNITED KINGDOM

Dublin •

GERMANY
BELGIUM
FRANCE   AUST HUNG
ITALY

PORTUGAL

GRE

LIBY

FRENCH WEST
AFRICA

TOGO   CAMEROON

CANADA

Windsor

USA

New York •

North Atlantic Ocean

BRAZIL

N
W   E
S

CHILE

ARGENTINA

South Atlantic Ocean

ANG

GERMAN
SOUTH WEST
AFRICA

UNION O
SOUTH AFR

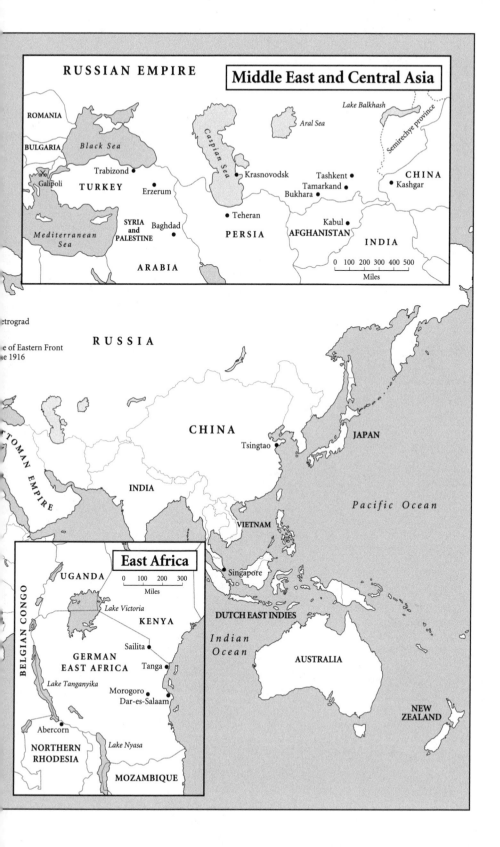

Middle East and Central Asia

RUSSIAN EMPIRE

ROMANIA

BULGARIA

Black Sea

Galipoli

Trabizond

TURKEY

Erzerum

Mediterranean Sea

SYRIA and PALESTINE

Baghdad

ARABIA

Caspian Sea

Aral Sea

Lake Balkhash

Semirechye province

Krasnovodsk

Teheran

PERSIA

Tashkent

Tamarkand

Bukhara

Kabul

AFGHANISTAN

CHINA

Kashgar

INDIA

0 100 200 300 400 500
Miles

etrograd

e of Eastern Front
e 1916

RUSSIA

OTTOMAN EMPIRE

CHINA

Tsingtao

JAPAN

INDIA

VIETNAM

Singapore

Pacific Ocean

DUTCH EAST INDIES

Indian Ocean

AUSTRALIA

NEW ZEALAND

East Africa

0 100 200 300
Miles

UGANDA

BELGIAN CONGO

Lake Victoria

KENYA

Sailita

GERMAN EAST AFRICA

Tanga

Lake Tanganyika

Morogoro

Dar-es-Salaam

Abercorn

NORTHERN RHODESIA

Lake Nyasa

MOZAMBIQUE

Introduction

On Sunday 6 July 1919, which was officially appointed to be a 'Public Thanksgiving Day' for peace throughout the United Kingdom, the Reverend John England preached a sermon in the small Irish Methodist Church at Athy, County Kildare, in which he meditated on the all-consuming nature of the recent war and its global compass.

> No matter where we went [he said], we could never get away – the thought was ever present & oppressive – newspapers, magazines, even picture houses & novels brought home constantly to minds that we were at war, that our men were laying down their lives on the far flung line of battle, that the best blood of youth & young manhood was being poured out like water on the plains of Flanders, the heights of Northern Italy, the wide spaces of Mesopotamia, the sacred spots of Palestine, hitherto unknown portions of Africa & the high seas.[1]

This book begins in Ireland, not just through this eloquent illustration of the extraordinary local and global impact of what rapidly became known as the 'Great War', but because events of the year 1916 are central to the twentieth-century creation and development of the states which now exist on the island of Ireland. The two most significant moments of the war for Ireland were Easter Monday 1916, when separatist republican nationalists launched a rebellion against British rule, and 1 July 1916, when the infantry assault at the battle of the Somme began, and men of the 36th (Ulster) Division, representing Unionism in Ireland, went over the top and suffered grievous casualties. Both of these experiences quickly became sanctified in their respective Irish political traditions and they have been stitched into the creation stories of both the Irish Republic and Northern Ireland.

The war provided both the moment and the mode for these Irish and Ulster demonstrations of devotion, commitment and military endeavour, both for and against the wider political objectives of the war. In this sense these specifically Irish events are just part of a much wider pattern, in which local loyalties, differences and antagonisms were everywhere affected and often amplified by the war itself. The experiences of the Easter Rising and the Somme thus exemplify the first main theme of this book, which is the inescapably global reach of the conflict.

The history of the First World War, as commonly understood in Britain and America, as well as France, has quite literally got stuck in the mud and trenches of the Western Front, in that blood-soaked frontier zone across the Low Countries and north-eastern France, which for centuries has been fought over by competing armies. This focus is understandable enough for the French and Belgians, for whom the conflict was above all a desperate war of national and territorial self-defence. The military involvement of the United States (as also of Canada) was primarily on the Western Front, and so for them, too, the focus is readily explicable. More British soldiers served and died here than anywhere else, and so, again, there is good reason for a concentration on this theatre of operations. In Britain, many schools organise tours to the easily visited battlefields of France and Belgium, and so many students study the 'war poets' (of whom Wilfred Owen has become the most deeply embedded in the national consciousness), that popular understanding about the war and 'the pity of war' is located in an imagined space in France and Flanders. Here, in the rich earth of the unforgettable Commonwealth War Cemeteries along the 'Old Front Line' is concealed the richer dust of the English fallen. For the most part, for most people, it is corners of French and Belgian foreign fields which are 'forever England'. Of course, Rupert Brooke, who coined these enduring images, did so before he departed, not for

France, but for the eastern Mediterranean, and, indeed, he perished before even arriving at any battle front.

Brooke's last journey east helpfully allows us to shift the focus away from Western Europe, for any study of the 1914–18 war which concentrates mainly on that region is profoundly flawed and limited. Only by placing the battles of France and Flanders in their wider context can we begin to approach a proper understanding of the First *World* War. My aim in this book has been to use emblematic events from each month of 1916 as hooks for a series of reflections through which the astonishing range, variety and interconnectedness of the wartime experience can be charted. Thus my exploration begins with Gallipoli (the destination Rupert Brooke never reached), where the future British prime minister, Clement Attlee, helped lay the plans for the evacuation completed in January 1916, and ends with Grigorii Rasputin sinking beneath the icy waters of the river Nevka in Petrograd at the end of December.

The impressively kaleidoscopic range of participants at Gallipoli – Turks, Arabs, French, Senegalese, Maltese, Indians, British, Irish, Anzacs – is characteristic of many other theatres and, here as elsewhere, I have endeavoured where possible to draw into the narrative sometimes marginalised participants in the war, non-combatants as well as soldiers, women as well as men. February and March take us to France – the iconic struggle for Verdun, where Germany aimed to bleed France dry (and very nearly succeeded) – and the crazy battle front along the Dolomites and Isonzo, where the Italians and the patchwork Habsburg army fought themselves to a standstill.

April brings the narrative to the Easter Rising in Dublin, imperfectly understood (not only in Ireland) as a First World War battlefield. Here the occasion of the Great War and the prevailing wartime mode of employing organised violence for national political ends provided for some separatists the most opportune moment to strike for freedom from the British Empire. The powerful infection of nationalism manifest in 1916, while temporarily blocked in Ireland, went on fatally to challenge Ottoman and Habsburg imperial systems. The battle of Jutland in May 1916 moves us away from terrestrial concerns to the maritime conflict which was worldwide from the very start, with naval engagements off the coasts of South America in the first months of the war. Here, too, we can explore the crucial (though debatably effective) naval blockade which was thought to have played such an important part in the Allied war effort. In part (but not solely) because of the blockade, the maritime struggle affected neutral countries and populations more extensively than any other aspect of the war. While Norway was neutral, for example, the Norwegians as a seafaring people could not escape the sufferings of the conflict. The port of Sandefjord in south Norway is famous particularly for whaling, but there is a First World War memorial even there with the names of thirty-two local men who were killed serving on ships lost during the conflict.

The Brusilov offensive in June takes the narrative to the Eastern Front where from the start there were colossal battles involving hundreds of thousands of soldiers and affecting further masses of civilians caught up in the wartime turmoil. It was the most successful Russian imperial offensive of the war, but one which helped terminally undermine the empire's capacity for further sustained involvement. The Easter Rising in Ireland, moreover, was far from being the only rebellion against imperial rule during 1916. In July a major revolt broke out in Russian central Asia, sparked off by the increasing war-prompted demands being imposed on the region's imperial subjects. This rebellion raised questions about the loyalty of Muslims, a concern which also troubled the British, who at the time ruled more Muslims than any other state. The wartime exploitation of colonial manpower by the British (and the French), as well as the Russians, threatened at times seriously to destabilise imperial rule and, as graphically illustrated in John Buchan's 1916 novel, *Greenmantle*, politicians and soldiers worried about the ominous threat of a German-backed Islamic holy war against the Allies.

Towards the end of August 1916 British Rhodesian and Indian troops captured the town of Morogoro in German East Africa (now Tanzania), which had been the German colonial administrative centre since the end of 1914. They believed in vain that the fall of the town would mark the end of enemy resistance, but in fact the Germans held out in Africa longer than anywhere else in the world, not surrendering until 25 November 1918. Although relatively small numbers of white troops were used in Africa, staggering numbers of indigenous Africans – totalling up to two million people – were conscripted and mobilised mostly for non-combatant duties, and perhaps 200,000 of them perished. The discussion of the war in Africa enables some consideration of this lost multitude of individuals who were war casualties as surely as the much more adequately recorded dead of Western Europe.

Although the first of July cannot (and is not) ignored, I have chosen to begin my exploration of the battle of the Somme in September, emphasising that (like Verdun) the Somme was a battle which lasted several months. At the battle of Flers-Courcelette on 15 September, moreover, the British first used tanks, a distinctive technological pointer to future warfare. The Somme, too, is for the British the most iconic of all First World War battles, characterised by Scott Fitzgerald as 'the last love battle', a moment when any residual public innocence about modern war was finally and brutally stripped away. October sees the Allied occupation of Athens, capital of a small neutral nation which was rather bullied by the British and French before coming into the war in 1917. Greece provided the main base at Thessaloniki for a huge Anglo-French army which toiled, to very little strategic effect, in a largely forgotten campaign against Austria-Hungary and Bulgaria in the southern Balkans. In the eastern Mediterranean, too, nationalist ambitions were encouraged by the British who backed the Arab Revolt of June 1916. But, hidden from the Arabs at the time, 1916 also saw the Anglo-French Sykes–Picot agreement, which partitioned the Ottoman Middle East between the Great Powers and laid the basis of the modern political map of the region.

The United States presidential election in November enables a discussion of the American dimension of the conflict which was to have so momentous an impact on the war. Although Wilson was elected on a 'keep America out of the war' platform, what in the end made the difference on the Allied side was the participation of the USA after April 1917. Over the first two years of the war much American opinion had become increasingly inclined towards the Allied side, and well before 1917 many Americans joined the war, both to fight and for humanitarian reasons. In some ways, the war came to the USA, too, through the covert activities of British and German agents,

the latter including saboteurs aiming to disrupt the supply of munitions and other war materiel across the Atlantic. At the very end of
1916 Grigorii Rasputin was murdered in Petrograd (St Petersburg).
This dramatic event, while it did not have the politically therapeutic
effects which its instigators hoped for, is symptomatic of how dysfunctional Russia had become, and (certainly with the ample benefit of
hindsight) it is clear that the old regime there was by this stage doomed,
and the appearance of revolutionary turmoil, as happened in 1917, was
only a matter of time.

This work is conceived as part of the growing appreciation and
understanding of the global dimension of the First World War apparent in recent scholarship. Even before the centenary of the conflict
prompted a rush of publications, Hew Strachan's magisterial study,
The First World War,[2] had laid down an impressively wide (and deep)
foundation. In *Fighting the Great War: A Global History*, Michael S.
Neiberg has shown what can be done in a single volume. Historians
of empire have valuably contributed to what might be called the
'global turn' in First World War studies. Nailing their colours firmly
to an imperial mast, Andrew Tait Jarboe and Richard S. Fogarty,
asserting that 'World War I was a conflict fought by empires to deter-
mine the fate of those empires', have described an 'imperial turn' in
the field.[3] Robert Gewarth and Erez Manela have edited an important
volume of essays which they (or their publishers) present as the 'first
history of the Great War as a global conflict of empires'.[4] This is a
little unfair on some older treatments by authors who themselves
were children of imperial states and well understood the broader
imperial ramifications of the conflict. Cyril Falls's *The First World
War* (published in 1960) is a good example of an earlier such study,
and it is absurd to imagine that such writers as John Buchan and
Arthur Conan Doyle did *not* understand that the war had an essential
imperial character. But Gewarth and Manela's chronology – 1911 to
1923 – valuably reminds us that a wider such perspective helps to
contextualise the conflict in significant ways. In this book, indeed, I
have sought to explore the longer-term ramifications and resonances
of events and developments identified in 1916. Here, in part, I follow
Jack Gallagher's location of a particular British period of 'imperial

crisis' which began in 1916 and lasted until 1922.[5] 1916 (not 1914) is also the starting point for Adam Tooze's mapping of the new global order of power which emerged following the war.[6]

A second main theme winds through the chronological exploration of 1916. The evidence of the year itself reveals a number of crisis points where the intensity of the war, often sharpened by a widespread sense that it might never end, began to cause fractures in the bodies politic of belligerent powers. Large-scale war can test states to destruction. This was undoubtedly true of the Great War, as shown by the fate, not just of the Russian empire, but the German, Ottoman and Habsburg empires too. The United Kingdom was not immune from this stress and did not itself escape unscathed from the war and its aftermath. The 1916 Easter Rising saw the first separatist shots fired in a campaign which was to destroy the United Kingdom of 1914 and lead to the secession of over twenty per cent of the country's land mass. And, if 'England's extremity was Ireland's opportunity' (as the nationalist mantra had it), other states' extremities equally provided opportunities for suppressed and unsatisfied nationalists (and others) to exploit the wartime situation.

The inevitable and progressive centralisation of control in all the belligerent states also put conditional loyalties under pressure. This was a special problem for multi-national states where dynastic loyalties could be strained by national ambitions. There is evidence, for example, of a crisis of legitimacy which from the winter of 1916/17 began to affect the Habsburg lands, though here socio-economic factors may have been as significant as national. The imposition, especially, of compulsory service – combatant or non-combatant – in places as far removed as Belgium, Vietnam, Nyasaland (now Malawi), Syria or Senegal alienated moderate opinion and stimulated resistance, which in some cases led to violent rebellion. When revolt occurred, moreover, the wartime circumstances almost inevitably led to draconian responses. Challenge was met with exemplary state violence, which in some places – Dublin, Trento, Beirut and Damascus, for example – produced martyrs whose memory helped sustain and amplify opposition.

In another sense, too, the increasing intensity of the war by 1916 had irrevocable consequences. The two titanic battles of the Western

Front, Verdun and the Somme, entailed such an investment of effort and sacrifice of life that the countries involved could afterwards scarcely conceive of any compromise peace. To be sure, the French were never going to be satisfied with anything less than the expulsion of the enemy from the national territory, including if at all possible Alsace and Lorraine, which the Germans had held since 1871. It was rather different for the British, yet the losses sustained on the Somme by the mass volunteer army raised in 1914 and 1915, far from provoking any widespread rejection of the war, seem to have produced a grim determination that the matter should be seen through to a finish, however great the cost. The Germans, too, despite the prodigious losses of Verdun and the Somme, dug in for a longer haul, encouraged in the east by the Russian offensive running out of steam and the unanticipated collapse of Romania.

The intensification of war was by no means limited to the battlefield. Increasingly, whole populations were drawn into a collective national effort in support of the war. In all the major belligerents the year 1916 saw efforts being stepped up to regulate domestic manpower and mobilise all sectors of the community behind the war. Women played a greater part than ever before, both at home and on the battlefield. This was a global phenomenon. African women stayed with von Lettow-Vorbeck's column to the very end in 1918. Azerbaijani women tried to stop troop trains carrying away their menfolk. French women unloaded stores in the Marseilles docks. American women campaigned for peace. Intrepid and skilled British nurses and ambulance drivers were to be found on the battlefields of Italy, Russia, Romania and Serbia.

Throughout this study I have also sought to investigate the human (and, happily, sometimes humane) dimension of the war experience. At the core of the story are the personal experiences of individual human beings, caught up in cataclysmic events which changed not just the world, but which affected and altered them, too, in ways which we sometimes can only guess at. It is one of the boons of military history that armies generally keep very good records, but these are often limited to the soldiers themselves. Those who carry weapons have been privileged by posterity; those who were killed in action especially so. The fallen in many cases have had their fate painstakingly recorded, most notably in the carefully tended war graves and memorials of the major belligerent powers. This is perhaps as it should be, but the focus on the dead sometimes occludes the fate of those who survived, and we can easily forget that some ninety per cent of the soldiers mobilised in the First World War survived it. So the historian must focus on the living as well as the dead.

The concentration on active combatants which characterises so many explorations of the war also serves to deflect attention from the shadowy masses of non-combatants, without whom the armies simply could not function. Many (though by no means all) of these men and women were very reluctant participants in the conflict, but I have attempted to include them in my narrative where possible. Among these people were huge numbers who were carried thousands of miles to the battle zone, from India, Africa and East Asia, for example, to the Western Front. They too deserve their history.

A final theme of the book, almost unavoidable now that we are marking the centenary of the conflict, is the 'memory' of the war. At intervals I have sought to explore the commemoration of some of the events and people of 1916. Spread across the world there are monuments of stone and bronze which survive to remind us of the war (if we have eyes to see them). Many of these are state memorials – like the graves of Unknown Warriors brought home to represent all their fallen comrades – which aim to embed the rituals of commemoration into a public and national narrative of dedication and service. Some are remote and not much cared for or visited, like the Northern Rhodesia monument by the Victoria Falls in Zambia, or the Habsburg cemeteries behind the old Isonzo front in Slovenia. And some, perhaps, are not yet built, nor may they ever be, for there are many hundreds and thousands of casualties of the Great War – men, women and children – who have no memorial at all.

I

Gallipoli

The Gallipoli campaign, which ended in January 1916, has a special resonance in the history of the First World War. It was the first Allied attempt to break away from the stalemate which had developed on the Western Front, and it was the first really integrated Anglo-French operation. Here, too, was the fullest mobilisation so far of British imperial resources, with manpower deployed from the United Kingdom, India, Newfoundland, and, above all, from Australia and New Zealand, whose Australia and New Zealand Army Corps – the 'Anzacs' – forged a particular reputation for dash and valour, as well as powerfully reinforcing the development of distinct national identities in Australia and New Zealand. On the opposing side, Ottoman and German forces proved to be more resolute and accomplished opponents than had been expected.

THE EVACUATION

For the Allies, the only unambiguously successful part of the whole ill-fated Gallipoli campaign was the evacuation, which occurred in two phases. The first, withdrawing the troops at Anzac and Suvla Bay, was completed over the two nights of 18/19 and 19/20 December 1915. The second phase involved the troops at Cape Helles and ended at about 4.30 on the morning of Sunday 9 January 1916. Despite dire predictions to the contrary, there were very few casualties, yet it still represented an ignominious defeat for the British and Allied war effort.

By the autumn of 1915 the forces on the Gallipoli peninsula had become bogged down in a sterile static campaign of trench warfare, rather like the situation which had existed on the Western Front since the autumn of 1914.[1] Unlike the Western Front, however, where withdrawal was not an option (at least for the French and Belgians whose territory had been occupied by the German invader), there was no national or military veto on evacuation from Gallipoli. Indeed, when General Sir Ian Hamilton, who had been in command from the start, was dismissed and replaced by Sir Charles Monro in the middle of October 1915, Monro was sent out with the express instruction from the secretary for war, Lord Kitchener, to report quickly on the alternative options of evacuation or a renewed offensive.[2] He arrived at general headquarters (GHQ) on the island of Imbros on 28 October and spent the next two days visiting the positions at Gallipoli and considering the problem. He doubted that any feasible new offensive could be successful. Apart from the Anzacs, he felt that the troops were 'not equal to a sustained effort', due to their inexperience, lack of training and 'the depleted condition of many of the units'.

Right from the start of the campaign the health of the troops had been a matter of concern. Miserable living accommodation, inadequate sanitary provision, poor diet and water shortages, not to mention unburied putrefying corpses on the battlefield, all contributed to a high sick rate. Dysentery was endemic. Writing in 1931 to Cecil Aspinall-Oglander, the British official historian of the campaign, Arthur Beecroft, who had been a signals officer, remarked on the chronic diarrhoea which everyone suffered. 'We had,' he wrote, 'a crude saying that the 11th Division went into battle grasping a rifle in one hand, and holding up its trousers with the other. There was hardly a man not so troubled, and I need not add what a depressing and devitalising effect such a malady has ... When one is rushing for the latrines dozens of times a day, as most of us were, esprit de corps soon oozes away.'[3]

Despite the fact that the headquarters staff had predicted that perhaps half of the troops and two-thirds of the guns would be lost in a withdrawal, at the end of October Monro recommended complete evacuation. Five years on, Major Orlando ('Orlo') Williams, the officer who had enciphered Monro's situation report, recalled the moment on 31 October when he had read it. 'Very few people knew the contents of that telegram,' he wrote. 'To those who did it gave the first ray of hope for the future – a hope that wise and definite decisions would be made at once, [and] that a waste of energy and lives on useless ends would cease.'⁴ Winston Churchill, whose brainchild the campaign had largely been, was more pithily grumpy in his war memoir. Monro, he wrote, 'was an officer of swift decision. He came, he saw, he capitulated.'⁵

But it was to be a while before London finally agreed. At first Kitchener favoured a renewed offensive. On 3 November he cabled Monro: 'I absolutely refuse to sign orders for evacuation, which I think would be the gravest disaster and would condemn a large percentage of our men to death or imprisonment.'⁶ He asked Monro to consult his three corps commanders. Only one, Sir William Birdwood, who commanded the Anzacs, opposed evacuation, principally on political grounds. He had spent most of his professional life in the Indian Army. 'From Indian experience,' he wrote, 'I fear the result in the Mohammedan world in India, Egypt and Mesopotamia.' This was 'the great bogy', as Orlo Williams put it: 'A triumph for the Turks, loss of British prestige, the East in flames, the Caucasus, Mesopotamia [Iraq], and Egypt overrun.'⁷

In the early twentieth century the British Empire was often celebrated as 'the greatest Muhammadan Power in the world'.⁸ Over 60 million of the 300 million inhabitants of British-ruled south Asia (comprising today's India, Pakistan, Bangladesh and Burma) were Muslim – and apprehensions about the potential of pan-Islamic mobilisation were common among the more 'Indian-minded' of British decision-makers. Throughout its whole existence – not just during the First World War – concerns about the ramifications which any decision anywhere in the British Empire might have elsewhere within its worldwide reach was a constant preoccupation for ministers, governors and generals. Fighting the Turks at Gallipoli, when the head of the Ottoman Turkish empire, Sultan Mehmet V, as caliph also claimed leadership of Muslims throughout the world, the worry was particularly acute. There was a wider problem of prestige, moreover, as A. J. Balfour (at the time First Lord of the Admiralty) noted. By abandoning Gallipoli 'we should lose credit in our own eyes, in those of our enemies, and in those of our friends. Quite apart from our prestige in the East . . . we have a character to lose in the West. To Russia the blow would be staggering.'[9]

Harsh military realities, however, overrode wider political concerns and, after Kitchener had inspected the theatre for himself, he decided that the two northern sectors at Suvla Bay and Anzac should be evacuated forthwith. 'Careful and secret preparations for the evacuation of the Peninsula are being made,' he reported to the prime minister, Herbert Asquith, on 15 November. But 'if undertaken it would be an operation of extreme military difficulty and danger'. A few days later Lord Curzon, a former Viceroy of India and now a Cabinet minister who certainly opposed evacuation on political grounds, painted a nightmare scenario of evacuation in a '"welter of carnage and shame", with panicking, frenzied men scrambling in the water, "being drowned by the hundred"'.[10] But opinion in London moved inexorably in favour of evacuation. Churchill, who had been under pressure for some time due to the failure of the campaign to deliver any breakthrough, resigned from the government on 15 November, removing the strongest opponent of the policy from the Cabinet. Exceptionally severe winter weather hit the peninsula during the last week in November, causing serious casualties (including 16,000 cases of frostbite and exposure) and reinforcing concerns about the costs of staying on over the winter months. Finally, on 7 December the Cabinet agreed to evacuate Suvla and Anzac, though they decided to hang on at Cape Helles for the meantime.

As Kitchener had noted, the staff at Gallipoli had already begun planning for an evacuation. Indeed, once the principle of withdrawal had apparently been conceded, Orlo Williams recalled that 'preparations were pushed on with the utmost haste, for the prospect of winter storms hung over us like an evil spectre'.[11] The preliminary evacuation plans envisaged three stages. The first, which could be implemented before a final decision was made, involved reducing the number of troops to that required 'for a purely defensive winter campaign'. The second stage would be implemented once the decision to withdraw had been made. At this point 'force and material would be reduced until there remained only a bare sufficiency to enable the positions to be held for a week against attack'. In the final stage 'this diminished garrison was to be withdrawn with the greatest possible speed, no special effort being made to save any more material'.[12]

But it was a tall order to see the safe withdrawal of just over 80,000 men, along with huge quantities of guns, stores and equipment. The 'main thing', as put in the instructions prepared by staff officers at Suvla, was 'to deceive enemy for ten days'. In order to cover the initial troop movements Brigadier General Brudenell White, chief of staff of the Anzac Corps, also devised a system of 'quiet periods' during which in the final days there were regular suspensions of firing (especially at night) from the Allied side, though if there were Turkish attacks these were to be strongly resisted. Thus the Turks, thinking that the Allies were merely settling into a defensive winter posture, would become accustomed to periods of inactivity along the front.

While most of the support formations and a fair number of the front-line troops were evacuated, various cunning schemes were devised to deceive the Turks into thinking that nothing unusual was under way. Supplies apparently continued to be moved in: 'Carts went up at night empty but returned full of trench stores, troops in the front line being fed from reserves already prepared.' Activity on the beaches was sustained as much as possible. The casualty clearing stations, which were in full view of the enemy, were 'evacuated and almost empty for several days'. Special parties of men were instructed to keep fires lit in the tents, while ambulances continued to operate 'as if to remove sick and wounded to casualty clearing stations at the usual hours. They were always nearly empty.'[13] Nevertheless, concerned that there might be serious casualties in the final stages, it was anticipated that some medical personnel would have to 'remain on the Peninsula until after the evacuation has been completed, to tend such wounded as cannot be embarked'.[14] 'It is,' wrote Walter Campbell, a headquarters staff officer, on 18 December, 'of course impossible to say how many men we may lose in the final withdrawal when the Turks tumble to what we are up to, and it will of course be inevitable if they attack heavily, that we must leave wounded behind.'[15]

The final withdrawal from Suvla and Anzac was set for the night of 19/20 December and in the end no-one was left behind. At Anzac, Brudenell White's careful planning paid off. Detailed timetables were prepared for the movement of over 10,000 men on the last night. In order to muffle the sound of the operation, the men were ordered to wear socks or sandbags over their boots, while torn-up blankets were placed on the floor of trenches. The 'drip rifle', a device which became embedded in Anzac folklore, was developed to deceive the enemy after the last troops had left the front line. The invention, ascribed to a Lance Corporal William Scurry from the Melbourne suburb of Essendon, involved dripping water into an empty bully beef or kerosene can attached to the trigger of a rifle left loaded and aimed towards the Turkish trenches. Thus sporadic fire could be maintained after the trenches had been evacuated. Another ruse at Suvla produced a similar effect. When the final party left the trenches on the last night, 'candles were left burning at intervals. In each candle there were two or three fuses which, as the candle burned to the point of juncture – fuse and candle – the fuse was set off and the noise very similar to a rifle shot was exploded.'[16]

Among the soldiers at Suvla was Captain C. R. Attlee of the 6th Battalion, South Lancashire Regiment, who in 1945 was to head the first Labour majority government in Britain. Clement Attlee was deployed as part of the rearguard and given the task of holding 'the last line, known as the Lala Baba defences' on the southern side of the Suvla sector. Attlee's job was to hold the line until the remainder of the withdrawal had successfully been accomplished. According to an admiring biography by Francis Beckett, 'Clem was the last but one soldier to leave Gallipoli', followed only by the divisional commander, General F. S. Maude. Attlee's own account is typically more downbeat. Late in the afternoon of 19 December, and in command of 250 men and six machine guns, he had to hold trenches around the small hill of Lala Baba just behind the front line. Parties of men withdrew through Attlee's position all night until 'about 3.30 [a.m.] word came that the parties holding the wire halfway had closed the gaps and were coming through . . . All this time everything was very peaceful though there were occasional shots to be heard from Anzac [just to the south]. Then we got the order to move.' Bringing up the rear, he sent his men up the communications trench, and on to the beach. Here they found 'a few military police, General Maude and a few of the Staff. We went on board lighters which seemed to go round and round. Flames shot up from the dumps of abandoned stores.' The unit war diary is even more laconic: 'Capt C. R. Attlee's party after remaining in the Lala Baba defences until the evacuation was completed then embarked his party on H.M.T. [His Majesty's Transport] Princess Irene & proceeded to Imbros.'[17]

The evacuation caught the enemy completely by surprise, though there had been rumours that the Allies might withdraw. The German general Hans Kannengiesser, who commanded the 9th Ottoman Division in the Suvla sector, recalled in his memoirs that when they noticed increased Allied activity over the night of 19/20 December they thought it 'must either indicate the commencement of the English retirement, or we had to expect a large-scale attack to-morrow'. At about three o'clock in the morning (just as Clement Attlee and his men were preparing to move down to the beach) a 'steadily increasing mist commenced rising which hid the full moon which so far shone, and clouded the English activities in a curtain which we were neither able to pierce nor penetrate'. While some Turkish colleagues continued to believe that the Allies were 'bringing new troops ashore', by about five o'clock or so, it had become clear to Kannengiesser that 'the enemy was actually evacuating'. The retreat, he conceded, had been 'splendidly prepared and very cleverly carried out . . . even if, as the opponent, I found their success rather painful'.[18]

On 27 December the Cabinet in London decided to evacuate the remainder of the troops from Gallipoli. The very success of the Suvla and Anzac withdrawals made any similar operation from Cape Helles more hazardous than it would otherwise have been. 'It seemed too much to expect that the same trick would come off twice running,' thought Eric Wettern, a sapper at Cape Helles. Charles Callwell (Director of Military Intelligence at the War Office in London in 1916) later described it as 'a decidedly more difficult affair'.[19] Partly this was because of the advance warning provided by the 19/20 December withdrawals, but the operation was also technically trickier. Writing on 4 January, Lieutenant Colonel Norman Burge of the Royal Naval Division reflected on the difference between Anzac and Cape Helles. Whereas at Anzac, for example, the front line was 'not, I believe, more than 1500 yards from the beach', at Helles, 'here we are about 4 miles, and you have to stick to single file in communications trenches practically all the way – that delays things and wearies heavily laden men frightfully'. Burge also believed that the secret was already out: 'I'm convinced they think we're going down here, because they've taken to shelling the beaches all night.'[20]

From the last few days of December 1915 onwards there was a staged withdrawal from Cape Helles. General Sir Francis Davies, who as commander of VIII Army Corps was in overall charge of the evacuation, immediately arranged the removal each night of 'as large a proportion as possible of stores, animals and vehicles not required for the final defence of the position'. Ancillary personnel were removed, men of the Greek Labour Corps being sent away 'under the pretext that the severe shelling of the beaches no longer made their retention justifiable', and told that they would return after the Turkish guns had been silenced.[21]

By 2 January, apart from a few guns, the last of the French troops on the peninsula had been evacuated and replaced with men from the Royal Naval Division. But in order to conceal the departure of the French, when the sailors 'got to exposed parts of the line' they 'had to don French caps, which did not suit our style of beauty at all. Considering that at certain points Johnny [Turk] had an excellent view, not only of our caps but of our boots as well, it was a somewhat feeble disguise.' On the other hand, in this sector, the French and Turks had evidently come to an accommodation for day-to-day survival. Their lines were on opposite sides of a precipitous gulley running down to the sea at points along which the communication trenches 'were in full view of the chaps opposite, without any possibility of protection'. The French and Turks, however, had placed two flags – one French, one Turkish – on trees down near the beach, and 'as long as nobody, from either side, ventured beyond these flags, there was to be no rifle fire during daylight hours in this particular region'. Eric Wettern thought that it made the line there 'an absolute rest-cure'. Here, in an olive grove, 'one found chaps placidly leaning over the parapet, or sitting on it'. Wettern 'then and there formed the resolve that if ever I should have occasion to run a private war of my own, I would organize it on similar lines. I am sure,' he concluded, 'it would be well attended.'[22]

The final evacuation was scheduled for the night of Saturday 8 January, but there was an alarm on the late afternoon of the 7th when the German commander of the Ottoman Fifth Army, General Liman von Sanders, launched a push at Gully Spur on the western end of the British line. Having been able to reinforce their artillery with guns from Suvla and Anzac, the Turks began the assault with an especially concentrated barrage. Fearing that the enemy had got wind of the planned evacuation, the weakened British garrison resisted fiercely and found the opposition unexpectedly reluctant to press home the attack. The Turks, moreover, interpreted the determined British defence as evidence that they intended to remain on the peninsula.[23]

Some of the units at Cape Helles, such as those of the 29th Division (though inevitably, and sadly, rather fewer of the men), had been on the peninsula from the very start. On 2 January 1916 the 1st Battalion, Royal Dublin Fusiliers – some of whom had been carried onto 'V' Beach in the armoured ex-collier *River Clyde* and suffered horrific casualties on the first day, Sunday 25 April 1915 – returned to the exact same place to be transhipped from the *Clyde* to a transport taking them to Mudros. According to the regimental history, of those who had 'stormed ashore' in April (some 900 men), 'there remained at the final evacuation no more than *eleven* noncommissioned officers and men who had served continuously throughout the campaign'.[24]

The 1st Royal Inniskilling Fusiliers had also landed on the first day, at 'X' Beach to the north-west of the Cape, but 'without a casualty'.[25] They, too, remained until the very last day, and their war diary provides one of the most detailed and vivid records of the evacuation. On 3 January 1916, having relieved the 1st Border Regiment in the firing line, they were making 'Improvements and repairs to Fire Trenches, Saps, etc, repairing Communication Trenches to facilitate retirement, preparing obstacles, clockwork Rifles etc.' On 5 January: 'Preparation of Obstacles and Booby traps, . . . blocking up side trenches, making Dummy figures, fixing up barbed wiring and removing surplus stores to Brigade Dump.' Just before midday on 8 January the battalion was told it was 'Z. day EVACUATION'. A strict timetable had been arranged for the withdrawal of the men in three more or less equal groups. Before dusk the first third moved out, followed shortly after by the second. 'Then a long wait ensued, the normal procedure was followed, firing and bombing allowed to die down and at 11.45 p.m. the final parties . . . commenced their move down to the Battalion control.' After the last men arrived, a party of sappers placed 'obstructions and devices behind the troops – The C.O. wired "all safely proceed" to the Bde [Brigade] Control, disconnected, destroyed the telephone line & proceeded to rejoin the party,' which made its way down to 'W' Beach, at the western end of the Cape itself. 'On the whole march down nothing was to be heard but a slight shuffle of the muffled feet and an occasional shot or bomb from the ever lengthening distant Turkish trenches shewing the enemy were still in ignorance that we had withdrawn.' They were taken off the beach at about 2.50 a.m. to a destroyer which left for Imbros about an hour later. 'There were no casualties.'[26]

As at Suvla, General Maude was one of the last men off the beach. Two brigades from his division had been taken from Suvla to help hold the final positions at Cape Helles, and he was personally determined to see them off safely. Despite the broadly self-congratulatory tone which suffuses many reports of the Gallipoli withdrawals – fuelled as much as anything else by relief at the almost complete absence of casualties – the story of Maude's experience reflects the anxiety and confusion which inevitably accompanied the operation. The last of Maude's troops to retire were scheduled to do so from makeshift jetties at Gully Beach, the most northerly and exposed beach on the western shore of the peninsula. Shortly after two o'clock on the morning of 9 January, in deteriorating weather conditions, one of the two lighters evacuating Maude's men ran aground and could not be moved. Judging that the rising wind would prevent any replacement vessel (which would take some time to arrive) from approaching the beach, Maude decided to march his remaining

160 men the two miles south to the more sheltered 'W' Beach. By this stage the front-line trenches had been evacuated for over two hours, and there were increasing fears that if the Turks cottoned on to the withdrawal the beaches would come under intense bombardment. At 'W' Beach, too, the worsening weather was making matters difficult. At about 3 a.m. the bulk of Maude's party arrived, but by 3.30 there was still no sign of the general himself. It turned out afterwards that some of Maude's luggage had been left on the beached lighter and he had gone back to find it.

Time now was running very short indeed. Along the shore, stores and equipment which could not be taken off had been mined and the forty-five-minute fuses had been lit at 3.15. One of the embarkation staff at the beach, a Newfoundlander, Lieutenant Owen Steele, was sent to find Maude and the rest of his men. 'I went up over the hill,' he wrote in his diary the following day, 'and shouted the General's name until I eventually found him and so soon hurried them on board the waiting lighter . . . However we got on board at just 5 mins. to 4, and within 5 mins. and before we had even untied from the wharf, the first magazine went off with a very heavy explosion.' Other mines soon went off: 'there were fires everywhere, and it was really a wonderful sight'. Steele thought it 'fortunate that we left when we did', as the wind was dead in-shore and 'increasing every minute . . . What we were afraid of more than anything was that the fires and the explosions would draw Turkish shell fire.' In fact, according to Cecil Aspinall-Oglander, one thing holding the Turks back from shelling the beaches was the deteriorating weather which helped persuade them that 'the embarkation of troops was out of the question'.[27]

William Birdwood recalled that Maude's panic over 'his valise' and the consequent hold-up was 'much to the annoyance of those waiting', one of whom wrote a parody of the famous Tennyson poem:

> Oh, come into the lighter Maude,
> The fuse has long been lit;
> Oh, come into the lighter Maude,
> And never mind your kit.
> The seas rise high,

> But what care I?
> I'd rather be seasick
> Than blown sky-high –
> So come into the lighter, Maude,
> Or I'm off on the launch alone!

'One can afford to laugh at such incidents now,' wrote Birdwood a quarter of a century later, 'but it was a night such as I should never wish to go through again.'[28]

General Davies reported after the evacuation that, while it had been 'an entire success', the 'gradually increasing strength of wind and sea throughout the night caused a great deal of anxiety up to the very last'. Writing notes for Aspinall-Oglander some years later, he recalled that on the last full morning, 8 January, he had been 'by no means happy about the weather'. When he got up he 'looked out on a glassy sea but there was an ominous swell coming in from the westward, the almost inevitable precursor of wind'. During the afternoon the sea conditions deteriorated, but by this time the evacuation orders were irrevocable and nothing could be done; 'we could merely watch the rising swell'. In order to take the minds of his staff off the situation Davies got them to play bridge, 'the only time in my life I have ever played cards by daylight'. Davies was himself 'not at all fond of bridge', but he claimed it was 'an excellent sedative . . . and it kept us all from fussing'. 'What a miracle the whole thing was. . .', he mused, and how the wind 'did blow after it was all over'.[29]

Davies was justly pleased about 'the withdrawal, and successful embarkation of 16,900 men and 35 guns from a position 8,000 yards in length at an average distance of 100 yards from the enemy and in some places within as near as 15 yards from his trenches'.[30] And the feared casualties did not materialise. Callwell reported that one sailor was 'killed by debris from a prematurely exploding mine'. Norman Burge left the peninsula thankful that in the Royal Naval Division there had been just one man with 'a stray bullet in the leg' and three with sprained ankles, 'so it was pretty marvellous'. And he did not hate the enemy: 'I'm sorry to part with the Turk – he's a whiter man than many I've met and all of us would be only too delighted to join up with him and

give the Greeks and Bulgars what they thoroughly deserve and ought
to get.'[31]

EASTERNERS AND WESTERNERS

The idea of launching an attack against Turkey was a direct result of
the static situation which had emerged along the Western Front in
Belgium and France from the autumn of 1914. After the great German
thrust into France had been halted at the battle of the Marne in
September 1914, French armies (with British and Belgian support)
turned back and sought to outflank the Germans and there was a race
to the northern French and Belgian coast. By the end of November
1914 both sides had established opposing lines of positions – the
Western Front – running from the Channel coast to the Swiss border
and which was to be the main battle zone in Western Europe for the
next four years. Reluctantly, the British were drawn into a land
commitment which inexorably, it seemed, required the deployment of
a continental-style mass army. British war planning before August
1914 had envisaged some military 'Continental Commitment', but it
had also been anticipated that, in the event of being drawn into a
conflict at the side of France against Germany, the military demands
could be limited and Britain's main contribution might be naval and
economic. 'Events', however, so often the driver of decision-making,
dictated otherwise. To be sure, Lord Kitchener, the towering imperial
pro-consul who had been appointed secretary for war at the outbreak
of hostilities, foresaw that something more than Britain's small professional army would be required and he immediately launched an
appeal – 'Britons! Your Country Needs You' – for recruits. But
Kitchener's 'New Army' would not be ready to fight for at least a year,
if not longer, and in the meantime on the Western Front the British
were largely restricted to acting in coordination with the French.

The entry of Turkey into the war in November 1914 on the side of
the 'Central Powers' (Germany and Austria-Hungary), however,
offered new opportunities both for striking at the enemy and also
exploiting Britain's naval power. Envisaged at first as a purely naval
operation, a scheme was devised to break through the fortified

Dardanelles – the narrows at the Mediterranean entrance to the Sea of Marmara – and move on to threaten the Turkish capital of Constantinople (Istanbul). Strongly backed by Winston Churchill (the First Lord of the Admiralty) and other senior ministers in Herbert Asquith's government, including David Lloyd George (Chancellor of the Exchequer), as well as Andrew Bonar Law (Leader of the Opposition), the proposal offered an attractive, and relatively low-cost, opportunity to knock the Turks out of the war. It would also bring strong encouragement to Britain and France's ally, Russia, and open up a supply route through the Bosphorus to the Black Sea. In January 1915 the British War Council agreed to proceed with the scheme. The French, concerned that a successful operation would put the British in an unassailably powerful position in the eastern Mediterranean, insisted on taking part, so it became an Allied, Anglo-French affair.

Like many imaginative schemes (civilian or military), with what in more recent times would be called 'mission creep', the extent of the operation and the resources required began to escalate. It was accepted that some troops would be required to complete the destruction of the shore batteries and secure the Gallipoli peninsula on the west side of the narrows, and units of the Royal Naval Division (an infantry division composed of Royal Navy and Royal Marine reservists not required at sea) were earmarked for this. Kitchener, moreover, was persuaded to commit additional forces should more extensive land operations be required. In Egypt, the Australian and New Zealand Army Corps, originally en route to Europe, were readied for deployment, and the regular 29th Division was sent out from Britain. The French also promised to supply a division. On 12 March 1915 General Sir Ian Hamilton was appointed to command what had now become the 'Mediterranean Expeditionary Force'.

Meanwhile the naval planners had underestimated the difficulty of forcing the narrows, which were strongly protected by mines and well-sited Turkish batteries. After a number of preliminary bombardments had alerted the Turks to the vulnerability of their positions, in mid-March 1915, an Anglo-French naval attack with eighteen battleships was beaten back with the loss of three capital ships (two British and one French) and three more badly damaged. Concluding that a purely naval operation could not succeed, it was decided to land troops on the peninsula in order to neutralise the guns before renewing the effort to send warships up the narrows.

Thus the Gallipoli campaign began on 25 April 1915 with simultaneous landings at Cape Helles, at the southernmost tip of the peninsula, and what became known as 'Anzac Cove', some twenty miles north on the western shore, where men of the Australia and New Zealand Army Corps were first blooded in the war of 1914–18. The experience of different units varied markedly. Around Cape Helles, there was a bloodbath at both 'V' Beach, where the Dublin Fusiliers and Munster Fusiliers, with some men of the Hampshire Regiment, were cut to ribbons, and 'W' Beach where the Lancashire Fusiliers famously 'won six Victorian Crosses before breakfast', while the subsidiary landings at 'X' and 'S' Beaches (west and east of 'W' and 'V') were achieved with negligible casualties. By the end of 26 April, nevertheless, beachheads had been secured at both Helles and Anzac. While the troops at Cape Helles were eventually able to push about four miles inland, those at Anzac, faced with precipitous slopes, never managed to capture territory much more than about a mile from the shore. In August 1915 there was an attempt to break the stalemate with coordinated attacks at Helles and Anzac and fresh landings at Suvla Bay, just north of Anzac, but this merely resulted in more troops being pinned down by increasingly well entrenched and supplied Turkish forces.

The decision in London to back what became the Gallipoli campaign marked the first stage of a strategical debate which was to continue for the rest of the war, and which became characterised as 'Easterners' versus 'Westerners'. For Westerners, the principal enemy was Germany, and the *only* important theatre of operations was the Western Front, in keeping with (as General Sir Henry Wilson put it) 'the old principle of decisive numbers at decisive theatre'.[32] Clearly for the French (as also the Belgians), whose territory had been invaded and occupied, expelling the Germans had always to be the chief war aim. Even though most British soldiers agreed that defeating the Germans on the Western Front was the primary task, among politicians, at least, Britain's traditional suspicion of continental European entanglements, combined with the global reach of British imperial interests, prompted them to look beyond North-West Europe. The apparent tactical paralysis of the Western Front, and its appalling human cost, powerfully encouraged decision-makers to explore any possible alternatives. The imperial world view of many British politicians and officials was also important. The involvement of the Ottoman Empire in the war focused British attention on its vulnerabilities in the Mediterranean and Middle East, along the vital line of imperial communications through the Suez Canal and Red Sea to India and beyond. After all, turbulence in the region had led to the British acquisition (with France) of a controlling interest in the canal, as well as the occupation of Cyprus in the 1870s and Egypt in the 1880s. It was no accident that the Anzac troops were available in the region since any forces coming from Australia or New Zealand would normally pass through the eastern Mediterranean, and being deployed against the Turks in Gallipoli could make as much, if not more, sense to people in the Antipodes than fighting Germans in France and Flanders.

THE ARMIES OF GALLIPOLI

In the concluding words of his book, *The Tragedy of the Dardanelles*, Edmond Delage, a prolific French author on military topics in the interwar years, reflected on the extraordinary range of combatants who fought on the Allied side in the campaign: 'Superb Anzacs, nimble Gurkhas, laughing Senegalese, sailors who fought under Guépratte and de Robeck [the French and British naval commanders], soldiers of France and of all the counties of old England, you! All of you, what heroes! But – to what end did you die?'[33] Many observers, indeed, remarked on the extraordinary variety of personnel at Gallipoli. Strolling round the rear area at Cape Helles, the Irish journalist-cum-soldier Ivan Heald likened it to being 'behind the scenes at a circus. There are Egyptian soldiers, Zouaves, Turcos, Senegalese, French cavalry – all sorts and colours of costumes.'[34] To a greater extent than anywhere on the Western Front, the mixture of nationalities cheek by jowl in the crowded beach-side camps, combined with the exotic, and to some romantic, foreignness of the Mediterranean location (with its inevitable Classical resonances), meant that Gallipoli exemplified the remarkable global reach of the Great War.

Despite the range of soldiers deployed on the peninsula, by far the largest proportion of the troops came from the United Kingdom. These men, moreover, included a representative sample of the types of soldiers who comprised the wartime British armed forces. Of the troops who landed at the start, the 29th Division were almost all regular soldiers: pre-war long-service professionals who had been assembled from garrison units scattered across the empire at the start of the war. The Royal Naval Division had been formed principally from naval reservists surplus to requirements in the sea-going navy. By the end of June 1915, they had been joined by Territorial divisions, composed of pre-war volunteer soldiers, and in August came 'New Army' divisions – 'Kitchener's men' – the volunteers who had enlisted after the outbreak of the war: the 10th (Irish), 11th (Northern) and 13th (Western) Divisions.

Deployed at the start, too, was the Anzac Corps, comprising the 1st Australian and the 'New Zealand and Australian' Divisions. Both British Dominions had rallied loyally to the flag on the outbreak of the war. The Australian premier, Sir Joseph Cook, had declared that 'when the Empire is at war, so is Australia', and the leader of the Labor Opposition, Andrew Fisher, promised Australia's 'last man and last shilling' in support of Great Britain. In Wellington, W. F. Massey undertook that the New Zealand government would 'send an expeditionary force to the assistance of the Mother Country' if required.[35] By the beginning of November 1914 the first contingents from the two Dominions had left for Egypt. In the end, of the total 407,000 'British Empire' troops in the campaign, some 50,000 Australians and 9,000 New Zealanders served on the peninsula.[36]

The forces at Gallipoli also included 4,500 men of the British-run Indian Army. The 7th Indian Mountain Artillery Brigade, manned by Sikh and Punjabi Muslim gunners, were 'the only allied Muslim troops [continuously] in action against the Turks on the peninsula'. They were joined by the 29th Indian Infantry Brigade, composed of two battalions of Punjabis, one of Sikhs and the 6th Gurkha Rifles, which landed at Cape Helles at the beginning of May 1915. But after some sharp fighting, the high command, worried about the significant proportion of Muslims in the two Punjabi battalions, replaced them with two Gurkha battalions. At the third battle of Krithia early in June, the 14th Sikhs suffered over eighty per cent casualties in a fight which greatly impressed the British commander-in-chief, Sir Ian Hamilton. Quoting from a letter 'which was published in the Indian press', he wrote: 'The history of the Sikhs affords many instances of their value as soldiers, but it may be safely asserted that nothing finer than the grim valour and steady discipline displayed by them on the 4th June has ever been done by soldiers of the Khalsa [the nation of the Sikhs].'[37]

The brigade, having suffered very heavy casualties on the Cape Helles front in June and July, was withdrawn and re-formed before being returned to Anzac, where it fought alongside British and Australian troops in the August battle for the Sari Bair ridge. Major Cecil Allanson of the 6th Gurkha Rifles recorded the savage intimacy of the fight: 'At the top we met the Turks; Le Marchand went down, a bayonet through the heart. I got one through the leg, and then, for about ten minutes, we fought hand to hand, we bit and fisted, and used rifles and pistols as clubs; blood was flying about like spray from a hairwash bottle. And then the Turks turned and fled, and I felt a very proud man.' But, pursuing the Turks off the hill, Allanson and his men appear to have come under 'friendly fire' (Allanson blamed the navy) which drove them off the summit and the position was lost.[38]

Another formation from British Asia was the Ceylon Planters' Rifle Corps, a volunteer unit originally formed by Europeans in Ceylon (Sri Lanka) in 1900. At the beginning of the war nearly three hundred members of the unit immediately volunteered for overseas service. Posted to Egypt, they were attached to the Anzac Corps, though many of them, being 'either University or English Public school men' (Charles Bean called them 'fine young Englishmen'), secured commissions in other formations. The remaining seventy-five or so, nicknamed the 'Tea Leaves', landed at Anzac on the first day and served through the campaign as General Birdwood's guard and personal escort; indeed they accompanied him to France, until the last few were disbanded in September 1916.[39]

By far the largest non-British contingent at Gallipoli was the French, who were committed to the campaign for political and strategic reasons. With historic interests in the Levant and eastern Mediterranean, the French were sensitive to any British encroachments in the region. When British plans for a purely naval attack on the Dardanelles Straits emerged early in 1915, the French insisted on being involved. As the French Minister of Marine, Victor Augagneur, later put it: 'Not to take part in the operation would have been, in case it succeeded, to witness the appearance of the English fleet alone before Constantinople.' Considering existing French involvement in the region, 'it would have been a very painful renunciation of our national pride and perilous for our interests'.⁴⁰ As a result, while conceding overall British command, a squadron of French warships (to which was attached the Russian cruiser *Askold*) took part in the naval operations. As the potential for military operations developed, the French determined to be involved with these too. Although there was inevitably very little enthusiasm in Paris for dissipating scarce French manpower away from the Western Front – Joseph Joffre, the French commander-in-chief, refused to release any men at all – Alexandre Millerand, the minister of war, pressed on with the creation of an 18,000-strong Corps d'Expedition d'Orient, formed of men 'whose distinctive feature was that they were not taken from the armies engaged in the west'.⁴¹ There were men from reserve units in France, together with colonial Senegalese from West Africa, Zouaves (light infantrymen from French North Africa), and Foreign Legionnaires. Again, despite French misgivings, this force was put under overall British control.

Initially used for a diversionary attack on the Asiatic shore of the Straits, the French forces were then deployed at the south-eastern corner of Cape Helles, which they occupied from April 1915 almost to the very end of the campaign. The French suffered very heavy casualties in the early days. Three weeks after the offensive had begun they had lost 12,600 killed and wounded out of a total 22,500 who had landed. The numbers of French involved escalated considerably, and a total of 79,000 men served, with a maximum of just under 50,000 at any one time. The French official history of the campaign records 3,706 killed and 6,092 missing between 25 April 1915 and 6 January

1916, though in the French cemetery at Morto Bay, Cape Helles, there are 3,236 graves, together with ossuaries containing the remains of an estimated 12,000 further unidentified individuals.[42]

Arriving at Cape Helles a week after the first landings, a gunner, Raymond Weil, found 'hundreds of corpses' marking the way up from the beach. 'Everywhere,' he noted, 'dead Turks lay one against another, having been mown down like corn by our 75s' – the famous French 75mm guns were much valued on the peninsula. In a 'sad spectacle', next to the Turks lay many Senegalese. Here, as French accounts of the fighting testify, they shared the privations and frustrations of their British and British imperial colleagues elsewhere on the peninsula. In July, Weil complained that the heat had got much worse, the flies had become 'legion' and the men's health was suffering. Every day they had to evacuate two or three men with dysentery and the 'brutal fevers' quickly transformed men to 'walking spectres'. Gaston-Louis Giguel, a sapper sent up to repair a front-line trench in a ravine – '*Le ravin de mort*' – at the extreme right of the French position in August, was hit by an appalling smell. Both the walls and floor of the trench consisted of corpses covered by just a few shovelfuls of earth. The hands and feet of the dead, moreover, seemed to reach out from the ground.[43]

Giguel, who could speak good English, struck up a friendship with Australian gunners manning an adjacent battery, and was able to smoke 'their excellent cigarettes' and negotiate various exchanges, including canned beef which he claimed when heated made a '*véritable bœuf à la mode*'. British jam was an especially valued commodity. Later on in the campaign, Guigel traded French army tins of sardines for 'jam and English cigarettes' from British soldiers, who for their part were pleased to do similar business. 'We did a lot of swopping with the French troops,' noted Eric Wettern, 'their vin rouge and coffee being much in demand, in exchange for our jam.' Although some British envied the riches of the French commissariat, the latter were not always well enough to enjoy it. On account of his '*dérangement d'ordre digestif*', Raymond Weil gave up meat and wine, confining himself to rice, potatoes, haricot beans and tea. Guigel was one of the very last Frenchmen to leave the peninsula. On 2 January 1916, under fire from Turkish guns on the Asian side of the Straits, he was on the beach below Sedd el Bahr where huge quantities of supplies had been stockpiled. The shellfire, he noticed, had scattered 'tins of jams of all sorts destined for officers'. There was, too, a store of cigarettes that should have been distributed to the troops as a celebration for the New Year. 'The unhappy expeditionary force,' recorded Guigel, 'had naturally never received them [but] everyone just digs into the pile; all you had to do was climb down to the landing-stage and help yourself.'[44]

There was national and ethnic variety on the Ottoman side, too. Several of the regiments in Mustafa Kemal's subsequently famous 19th Infantry Division were composed of 'Arabs'. The 77th Regiment, for example, had been mobilised in Aleppo, Syria, and was strongly Nusayri from the Alawite community together with Yezidi Kurd. Although official Turkish narratives of the campaign do not take into account ethnicity as a factor influencing operations, Edward Erickson, historian of the Ottoman military campaign, notes that the 'Arab' regiments were criticised by some senior officers for losing cohesion during the night attacks of 25 April.[45] Not only did the regiment mainly consist of Arab soldiers, but it was reported that many of them were 'quite old', most did not speak Turkish and that they were 'highly volatile under fire, often discharging their rifles wildly'. During the night of 25 April, indeed, their firing was so erratic that the Turkish units on either side, apparently unaware that the 77th Regiment was between them, thought that they were firing at each other in error.[46] Over recent years there has been some official recognition of the multi-ethnic composition of the Ottoman army. In March 2013, for example, speaking at a war cemetery the Turkish prime minister, Recep Tayyip Erdoğan, said that the 'martyrs' of Çanakkale (the Turkish name for the campaign) included 'children of people from all over Turkey, the Balkans, the Middle East and Africa. There are Turks here at this cemetery, and Bosniacs, and Kurds.' Latterly, too, the Turkish Armenian newspaper *Agos* urged its readers not to forget the Armenian military doctors who served on the peninsula.[47] The overwhelming majority of the troops, however, were Anatolian Turks who proved to be especially tough and resilient fighters. In his memoirs, General Liman von Sanders reflected that 'the preparations of the enemy were excellent, their only defect being that they underestimated the powers of resistance of the Turkish soldier.'[48]

Beyond the fighting men at Gallipoli were a host of non-combatant personnel whose histories are sadly much less well recorded. Charles Bean asserted that the Turks employed 'bodies of Greeks or Armenians' as labour units, but he provided no further details.[49] The German General Kannengiesser recalled that for the most part the fighting troops 'were pure Turkish-Mahommedan'. Christians and Jews were enlisted 'into labour battalions or used in other ways behind the front'.[50] Gallipoli had been the historic home of many thousands of Greeks. As during the Balkan War of 1912, ethnic Greeks were thought by the Ottoman government to be potentially unreliable, and there was a history of poor inter-communal relations in parts of European and Anatolian Turkey. After the peninsula had first come under attack in March and April, therefore, the army removed some twenty thousand Greeks, principally to other Greek settlements on the Asian side across the Sea of Marmara.[51]

According to one Turkish veteran, Mustafa Yildrim from Central Anatolia, interviewed many years after, the Allied troops themselves were thought to have been Greek. He asserted that 'men volunteered in the belief they were fighting "infidels come to destroy the Muslim people"'. Never having heard of British or Australians, Yildrim said that in 1915 'we all believed it was the Greeks we were fighting against at Gallipoli'.[52] Seven years later, in 1922–23, almost the entire Greek population of Anatolian Turkey fled or was expelled, in a massive exchange of minorities between the two countries (Greek Orthodox Christians from Turkey and Muslims from Greece). The Allies certainly hoped to exploit ambivalent minority loyalties within the Ottoman Empire. From early 1915 a British intelligence network operating out of Athens began to recruit Asiatic Greeks as agents to work in Turkey itself. In May 1915 it was reported that Christians in the Turkish forces had been disarmed and were now employed purely in labour units. It was thought, however, that they could do good work for the British 'as guides and soldiers. All the local Christians ask is 24 hours' grace to pay off old scores on the Moslem population.'[53] Almost the only reminder of their presence in the region now are the

Greek-derived names still used in Anglophone histories of the campaign: 'Chanak' for the modern Cannakale; 'Krithia' for Alçitepe, and so on.

The British official history contains just three mentions of labour units. Aspinall-Oglander wrote that 'special recognition' was 'due to the infantry transport personnel, the Indian mule-cart drivers, and the Zion Mule Corps for their untiring energy' in helping clear the battlefield after the third battle of Krithia, above Cape Helles in early June 1915. A footnote to an account of operations in the autumn of 1915 records that both the Egyptian and Maltese Labour Corps worked at the Anzac beaches, and '1,255 Greek labourers' were installed at Helles by the end of October. Finally, 'the Indian Mule Corps carried out particularly valuable services in getting up supplies during the blizzard in November'. Egyptian and Maltese labourers were billeted in camp sites at the north end of Anzac in full view of an enemy post and sustained casualties there. Precise numbers are difficult to obtain for labour units, though one account of the Indians at Gallipoli reckons that there were 650 men and 1,086 mules in the Indian 'mule transport train'.[54] In September 1915 over a thousand men (of whom 864 were chosen) responded to a call in Malta for volunteers to take on stevedore duties at Gallipoli. These individuals are not quite forgotten. One casualty from the Maltese Labour Corps, twenty-seven-year-old Giuseppe Camilleri, 'only son of Filippa Camilleri, of Strada, Santa Elena, Sliema, Malta, and the late Angelo Camilleri', lies in the Ari Burnu cemetery overlooking Anzac Cove. He died on 7 December 1915, having very nearly made it to the end.[55]

One unit, recruited for labour duties, but which also saw action in battle, was the Assyrian Jewish Refugee Mule Corps, raised in Egypt in March 1915. Better known as the Zion Mule Corps, and celebrated as the 'the first regular Jewish fighting force' of modern times, it comprised 650 or so men, drawn from the large Jewish refugee community in Alexandria. Late in 1914 some 18,000 Jews had been expelled from Palestine by the ruling Turkish authorities, of whom 11,000 ended up in Egypt. With the aim of forming a Jewish legion, a group of Jews led by the radical Russian journalist and Zionist, Ze'ev

(Vladimir) Jabotinsky, and Victor Trumpeldor, a one-armed former captain in the Imperial Russian Army, offered their services to the British. While dismayed that the British would only permit the formation of a volunteer transport unit, they eventually agreed to organise on that basis, under the command of an improbable forty-eight-year-old Irish Protestant soldier, adventurer and inveterate self-promoter, John Henry Patterson.

Patterson, whose family background is unclear – one source suggests that he was the illegitimate son of an Anglo-Irish aristocrat – had served with distinction in the Boer War and had made a name for himself as a big-game hunter in the early 1900s, prompting an invitation to the White House from his fellow field sportsman, President Theodore Roosevelt.[56] Lobbying for a war job in Egypt in the spring of 1915, Patterson found himself with five British and eight Jewish officers in charge of the new unit. From the start Patterson was determined that it should be a fighting formation, and he saw that it was well equipped with 'excellent rifles, bayonets and ammunition, all captured from the Turks when they made their futile assault on the Suez Canal [in February 1915]'. The unit was organised at astonishing speed, and just over a month after its establishment, Patterson and a contingent of some 300 men were landed at Cape Helles on 27 April and immediately deployed under fire to move supplies and ammunition up to the front line. Although officially prohibited from fighting, on 1 May, Patterson's men helped the 1st Battalion Royal Inniskilling Fusiliers repel a 'severe night attack', thus (at least in their own eyes) winning a battle honour on Gallipoli.[57]

According to Patterson (who had a reputation as a raconteur) the irregular nature of the Zion Mule Corps caused problems on a couple of occasions. Shortly after they had landed, one of his men was guarding stores on 'V' Beach when he was challenged by some French soldiers. Since he could only speak Russian and Hebrew, and 'seeing that he was armed with a Turkish rifle and bayonet . . . he was taken for a daring Turk who had invaded the beach to spy out the land'. A drumhead court martial sentenced him to death and he was about to be executed when a Mule Corps colleague who spoke French was able to rescue him. 'After this,' wrote Patterson, 'I allowed none of my men to leave camp unless they could speak English or were accompanied by someone who could act as an interpreter.' Later on in the campaign a detachment of the corps came upon a battalion of French colonial Zouaves. A Mule Corps sergeant 'took them for Turks', and, Patterson claimed, 'only that I was happily on the spot when he made this startling discovery, he would undoubtedly have opened fire on the Frenchmen. I must say,' he added, 'they looked exactly like Turks owing to their semi-barbaric uniform.'[58]

Patterson was invalided home in December 1915 and spent a month in a London hospital writing an account of the corps. He had an explicit political agenda, 'to interest the Hebrew nation in the fortunes of the Zionists and show them of what their Russian brothers are capable, even under the command of an alien in race and religion'.[59] Patterson, indeed, went on to command the all-Jewish 38th Battalion of the Royal Fusiliers – which with two further battalions (the 39th and 40th) approached Jabotinsky's original vision of a Jewish legion and which served in the final Palestine campaign of 1918. Here Patterson (who progressively became more Zionist than many Zionists themselves) and his unit encountered much open anti-semitism, which, he noted, contrasted sharply with his earlier experience on Gallipoli. He even claimed that if an Australian, English, Irish or Scottish battalion had been treated as his had been, the divisional headquarters 'would have gone up in flames and the General himself would probably have gone up with it'.[60]

Pondering in 1917 on the losses at Gallipoli, Bryan Cooper, an Irish officer who had landed at Suvla in August 1915 with the Connaught Rangers, reflected that 'Death had made strange bedfellows: in one little cemetery high up at the Chailak Dere behind Rhododendron Ridge there lay side by side Private John Jones, Royal Welsh Fusiliers, and Sergeant Rotahiru of the Maoris. From the two ends of the earth Christian and Buddhist and Sikh had come to fight in the same cause, and in death they lay together.'[61] And as Kemal famously declared in 1934, these men also lie together with their one-time enemies. 'You are now lying in the soil of a friendly country,' he said. 'Therefore rest in peace. There is no difference between the Johnnies and the Mehmets to us where they lie side by side now here in this country of ours.'[62]

Remembering Gallipoli

The commemoration of Gallipoli naturally focuses on the date of the first landings, 25 April (1915), enshrined by statute in both Australia and New Zealand as Anzac Day. Indeed, apart from 1 July 1916, the first day of the battle of the Somme, and perhaps 11 November 1918, no other single date through the whole war has such an iconic status (at least in the 'British world'). Even the very instant of the first landing is embedded in the public memory of the event. Across Australia, and at Gallipoli itself, dawn services are held each year on 25 April to coincide with the early morning landings. The First World War memorial at Cairns in Queensland, Australia, includes a column with four painted clock faces, each of which shows 4.28 [a.m.], believed to be the exact time when the first Australian soldier set foot on the shore at Anzac Cove. All over Australia, and New Zealand too, there are memorials which commemorate service in the First World War, but, despite the fact that a majority of those who served during the war did *not* do so at Gallipoli, Anzac dominates popular perceptions of the Great War experience and much of the annual commemorative ritual.[63]

This is especially so in Australia where 'Anzac' developed into a kind of secular religion and became part of the creation myth of an autonomous Australian nation. As a country, Australia only dates from 1901 when the six Australian colonies joined together in a 'Commonwealth' federation. Thus, the soldiers despatched to the war in 1914 and after were the first to serve in an explicitly *Australian* formation. As Jenny Macleod, one of the most thoughtful commentators on the Anzac 'legend' has put it, it was 'Australia's first major appearance as a nation on the world stage. It was the Australians' "baptism of fire", the "birth of a nation".' 'In no unreal sense,' concluded Charles Bean in *The Story of Anzac*, 'it was on the 25th of April, 1915, that the consciousness of Australian nationhood was born.'[64]

Charles Bean's contribution to the heroic-romantic myth of Anzac has been extensively discussed by Australians trying to make sense as much of Australia's part in the First World war as of the war's part in Australia.[65] The process began even during the campaign itself, with newspaper reports celebrating the valour and achievements of

Australian soldiers on the battlefield. This myth, or legend, of Gallipoli was powerfully stimulated by *The Anzac Book*, edited by Charles Bean, which gathered together contributions written by the troops themselves. It had originally been conceived as a morale-boosting magazine – like the trench newspapers, such as the *Wipers Times*, which flourished on the Western Front – aimed to amuse them over the winter of 1915/16. The decision to evacuate the peninsula transformed the venture into a commemorative souvenir which, when published in May 1916, was a stupendous success. By September over 100,000 copies had been sold. The contributions which Bean selected for publication exemplified the quintessential Anzac features which have survived ever since. Bean – not a soldier himself, but a journalist – had a very specific vision of what constituted the essential national character of the troops he so admired, much of it drawing on a belief that it was moulded by the natural environment of Australia. This produced resilience, independence, enterprise, self-sufficiency and a fierce loyalty to comrades, encapsulated in the Australian concept of 'mateship'. In a single-volume history of Australia in the First World War published in 1946, Bean wrote that 'Anzac stood, and still stands, for reckless valour in a good cause, for enterprise, resourcefulness, fidelity, comradeship, and endurance that will never own defeat'.[66]

Although Anzac means more to Australia than to New Zealand, there is a similar specificity to the New Zealand involvement with the campaign. As with Australians, there is a popular perception that Anzacs took the major part. Reflecting on Gallipoli in 1994, General Sir Leonard Thornton, a former chief of the New Zealand general staff, suggested that most New Zealanders would 'acknowledge that the British were there, but would reject the assertion that they outnumbered the Anzacs by a factor of ten to one'.[67] As with Australia, too, the experience of the campaign also represented a coming-of-age for the smaller dominion. 'Gallipoli,' wrote Alan Mulgan in the late 1950s, 'was the birth of a nation . . . It taught us to think more of ourselves and more about ourselves. New Zealanders began to see more clearly that their country was not just another Britain, but a different land, with a history and destiny of its own.'[68]

The prominence of Gallipoli in Australian and New Zealand perceptions of the First World War reflects a progressive general sense of
disaggregation in the British imperial war effort. What began as an
apparently united and coherent endeavour – 'when the Empire is at
war, so is Australia' – ended up with a perception of partnership
between imperial, albeit certainly still British 'nations', so much so
that as part of a 'British Empire Delegation' the dominions (and India,
too) separately signed the postwar peace treaties. But, a century on,
with Australia and New Zealand now in effect fully independent
nations, the prevailing Antipodean narrative focuses relentlessly on
the Anzac involvement, scarcely acknowledging that the great majority of troops on the peninsula were British. Even in the late 1920s
Aspinall-Oglander had noted the extent to which 'Anzac' had come to
dominate narratives of the campaign: 'The anniversary of the landings
at Gallipoli is called Anzac Day,' he noted, 'and very many people
would be surprised to learn that any other troops but Australians took
part in the landing operations in Gallipoli.'[69]

This disaggregation process has happened within the United
Kingdom, too, reflecting modern and contemporary political developments, as well as changes in our understanding of 'British' and
'Britishness', both in a political and cultural sense. As the United
Kingdom breaks up – or tends towards breaking up (a process which
was powerfully stimulated by the strains of the First World War) – so
researchers increasingly endeavour to discover, for example, particular
'Irish' and 'Scottish' elements in the British war effort,[70] a trend which
helps obscure the fact that the majority of the troops at Gallipoli were
not just British, but *English*.

The role of Gallipoli in defining perceptions of Australia and New
Zealand as distinctive and autonomous nations was mirrored on the
Turkish side. The victory of Gallipoli, and the role played in that
victory by Mustafa Kemal, was central to the creation and sustaining
of a secular Turkish Republic after the war. The triumphs of Turkish
arms against the might of the British and French empires – if only
temporarily – became part of the creation story of Kemalist Turkey.
Today on the peninsula, away from the excitements of Anzac Day, one
is as likely (if not even more likely) to encounter parties of Turkish

schoolchildren being taken round the battlefields and instructed about their country's glorious military history as Australian backpackers looking to find some remaining resonances of that 'mateship' which Charles Bean so memorably identified as the key component of Anzac's fabled spirit and resilience.

There was one unexpected, long-term effect of the withdrawal from Gallipoli, when the recollection of its success raised spirits in the early summer of 1940. Less than three weeks after Clement Attlee, as leader of the Labour Party, had been brought into Winston Churchill's wartime coalition government, Hitler's Blitzkrieg drove the British Expeditionary Force back to the Channel, where the evacuation from Dunkirk began on 27 May. Years later Attlee was interviewed by Francis Williams about that perilous moment:

> *Williams*: How grim did things look to you when you came in?
> *Attlee*: Pretty grim. I didn't take so gloomy a view as some about our chances at Dunkirk. Dill, who'd been made CIGS [Chief of the Imperial General Staff] thought we'd get practically none of our men away. Having served through the evacuation of Gallipoli I thought we would.[71]

And so they did.

2

Verdun

For the French the two most iconic battles of the First World War are the Marne in 1914, when the initial German strike towards Paris was turned back, and the desperate struggle at Verdun, a historically important fortress in Lorraine, which began on Monday 21 February 1916 and continued for much of the year. It was the longest and most costly of all the battles of 1914–18, claiming nearly 700,000 casualties from both sides. In France and beyond, 'Verdun' – in the title of one French work, 'the greatest battle of history' – became a byword for the manifest horrors of industrialised, 'total' war, as well as the courage and steadfast endurance of armies and people on both sides.[1]

THE BATTLE

By following English-language press reporting of Verdun over the first days of the battle we can get some idea of what the wider general public knew about First World War fighting. By focusing primarily on the coverage in *The New York Times* we can, moreover, get a sense of how the war looked to still-neutral Americans receiving reports from all the European belligerents. Though undoubtedly sympathetic to the Allied side, *The New York Times* endeavoured to be as even-handed as possible in its treatment of what it called 'the world's catastrophe'.[2] The paper had its own correspondents in London and Paris. Their man in Berlin, a Briton who also worked for the London *Daily Mail*, was expelled at the start of the war, but from September 1914 Cyril Brown reported from Germany and, as *The New York Times*'s own history claimed, 'succeeded in presenting probably the best picture given in the American press of the operations of the German Army on all fronts'. During the Verdun campaign, as well as transmitting official communiqués from Berlin, Paris and London, the paper also took reports from the correspondents of several Berlin dailies. In addition to the daily *New York Times*, from December 1914 there was also a monthly magazine of war news, *The New York Times Current History of the European War*, which reproduced articles from the daily paper as well as more extended pieces drawn from other sources. Thus *The New York Times*'s stable of publications provides us with a pleasingly wide range of reporting.

Heavy artillery duels and a 'series of extremely vicious infantry actions' in the Verdun area were reported on 22 and 23 February. French sources were guardedly optimistic (as was so often the case on all sides at the start of Great War offensives). Some German attacks had 'gained a footing in some of our advanced trenches . . . but our counterattacks drove them out . . . [and] we took about fifty prisoners'. At another point the Germans had occupied some trenches but only 'with large losses'.[3] The following day it was asserted that the Germans had 'been making preparations for a big stroke at Verdun so openly during the past month that the French had every chance to get ready for them'. Because of the strength of the local defences, military opinion in Paris was 'inclined to doubt that the Germans will attempt to carry Verdun by storm'. By 24 February it was understood that 'the most ambitious offensive since the French advance in Champagne [the previous autumn] is now in progress to the north and northeast of Verdun' and it had 'so far resulted in German gains of nearly two miles at various points along a twenty-five-mile front'. The French, nevertheless, were still claiming to have 'inflicted heavy losses upon their assailants'.[4] At this early stage *The New York Times*'s reporting comprised mostly verbatim quotations from official British, French and German communiqués, and, while it was now apparent that a major battle was under way, it was not yet clear which (or indeed if either) side had the upper hand.

The tone of the reporting began to change as the battle intensified, and with significant advances on 24 February and the capture of Fort Douaumont the following day, German reports took on a triumphant quality. Although it was not generally realised at the time, Douaumont, four and a half miles north-north-east of Verdun, and which was regarded by some as the strongest fort in the world, had been left virtually undefended. Over the winter of 1915/16 the defences in the region had been run down. As it was a quiet zone, and no German attack was anticipated, guns and men had been withdrawn for deployment in more active sectors further north. Moreover, following the experience in 1914 of the great Belgian fortifications around Namur and Liège, which the Germans had relatively easily overrun, forts such as Douaumont were widely regarded as indefensible death traps. The loss of the fort to the Germans, nevertheless, was a striking and undeniable defeat for the French.

On 28 February a 'staff correspondent' in Berlin reported that flags were 'beginning to appear in celebration of the news of the fall of the first fort at Verdun'. The German public, however, were 'still in the dark as to whether it really marks the beginning of the long-expected great offensive, or is a great demonstration to cover one elsewhere'. It was difficult to judge the chief aim of the offensive as military experts in Berlin were 'observing the utmost reticence in discussing the event'. There were several eyewitness reports from the front line in the same edition. One, dated 25 February, from Max Osborn of the liberal-leaning Berlin *Vossische Zeitung*, described a steady advance down the Meuse river valley due north of Verdun and into thickly wooded territory around the villages of Haumont and Beaumont to the north-east. Osborn stressed the immediacy of his report. 'I had an opportunity this noon from several high points in the firing line of surveying the mighty battlefield over which the thunder of cannon rolled . . . You must see for yourself,' he added, 'the bare ridge that runs south from Consenvoye to Brabant to realize what it means to capture such terrain by storm.' He concluded his despatch with a word about the soldiers: 'The driving power, endurance, and discipline of our troops was incomparable. Commanders and officers never tire of giving praise and recognition of their performance. Our losses, happily, were not very great.'

Another report, of 26 February, from the *Berliner Tageblatt*'s correspondent at the 'German Great Headquarters before Verdun', bluntly
announced that 'the giant block of cement and steel armorplate that
was Douaumont lies in ruins'. A key factor in the success had been the
German guns. French prisoners had 'said that the effect of our artillery
was indescribably frightful; nobody could hold out long against it'. In
a 'special cable' to *The New York Times*, Karl Rosner of the more
conservative *Berliner Lokal-Anzeiger* noted that the 'brilliant feat of
our Brandenburgers in the splendid storming of Fort Douaumont'
had been 'preceded by the no less glorious work of our artillery', and
he detected a rekindled spirit of patriotism among the German troops.
'In these days,' he wrote, 'I have seen men who have been in the fierce
Verdun fighting whose eyes have flashed as in those August days of
1914.' A few days later (in a report which had been transmitted directly
through the German Telefunken wireless station at Sayville on Long
Island), Major Ernst Moraht, military correspondent of the *Berliner
Tageblatt*, paid 'tribute to the bravery of the French troops in coming
to "iron grips" with the Germans', but added that 'a race of military
valor perishes before Verdun or drags itself crippled home'.[5]

These front-line despatches demonstrate some constants of modern
war reporting. In the first place was the essential presence of the
reporter on the battlefield itself, thus reinforcing the immediacy and
veracity of the writing. 'I was there' conveyed a powerful message to
the families back home, desperate for news of their loved ones at the
front. There was a clear implication, too, that (at least to some extent)
the writer was sharing the dangers of the troops involved. The substance
of the articles then generally contained three key characteristics. First
was factual information, evidently derived from official army sources:
numbers and units involved; place and direction of assault; ground
gained (or lost); casualties suffered, and so on. Second was often highly
coloured descriptions of the fighting itself, stressing the intense nature
of the conflict. Finally, no battlefield report was complete without
some admiring celebration of the fighting men involved with a
comment on their effectiveness, courage and spirit.

The valour of the troops was not a monopoly of one side or the
other, as testified by the combatants themselves. *The New York Times*

had an eye for individual soldiers' stories and on 28 February its correspondent in Paris cabled the tale of a wounded French 'Colonial infantryman' who had been at Fort Douaumont. Describing the moment when a concentrated German attack was driven off, the soldier said: 'we hurled ourselves at them with the bayonet, among the shell holes and ruined emplacements. This was real war as I had never seen it. For a moment it was furious and equal.' And he generously praised his opponents for 'coming on incessantly'. 'Truly they are brave, those Boches,' he said. 'I would never have believed that human beings could face such a terrible fire. Yet they knew it was certain death, for the wounded were stifled under corpses or torn in pieces by fresh shells.' The paper picked up this account in an editorial, claiming that it demonstrated 'the human lust for fighting' and embodied 'a heroic ecstasy'.[6] But did it? Safe enough in their Times Square offices, far away from the battle front, the editorial staff of *The New York Times* could readily speculate as to the soldiers' emotional engagement with the fighting.

Despite the imposition of censorship on all sides, newspaper reports of fighting at Verdun included much about the personal dangers and horrors involved in the fighting. The predominance of reporting, however, came through official channels, and, despite individual by-lines and some undeniably graphic 'human interest' stories, there was a level of generality and abstraction about the coverage and the language used which insulated the civilian reader from the actual front-line experience. Phrases such as 'vicious fighting', 'heavy casualties', and even 'at ghastly cost', only partially communicate the realities of the fighting (though, to be sure, *absence* of detail could stimulate the imagination and worst fears of the reader at home). Assuming that those realities can be communicated at all (which has been a matter of considerable debate among historians of the First World War), it is understandably assumed that the diaries, letters and memoirs of soldiers themselves must take us closer to the war, in Leopold von Ranke's resonant phrase, 'as it actually was' (*wie es eigentlich gewesen*).[7]

Henri Desagneaux's especially vivid diary illustrates the horrors of Verdun for the soldiers involved. In peacetime, Desagneaux had been a railway company lawyer. By June 1916, when his unit was posted to Verdun, he was a lieutenant commanding a company in the 359th Infantry regiment. Although they spent little more than a fortnight in the front line, the evident pressures pushed him and his men close to, and in some cases beyond, breaking point. Indeed, the very brevity of their spell at the front demonstrated the wisdom of the French system of rotating troops in and out of action before they were utterly destroyed.

Desagneaux and his men arrived at Nixéville, about seven miles from Verdun, on Tuesday 13 June. It was cold and pouring with rain and 'we bivouac in a wood in a lake of mud'. At 5 p.m. orders arrived sending them to the Citadel of Verdun: 'Faces are grave. The guns are thundering over there. It's a real furnace, everyone realises that perhaps tomorrow death will come.' There were rumours that they might be sent to 'Mort-Homme' or the Fort at Vaux. 'What is certain, nothing good lies in store for us.' They spent a day in the Citadel. Underground it was safe 'but very gloomy'. Desagneaux walked around the ruined town but could not 'stay outside for long as shells are dropping every-where'. Going up to the front – they were being deployed in the Ravin de la Dame just west of Fort Douaumont – Desagneaux's uncomplain-ing glum fatalism seems typical of the ordinary soldier's experience on the battlefield. Ordered to advance, 'we leave, not knowing exactly where we are going; and no one has a map . . . Guides are rare in this area where death stalks at every step.' Meanwhile they had not eaten for twenty-four hours. Not quite at the front line, they came under German shellfire. 'There are so many explosions around us that the air reeks of powder and earth; we can't see clearly any more. We wait anxiously without knowing whether we shall be alive an hour later.'

By Sunday 18 June Desagneaux and his company, still without food, were 'stuck at the top of a ridge in a half-collapsed trench, without any shelter', apart from 'small crannies in which one must curl up'. 'It's a void,' wrote Desagneaux, 'we are no longer in a civilised world. One suffers, and says nothing.' On Monday morning they discovered that a squad of machine-gunners of the 5th Battalion had been buried all along their trench, leaving 'corpses, then legs and arms protruding out of the ground'. They tried to make themselves 'as comfortable as possible', but the more they dug the more bodies they found: 'We give up and go elsewhere, but we just leave one graveyard for another.' Early on Tuesday morning food supplies at last arrived, though without any water, and since the weather had turned warm they were very thirsty. The heat was 'overpowering', with flies and corpses which gave off 'a nauseating smell'.

There were two more days of almost unbearable waiting for orders to move up to the front line. The pressure began to tell under the constant bombardment. 'The shells, the shrapnel, the 210s fall like hail for twenty-four hours non-stop', wrote Desagneaux on 21 June, 'only to start again; everything trembles, one's nerves as well as the ground. We feel at the end of our tether. . . . We are haggard, dazed, hungry, and feverishly thirsty, but there is no water. In some companies there have been cases of madness. How much longer are we going to stay in this situation?' Such was the strain, that when, at 11 p.m. on 22 June, the order finally came to leave the trench and move up to the front line it was a great relief, even though they had to advance across 'a plateau, swept continuously by machine-gun fire and flares. Every ten steps one has to fall flat on the ground so as not to be seen.' But the terrain was littered with bodies. 'One falls down flat and it's a corpse. It's awful; we start again with only one desire – to get there.' They crossed 'ground where there lie forever men of the 106th, of the 359th, still others of regiments which preceded us. It's a graveyard, a glimpse of hell.'

On 24 June, after just a week in the front line, Desagneaux began to worry about the demoralisation of his men. The word 'prisoner' was being whispered, as capture by the enemy 'for many would seem salvation'. 'We must fight against this notion,' wrote Desagneaux, 'raise morale. But how?' Their state of nerves now made it impossible to eat, and 'if we have a call of nature to satisfy, we have to do it in a tin or on a shovel and throw it over the top of our shell-hole. It's like this every day.' The next two days were 'terrible day and night'. At three o'clock in the morning on 25 June, 'without warning, our own troops attack us from behind'. They had been sent to recapture ground lost the day before, but 'without precise orders, without maps, without even knowing where our lines are, ventured off [and] . . . fell upon us, believing they had found the Boches'. At six o'clock 'to add to our plight' the French 75s fired on them: 'Terrible panic; six wounded at one go from a shell-burst, everyone wants to run for it. Agnel and I have to force these poor devils back by drawing our revolvers.' Two days later under similar conditions some more men tried to flee and the officers had to 'get our revolvers out again and stand in their way'. And there was unsettling news from an adjoining unit that two of their men had committed suicide.

In the early evening of Wednesday 28 June, spirits were astonishingly raised by a German attack. They advanced 'in massed formation'. Desagneaux's men held their fire until they were fifteen yards away, 'then let them have it' with grenades and a machine gun, and drove them off inflicting heavy casualties. But the artillery bombardment continued with particular intensity on 30 June, by which stage even Desagneaux began to think they had had enough. 'There's death everywhere,' he wrote. 'At our feet, the wounded groan in a pool of blood; two of them, more seriously hit are breathing their last.' Not a moment too soon, early in the morning of 1 July his unit was withdrawn from the line, after sixteen horrific days, and returned to the very same camp from which they had departed in early June.[8]

French soldiers' diaries also encapsulate a variant of the Anzacs' 'mateship' demonstrated at Gallipoli, that close binding of individuals together, supporting each other, and creating a powerful loyalty and cohesiveness arguably greater than any sense of patriotic service or national sacrifice. Eighteen months into the war, Louis Mairet, an infantryman at Verdun, concluded that 'the soldier of 1916 is fighting not for Alsace, nor to destroy Germany, nor for his country. He fights from honesty, from habit and because he is forced to. He fights because he cannot do anything else.' After the initial enthusiasm of the war, and the discouragement of the first winter, by the second winter he had become resigned. He had 'exchanged his house for a hovel [and] his family for his soldier comrades'.[9]

In a thoughtful exploration of French soldiers' testimony of the Great War, however, Leonard V. Smith has argued that this was a false dichotomy, and that small-group dynamics could 'simply reproduce the ideology in microcosm'. In André Pézard's war journal (which comprises one of the most remarkable records of French army life during the Great War) Smith identified 'a miniature version of the [French] Republic, based on a small group of men totally and individually committed to one another', and 'the more Pézard and his comrades suffered, the more they considered themselves committed to one another and through one another to the war'.[10] If this be true – and the argument seems particularly persuasive over the long-drawn-out battles of Verdun and the Somme in 1916 – far from disenchanting or disillusioning soldiers (of either side) from the war, the longer and more intense the suffering, the more determined the participants might be to see the issue through to the end.

At the start of the war André Pézard was a twenty-two-year-old student of medieval Italian literature. In February 1915, as a junior infantry officer, he was posted to Vauquois, fifteen miles west of Verdun.[11] At one point in June 1915, on a quiet, beautiful early summer evening, when it would have been 'good to be lovers', Pézard recorded a discussion with a fellow lieutenant, René Fairise, who had been a student friend at the elite École Normale Supérieure in 1914. After visiting a wounded colleague in hospital who had exulted in the killing of Germans, Pézard worried about this brutalisation, and their apparent acceptance of such behaviour. Was their experience in the war, he asked, going to make them all depraved? Fairise denied this, arguing that the hardness and brutality which some soldiers manifested (especially when they first arrived at the front), stemmed from what they felt they *ought* to feel, rather than any genuine emotion – a state of mind, furthermore, which was encouraged by 'official journalists' who had no proper experience of the real war. In fact, suggested Fairise, the longer one was in the front line the more one was likely just to be resigned, and thus able to 'wage war as they [civilians behind the lines] wanted us to do'.[12] For Fairise and Pézard there was an unbridgeable space of experience and emotion between the soldiers at the front and everyone else. In the end, no-one who had not been there could ever know what it was really like, or how those men actually endured it – which is not to say that they did not try to describe and explain the experience, as Pézard did himself in his journal, first published in July 1918. Fairise, alas, was denied any such opportunity. He was killed on

21 July 1915, the day before their unit was moved out of the front line for a brief rest.

In February 1916, once more at Vauquois, Pézard endured the German barrage at the start of Verdun. On the 25th, sheltering with his men in tunnels below the Butte de Vauquois, he thought it 'odious' that they should be caught up in the hurricane which was battering their neighbours to the east, but 'we will defend ourselves despite the terror, like them. For our Country.' Perhaps as befits one who was to become a well-known Dante scholar after the war, Pézard had a particular eye for the grotesque. At Vauquois, where French sappers were digging to undermine the German positions, the shelling buried two men in a mineshaft. It took two days to dig them out, when they were discovered one on top of the other. The man on top had hands with 'blood and sand beneath fingernails, between fingers and in his sleeves', the face of the one below was 'black and sticky with a mixture of blood and mud'. One 'witnesses atrocious things', wrote Pézard.[13]

The shocking presence on the battlefield of what Fernand Léger, the pioneer Cubist painter, called 'human debris' constantly recurs in the writings of front-line soldiers. Léger, who served as a stretcher-bearer at Verdun in the autumn of 1916, thought the battlefield was an 'academy of cubism', in which human bodies and the ordinary countryside had been shattered and rearranged in grotesque new ways. Here he found 'excessively curious things. Almost mummified heads of men emerging from the mud . . . The hands were most extraordinary. There were hands I would have wanted to photograph exactly.' Worse still, several of the heads 'had fingers in their mouths, fingers bitten off with the teeth', something which Léger had seen a few months before when serving in the Argonne sector to the west of Verdun, a soldier who had been 'in so much pain he ate his own hands'.[14] Black humour was one coping mechanism for the men in the front line. A French officer described how a 380mm artillery shell (fired from a battery some six or seven miles behind the lines) had landed plumb in the middle of an advancing party of Germans in front of Douaumont village. 'It landed right among the German mass,' he said. 'I never saw such a sight. You can judge the effect from the fact that a man at my right was stunned by a gray-sleeved arm. It made the rest of us laugh.'[15]

Many Germans had similar experiences. In mid-July Anton Steiger, a theology student before the war, was deployed near Douaumont, not far from where Henri Desagneaux had been the previous month. In a letter home on 17 July, Steiger reported that even getting to the front line had been costly. Six out of seventeen men in his party were killed on the way up, including an old school friend: 'Reifer, who had lolled on a school-bench beside me for nine years.' At the front their dugout 'was an old half-blown-in, French casemate', just by the fort of Thiaumont. As they approached it, it 'had looked like a mere hummock of earth. The entrance was like that of a fox's hole.' There they stayed for four days in a chamber where French ammunition was stored and next to one full of explosives. 'Dead bodies were lying under the soil, one with its legs protruding up to the knees,' and for the most part they were in the pitch dark as they only had a few candles for lights. There was, too, 'a horrible smell . . . the reek of decomposing bodies; I could hardly eat anything the whole four days'. On the third day the French started such a heavy artillery barrage that they thought the dugout 'would certainly be blown in altogether'. Next day there was continuous shellfire: 'ten hours in the expectation of death either through being buried alive, or of being blown into the air if a shell should happen to fall where the explosive is stored'.[16]

WAR ON TWO FRONTS

The Verdun strategy was part of an 'Easterner–Westerner' debate in Germany, rather as Gallipoli had been in France and Britain. At the beginning of the war the German high command was fully alive to the dangers of fighting simultaneously on western and eastern fronts against major opponents. In what became popularly known as the Schlieffen Plan (though German war planning in 1914 owed little in detail to the work of Schlieffen, who had been chief of the German general staff ten years previously), in August 1914 the Germans launched an offensive through Belgium into northern France aiming to outflank the main French forces and rapidly envelop Paris. Hoping that a successful short campaign in the west would be sufficient to defeat France, the Germans could then turn their attention to the east, where the more slowly mobilising Russians would not immediately have been able to launch their own offensive against Germany.[17] But the 'Miracle of the Marne' extinguished German hopes of a quick victory in the west. During 1915 the French and British launched a number of attacks on the Germans, particularly in Artois and Flanders towards the northern end of the front, none of which met with any great success. In December 1915 a real effort was made for the first time to coordinate Allied war policy and a conference at Chantilly, north-east of Paris, agreed that in 1916 there should be a synchronised series of Russian, French and British offensives.

On the Central Powers' side, the inconclusive engagements of 1915 (during which Germany had primarily been on the defensive), led the German chief of staff Erich von Falkenhayn, a 'Westerner', to consider an attritional offensive against France. In a memorandum for the Kaiser apparently drawn up in December 1915 (the only copy that has been found is one published in his memoirs after the war), he argued that although Great Britain was the principal enemy, its main strength was imperial, naval and financial. 'For England [sic],' he argued, 'the campaign on the Continent of Europe with her own troops is at bottom a side-show.' England's 'real weapons' were the French, Russian and Italian armies, and Germany's best strategy would be to knock them out. Thus he proposed an assault against either one of two French strongpoints: Belfort (near where the Franco-German frontier reached Switzerland) or Verdun, where he proposed that 'the forces of France will bleed to death'.[18] Late in the month it was decided on Verdun, and planning began with the German crown prince, commander of the Fifth Army which was deployed opposite the city. Far from an attritional campaign, the Fifth Army's plans were for a massive lightning strike backed up with a greater artillery barrage than ever before and innovative use of all the latest technology, from aircraft, employed in an embryonic combined operations role, to flamethrowers, which the Germans had used with modest success in 1915.[19]

The concept of a swift 'push', as was so often the case in France and Flanders during the war, did not survive the first few days of the offensive. After initially conceding some ground, and losing Fort Douaumont, the French, under Philippe Pétain, grimly dug in for a prolonged defensive campaign. Pétain was exactly the right man for the job. Although an able and thoughtful officer who had been an instructor at the École de Guerre, he was a fifty-nine-year-old colonel, close to retirement at the start of the war. He had missed promotion through not subscribing to the prevailing French military orthodoxy of faith in the 'spirit of the offensive'; the idea that, even in conditions of modern war where the defence was greatly favoured over the offence, battles could be won by properly inspired and trained soldiers. Pétain, well schooled in defensive tactics and the potential of artillery (unusual for an infantryman), was not so sure. Among his aphorisms were 'cannon conquers, infantry occupies' and 'audacity is the art of knowing how not to be too audacious'. The war gave him his opportunity. With rapid promotion, by July 1915 he was commanding the French Second Army, which in February 1916 was in reserve, training for a planned Franco-British offensive. At the start of the German attack on Verdun, the French high command decided that the city could be saved and ordered the Second Army under Pétain to take charge. General de Castelnau told Pétain bluntly that Verdun 'must be defended at all costs'. The precise circumstances of his appointment are the stuff of legend. Pétain, a bachelor, was something of a ladies' man. On the night of 24/25 February, when the call came, he could not immediately be contacted. But a well-informed staff officer who knew his habits found him with a female companion in the Hôtel Terminus du Nord in Paris.[20]

For the next two months Pétain remained in direct command at Verdun, during which he steadied the French defences and focused on three main areas: artillery, supply and, above all, husbanding the lives of his troops. Appreciating the critical importance of artillery, he deployed his batteries along the west bank of the Meuse where they were able to rake the slopes opposite. There was only one supply route into Verdun, running along a thirty-mile country road and narrow-gauge railway north and north-east from the town of Bar-le-Duc. Organised by Pétain's transport chief, Major Richard, this became the famous 'Voie Sacrée' – a name coined by the nationalist journalist and

politician Maurice Barrès in April 1916 – along which a stream of
trucks, guns, men and materiel moved around the clock. There were
horses, too, though being unable to take cover (as men could when
they detected incoming artillery shells), they were massacred in great
numbers.

Pétain set up his headquarters along the route in the Mairie at
Souilly, and when he had a moment he would stand on the steps to see
(and be seen by) the men on their way to and from the front. Pétain's
special concern for the welfare of his men was reflected in the roulement system of rotating units he introduced at Verdun.

Called a 'noria' (an endless chain of buckets on a loop), troops
ideally were to spend a maximum of eight days in the front line. In its
favour, this arrangement had obvious attractions in limiting exposure
to the dangers and strains of front-line service. But it had drawbacks,
too. Actually moving in and out of the front was dangerous, and the
risk of casualties was increased the more frequently units had to do
this. Ian Ousby has argued that 'some of the blunders at Verdun, and
the appalling casualty rate that always went with them' resulted from
troops being inadequately prepared or experienced, and deployed in
situations where they had not had sufficient time for proper reconnaissance.[21] It was very different on the German side, where units
stayed in the line for much longer periods. General Hans von Zwehl's
VIIth Reserve Corps remained at Verdun for the full ten months of the
battle, and he wrote afterwards of a 'kind of psychosis' which afflicted
his men in that terrible place.[22]

One result of the constant turnover of units under the noria system
was that a huge proportion of the total French army passed through
the Verdun sector. There was scarcely a family in France untouched by
the battle, which became embedded in French society more completely
than any other engagement. 'Of all the battles of the First World War,'
wrote Alastair Horne, 'Verdun was the one in which the most
Frenchmen had taken part.'[23] Among them was Pétain's own regiment,
the 33rd, at Douaumont, where at the beginning of March one junior
officer, Captain Charles de Gaulle, later leader of the Free French in
the Second World War and president of France, was wounded and
taken prisoner, where he remained for the rest of the war, despite
several attempts to escape.

Reflecting on Verdun a few days into the battle, *The New York Times* argued that the Germans could not afford a 'contest in attrition' with the French on the grounds that Germany was numerically weaker than her enemies and must inevitably lose an extended attritional contest. In the circumstances of the Western Front, moreover, where defensive positions were so strong, the attacking side was always bound to suffer much heavier losses than the defenders. Having failed to take Paris at the start of the war, the Germans had now 'elected to hit the French line at its strongest point, to put forth the supreme effort there, on the heroic calculation that success, besides entailing the maximum of military advantage, would have a particularly depressing effect upon French morale'. Yet, having made this 'fateful cast' at Verdun, and 'willing, perhaps, to risk the war upon the outcome', for the Germans, too, 'failure would be disastrous, in a moral if not a military sense'.[24]

As the battle continued into March 1916, commentators remarked both on its titanic scale and grinding nature. On 5 March, the American journalist Garet Garrett, who had toured Germany from mid-November to the end of December 1915, shrewdly observed that the problem with attempting a 'decisive result' was 'whether the cost would be such as a civilized people could afford to pay'. The offensive against Verdun represented a 'moral and political risk' for Germany since it had smaller reserves of manpower than the Allied side. Failing to win at Verdun, he argued, could 'end for ever the hope for Germany of being able to get a decision on the Western Front'. A fortnight later an unnamed 'military expert', reviewing the previous week's war events, confirmed the view that Germany 'must keep on until Verdun falls'. The following week the same commentator drew a parallel with the American Civil War. With superior resources (like the Northern side in the war), the Allies must inevitably defeat Germany. 'The probabilities are,' he wrote, 'that the battle of Verdun will prove the Gettysburg of the war . . . It is now a case [for the Germans] of taking Verdun at all costs.'[25] This was very perceptive, and identified the same belief in German strategists' minds as in Allied that the war could only be won by defeating the enemy at what might be their strongest point – 'the old principle of decisive numbers at decisive theatre'.

Some ominous conclusions were also drawn. Just a week into the battle, the Paris correspondent of *The New York Times* reported the opinion of the French military authorities that infantry had 'become once more, as throughout history, the decisive factor of warfare'. The French argued that under the German artillery barrage at Verdun 'even the strongest trenches' had been 'smashed into a defenceless chaos', and machine-gun emplacements, which previously had 'rendered the heroism of infantry fruitless', had been 'blasted into nothingness'. The destruction of the French trench lines had enabled such advances as the Germans had made, albeit at terrible cost – 'an orgy of slaughter' – with the chilling conclusion that 'if sacrifices are ignored and reserves are sufficient, infantry can advance'. The 'bloody lesson' which the Allies had learned was that, with their superior manpower and industrial strength, they would have the capacity to launch 'a series of these blasting attacks, terribly expensive, but culminating inevitably, according to opinion here, in Germany's downfall'. In the 'last resort' only, Germany's infantry – that is to say the numbers of fighting men available – could 'save her, but her infantry has been wasted like sand from the banks of the Marne to the Riga swamps'.[26] This, if the Allies were truly to 'learn this lesson', was a bleak prediction indeed, by which terribly expensive blasting attacks would surely 'waste like sand' both Allied and German manpower.

What might be called the 'normalisation' of the Western Front experience soon set in, even at Verdun. Increasingly throughout the war an attitude emerged that the casualties which occurred even on quiet days constituted a perfectly normal and apparently acceptable state of affairs. This was precisely encapsulated by the German veteran Erich Maria Remarque in his famous novel *All Quiet on the Western Front*, published in 1929. The report, 'All Quiet', was issued on the day when Remarque's hero, Paul Baümer, was killed, an event so utterly unremarkable as not to trouble the military commentators. Indeed, the original German title of the novel – *Im Westen nichts Neues* – has even greater resonance: 'In the West Nothing New', just the same old thing, time after time after time. We can see this phenomenon in a report from *The New York Times*'s man in Berlin, Cyril Brown, who visited the crown prince's headquarters two months after the battle had begun. By then the German attitude had become one of patient endeavour. 'As seen at close range,' wrote Brown, 'it seems incorrect to call the German attack on Verdun a drive, except in the sense that one speaks of driving a tunnel through solid rock by slow blasting and boring operations.' Indeed, the Germans had apparently settled down for a long haul. Their side 'resembles the humdrum and well-organized routine of a great engineering enterprise'.[27]

The engineering analogy was apt for a battle which exemplified the latest developments in technology. Machine guns, the fabled French 75mm guns, flamethrowers and the rest were all products of the advanced industrial 'civilisation' which had developed so rapidly through the nineteenth century. Poison gas, too, was a technologically advanced industrial product which was refined and developed (by both sides) from the tear gas used at the start of the war to chlorine in 1915 and diphosgene, a slightly less effective variant of phosgene, which the Germans used against strongpoints at Thiaumont and Froideterre, protecting Fleury and Fort Souville in front of Verdun in June 1916. Unlike the easily detectable chlorine, diphosgene was colourless, smelt faintly of silage and caused no spasm when inhaled. On 22–23 June, the Germans fired an estimated 116,000 gas shells. As on other occasions, it was initially a success. French gas masks proved inadequate and there was immediate, if patchy, panic. Nevertheless, once the surprise had worn off and the gas dispersed somewhat, the French defenders were able to hold out at Froideterre. Again backed with conventional artillery fire and diphosgene, a renewed German attack on 11–12 July pushed through Fleury to Fort Souville, and while a handful of Bavarian Alpenkorps assault troops reached the fort, it was never taken. By this stage the French had been supplied with more effective masks and the gas had only minor impact.[28] Although ostensibly a game-changing innovation, gas always promised more than it could deliver. The comparatively rapid development of effective counter-measures, moreover, embedded further the superiority of the defensive over the offensive which so characterised the land battles of the Great War. All the same, the peculiar, insidious horror of the weapon's effects on the battlefield, somehow magnified by knowledge of the careful scientific process by which it was developed, remains as one of the most powerful and enduring images we have of the war.

There were other innovations. Verdun was not just a land battle, but operations there (and later on the Somme) 'marked the true beginning of aerial warfare'.[29] At the start of the battle the Germans had assembled 'the greatest concentration of air power yet seen', comprising 168 planes, fourteen observation balloons, and four Zeppelins.[30] With the planes primarily being used for observation, they were deployed rather statically and proved vulnerable to French attack. But the balance of advantage swung back to the Germans after a new commander, Oswald Boelcke, reorganised his planes in 'Jagdstaffeln' ('hunting packs', called 'flying circuses' by the British) and developed air fighting tactics (such as attacking from the rear, if possible with the sun at one's back) which still apply today. The French, however, managed to maintain sufficient air superiority in June and July 1916 to provide vital reconnaissance for their artillery. The new war in the air – romantic, individual, *free* – appeared very different from the terrestrial slogging match below. In the sky over Verdun, German and French pilots fought gladiatorial battles and the air aces became the superstars of their day: Boelcke, Max Immelmann and Manfred von Richthofen on the German side; Georges Guynemer, Jean Navarre, Felix Antonin Brocard on the French. But the costs of air combat were high, too. Boelcke was killed in October 1916; Immelmann in June; von Richthofen in April 1918; Guynemer in September 1917. Navarre, 'the sentinel of Verdun', survived the war with his nerves shot and died in an air accident in 1919. Brocard was wounded in the jaw by a machine-gun bullet during a dogfight over Verdun in March 1916, but recovered and later commanded the famous elite 'Groupe des Cigognes' ('the Storks'), based near Villers-Bretonneux on the Somme.

The German attacks around Fleury and Fort Souville in June–July 1916 marked the high point of their advance. Although the battle of Verdun continued until November, from this moment on the Germans were on the defensive. Needing to deploy troops on the Somme from 1 July, there were no forces available to sustain any sort of offensive. The French, too, began to regain ground. Under a creeping artillery barrage (a technique first applied on the Somme by which the line of shellfire was moved forward at predetermined intervals) and with air superiority, which crippled German artillery spotting, French infantry retook Fort Douaumont on 24 October and Fort Vaux on 4 November. It was France's 'most brilliant victory since the Marne'.[31] Although the battle officially ran on until 18 December, it was effectively over. There had been prodigious casualties on both sides. The French lost 351,000 men, of whom 150,000 were killed; the Germans 330,000, of whom 143,000 were dead or missing.[32]

Even in 1916, and certainly after the war, Verdun came to represent the accumulated suffering and hardships of the entire war as it was fought along the Western Front. One of the outstanding features of the whole battle was its tight geographical extent, especially on the north-east of the city where the initial German assault fell. All the horrors of the Western Front seemed focused in one tiny area. Barely a week after the battle had begun, an American correspondent argued that 'what makes the Verdun struggle so appalling is it[s] final concentration from a twenty-five-mile front into two short sections, each barely a mile across'.[33] Here ground was occupied and re-occupied, invariably at appalling cost. Fleury-devant-Douaumont, one of the nine 'lost villages' of the battlefield, was obliterated between June and August 1916 when it changed hands sixteen times. The hill village of Vauquois, in a commanding position to the west of Verdun, had been captured by the Germans in September 1914, but a French counter-attack left the opposing trench lines just yards apart through the village along the crest of the hill. In 1915–16 an underground war developed with each side seeking to undermine the other. Between March and May 1916 a series of mines blew both the hilltop and the village to smithereens.

Laurence Binyon, the poet who early in the war wrote 'For the fallen' ('They shall grow not old, as we that are left grow old'), worked as a medical orderly in a hospital receiving casualties from Verdun during 1916. The following year he was commissioned by the Red Cross to report on the work being done in France by British volunteers, and, in the spring of 1917 visited Verdun itself. 'Beyond the town,' he wrote, 'in the afternoon brightness, rose the encircling hills, their slopes zigzagged with communication trenches. There was the

Côte St-Michel; and beyond it, I knew, lay Fleury, and Fort de Vaux, and Douaumont . . . names for ever scored into the history of Europe.' They were all 'scenes of hideous slaughter and of indescribable valour; fought for with desperate tenacity, lost and won, and lost and yet again won, in the hugest and most fiercely protracted battle that this earth had ever seen'.[34]

THE WOMEN (AND MEN) OF FRANCE AND ITS EMPIRE

In a resonant recollection first written up from memory in 1917 (and revised in the 1930s), the Gallipoli veteran, New Zealander Alexander Aitken, remarked on the absence of men as he travelled through France in the spring of 1916, en route from Egypt to the Western Front. In the marshalling yards at Marseilles, 'at first, no men were to be seen, only women and girls, at the heavy work of loading and unloading railway trucks in sidings; and when at last some Frenchmen appeared, they were past middle age, reservists on home guard, superintending batches of German prisoners'. On a train slowly creeping along the coast of north-eastern France, he 'had time to perceive at leisure the scarcity of men – none to be seen except soldiers on leave, sitting in pairs on seaward-facing seats in utter blankness and *cafard* – and the large proportion of comely young women wearing deep mourning. Here,' he remembered, 'Verdun began to shape for me, as Ypres did later, in great black letters.'[35]

The war – not just in the matter of military casualties – affected women's lives in many different ways, and brought opportunities as well as losses. In common with all the principal belligerents, the French government increasingly intervened in economic and social affairs in order to exploit national resources to the greatest possible extent. The conscription of a huge proportion of the male labour force inevitably produced labour shortages in all parts of the economy. Rural France coped quite well at the start of the war, and a combination of older men, women and children helped to bring in the 1914 harvest. In subsequent years the agricultural labour force was boosted by prisoners of war and large numbers of temporary Spanish migrants, and rather smaller numbers of Greeks and Portuguese. Over the whole war, some 230,000 Spanish, 24,000 Greeks and 23,000 Portuguese came to work in France. French industry, which had to contend with the escalating and apparently insatiable demand for munitions of all sorts, coped less well. During 1915 the state introduced regulations to keep men in essential, 'reserved' occupations, though this practice was limited by the need not to undermine the longstanding French principle of equality of service, whereby all male citizens were obliged to bear arms for the defence of the state. Foreign workers were also employed in industry, but an important additional consequence (as in Britain) was the increasing mobilisation of women and their employment in jobs hitherto generally reserved for men.[36]

The initial impact of the war had been to throw many women out of work. This was especially so in Paris where large numbers of women – seamstresses and the like – worked in luxury trades. But by July 1916 general labour shortages led the government to adopt an official policy of using women wherever possible to replace military workers. Between 1914 and 1918 some 684,000 women were employed in French armaments factories. Although General Joffre, the French chief of staff from the start of the war until December 1916, asserted that France would have lost the war without women's work in munitions factories, it was by no means all plain sailing. Women, like their male counterparts, were exploited; hours were long; working conditions often dreadful; and inflation eroded the value of even enhanced wartime rates of pay. A petition in August 1916 from women workers in an armaments factory to Alphonse Merrheim, secretary of the Metalworkers Union, asserted that 'many of us can't sleep, so great are the sufferings we endure and feel in our arms and in our stomachs from this overwork, at the end of our laborious day or night of work'. A trickle of worker militancy in the autumn of 1916 developed into a wave of serious strikes in the early summer of 1917, reflecting on the civil side a breakdown in relations similar to that which produced the much more alarming French army mutinies at much the same time. Many of the most active participants in these strikes, moreover, were women, with clothing workers being especially militant.[37]

Women in France could support the war effort in more traditional ways. Upper- and middle-class women threw themselves into a wide range of charitable voluntary work. A scheme based in Marseilles called 'Godmothers for the Soldiers of the Invaded Regions' was set up to help soldiers establish and sustain contact with their families in the German-occupied part of France. As in Britain, there was a multitude of organisations devoted to providing 'comforts' for front-line troops. Women were encouraged to adopt a 'godson' in the army, to whom they could write letters and send gifts. Nursing was an obvious wartime occupation, conferring in France (as in all the belligerent nations), perhaps the highest status for women, as it combined an apparently irresistible combination of practical caring, patriotic devotion and noble service.

Inevitably, too, there was a huge expansion in prostitution to meet the demands generated by tens of thousands of young men mobilised and away from home, many desperate for human comfort of any sort. Prostitution was legal in France, and in towns behind the lines, such as Amiens or Rouen, as well as Paris, the number of brothels increased dramatically. But there was much unregulated activity as well. In Marseilles in 1917, while the local authorities had some 700–800 women registered, there were thought to be an additional 7,000 active sex workers in the city. Reflecting that their clientele included more than just Frenchmen, in one Paris brothel near the Etoile the women took English classes in their spare time.

Prostitution, however, as James F. McMillan has observed, was 'only one particular instance of the heightened sexual activity generated by the war', and he quoted the improbable assertion by Anatole France, the anti-militarist and socialist sceptic, that a major reason for the prolongation of the war was because wives were enjoying themselves so much in the absence of their husbands.[38] If some censorious observers are to be believed, there was a huge increase in extra-marital sexual relations. Indeed it seems clear that the wartime relaxation of social and moral restraints brought enhanced opportunities for mutually beneficial relationships between men and women (and homosexual ones too). Not everyone necessarily disapproved. The radical sex-education pioneer, Ettie Rout, who travelled to Egypt in February 1916 to help care for New Zealand soldiers, appreciated the value which sex had for many soldiers, while deploring the ignorance which resulted in high rates of venereal disease. Devoting herself to the provision of prophylactic kits containing ointment and condoms, she later worked in London and Paris, where she set up 'a one-woman social and sexual welfare service for soldiers'. She met troop trains arriving at the Gare du Nord and handed out a card recommending one particular brothel which had agreed to operate on hygienic lines.[39]

The French empire was thought by many to provide a virtually limitless reservoir of manpower for both military and civilian demands. In 1910 Charles Mangin, a French army officer with extensive colonial experience, had claimed in his book *La force noire* that French West Africa could provide up to 400,000 troops. In the event, this was an over-optimistic prediction. Nevertheless, during the war many thousands of colonial soldiers were mobilised in West Africa and elsewhere. At first mainly deployed in Africa, by the end of the conflict, they had served in every significant theatre involving French troops. Both the empire and China were also tapped to help meet labour shortages in industry and agriculture, as well as the constantly increasing demands of the military supply services behind the battle lines. The Voie Sacrée at Verdun was maintained by colonial labour battalions, including 'powerful Senegalese' and 'industrious little Annamites'.[40]

Recruitment for these units was systematised from January 1916 when the War Ministry established a 'Colonial Labour Service' (Service des Travailleurs Coloniaux) which began to import Chinese labourers from the spring of 1916 and by the end of the war had recruited nearly 40,000 men. While the Chinese were enlisted more or less voluntarily, men from French-controlled territories in North Africa (Algeria, Morocco and Tunisia – which supplied 79,000, 36,000 and 18,000 men respectively) and the French eastern empire in Indochina (49,000) were increasingly conscripted, or recruited under the threat of possible compulsion. Towards the end of 1915 the Munitions Ministry asked the Algerian authorities to supply up to 30,000 workers, but when by July the following year fewer than 5,000 had been assembled the government introduced a decree laying down quotas of Algerian labour to be supplied and providing for conscription to be applied if the numbers were not met voluntarily. Similar provisions were applied in Tunis. In Indochina, where the colonial authorities ran an extensive publicity campaign, putting up recruiting posters across the territory, quotas were also set, but the central administration left the actual recruitment to local village headmen who in many cases coerced individuals to meet their numbers.

In both North Africa and Indochina the imposition of progressively more stringent manpower demands, for both military and labour recruitment, on communities with (at best) only conditional loyalties to the French state provoked resistance. The fabled 'Union Sacrée', which from August 1914 was claimed to have bound French people of all political stripes together against the German invader, applied only patchily (if at all) in the colonies. It was, wrote the Algerian Director of Native Affairs in October 1915, 'puerile to believe that the natives wish to serve France, that they join up through patriotism or loyalty'. In August 1916 the imposition of conscription across Batna Province in the highlands of north-east Algeria sparked off widespread protests. Men in one village were reported to have declared: 'We will not give our children away! You will have to take them!' By November the grumbling resistance had turned into open rebellion. A band of insurgents, estimated at between 1,000 and 1,500-strong, sacked a French settler farm, cut telegraph wires and went on to kill two colonial officials. On 30 November a French military party escorting Algerian conscripts to barracks was attacked by a band of rebels seeking to 'set their brothers free'. In December the insurgents withdrew into the mountains and fought off attempts to prise them out. It was not until well into the New Year, and a force of over 14,000 troops had been deployed, that the insurrection was finally quashed.[41]

This Algerian outbreak was a relatively minor affair, ill-led and sustained mainly by a general unease about the imposition of military and civil conscription. Yet it also suggested that there were real limits to French colonial power, particularly in the circumstances of the Great War. In responding to an existential threat to the state itself, and by making increasing demands on the state's resources, at home and in the empire, there was a risk of pushing matters close to breaking point. Episodes, such as the rising in Algeria, were perhaps symptoms of a system, or a part of a system, which could not easily cope with the demands made upon it.

Similar events occurred further afield. The colonial prisons historian, Peter Zinoman, has noted that heavy-handed attempts to recruit soldiers and labourers by the French colonial authorities in Indochina 'provoked an un-coordinated but widespread movement of resistance to forced conscription'. Large numbers of draft-evaders were jailed, putting the prison system under particular pressure. Before the war the French authorities had been accustomed to pack off troublesome colonial subjects to the famous Devil's Island prison colony in French Guiana, an option no longer available during the war. On 25 January 1916 a mob stormed the prison at Bien-Hoa, near Saigon (Ho Chi Minh City), aiming to release draft-evaders. Several guards were killed and all the prisoners were freed. Three weeks later another mob attacked the central prison in Saigon, aiming to free Phan Xich Long, a mystic who claimed to be emperor of Vietnam. Forewarned, the French beat off the attack with the loss of ten lives. Various other attacks in February served merely to heighten fears of further insurgency among the white French population, already anxious following the withdrawal to Europe of thousands of troops from the colonial military garrison and beset by talk of a German plan to invade the colony. Real and imaginary war-induced fears served to stiffen attitudes and underpinned a wave of arrests of anyone remotely suspected of sedition. Between February 1916 and May 1917 over five hundred suspects were brought before a *conseil de guerre* which handed down numerous death sentences. In all, some fifty-eight individuals were executed for the attacks at Bien-Hoa and Saigon.[42]

Once they reached metropolitan France, non-white workers from the colonies and China were very closely controlled under a system known as '*encadrement*' (supervision), which was organised to keep them as isolated as possible from the French population. While the workers' travel costs to and from France were met, free health care was provided and bonuses awarded for re-enlisting, their freedom of movement was closely regulated and they had to agree to return home

on the expiry of their contracts. Although pay rates were initially set
to match those of equivalent French workers, in practice incomes were
reduced by wartime inflation and non-negotiable deductions for often
sub-standard food and housing. Indeed, some of the workers were
very unhappy, as revealed in letters monitored by the French postal
censors. 'Misery descends on us day and night,' wrote Khalifa Ben
M'Hamed, a Tunisian working on a farm near Montreaux, south-east
of Paris, 'and I can no longer sleep because of overwork. We are six
workers on a large expanse of land covered with a plant which they
call sugar-beet, and for such work you need camels, not men.' There
were difficulties, too, with the observance of religious dietary rules.
'Today I drank wine and ate pork,' wrote Mohammed Baccouch. 'I
intend to eat during the month of Ramadan, for we take our meals
with Christians, and what's more the kitchen utensils which we use are
soiled with pork and all that comes from it, grease, lard etc. I really
don't know what to do, short of dying of hunger and thirst.'[43]

Tensions between colonial workers and French people sometimes
broke into violence. In Le Creusot, a small town in Burgundy, foreign
workers were accused of taking local jobs and driving Frenchmen back
to the front. 'Our men,' claimed one woman, 'are being driven out of
factories by Chinamen, who should rightly be sent to the front and
our husbands allowed to stay in the workshops.' In September 1916 a
fight between Chinese and locals ended with a café being ransacked
and one of the Chinese men being shot dead. As one of the colonial
workers put it: 'We love French, but French no good.'[44]

A particular concern for the authorities was the matter of sexual
relations between immigrants and French civilians. In an engrossing
study of immigrant workers in France during the war, John Horne has
observed a 'curious reversal', that whereas in North Africa and
Indochina, French colonists, administrators and soldiers had frequent
access to local women – prostitutes or not – suddenly significant
numbers of colonial males temporarily in metropolitan France could
in their turn develop and enjoy liaisons with French women. A report
on Indochinese workers in Marseilles in 1917 said that their conduct
'leaves a lot to be desired. Our customs, it must be admitted, lend
themselves admirably to their natural lewdness. Prostitution in the big

cities offers them the pleasures of the flesh.' Worrying about the subversion of metropolitan–colonial relations, the censors thought that after their experience in Marseilles, it would be difficult 'to keep intact in Indo-China the prestige of European women'. There was certainly much evidence of interaction between Indochinese and French women. One sergeant-interpreter (and many of the interpreters were well-educated men who joined up in the hope of self-improvement), Pham Van Nhuong, was reported as receiving 'letter on letter from his faithful fiancée' in Toulouse, while additionally being reproached by 'another young girl whom he dishonoured after promising to marry her'. The censors also fastidiously counted and catalogued the number of 'dirty postcards' intercepted; in August 1917, for example: '3 obscene photographs, 137 nude scenes, 29 undressing scenes, 20 bathing scenes, etc.'.[45]

Unknown soldiers

In the immediate aftermath of the Great War, several countries, beginning with Britain and France (but later including others on the Allied side, the USA, Italy, Belgium and Portugal), commemorated their many thousands of unidentified dead with a single 'Unknown Soldier', ceremonially selected and then entombed in a place of special national significance. Since so many of the wartime casualties were unidentified, it was one way of providing, as Jay Winter has put it, a 'site of memory and mourning' for individuals with no known grave, as well as democratically commemorating the host of humble 'ordinary soldiers' who had served and died in the war. This was a novel form of war memorial, which before 1914 had tended to commemorate national victories and leaders such as kings and generals. In Britain and the British Empire, after the Crimean War and especially the Boer War of 1899–1902, regimental memorials became common, but the notion of communities commemorating their own fallen, let alone the burial of any emblematic individual representing 'Everyman', only really emerged during the First World War.

The ways in which these Unknown Soldiers were selected, and the ceremonials which accompanied their re-burial, varied from country to country. In each instance, however, the careful thought which accompanied these processes reflected what those involved perceived to be the essential requirements of national and communal commemoration. Thus the British individual was carefully named as an 'Unknown *Warrior*' ('Soldier' being too limiting for a maritime nation), yet he was almost certainly a soldier, being selected randomly from six unidentified bodies disinterred from representative locations in France and Belgium: Ypres, the Somme, Cambrai, the Aisne, the Marne and Arras.[46]

Inevitably the French commemoration began at Verdun, to which, as reported by *The Times*, had been entrusted on 10 November 1920 'the sad and glorious task' of selecting one from the coffins of eight unknown soldiers destined for a 'perpetual resting place' in Paris. Although André Maginot, a deputy for Lorraine and minister of pensions, who himself had been wounded at Verdun in 1914 and who as minister of war in the 1930s presided over the construction of fortifications along the Franco-German frontier named after him, initially wanted one body to be taken just from the Verdun battlefield, eventually eight bodies were collected from different sectors along the Western Front. The final selection was made by a young private soldier of the Verdun garrison who indicated his choice by placing a posy of wild flowers gathered from the battlefield on one of the coffins. In a short speech, M. Schleiter, the deputy mayor of the city, wished the *poilu inconnu* 'God speed': 'Go, Soldier of France, to the glory that a grateful country reserves for its great men. Go to receive for ever in glory the admiration of future generations. Verdun salutes thee with emotion.'

The next day there was a double ceremony in Paris, as 'France's homage to the men of 1914 and the other years of the war' was combined with celebrations marking the fiftieth anniversary of the founding of the Third Republic. The coffin of the Unknown Soldier was accompanied by a casket containing the heart of the French statesman, Léon Gambetta, who had championed the Republic in the aftermath of French defeat in the Franco-Prussian War. Gambetta's heart was placed at the Panthéon, and before the Unknown Soldier was carried on to rest at the Arc de Triomphe, the French president

Millerand eulogised the part both men had played in the defence of the nation. Gambetta, he said, had 'laid the foundations of the Republic, and the Unknown Soldier, the anonymous and triumphant representative of the collective heroics of the poilus', should 'rest in peace. You have fulfilled your destiny. France and civilisation have been saved.'[47]

The British Unknown Warrior was carried from the battlefield to London with equal pomp and circumstance. On 10 November 1920 he was taken across the Channel on the specially chosen British V-class destroyer HMS *Verdun*, named in 1917 'after the French victories at that place'. With full military honours at every stage, the coffin was taken by train from Dover to Victoria Station where it rested overnight. The following day the funeral party moved from Victoria to the newly erected Cenotaph in Whitehall in time for its unveiling by King George V at eleven o'clock, the exact second anniversary of the Armistice. Enormous crowds attended at every stage, representing, as *The Times* put it, not just London and 'the people of the United Kingdom, but . . . all the kindred peoples of the British States, Governments, and Dependencies beyond the seas'. The Unknown Warrior himself, moreover, might have been 'an Englishman, a Scotsman, a Welshman, an Irishman, a man of the Dominions, a Sikh, a Gurkha. No one knows. But he was one who gave his life for the people of the British Empire.' There were no speeches on the day (nor any sermon), merely a funeral service in Westminster Abbey in the presence, not just of the 'Good and Great', but also injured ex-servicemen and nurses, as well as bereaved relatives, who had been allotted places by ballot. In keeping with the studied symbolism of the day's events, when the words of the committal reached 'Earth to earth, ashes to ashes, dust to dust', the king scattered some of the soil gathered from French battlefields which had been brought to London as filling for the grave.[48] Thus rich English – or British – dust, brought home to represent all of the empire's dead, was to lie for ever, not just at home, but also in the rich, foreign earth of France.

The concept of an Unknown Soldier (or equivalent) as a representative national icon continued to resonate long after the end of the Great War. In Washington DC, there are now 'Unknowns' from the

Second World War, Korea and Vietnam, and a Tomb of the Unknown
Soldier outside Ho Chi Minh City commemorates those who fought
against the Americans. By the late twentieth century the notion of a
single Unknown Warrior buried in Westminster Abbey, London,
representing all those who served from within the British Empire,
was no longer felt to be satisfactory in Australia, and on 11 November
1993, in the Hall of Memory at the Australian War Memorial in
Canberra, an Australian Unknown Soldier was interred. And,
although Ken Inglis, historian par excellence of Australian war
commemoration, thought that this tomb would 'surely hold another
record, as the last to be built over the remains of a man who died in
the Great War',[49] there were more yet to come. In May 2000 an
unidentified Canadian soldier, exhumed from a cemetery near Vimy
Ridge, where the Canadian Corps fought in 1917, was reburied next
to the Canadian national war memorial in Ottawa. On 11 November
2003, a New Zealand serviceman was re-interred in a 'Tomb of the
Unknown Warrior' in Wellington. This man was another Great War
casualty, originally buried near Longueval, where the New Zealand
Division fought during the battle of the Somme in 1916. Marking a
change in how war dead are commemorated over the eighty years
since the Westminster Abbey ceremony, the rhetoric accompanying
this re-burial not only stressed purely national endeavour, but also
contemporary international peace-keeping operations. 'By bringing
this one warrior home to rest in a place of honour,' wrote the New
Zealand prime minister Helen Clark, 'we give thanks to all those who
have served New Zealand overseas.' Furthermore, by providing 'a
peaceful place to pay tribute to the ultimate sacrifice [of] New Zealand
servicemen and women', fellow citizens could also 'contemplate the
tradition of service which continues today with New Zealand's
commitment to bring peace to troubled places around the world'.[50]

3

On the Isonzo

The fifth battle of the Isonzo, which began on 9 March 1916 and continued for eight days, was one of a long series of twelve battles fought between Italian forces and those of the Central Powers between June 1915 and November 1917. Five of these largely inconclusive engagements (the fifth to the ninth) were fought in 1916, on the south-eastern end of a 400-mile front which ran from crazy, mountain-top trench lines in the Dolomites to more conventional positions in Friuli, along the river Isonzo (Soča) down to the Adriatic Sea coast just north of Trieste.[1]

BRITISH AMBULANCES AND ITALIAN WOUNDED

On 10 January 1916 the *Manchester Guardian* published what it claimed was the 'first account by an English eyewitness' of the Isonzo battle front. It was written by the 'well-known man of letters', Edward Garnett, an author, playwright and literary editor who had encouraged writers including Joseph Conrad and D. H. Lawrence at the start of their writing careers (though he was also one of the editors who turned down James Joyce's *A Portrait of the Artist as a Young Man* for publication). In 1915, Garnett, by then in his late forties, had joined an ambulance unit destined for Italy, sponsored by the Society of Friends and the British Red Cross. Garnett described how, since the summer of 1915, the Italians had been besieging the town of Gorizia, situated on the river Isonzo, twelve miles on the Austrian side of the frontier with Italy and about the same distance from the Adriatic Sea. Protected by the inhospitable limestone plateau of the Carso to the south and west, and hilly country to the north-west where the Austrian artillery was well dug in, Gorizia was a hard nut to crack. Directly in front of the town, moreover, was another 'rounded, shaggy hill, Podgora, the scene [as Garnett put it] of the bloodiest fighting in the war'. Here the Italian and Austrian trenches ran 'side by side, bisecting the hill slopes; time after time the Italians have made advances of desperate bravery, only to be held up at this segment or thrown back at that'. In a second article published four days later Garnett wrote about his experiences as an orderly working at 'the English Hospital' in the Villa Trento (the Count of Trento's rambling country residence) at Cormons just inside the Italian frontier in the fertile plain west of Gorizia. He said relatively little about the actual work of the hospital, merely describing the movements of troops and waxing lyrical about the physical surroundings. 'Endless convoys' passed by the villa gates, winding onwards 'to where the Austrian hills and plain were ringed with trenches'. And in the distance was 'the great mountainous wall of snowy Alpine crests, terrible in their beauty and inaccessible purity'.

Recounting, however, an offensive the previous October (the third battle of the Isonzo), he described the constant stream of sick and wounded, 'batches of men, then more batches, limbs splinted, bloody head-cloths, back and chest wounds, arms in slings, men walking, limping in, hobbling on sticks, carried in friendly arms or pig-a-back, others borne in on bulging stretchers which are lowered on trestles till the whole floor is thick with wounded'. To the operation theatre 'in the white naked light' came 'nurses and assistants ready with instruments and anaesthetics. The surgeons come; the doors are shut . . . So here behind the Isonzo,' he concluded, 'flows the tide of war, where life grapples with life, and life goes out in death.'[2]

The British Ambulance Unit on the Italian front had its origins in August 1915 when it was sponsored by the British Committee in Aid of the Italian Wounded and the British Red Cross. The prominent historian and Fellow of Trinity College, Cambridge, George Macaulay Trevelyan, was put in charge. Having written a very successful three-volume study of Garibaldi, whom he celebrated as a great champion of freedom and liberal nationalism, he was well known in Italy and an apt choice to head the unit. Trevelyan came from a high-achieving family of public intellectuals and Whig-Liberal politicians. His brother Charles, a junior minister in Asquith's government, had resigned in August 1914 as a protest against Britain entering the war. 'G.M.', as he was widely known, initially shared his brother's non-interventionist sympathies, but changed his mind after the Germans invaded Belgium. 'The present awful struggle,' he wrote to a friend on 2 September 1914, 'is to save England, Belgium and France from the Junkers, and to save our island civilisation, with its delicate economic fabric, from collapse.'³ Disbarred from active service due to his poor eyesight, the thirty-eight-year-old Trevelyan threw himself into relief and propaganda work, and spent the spring of 1915 promoting British war aims in the USA.

The personnel Trevelyan assembled for the unit included a mixture of individuals like himself who were not fit for active service, conscientious objectors, and others both above and below military age (among whom were an Irishman called Pringle and his seventeen-year-old son). Key early recruits came from a group of volunteer pacifist Quakers who had run a Friends' Ambulance Service in Flanders early in the war until official medical services supplanted them. One was Geoffrey Winthrop Young, who had been an undergraduate at Cambridge with Trevelyan in the 1890s. He was a celebrated mountaineer and had been sacked from a teaching position at Eton in 1905 for homosexual activity. Another volunteer was Philip Noel-Baker, also a Cambridge man (King's College), who had been president of the Cambridge Union and a finalist in the 1,500 metres at the 1912 Stockholm Olympics. After the war he had a long career as a Labour politician and committed liberal internationalist, being awarded the Nobel Peace Prize in 1959. Others included the sculptor Francis Sargant (who had a studio in Florence) and the artists Elliott Seabrooke and Henry Tonks, the latter as 'assistant surgeon'. Tonks had given up a promising surgical career in the 1890s to become assistant to the Slade Professor of Fine Art at University College London. On the outbreak of war he returned to medicine, but did not really have the stomach for it. Nor did he take to the rather high-minded austerity of G. M. Trevelyan's regime. 'It always seems to be my fate,' he wrote to a friend just after he had joined the unit, 'to work with water-drinkers and virtuous men, whereas my natural leanings are towards drunkards and lewd persons.' Tonks, who only stayed in Italy for a month, never entirely abandoned art and ended up as a British official war artist in 1918.[4]

Trevelyan's party of fifty-five 'officers, interpreters, medical men, drivers, mechanics, orderlies, and cooks', with twenty ambulances, was shipped across the Channel and drove through France to northern Italy during the last days of August 1915. Although welcomed along the way, and given a formal official reception at Turin, Geoffrey Young recalled what he regarded as a strikingly ill-judged and pompous speech at Vicenza from Lord Monson, commissioner of the British Red Cross in Italy (though one which was perhaps painfully close to some realities of battle-zone experience). Monson told the British contingent 'that whoever raped or looted or got drunk would be sent home at once', and so offended Young that he walked off the parade. 'No man,' he confided to his journal, 'would talk to a reformatory as he did to our distinguished middle-aged set of English volunteers and gentlemen.'[5]

The unit was quickly established at the Villa Trento, and the ambulances were deployed in a series of advanced stations behind the lines facing Gorizia. Geoffrey Young was posted with a detachment to Quisca, in the hills north of Cormons. From here the mountain road up to the front was in places open to Austrian shellfire. Even in vehicles prominently marked with large red crosses, the ambulances were at risk. 'Coming up today,' wrote Young on 4 October 1915, 'it was gorgeously, murderously clear.' Although he thought his red cross was 'clear as noon', the Austrians 'shelled me at both salient corners, where one has to slow up to round the cornice-cliff overhanging the precipice. It is the worst sensation I have ever had.' There was much driving at night, under orders not to use headlamps. On one terrifying evening Young noted 'an all-night grim running in pitch dark on worsening slime' on roads along which other military traffic was running. He 'had 11 in my first load; mudguards down to the wheels', when a mule cart ran into him and pushed the ambulance forward so that one wheel hung over the edge of the cliff. Young had to get all the wounded out before carefully reversing the car back onto the road. On his second journey he 'was charged by an ammunition waggon and again got out without bad damage'. Thereafter, however, 'for later runs I put on *full* lights, swore at objecting sentries, and took the offensive in collisions, which gives the car the advantage of impetus and head-on attack'.[6]

Because of the parlous state of the roads, badly cut up on account of the winter weather, the British ambulances were reckoned to be more comfortable than the available Italian army trucks, so they got the most serious cases to carry. 'The business of carrying grave cases by the only available road for ambulances over some 20 miles of surface cut to pieces by traffic,' reported Trevelyan in January 1916, 'has it is to be feared been very painful to the wounded, although it is considered that they suffer to the least possible degree in our cars.' Even over a relatively quiet period, Trevelyan noted that his ambulances had carried nearly 850 casualties in the first fortnight of 1916. And, although the poor weather made driving difficult, the wet misty conditions had resulted in 'very little firing on the cars or stations'.[7]

Among the most dangerous and dramatic experiences of the Ambulance Unit was the entry into Gorizia of cars from Geoffrey Young's detachment after the Italians had captured the town in August 1916, at the start of the sixth battle of the Isonzo. On the evening of 8 August Young was asked if he could get some wounded Italian cavalrymen out of the town and back over the damaged iron bridge which carried the main road sixty feet above the Isonzo. Later that night, walking ahead in the moonlight, Young led a convoy of a Ford car and three ambulances carefully over the bridge. 'Every ten feet or so,' he reported, 'there were shell breaches through the bridge' which, in the dark, it was 'next to impossible to see'. At places 'soldiers, mules and carts fell through during the night' and at two points the bridge was so badly damaged that there were 'only narrow passages along the edge . . . slightly but insecurely widened by a few loose planks'. The bodies of soldiers killed in the assault across the bridge that morning had not yet been cleared away. 'Each of our cars had to be piloted across, on foot, inch by inch.' Young managed to get all four cars into the town, where he distributed medical supplies and loaded up with wounded.

Getting back across the 250-foot-long bridge was even more hazardous. Not only were the ambulance men now faced with a steady stream of guns and supplies moving into Gorizia, but the bridge itself was breaking up under the pressure of the traffic. 'The moon had now sunk,' wrote Young. 'The gaps in the iron bridge had opened further. The traffic was all from the other bank, and the munition carts were all successively breaking through and necessitating lengthy rescue operations.' Young managed to get the Ford and a small ambulance over, though it took two hours to do so, temporarily leaving two heavier ambulances behind. On the Italian side the traffic was so jammed that they had to proceed on foot to the nearest ambulance station where Young and one of his drivers, Lionel Sessions, picked up fresh medical supplies and thermos flasks of hot coffee for their colleagues left at the Gorizia end of the bridge. By this stage it was nearly daybreak, when the Austrian artillery would resume shelling. As Young approached, the road and bridge began 'clearing like magic' as gun crews and carts rushed for cover as the light improved. This gave Young's two remaining ambulances the chance to cross. First over was a Crossley, then a heavier Buick, which 'had to be carefully piloted over, [the driver] Christie winding through the gaps and rushing the awkward, skew, narrow traverses with skill and nerve'. It was the last car back across the bridge, and it had been the first over the previous evening. 'We were barely clear of the bridge, perhaps not four minutes,' reported Young, 'when the first big shell exploded, at the Italian end.'[8]

George Trevelyan claimed at the time that the events of August 1916 had represented 'the principal crisis of the history of the Unit', in which the results had 'been in the highest degree satisfactory'. After the heroics of the first day, ambulance stations had been established in Gorizia itself under Young's command, and up to sixteen vehicles were carrying wounded across the Isonzo bridges, often under fire. At the end of the month he reported that, since 10 August, six cars had been 'perforated by shrapnel'. The dangers of the work were vividly illustrated a year later when Young's car was hit by Austrian shellfire on a mountain road north of Gorizia, and he was so badly injured that he had to have his left leg amputated at the thigh. He survived into his eighties, and continued mountaineering on a special 'climbing leg' he designed for himself. A few days after Young's injury, Lionel Sessions's car was hit on the same road and he, too, lost a leg. The same day, Victor Silvester, under age for front-line service and serving as an orderly, sustained a shrapnel wound on his leg from which he fully recovered, a happy outcome bearing in mind his future career as a ballroom dancer and dance-band leader.[9]

The Villa Trento eventually expanded to contain a hospital of 180 beds, with a British nursing staff of twenty or so women, comprising both professionals and VADs (Voluntary Aid Detachment volunteers with some elementary training). This provoked a change in the Italian regulations which before August 1915 had prohibited female nurses from serving so close to the front. Between the intense periods of activity accompanying pushes and flare-ups along the front, and even though the constant artillery fire was both visible and audible from the villa, life there seems to have been pretty enjoyable. 'In the evening when work is done,' wrote E. V. Lucas, *Punch* journalist and travel writer, who visited the unit in late 1916, 'the Villa turns into a social club.' In the spacious saloon were 'sofas, a piano, English papers, and the works of Jack London, who seems to be the most popular writer wherever ambulances are driven'.[10] In March 1916 members of the unit produced a parody house magazine: *Trento – Journal and Organ of the Anglo-Italian Nursing and Automobile Association*. One advertisement extolled the charms of the 'Grand Hotel des Anglais' at the Villa Trento. Every visitor was 'met by a luxuriously appointed automobile and he enjoys this convenience (so restful after a long journey) absolutely gratis, a small fee only being charged when stretchers are required'. The hotel was equipped 'with every convenience' and 'the most costly fireworks are visible every evening' from the saloon. Visitors, it declared, 'have the opportunity of trying their skill as motor drivers and even as hospital nurses . . . and special trips to the trenches are conducted by Mr Elliott Seabrooke.' The whole was signed by 'G.M.T. Business Manager The Italian Picnics Co.'[11]

The nurses and VADs at the Villa Trento were not the only females on the battle front, which provided opportunities for activist British women to contribute to the war effort in ways not always available elsewhere. From January 1916 Mrs Henry Watkins, helped by Bridget Talbot and two female assistants, ran canteens at Cervignano and Cormons providing refreshments for Italian soldiers in passing hospital trains. In one six-month period they calculated that 50,000 troops had passed through their hands. For Talbot, twenty-nine years old in 1914 and granddaughter of the Earl of Shrewsbury, her war work began a career of social and political activism, some of which took her a fair way from her upper-class origins. While she spent much time lobbying the National Trust to help preserve English country houses, between 1920 and 1922 she also worked in Turkey to help Russian refugees. Between the wars she campaigned to improve the safety of merchant seamen, and in 1931 joined the National Labour Party to help promote this cause.[12]

There was also an X-ray unit run by the painter Helena Gleichen, and her long-time friend and companion, Mrs Nina Hollings. Having worked in an English hospital in France between February and May 1915, Gleichen and Hollings spent six months in Paris training as radiographers while supporters back home raised funds to provide, as Gleichen recalled in her memoirs, 'a portable X-ray apparatus' for use at the front. They initially offered their services to the British authorities, but the War Office responded 'that as no women had ever been known to be radiographers, we could not be employed as such'. Undeterred, they went to the French who initially welcomed them, but once they arrived in France attempted to requisition their vehicles and send the women away. Gleichen and Hollings managed to hold on to the cars and were finally accepted by the Italians, who, giving them each the rank of major in the Italian army, deployed them on the Isonzo front from December 1915 until October 1917. Here they provided the only X-ray service, initially for eleven field hospitals (which had increased to twenty-seven by July 1916). The unit worked long days, driving, regularly under shellfire, between hospitals, sustained, among other things, with 'hot coffee or *zabaione* (a raw egg beaten up either in Marsala or coffee)'. Not only did they perform the delicate and specialised radiography work, but they also had to maintain and repair the X-ray equipment and dynamos, and, although they had male drivers, they were not all very satisfactory and the women regularly drove their vans themselves. One driver sent out by the Red Cross from England, indeed, complained that 'he had not been sent out here to be taken to nasty dangerous places by ladies'. After they got home, often late in the evening, they had to develop plates in time for distribution to the hospitals early next morning.

Quoting letters written home from Italy in her memoirs, Gleichen apologised that for 'some to whom the War brought sorrow and nothing but sorrow' these showed 'an unfeeling light-heartedness at such a time'. She explained that the constant high pressure under which they worked, combined with 'the excitement of a certain amount of danger', seemed to have 'a tonic effect' which enabled people 'to take their part in scenes which in ordinary times they could not have borne to witness'. In effect, they laughed lest they wept. 'We found that if we allowed ourselves . . . to relax for a moment and feel and show sympathy to the patients, both would crack and both would suffer for it in the long run.' But the tone was not all light-hearted. 'Today,' she wrote on 31 August 1916, 'we were working in a big building where they bring the worst cases before sending them on to hospital . . . The hustle and noise, the groaning, the cries for "Mamma mia," the smell of disinfectants and the smell of blood all help to make the place a nightmare, never to be forgotten.'

When the fighting intensified the pressure of work was continuous. The previous autumn during the third battle of the Isonzo, Geoffrey Young recorded that in one week the ambulances had carried 1,500 casualties to the hospital at Cormons. 'The Italian surgery is brilliant, but savage!' he noted. 'I saw an arm amputated and a finger taken off and the hand shaped and re-made – all without anaesthetics! They haven't time for anaesthetics here at the front.' A year later, during the build-up to the eighth battle of the Isonzo, George Barbour noted similar conditions: 'The operating room was one of the ghastliest sights I've ever seen, almost unimaginable to anyone with an idea of a modern hospital theatre.' There was only one surgeon having to cope with a

stream of casualties: '3 amputations going on at once without anaesthetics & the next patients awaiting treatment already in the room
watching it all'.[13]

In October 1916, Gleichen's unit was posted forward to Gorizia, a
health resort (described as 'a kind of Harrogate' by E. V. Lucas) which
as yet was largely undamaged by the war. Geoffrey Young remarked
on its 'superficially unspoiled beauty of white palace and pleasure
garden'. But from August 1916 it had come under constant Austrian
shellfire. Gleichen cheerily dismissed Young's concerns about how
dangerously exposed their building was. 'You see,' she said, 'the Park
Hotel is just in front of us, and that *stops* the shells!' Young noted that
it had indeed 'stopped three' just the day before, and hoped that 'it
would go on stopping them'. After an Austrian counterattack in
November, Gleichen described the sound 'as being just like the over-
ture to *Tannhäuser*'. They were briefly joined in Gorizia by Nina
Hollings's sister, the chain-smoking feminist composer Ethel Smyth,
whose dynamism affected them all. 'I shall shoot Ethel soon,' wrote
Gleichen in one of her letters home, 'so kind, so persistent and so
damnably energetic.'[14]

The widespread sense of the war being never-ending, which in so
many places was such a feature of 1916, affected the Ambulance Unit
too. Geoffrey Young remembered that year's Christmas revue (which
he produced) as being 'exceptionally artistic'. In the final scene, Old
Time, played by Young himself, 'relented at last and let the war end'.
Thus 'the members of the aged Unit, white-bearded and white-locked,
woke up in the moonlit cavern of the years to a last Italian chorus and
their way home'. Young had endured weeks of strain running the
exposed advanced post in Gorizia, and the amateur dramatics proved
a welcome diversion (and perhaps not only to him). The Christmas
play, wrote George Barbour, gave 'a much-needed occupation' to
Young '& cheered him up immensely'.[15]

Trevelyan, too, remarked on the festivities in his December 1916
report to the Red Cross back home, and 'a particularly good play or
revue about ourselves' which had 'helped make Christmas a very
pleasant occasion for the members of the Unit'. Evidently conscious
of the need to reassure the unit's funders and supporters about their

work, Trevelyan concluded with some striking statistics. They had carried 4,245 patients in the previous month and 60,138 since September 1915, 'while the total number of kilometres run is 512,206'.[16] In the autumn of 1916 their work was inspected by Sarah Swift, the matron-in-chief of the joint war committee of the St John Ambulance Association and the British Red Cross Society, who was in overall charge of the nursing at the 1,500 or so Red Cross auxiliary hospitals. Reporting on her visit, the *British Journal of Nursing* remarked that 'the patients, of course, are all Italians, and they much appreciate all the care and good nursing which they receive from the British Sisters'. Standards at the Villa Trento were undoubtedly good, but with evident faith in the superiority of British nursing, the report added that 'to receive such skilled attention has possibly never been their experience on any previous occasion'.[17]

ITALY'S WAR

Italy entered the war in stages. Unlike the belligerents of July and August 1914, Italian leaders took some time to debate the issues and contemplate the costs and benefits of participation. While there was a strong party in favour of participation – including General Luigi Cadorna, who had been appointed chief of staff of the Italian army at the end of July 1914 – others counselled caution, an approach which the foreign minister, Antonio di San Giuliano, argued might 'not [be] heroic but [was] wise and patriotic'.[18] There was, moreover, some doubt as to which side Italy might join. Since 1882 Italy had been part of the Triple Alliance with Germany and Austria-Hungary, a defensive arrangement which committed each of them to support any other ally if it were itself attacked. But despite their joint membership of the alliance, there was unfinished business between Italy and Austria-Hungary, since the latter still occupied part of what Italian nationalists regarded as the legitimate national territory. Since its creation as a unified national state in 1861, Italian nationalists had sought to make the new nation state coterminous with the Italian peninsula, right up to the mountain barriers of the north and north-east. By 1870, when Rome (excluding the Vatican City) was occupied, this had been achieved with the exception of ethnically Italian areas in Trento, the Alto Adige and along the Dalmatian coast which remained within the Austrian Habsburg Empire.

Since the Triple Alliance was a mutually defensive pact, the Italian premier, Antonio Salandra, offended by the German invasion of Belgium and France, had a strong case for keeping Italy out. Nevertheless, amid the diplomatic jockeying in the summer of 1914, the glittering prospect of finally possessing '*Italia irredenta*' led Rome to propose territorial compensation from Austria-Hungary as a reward for participation on the Triple Alliance side. Vienna, however, was not prepared to concede anything more than the possibility of some frontier adjustments after the war had been won. Meanwhile the Allied powers of Britain, France and Russia had more to offer, and by the spring of 1915 were promising Trentino, the Alto Adige, Trieste and a considerable amount of territory in Dalmatia, as well as a pocket of land around Valona (Vlorë) in Albania and sovereignty over the Dodecanese Islands (which the Italians had occupied in 1912), if Italy came in on their side.

Other factors delayed the Italian decision for war. A strong body of opinion opposed any participation, on various grounds including the manifest unpreparedness of the army and the weakness of the Italian economy. Socialists and Catholics, too, had ideological objections. In the end, however, the Allies' offer (which was embodied in the Treaty of London signed on 26 April) tipped the balance in their favour, though even then the Italians did not immediately go to war against all three Central Powers. Assuming that the moment was propitious to take on the Austrians, preoccupied with fighting against Russia on the Eastern Front and Serbia in the Balkans, on 23 May Italy declared war just on Austria-Hungary. While hostilities against Turkey followed on 28 August, the Italians (much to the Allies' annoyance) did not declare war on Germany until 28 August 1916, at which stage Rome calculated that the diplomatic benefits of so doing would outweigh any military costs. G. M. Trevelyan, always ready to put as positive a construction as possible on anything the Italians did, had been deeply concerned at the start of the war that they might honour their Triple Alliance obligations and enter the conflict at the side of Germany and

Austria-Hungary. Relieved that they did not, he argued that even non-intervention had an impact and claimed that Italy's neutrality had 'saved France on the Marne' by permitting her 'to strip her Alpine frontier' of troops.[19]

Although the military authorities had stepped up preparations for action from the summer of 1914, the Italian army was by no means ready for action in May 1915. Some troops had battle experience from fighting in the Libyan war of 1911–12, though the desert operations there against scattered Ottoman units and tribal forces scarcely provided adequate preparation for the mechanised warfare against the well-equipped opponents they encountered on the Isonzo. But Italy did mobilise a mass army of a million and a half men, of whom two-thirds were deployed at the front. Partially trained and under provided with machine guns and artillery, their experience of war was to be decidedly mixed.[20]

The strongpoint of Gorizia was a target from the start. There was an initial limited push in the Alps to the north, after which the forces in that sector remained largely on the defensive, and the main focus of the Italian effort was on the front north-east of Venice. In the first four battles of the Isonzo (fought at intervals between June and December 1915), the Italians managed to push forwards a few miles into Austrian territory. General Cadorna, who had begun with ambitious and wildly over-optimistic notions of a swift advance to Ljubljana and Trieste, hoping even to reach Vienna, was soon faced with a stalemate every bit as frustrating as that on the Western Front in France and Flanders. Unlike the rolling countryside along most of that front, however, the Italian lines encompassed high Alpine mountainsides and deep river gorges as well as the lower-lying ground towards the Adriatic coast. Like their fellow soldiers in every other belligerent at the start of the war, Italian generals believed that no matter how much the apparent balance of advantage lay with the defending troops, backed up in modern warfare with artillery, machine guns, barbed wire and concrete strongpoints, if the attacking forces were sufficiently imbued with the 'spirit of the offensive' then they would prevail. Like every other belligerent, the Italians learned through painful and costly experience that this was not so. And although by mid-1915 the evidence from the Western Front was there for all to see, even the German, French and British generals involved did not fundamentally alter their offensive tactics. Instead they trusted (vainly, as it turned out) in the ever-increasing weight of artillery to destroy the enemy's defences before launching mass infantry assaults across the killing zone of no-man's-land. By the end of 1915 the Italians had suffered over 200,000 casualties, killed and wounded, and made only insignificant gains along the front.

The fluctuations of the fighting on the Italian front demonstrate the international interconnectedness of the Great War. Uniquely of all the major belligerents in 1915 (and for most of 1916), Italy was only engaged on one main battle front, yet, even so, it was affected by events elsewhere. This was especially so as the Allies endeavoured to harmonise their strategic plans. Even though they were not at war with Germany, the Italians were invited to an Allied conference at Chantilly in December 1915 where the French commander Joffre aimed to organise coordinated offensives for 1916 on the main fronts – Western, Russian and Italian – with the primary focus on the principal enemy, Germany. British and French pushes, for example, were planned for north and south of the Somme river. This plan was upset by the German assault on Verdun, which sucked in more and more French troops, as well as delays on the part of the Russians to act on the Eastern Front. In March 1916, nevertheless, French requests for action to relieve German pressure at Verdun (by tying down Austrian troops which might otherwise have been able to assist their ally) led Cadorna to mount the inconclusive fifth Isonzo battle between 9 and 17 March. Another Allied meeting at Chantilly the same month confirmed the intention to mount 'contemporary' action.

On the Central Powers' side, Austria's defeat of Serbia in November 1915 released troops to be deployed against Italy. Determined to punish Austria's former Triple Alliance ally, the Austro-Hungarian army chief of staff, Franz Conrad von Hötzendorf, conceived his planned offensive as a *Strafexpedition* or punitive operation. Conrad drew troops from Austria-Hungary's eastern front, but failed to get any help from the Germans who were concentrating their forces for the attack on Verdun. He proceeded nevertheless and launched an offensive in the Trentino towards the Asiago plateau north-east of Lake Garda on 15 May 1916. Although the Habsburg forces were at first strikingly successful, the Italians managed to transfer nearly 180,000 men from the Isonzo and were able to stem the advance. Conrad, meanwhile, had to cope in the east with the initially successful Russian Brusilov offensive at the beginning of June, itself facilitated by the transfer of Austrian troops to the Italian front. He called a halt in the Trentino and deployed his forces in strong defensive positions, from where they were able to repulse a series of bloody and hopeless Italian counterattacks which dragged on until late July.

The sixth battle of the Isonzo, 6–17 August, during which Gorizia was captured, was, for the Italians, the most successful of all the 1916 battles.[21] From the spring of 1916 Cadorna began planning to take the town, depending on a concentrated and massive preliminary artillery bombardment, which he believed should principally be directed at the physical defences along the enemy's front line in order to open up the way for the Italian infantry to advance. The bombardment was the greatest yet inflicted in the Italian theatre. Over the period of the battle, 1,260 Italian guns and 768 heavy trench mortars fired 535,000 rounds. It was quite a propitious moment for an Italian push. The enemy defences were weakened by the withdrawal of troops to the Eastern Front, and the Austrians could expect no great assistance from the Germans, preoccupied as they were both at Verdun and with the great Anglo-French Somme offensive which had begun on 1 July. The Austrians, moreover, did not anticipate how quickly and efficiently the Italians could transfer units from the Asiago to the Isonzo front for the offensive. Before Gorizia itself could be attacked, the Austrians had to be pushed off the 2,000ft Monte Sabotino to the north of the town. This was achieved in a brilliant, well-prepared attack on 6 August directed by Colonel Pietro Badoglio, a rising star who made his name with the operation and went on to an extremely successful career taking him to the highest ranks of the Italian army, and a spell as prime minister of Italy after the fall of Mussolini in 1943.

Combined with Badoglio's success, the capture of Podgora, which Edward Garnett had identified in March as the scene of particularly bloody fighting, and Monte San Michele, another strongpoint to the south-west, made Gorizia indefensible. Bowing to the inevitable, the Austrians began a well-executed withdrawal early on 8 August to prepared defensive positions to the east, and the following day the Italians entered the now undefended town. The powerful British press baron and proprietor of *The Times*, Lord Northcliffe (who as Alfred Harmsworth had founded the immensely successful *Daily Mail*), was touring the Italian front in August 1916. Reaching Gorizia the day after its capture, he seized the opportunity for a typically dramatic report with the impressive dateline: 'Gorizia, Aug. 10'. 'To have broken bread well inside enemy territory is a quite a new experience in the war,' he wrote. 'This afternoon I had an excellent meal at the Grosses Café in Gorizia. As recently as Tuesday [8 August] this despatch would have been dated Gorizia, Austria. To-day, though pink and white Austrian shrapnel is still bursting fitfully over the town, Gorizia is firmly Italian.'[22]

The capture of Gorizia was (for the Italians) an unusual bright spot in an otherwise largely unrewarding and wasteful campaign. The ten-day battle cost them 51,000 killed, wounded and missing as against 37,000 on the Austro-Hungarian side. Three more battles of the Isonzo (the seventh to the ninth) were fought in 1916, at a cost of 125,000 further Italian casualties, and with minimal rewards. That year, as in 1915, it never looked as if Cadorna's wild ambitions of striking through to Ljubljana (sixty miles on through difficult country) and Vienna would remotely be achievable. In 1917 there was more of the same. The tenth and eleventh battles, in May and August–September, nibbled away at the Austrian positions, without significant gains, and with continued high casualties, the eleventh battle costing Italian losses of 143,000 dead, wounded and missing, to the Austrians' 110,000. In the late autumn, the advantage turned to the Central Powers, as the collapse of the Russians in the east enabled reinforcements to be moved to the Italian front. For the first time these included significant numbers of battle-hardened Germans, among whom Stürmtruppen units brought new offensive tactics, combining a short but intense artillery and gas bombardment with small-unit penetration in depth. Launched on 24 October 1917 through the town of Caporetto (Kobarid) on the Isonzo, about twenty miles north of Gorizia, these tactics worked spectacularly well, turned the flank of the Italian forces on the lower Isonzo and precipitated a full-scale retreat which quickly turned into a rout. Infected by panic, in just over a fortnight the Italians had been pushed back ninety miles to the river Piave, where they dug in and were at last able to hold up the enemy forces, who were themselves running out of momentum. Reinforced with British and French troops, there they remained until in a final advance in October 1918 – the battle of Vittorio Veneto – they managed to recover the territory lost after the Caporetto catastrophe and at the end of the war finished up just short of Gorizia.

How did the Italians soldiers survive? John Gooch has argued that before Caporetto, at least, the army's 'dogged commitment to the war' had become 'instinctual', rather than based on any intellectual (or even emotional) calculation of national interest. The left-wing historian Piero Melograni asserted that alcohol and 'casa di toleranza' (military brothels) were indispensable in sustaining morale. In his sardonic fictionalised memoir of the war, the Sardinian junior officer Emilio Lussu recalled conversations with the fifty-year-old Lieutenant Colonel Abbati up a mountain on the edge of the Asiago plateau. Abbati is staggered when Lussu refuses a glass of brandy. '"You don't drink spirits?" he asked in an anxious tone, and taking out his pocket-book he noted down: "June 5, 1916. Met lieutenant who drank no spirits." ... "Perhaps you belong to some religious sect?" he inquired.' Abbati, who came from an old army family, told Lussu that he protected himself by drinking and that if drinking were prohibited 'no one would go on with the war. The moving spirit of this war,' he proclaimed, 'is alcohol.' As for sex, army policy reflected contemporary socio-medical thought which held that too much sexual abstinence might lead to such activities as homosexuality, rape and sadism. The high command were also worried by the incidence of venereal disease. In June 1915 'in case the war lasts a long time', official military brothels were established to restrict the use of unregulated prostitutes. Significant numbers of these brothels were established and, apparently, were well patronised. In 1916 one establishment in Palmanova, west of Gorizia, was reported as having 700–900 customers every day.[23]

If men chose to console themselves with drink and sex, it was an understandable response to the brutal conditions of army life. At

times, indeed, Italian soldiers were as much at risk from the actions of
their own side as from anything the enemy might throw at them.
Cadorna was a martinet who considered that good discipline was more
important even than training or tactical expertise, and under his
command Italian soldiers endured perhaps the most brutal disciplinary regime of any First World War army. In his definitive study of the
Italian army in the war, John Gooch has concluded that the harsh
enforcement of military discipline during the war forms 'one of the
darkest pages in Italy's military history'. At the beginning of hostilities
the state police, the Carabinieri, were, among other things, given the
task of maintaining discipline behind the lines. In November 1915
they were even given the power to use artillery against 'recalcitrants'
and they were instructed to set up a line of posts behind the front line
with orders to shoot soldiers who failed in any way to follow orders.
Mark Thompson recounts the story of an army doctor working in the
Dolomites who, after one minor engagement, 'matter-of-factly
recorded treating 80 casualties of enemy machine-gun fire, and another
25 shot in the buttocks by the carabinieri'.[24]

Emilio Lussu related an incident where the clearly deranged (but
sadly typical) General Leone overheard a soldier ordering an advance
party to pause at a dangerous point in the line where a scout had just
been killed. Assuming cowardice, Leone ordered that the man should
immediately be shot. The soldier's commander, Captain Zavaratti, an
officer in the reserve who in peacetime had been a senior civil servant,
was staggered by the order. Having investigated the circumstances, he
reported to Leone that the soldier had actually been following orders
to take care while advancing. 'Have him shot all the same,' insisted the
general. 'An example must be made.' Zavaratti demurred. 'How can I
have a man shot when he's committed no crime, and without any sort
of trial?' he asked. This merely enraged Leone who threatened to have
the captain shot as well. Appreciating that further objection was futile,
Zavaratti went forward, out of sight of the general, and 'ordered a
firing party to fire a volley at a tree-trunk'. He then got men to place
the body of the dead scout on a stretcher and 'returned to the general,
followed by the stretcher-bearers and their burden . . . "The man has
been shot," reported Zavaratti. 'Seeing the stretcher, the general came

to attention and saluted it proudly. He appeared deeply moved. "Let us salute our country's martyrs! In war, discipline is a grievous necessity. Let us honour our dead!"[25]

From May 1916 there were reliably documented instances of 'decimation', the shooting of soldiers by lot for exemplary effect which Cadorna described as 'an essential weapon in the hands of army command'. Early in July 1916, for example, soldiers of the 89th Infantry Regiment, which had taken many casualties in heavy fighting on the Asiago, attempted to surrender to the enemy. The divisional general had his artillery and machine guns fire on them, before withdrawing the unit from the front. After this, two men were selected by lot from each of the four companies involved and summarily shot. At the beginning of November 1916 Cadorna issued orders formally instructing commanding officers to draw lots for summary executions, which immediately resulted in a number of exemplary punishments. John Gooch calculates that in 1916 there were 'at least 83 summary executions and 242 "regular" executions after trial, 76 accused were found not guilty, and a further 761 soldiers were sentenced to death in absentia'. Cadorna dismissed political concerns about the practice as 'morbid sentimentalism'.[26] There is little objective evidence that this and other draconian measures were particularly effective. Indeed, the degrading and demoralising impact of such brutality (on officers as much as on enlisted men) may well have contributed to the spectacular fragility which Italian units eventually demonstrated in the face of the Austro-German offensive at Caporetto in November 1917.

Austria-Hungary's war

Austria-Hungary, the Great Power apparently keenest on war in the summer of 1914, was the least fitted to survive the strains of prolonged full-scale conflict. Not only (as with Russia, Germany and Turkey) did the war topple the regime which had been in power at the start, but the imperial territory itself disintegrated into a series of successor states. In some ways the surprising thing is quite how long the ramshackle Habsburg state survived at all. Well within living memory of the end of the Habsburg monarchy, A. J. P. Taylor asserted that from the beginning of the monarchy the Habsburgs had lived 'on the verge of ruin'. 'There was never a time,' he wrote, 'when men did not expect the speedy dissolution of the Habsburg monarchy, and it was this familiarity of impending doom which enabled the Habsburgs to meet successive dangers, if not with wisdom, at any rate with calm persistence.'[27] But calm persistence was no use in the face of the First World War combination of external challenge and internal disintegration which proved fatal to the empire. Indeed, by 1916 it was evident that Austria-Hungary was no longer an independent entity and only survived by dint of German support. When its last independent campaign – Conrad's offensive in the Trentino – ran out of steam in June 1916, and German help was required to meet the Russian Brusilov offensive, thus effectively went the empire's autonomy.

Over the last century or so of its existence, the main challenge for the Habsburg monarchy was reconciling imperial rule over its vast central European territories with increasing demands for national self-determination among its eleven constituent nationalities. While the Dual Monarchy of Austria-Hungary established in 1867 had been a device to meet Magyar national aspirations, in the years running up to 1914 rising demands among Slavs within the empire proved difficult to accommodate. Indeed, Serbian support for some of these groups exacerbated international tensions in the Balkans and materially contributed to the tough line which Vienna took towards Belgrade after Serbian nationalists assassinated the Archduke Franz Ferdinand in Sarajevo on 28 June 1914.[28]

The high command worried about national minorities undermining the unity and efficiency of the army.[29] Before the war, twenty-seven per cent of the army were Austro-Germans, twenty-two per cent Hungarians, fourteen per cent Czechs, and the remainder Poles, Croats, Serbs, Romanians, Slovaks, Slovenes, Ruthenes and Italians. Although the Germans were slightly over-represented in the military, the ethnic composition of the army roughly reflected that of the empire as a whole. At officer level, however, the proportions differed significantly: seventy-nine per cent Austro-German, ten per cent Hungarian and five per cent Czech. The highest levels of command were even more dominated by Austro-Germans, though the commander of the Habsburg Fifth Army on the Isonzo was Svetozar Boroević, born of a Serb family from Croatia, the highest-ranking non-German in the army. The under-representation of Hungarians in the officer corps reflected national feeling and a widespread reluctance of Hungarians to commit fully to imperial institutions. The Hungarians were evidently not against military service per se, since at reserve-officer level, where individuals could serve close to home in a specifically Hungarian formation, their proportion aligned much more closely to their share of the population. There had been nationalist-inspired disturbances in Czech districts during partial mobilisation exercises in 1908 and 1912 which raised the unsettling possibility of something more serious happening when the general mobilisation was ordered in July 1914. But in fact mobilisation went remarkably well. Carried along in an unexpected groundswell of dynastic loyalty, it proceeded smoothly, even among Czechs and Serbs.

Although the Habsburg army on the whole remained notably cohesive and resilient until the very last months of the war, the nationalities problem did affect the way it could be used. Real or imagined fears of national disaffection constrained its deployment. Broadly, the only units which could be used freely on any front were German, Hungarian and Bosnian regiments. Italian units, for example, were in general not deployed on the Isonzo and at the start when Austria-Hungary went to war against Serbia some commanders had Serbian soldiers moved well away from front-line units.[30] Nationally inspired instances of disaffection, or even mutiny, while celebrated by some nationalist historians after the war, were comparatively rare in the first two years of war, though the pressures of mass mobilisation increasingly began to provoke what Mark Cornwall has called 'counter-mobilisations against the Empire', based on a combination of nationalist and socio-economic regional grievances together with a 'crisis of legitimacy' which began to gather momentum in the winter of 1916/17 and in the end proved fatal to the monarchy.[31]

The memoirs of one enlisted man, Joseph Gál, illustrate both the common experience of front-line soldiers in the First World War as well as some of the special characteristics of service in the Habsburg army. Gál was a Transylvanian Magyar, born in Székely-Udvarhely (now Odorheiu Secuiesc in Romania), whose infantry regiment was deployed on the Isonzo front. Having emigrated to the USA after the war, he completed his memoir in 1937. In it he aimed to lead the reader 'through the world war with events beyond the imagination, bloody roads, filled with sufferings, where I wandered [as] a twenty year old'. While he claimed to have written the work 'on the basis of real episodes', it has a melodramatic tone and should be taken more as an impressionistic survey of his war service (punctuated with passages of improbably detailed narrative and conversation) than a precisely factual account of events.[32]

The narrative takes Gál from being a raw recruit through his induction into military life (complete with an ill-fitting uniform), preliminary training and the beginnings of a group identity with three new good friends – Stein, Faluvégi and Bajko – 'faithfully swearing to remain together'. In April 1916 the regiment took a week to travel to Samatorca, a village behind the lines about halfway between Gorizia and Trieste, where the four men dally with two initially unfriendly Italian girls. Moving up towards the front line at Doberdo, about five miles south of Gorizia, Gál, calling himself a 'boy-man', muses on a battlefield 'where hundreds and thousands have bled for some incomprehensible goal that most people will never know the achieving of anyway'. Taken away with Stein and another soldier from his unit for 'patrol training', Gál came up against the language problem endemic in the imperial army. The primary language of command was German (which increasingly became an issue with the Magyars), and every soldier was supposed to know the eighty or so words required for drill, as well as some technical military terms. At regimental level, however, whatever language the enlisted men spoke was otherwise used. This system worked adequately in peacetime, but during the war, with the mixing of units, the loss of experienced junior officers and technical developments requiring enhanced training, it proved to be more problematic. Gál found that, of 150 men undergoing training, they were the only three Magyars and they became the butt of barrack-room jokes. 'Like three Hungarians broken off the same branch,' he wrote, 'we sit down on the edge of the bunk and listen to the talk buzzing about us in the German and Czech languages.' They have to tolerate the 'barking,

stupid, sarcastic jokes' of one Czech soldier 'because we don't understand anything apart from German commands'.

At the end of April, reunited with his three pals, Gál went up to the
front line for the first time. There they spent ten days in trenches deep
enough to shelter them from rifle and machine-gun bullets, but not
mortar and artillery fire, which caused constant casualties. In this
'hellish place' – 'Death's Fortress' he called it – 'our nights are spent
observing and our days are spent in dangerous, tiring work', improving the barbed-wire defences in no-man's land and renovating the
trenches. They spent a period of time alternating ten days in the line
with ten days' rest, and when Gál had to return to the front he was
'more afraid now than I was the first time because I know where my
road is leading me'. Nevertheless, by May he was beginning to get
used to trench life: 'Seeing the dead and the wounded anymore leaves
me cold. The sight of blood, which at the beginning brought forth
such a terrible impression, we have also become accustomed to.
Around me men are dying who I cannot feel sorry for anymore.'

On 4 August in the artillery barrage at the start of the battle for
Gorizia Stein was seriously injured. Gál and Bajko took him back to a
dressing station where they learnt that his wounds were fatal (though
it was eight more days before he died). Five days later, after the Italian
breakthrough at Gorizia, they were ordered to retreat. 'Our joy must
be imaginable,' wrote Gál, since 'we are going to be free from this
endless flood of suffering'. From new positions a couple of miles back,
they saw the Italians as 'little, black spots . . . fleeing in every direction'
under Austrian shellfire. They 'watch with pleasure the slaughtering
work of our artillery and contentedly laugh at the retreat of the little,
moving spots'. Like many front-line soldiers, Gál contrasted the beau-
ties of nature with the horror of the war. He recalled one pale-pink
early morning, looking across the apparently empty countryside:
'How beautiful nature's enchanting panorama is! How spectacular
daybreak is. And how horrible life is here!'

Deployed to counter Italian attacks, Gál became excited by the
prospect. 'The blood-thirsty desire in the hunting of men awakens in
me,' he wrote, and having shot an Italian, who fell behind a wall with
only his two feet showing, 'I feel like a lusty hunter in a primeval

forest . . . The thought makes me happy that there is one less Italian soldier who is searching for me. To be certain of our work we shoot the Italian's feet. . .' – a chilling, final detail which reminds us how locked into the business of killing these ordinary young men had become. Bajko then was killed beside him and, 'with teary eyes and burning vengeance' in his heart, Gál shot at the enemy with renewed vigour. After an intense and desperate series of engagements, the Italians were driven back. Sent back to the front on 20 August, after a few days' rest, Gál reflected that for several months he had 'been walking calvary's thorny road, where death's scythe amply harvests the rows of suffering men'.

In late August, Faluvégi was wounded by a shot through the top of his right hand. It was what British soldiers on the Western Front cele-brated as a 'Blighty one'. Gál thought it a 'nice wound', minor enough not to be life-threatening but serious enough to get his friend out of the line. Indeed, within minutes Faluvégi was 'thinking of a white hospital bed and the slender, lean nurses'. Gál, now the last of the four-some, sighed 'contentedly in the knowledge that at least one good friend of mine has been luckily rescued from the cauldron on Death's Fortress'.

Writing home on 2 July 1916, Helena Gleichen remarked on the odd mixture of nationalities in the Austro-Hungarian army. She had been talking to an Italian woman about her husband: 'he is an Austrian and in the Austrian Army, but can only speak Friulani [the local language] and not one word of German or Italian'. The previous day 'we had six Austrian prisoners to radiograph and only one could speak a few words of German. There are Hungarians, Croats, Slavs, etc., and they all seem very glad to be in hospital making friends with the Italian orderlies.'[33] Eight hundred thousand Italians lived in the empire, comprising 1.5 per cent of the total population. There was a similar proportion of Italians in the imperial army, who were mobi-lised like the rest in 1914 and over 100,000 served in reserve formations, as well as on the front line, mainly in the east. After Italy came into the war in May 1915, apprehensions about the loyalties of these troops proved largely unfounded. Some active irredentists, dedicated to achieving the final unification of Italy, left Austria-Hungary to join the Italian army, but they constituted a tiny number – perhaps fewer than 3,000 – compared to the 'tens of thousands of Habsburg Italians [who] dutifully served in the Austro-Hungarian army and navy'.[34] Worrying about the dependability of the local civilian population, however, the Austrian authorities evacuated 114,000 Italian inhabitants of the Trentino (about a third of the total population) and removed them to internment camps well away from the battle zone. Ironically, after the Italians occupied Habsburg territory they also interned some 30,000 civilians in camps in Lombardy, themselves equally concerned about the uncertain loyalties even of ethnic Italians.

Some of the irredentists who joined the Italian forces, however, became causes célèbres. In May 1916 artillery lieutenant Damiano Chiesa was taken prisoner by the Austrians. Chiesa, whose father was a member of the Tyrolean state assembly, had been a student in Turin before the war and to avoid being conscripted into the Habsburg army escaped to Italy and joined up there. Rather than treat him as a prisoner of war, the Austrians charged him with high treason and executed him three days later.

A similar fate befell Cesare Battisti, a Trento-born irredentist who had been elected as a socialist member to the imperial parliament in Vienna in 1911. In 1914 he had gone to Italy and taken a prominent part in the campaign to bring it in against Austria-Hungary. The Austrian authorities, meanwhile, tried and condemned him to death in his absence. When Italy went to war Battisti enlisted in the elite Italian Alpini and on 10 July 1916 was captured at Monte Corno on the Trentino front, along with another Italian emigré, Fabio Filzi, who came from Istria. Both were convicted of high treason by military court martial and sentenced to death by hanging. The circumstances of Battisti's execution in his home town on 12 July were widely publicised, initially by the Austrians for their intended propaganda value, but subsequently by outraged Italian nationalists and other observers. Presenting himself as a soldier, Battisti requested a military execution, in uniform and by firing squad, but this was denied. Postcards were produced of the execution, including one picture of the executioners posing cheerily with Battisti's corpse, and widely distributed before the authorities realised they were having completely the opposite effect to that intended. There were international protests about the brutality of the execution. In London, for example, a 'solemn commemoration' was held for 'Captain Battisti, the martyr of Trent'.[35]

The cases of Battisti and other executed irredentists (he, Filzi and Chiesa were not the only ones) demonstrate the extent to which the circumstances of war magnified and sharpened patriotic loyalties, individual actions and official responses. Commitment to wartime objectives eroded any of the space for political manoeuvre and compromise which might have existed in peacetime. While Battisti's devotion to the goal of a unified Italy had been well established before 1914, once the Habsburg monarchy was fighting for its existence, and Battisti had explicitly joined the empire's enemies, his behaviour could no longer be tolerated or accommodated as before. What is more, it was impossible for the Austrian authorities to concede any measure of legitimacy to his actions, hence the grotesque circumstances of his execution. But the political necessity of treating him as a common traitor came at considerable political cost, since it also made him a national hero as a martyr in the high cause of Italian national liberty.

G. M. Trevelyan welcomed the destruction of Austria-Hungary by the war, especially because of the ruthless methods they had used to keep control in their polyglot empire. 'The fondness of the official Austro-Hungarian mind for gallows work is amazing,' he wrote, evidently with the Battisti and Filzi executions in mind. Accompanying the pursuit of the retreating Austrians in November 1918, he noted that 'we found in their quarters, more than once, collections of photographs and negatives of various pitiful executions of Czechs, Bosnians, Serbs, etc.'. With defeat, internal collapse and expulsion from Italy they had been 'justly paid; they and their worm-eaten bogey-show of medieval gibbets have been kicked bag and baggage over the Brenner, and trampled out of sight by their own subjects in every corner of the ramshackle empire which they have filled with blood and wailing and oppression for too many generations past'. Austria-Hungary, he concluded, was now just 'an "historical expression"'.[36]

LEGACIES OF THE ISONZO FRONT

Dominating the Slovenian town of Kobarid is a massive Italian ossuary containing the bones of over 7,000 dead from the Great War. It is one of three such monuments to Italian war dead on this front, the others being at Oslavia near Gorizia, and Redipuglia, between Gorizia and Trieste on the Carso plateau. Kobarid sits on the Isonzo river north of Gorizia and lies in one of those European frontier zones which changed state several times during the twentieth century. As with Kobarid, this is usually associated with name changes. Known in German as Karfriet when it was part of the Austro-Hungarian Empire, it became Caporetto under Italian rule from 1919, the name with which historians of the First World War are most familiar, recalling the catastrophic Italian defeat of November 1917. The Habsburg territories of Istria, Gorizia and the Tyrol, long desired by Italian nationalists as 'Italia irredenta', became the spoils of victory, and the remains of tens of thousands of Italian soldiers who had fallen in the battles for these lands were preserved (and their sacrifices celebrated) in bronze and stone monuments. After the Second World War – more costs of defeat than spoils of victory this time – with its Slovenian name of Kobarid, the town became part of Yugoslavia, and from 1991 the independent Republic of Slovenia. While there are also Austro-Hungarian cemeteries throughout the battle zone – filled with the plural nationalities of the empire – they are much more modest and less well cared for than the Italian monuments.[37]

The fact that Italy's entry into the war had been based principally on political calculation, coupled with its staggering human and economic cost, meant that the rewards had to match up to the sacrifices made. Yet this could never be the case, as Italian ambitions (as with Italian capabilities) wildly exceeded any possible compensation. The few crumbs which Italy got from the peace-makers' table during the Paris peace conferences – territory in the Trentino and Trieste (less than had been offered in the 1915 Treaty of London), as well as the Dodecanese Islands – scarcely met the bill and left Italian nationalists deeply dissatisfied. This in turn fuelled the aggressive and expansionist ambitions of the fascist movement which helped sweep Mussolini to power in 1922. In this way, therefore, the unsatisfactory results of the so-called 'Fourth War of the Risorgimento' contributed directly to the delusional and ultimately self-destructive dreams of fascist Italy.

In his extravagantly dictated 'autobiography', written up in the late 1920s by the sympathetic American writer, Richard Washburn Child,

Mussolini waxed lyrical about the steadfastness of the army in 1916, the shock of Caporetto in 1917 and the glorious finale in 1918, which was 'a victory for the whole Italian race ... New generations of Italians rejoiced, for the Italian cities were once again rejoined to the Country!'[38] In 1938 Mussolini came to dedicate the ossuary at Kobarid/Caporetto himself, and on 20 September, having driven up from Trieste, he told the people of Gorizia how one could not cross the Carso without deep emotion, 'where the Italian army had written immortal pages of blood and glory'. The children of today, he added, would tomorrow be 'ever-victorious Italian soldiers'. But the non-Italians in the region did not quite see it like that. The Slovenian revolutionary movement 'TIGR' (from the initial letters of Trieste, Istria, Gorizia and Rijeka), formed in the late 1920s, had a plan, which was aborted at the last minute, to assassinate the dictator when he visited the region.[39]

And was it all worth it? G. M. Trevelyan, the passionate Italophile who had witnessed the prodigious human costs of the war at first hand, thought so. Writing in the autumn of 1918 and evidently reassured that the outcome of the war was clear, he claimed that along the Isonzo front were 'the scenes famous now for ever in Italian history, where hundreds of thousands of the best youth of Italy shed their blood in attacks that were not fruitless, for a cause which time has crowned with success'. Borrowing an allusion from Thomas Hardy's verse-drama about the Napoleonic Wars, Trevelyan asserted the democratic case for defeating the Central Powers. 'This time,' he wrote, 'it was the Peoples warring the last great war to tame and bind the Dynasts.'[40]

4

'Ypres on the Liffey'

On 24 April 1916 – Easter Monday – armed parties of Irish republican men and women seized a series of strongpoints in central Dublin, proclaiming the establishment of 'the Irish Republic as a Sovereign Independent State', and asserting the Irish people's right to 'national freedom and sovereignty' against 'long usurpation . . . by a foreign people and government'.[1] The 1,500 insurgents held out for six days against increasingly overwhelming forces, including artillery and shellfire from a gunboat on the River Liffey, leaving widespread destruction in central Dublin. Although the total number of people killed (132 troops and police, sixty-four insurgents and 254 civilians, the latter mostly caught in crossfire), along with 2,614 wounded, was tiny in comparison to Western Front casualties – in the same week units of the 16th (Irish) Division *alone* at Hulluch in the Pas-de-Calais region of France suffered 570 men killed and over 1,400 wounded in a gas and artillery attack – the human cost was profoundly shocking in what many regarded as the 'second city' of the British Empire, and the serious damage done to the city centre was likened afterwards to the shattered Belgian city of Ypres.

ROGER CASEMENT AND THE RISING

On 17 April 1916 Liam Roche, an active Irish republican teacher based in Cork city (who was later to adopt the Gaelic form of his name,

Liam de Róiste), wrote in his diary of a report that Roger Casement
had been arrested in Germany. Reflecting on other news, he noted 'an
incident of, perhaps, some significance': that the socialist paramilitary
Citizen Army in Dublin had 'raised a Green Flag over their headquarters at Liberty Hall'. He also recorded how both government and
employers were intensifying their prosecution of the war. In London
there was a political crisis on the subject of conscription. Lord Derby's
military recruitment scheme of 1915 (by which men could register
voluntarily and only be called up when required) had been, he wrote,
'a muddle and a failure', and Sir Edward Carson, the Unionist leader,
with the backing of *The Times* and the *Daily Mail*, was now campaign-
ing for universal conscription to be introduced. Meanwhile, building
employers in Dublin were invoking the wartime Munitions Act against
striking workmen. Finally, he observed 'a fine statement of Cardinal
Mercier, replying to General Moritz von Bissing, German Governor
in Belgium', which had been reported in the Cork *Evening Echo*.
Cardinal Mercier, the Archbishop of Malines, had become an outstanding symbol of Belgian national resistance to the German occupier.
'Even though we may be smitten with admiration at the panoply of
war surrounding you,' he had written, 'and at the brilliant staff that,
like King Saul, you have attached to your person, we should preserve
entire freedom of judgment. In the troublous times through which our
country is passing, we cannot, and will not, alienate this liberty.'
Mercier said that the Pope had 'freed us from obeying the civil powers
as soon as they give orders contrary to the law of God and man ... We
can,' he continued, 'give you the silent homage due to force, but we
preserve, closed against your attempts, the sacred domain of our
conscience, the last refuge of oppressed right.' Inspired by Mercier's
'brave and splendid words', Roche thought they were 'applicable not
alone to Belgium, but to all oppressed countries, not least to Ireland',
where 'every effort' was being made 'to stifle expression of free
opinion', not only by the British government, but also 'by those of our
own people who support that government'.[2]

Writing thus in the week before the Easter Rising, Roche neatly
assembled some of the key factors which were to apply in the unfold-
ing tragedy of Ireland's Easter week in 1916: Sir Roger Casement and

some link with Germany; politico-military activity in Dublin; the progressively increasing burden of wartime demands; and the close parallel which Irish separatist republicans drew between Ireland's situation as an 'oppressed country' and that of Belgium.

Casement, in fact, had not been arrested in Germany at all. At the time Roche was writing his diary he was en route to Ireland in a German submarine. Although his original ambition had been to help lead an Irish republican insurrection against British rule, by April 1916 he was actually travelling to Ireland to try to prevent the planned rising from taking place. Casement was the most exotic and cosmopolitan of the Irish republican leaders. Left orphaned by the age of thirteen, he was brought up by Ulster Protestant relatives and educated at Ballymena Academy. He left school at fifteen and began a series of jobs which took him from Liverpool to West Africa and the Congo. From the mid-1890s he was employed in the British consular service in Mozambique and the Congo, where he reported on widespread abuses associated with the collection of rubber, including forced labour, mutilation and murder. During the early 1900s, while taking long-term sick leave in Ireland and Britain, he became a fervent Irish nationalist. Following a second spell in the consular service posted to Brazil, in a widely publicised report of 1911 he exposed more atrocities among the remote Putumayo Indians, where the Peruvian Amazon Company collected rubber. The report made him internationally famous as a humanitarian activist and earned him a knighthood from the British government. In 1913 he retired from the consular service and threw himself wholeheartedly into working for Ireland, becoming an enthusiastic propagandist and serving on the executive committee of the paramilitary Irish Volunteers.[3]

On the outbreak of war Casement was in the USA seeking to raise funds for the Volunteers. He immediately took the German side, and began to seek German support for an Irish rebellion. 'Germany fights today,' he wrote, 'as the champion of Europe' against 'the hordes of Russian barbarism, the sword of French hatred and the long purse of British greed . . . as an Irishman I say from my heart – God Save Germany'.[4] By October he was on his way to Berlin, tracked by the British authorities who were getting information from Casement's bisexual manservant and lover, a Norwegian-American called Adler Christiansen. Backed up with postal censorship and signals intelligence (decrypting telegrams between Berlin and the German embassy in Washington), British Naval Intelligence and the domestic security agency (from January 1916 'MI5') were able to keep track of Casement's activities.[5]

Casement remained in Germany for eighteen months from November 1914. During this time he tried to persuade Irish prisoners of war captured on the Western Front to join an 'Irish Brigade' dedicated to fighting for 'the national freedom of Ireland'. While the formation would ideally be transported to Ireland, Casement recognised that this would be difficult without a decisive German naval victory and so he allowed that they might be employed 'to assist the Egyptian People to recover their freedom by driving the British out'. Why Egypt? Casement, above all, with his internationalist anti-imperialism, appreciated the interconnectedness of the British imperial world system. Underlying this suggestion was his belief that pressure in both Ireland and the Middle East could combine to undermine the whole British imperial edifice. If the Suez Canal and Egypt went, he reflected in November 1914, it would encourage an uprising in India which 'must tax "the Empire" to its limit'. Furthermore, German pressure on the Western Front, combined with an uprising in Ireland, would leave the British with insufficient troops to hold India, unless they appealed to their ally Japan for help. But that would spell their 'own sure and certain eviction from Asia later on. Once India falls,' he concluded, 'the whole house collapses – for it is chiefly on India and its plunder the Colossal [British] scheme of robbery depends.'[6]

The effort to raise a brigade from Irish prisoners of war was a dismal failure. By the end of 1915 he had managed to recruit fewer than sixty men and when Robert Monteith (who arrived from New York in October 1915 to command the brigade) asked for volunteers to 'strike a blow' against England in the Middle East and help 'to free another small nationality' (Egypt), scarcely forty men responded. In mid-February 1916 the German ambassador in Washington, Count Bernstorff, told Berlin that a rising was planned in Ireland for Easter 1916 and enquired if Germany could offer any help. The Irish

separatists in the USA asked for 100,000 rifles, some artillery and
German gunners, but Berlin decided only to send 20,000 rifles, ten
machine guns and 5 million rounds of ammunition. Casement,
depressed and unwell, now thought the time inopportune for a rising.
Hoping both to ensure the arms got safely to Ireland and also (for the
moment) to delay the rebellion, he reluctantly agreed to travel to
Ireland with Monteith. The arms were sent on a 1,200-ton coaster, the
Aud, while Casement and Monteith went by submarine. Both vessels
were due to rendezvous at Tralee Bay off the coast of County Kerry at
midnight on 20 April but failed to do so and during the late afternoon
of 21 April – Good Friday – the *Aud* was intercepted by a British navy
sloop, HMS *Bluebell*, but was scuttled while being escorted to port.
Unfortunately for Casement and his companions, the British knew all
about the *Aud* and Casement's mission (though not his desire to delay
the rising). The Royal Navy's signals intelligence department, 'Room
40' in the Admiralty, had intercepted and deciphered cables between
North America and Berlin revealing that German arms were to be
landed during the week before Easter and that Casement was following by submarine.[7]

Sometime after two o'clock on the morning of Good Friday, the
German submarine U-19 dropped Casement, Monteith and an
ex-prisoner-of-war member of the Irish Brigade (whom they knew as
Julian Beverley) in a collapsible boat two miles off Banna Strand in
Tralee Bay. The boat foundered in the surf close to the shore and they
had to swim the last few yards. Casement and Beverley (whose real
name was Daniel Julian Bailey) were soon arrested, while Monteith
evaded capture and eventually escaped back to the USA. Casement
was taken to London where on Easter Sunday he was interrogated by
Scotland Yard's Basil Thomson, along with Captain Reginald 'Blinker'
Hall (Director of Naval Intelligence) and Major Frank Hall (no rela-
tion) of MI5. According to one report, Casement 'begged to be allowed
to communicate with the leaders to try and stop the rising', which he
'considered a fatal mistake'. His interrogators 'refused, saying, "It's a
festering sore, it's much better it should come to a head"'. Although
Thomson conceded that Casement had asked that there be a public
announcement of his arrest since he believed that 'if they know that I

am taken nothing will happen, they will know that the game is up', he flatly denied that anyone had suggested deliberately letting the rising go ahead. He claimed that they *had* decided that it would be better not to announce Casement's arrest, but on the flimsy grounds that this 'would be useful to the Germans, who at that time were thought to be planning an invasion'.[8] Even though it is most likely that Thomson and his colleagues did believe in letting Irish matters 'come to a head', any announcement about Casement's arrest would probably have made no difference whatsoever. Despite their evident hopes for German assistance, the leaders of the rising were quite determined to go it alone if necessary, as, in the end, they did.

Casement's capture, and the interception of the *Aud*, which became publicly known on Easter Tuesday, merely fed widespread assumptions of German support for Irish republican endeavours. Writing from Dublin the same day, Mary Louisa Norway, wife of the secretary to the Irish Post Office (whose own head office had been occupied by the rebels) told her sister that since the beginning of the war the separatist republican movement, 'encouraged no doubt by German intrigue and German money', had 'grown by leaps and bounds'. Only a month previously, she added, a party of Volunteers had marched down Grafton Street in Dublin 'singing "Die Wacht am Rhein" and revolutionary songs'.[9] And while the Irish Citizen Army famously adopted the slogan, 'We serve neither King nor Kaiser, but Ireland!', its leader, James Connolly, signed the 1916 Proclamation which explicitly asserted that the rebels were 'supported by gallant allies in Europe'. Casement's doomed mission to delay action, moreover, was not through *absence* of German support, but simply because he thought it was as yet insufficient. Beyond Ireland, too, there were suggestions that the encouragement of rebellion in Ireland was a deliberate German policy. Early in May the British ambassador in Sweden, Sir Esme Howard, sent a report to London quoting a local political informant that 'whenever a big military movement came to naught the Germans promptly turned to political intriguing, in order to create a diversion both at home and in the field'. Since the attack on Verdun had failed, 'the nearest result was the uprising in Ireland'. Now it had failed, 'something else has to be thought of. Undoubtedly the turn has now

come to Finland and Sweden.' Thus Germany was to blame for encouraging current agitation for Sweden to go to war against Russia to secure
the disputed Åland Islands in the Baltic for Sweden.[10]

The Dublin rebels held out until the afternoon of Saturday 29 April
when, 'in order to prevent the further slaughter of Dublin citizens,
and in the hope of saving the lives of our followers now surrounded
and hopelessly outnumbered', the leaders of the insurgents surrendered. The Volunteers, moreover, saw themselves as soldiers
surrendering as prisoners of war. But the authorities saw matters
differently. As mere insurgents or rebels they had no formal belligerent rights, and the leading rebels were tried in secret by military courts
martial under the wartime Defence of the Realm Acts, with dubious
legality and inadequate process. Of the 186 men and one woman
(Countess Markiewicz) who were tried, eleven were acquitted and
eighty-eight sentenced to 'death by being shot'. The great majority of
these sentences were commuted, but fifteen individuals (including all
seven signatories of the Proclamation) were executed between 3 and
12 May 1916. In London, Sir Roger Casement was tried in an open
criminal court, convicted of high treason, sentenced to death and
(despite an international campaign for clemency) hanged in Pentonville
prison on 3 August. Daniel Bailey turned king's evidence and was
found not guilty.[11] It could be argued that, unlike Casement, each of
the men executed in Ireland died a soldier's death. The maverick and
dissolute adventurer John MacBride was reported to have said to his
firing squad: 'Fire away, I've been looking down the barrels of rifles
all my life.'[12] In later years the casualty list of Easter 1916 in Ireland
was compared to that of the Western Front. In a mid-1930s novel
strongly sympathetic to the republican side, written by a woman who
had witnessed the events of the Rising, one character reading 'those
terrible lists [of executions] in the newspapers' regarded them as 'the
superb Roll of Honour' which would be 'enshrined forever on Irish
hearts'.[13]

Rather than seeing the Easter Rising as some uniquely Irish event,
sui generis, and only peripherally part of the wider conflagration, it
can only be properly understood in the context of the Great War,
which provided both the moment ('England's extremity') and the

mode (war, as Clausewitz affirmed, being 'politics by other means') for its planning and execution.[14] As surely as Verdun or the Somme, Dublin in 1916 was a First World War battlefield. The actual fighting, too, echoed that of the war. Once the strongpoints in Dublin had been occupied, it became a static struggle of attritional conflict. Cavalry made a brief and inglorious appearance in the early afternoon of Easter Monday when a squadron of men from the 5th (Royal Irish) and the 12th (Prince of Wales Royal) Lancers came down O'Connell Street en route (as they thought) to investigate a disturbance which had been reported at Dublin Castle, some distance further away. As they came past the General Post Office, the Volunteers fired on them, killing three soldiers instantly, mortally wounding a fourth and killing a horse. Cavalry was useless in this modern urban battlefield, but (as in France) artillery proved to be important. The British use of field guns, as well as a 300-ton gunboat, HMS *Helga*, positioned on the River Liffey and armed with two naval twelve-pounders, was decisive in bringing the rebels to surrender.

Reflecting on the Dublin events, Charles Townshend explicitly drew a parallel with the Western Front. The fierce fighting at Mount Street Bridge on Wednesday 26 April, he observed, saw raw British soldiers hurriedly brought in from England, 'as inexperienced as the Volunteers themselves' suffering heavy casualties 'in New Army-style shoulder-to-shoulder attacks that prefigured the Somme in miniature'.[15] As one of their officers noted, most of the Sherwood Foresters who saw action at Mount Street Bridge were 'merely boys, Derby Recruits, who had been in uniform about 6 or 8 weeks. They had not fired their musketry course and many had never fired a rifle.'[16] Some of the British reinforcements actually thought they *were* in France. Albert Mitchell, an Irishman who served as a Red Cross ambulance driver during the Rising, recalled working with an English sergeant who had 'thought he was again being sent to France and wondered how everyone he met spoke such good English'.[17]

Whether in Ireland or France, most British soldiers believed they were still fighting Germany. One soldier whose comrade had died at his side told a sympathetic nurse that 'the only thing which made it possible to bear was the certainty they were fighting Germany as truly as if they were in France. In his opinion, the Rebellion was Germany's last trump card, and would prove the turning point of the war.'[18] General Sir Henry Wilson, a southern Irish Unionist commanding IV Corps in France, was less optimistic (and more realistic), thinking it 'a marvellous state of affairs, & I should think almost equal to the capture of Verdun from the Boch point of view'.[19]

Whoever was to blame, the damage to Dublin was widely compared with that of France and Flanders. Inspecting the gutted GPO building on 1 May, Mary Louisa Norway said it passed 'all my powers of description, only one word describes it, "Desolation". If you look at pictures of Ypres or Louvain after the bombardment it will give you some idea of the scene.'[20] A soldier told the Belfast-born literary critic St John Ervine (who at the time of the Rising was manager of the Abbey Theatre in Dublin) that 'Ypres was not much worse than O'Connell Street', and 'an American lady who had seen Louvain said that the town was not more battered and broken than the heart of Dublin'.[21]

MOBILISING IRELAND FOR WAR

To observers who see the history of modern Ireland primarily as one of violent conflict against British oppressors, the painful and progressive achievement of independence for three-quarters of the island, and continued violence for thirty years at the end of the twentieth century, the astonishing thing about the First World War is the extent to which the Irish people as a whole appear to have thrown themselves behind the British war effort from the beginning of the conflict. Across Europe, popular conceptions of the beginning of the war are dominated by images of 'war enthusiasm', with cheering crowds and long lines of men queuing to enlist. Recent scholarship on the 'spirit of 1914', however, has modified this simultaneously affirming and troubling picture, telling us that, while masses of people did patriotically support the war effort of their respective countries, they did not necessarily welcome the war (though some did), and that underneath the bright public effusions were many darker worries about the direction of the war and its potential costs.[22]

In the summer of 1914 Ireland appeared to be on the brink of civil war over the issue of Home Rule. For two generations Irish national-ists (who were overwhelmingly Catholic by religion) had sought to repeal the Union between Great Britain and Ireland which had been created in 1800. In 1914, at last, the Irish Party in the United Kingdom Parliament, led by John Redmond, seemed to have achieved this aspi-ration. In 1912 a statute giving Ireland domestic autonomy, with its own parliament in Dublin, had been passed in London, though last-ditch resistance from the upper House of Lords delayed the application of the measure until the autumn of 1914. Meanwhile opposition from the predominantly Protestant Unionists, who constituted a majority of the population in the north-east of Ireland, backed up by allies in Great Britain, was progressively more strident and by 1913 had begun to threaten violence in support of their aims. A paramilitary 'Ulster Volunteer Force' (UVF) was established, which by the summer of 1914 had enlisted over 100,000 men and women, and had in part been armed by guns purchased in Germany and brought into Ireland in a dramati-cally successful clandestine operation in April 1914. On the nationalist side, the parallel 'National Volunteers' was founded in November 1913 in Dublin. Although by the summer of 1914 it had up to 180,000 members, it was less well organised and armed. In July 1914 it, too, imported guns from Germany, though on a smaller scale than its northern compatriots.[23]

The Irish stand-off was exacerbated by wider military and political considerations. In March 1914 the ability of the British government to maintain order in Ireland was seriously circumscribed by the so-called Curragh Mutiny, when sixty officers at the Curragh Camp near Dublin resigned from the army rather than accept orders which they thought were aimed at suppressing the Ulster Unionists. This was so badly handled by the authorities in London that it effectively denied them the use of the army to back up the civil power in Ireland. The divisions over Ireland were sharpened by especially poor relations between the Liberal government and the Conservative opposition, who believed that the former had lost legitimacy. Even after the Sarajevo assassina-tion on 28 June, the Irish issue dominated British political debate, and it was not until the last week of July 1914 that it was supplanted by concerns about the increasing likelihood of war, and, when war was declared, Ireland (for a time) almost entirely disappeared as a political concern.

Glumly reviewing the international situation to Parliament on 3 August 1914, after Germany had declared war on France and invaded Belgium, the British foreign secretary, Sir Edward Grey, said that, while British involvement was now almost inevitable, 'the one bright spot in the whole of this terrible situation is Ireland'. Intending his message to get through to Berlin and Vienna, where there was reason to believe politicians thought Britain's freedom of action might be limited by the Irish crisis, he confirmed that 'the general feeling throughout Ireland – and I would like this to be clearly understood abroad – does not make the Irish question a consideration which we feel we have now to take into account'. It was, indeed, a moment when all the British parties closed ranks. The Conservative leader, Bonar Law, offered his party's 'unhesitating support'. John Redmond, acknowledging the existence of the Ulster and Irish Volunteers, believed that they could combine to defend Ireland. He said that the government could 'to-morrow withdraw every one of their troops from Ireland. I say that the coast of Ireland will be defended from foreign invasion by her armed sons, and for this purpose armed nationalist Catholics in the South will be only too glad to join arms with the armed Protestant Ulstermen in the North. Is it too much to hope,' he added, 'that out of this situation there may spring a result which will be good not merely for the Empire, but good for the future welfare and integrity of the Irish nation?'[24]

The invasion of Belgium was the specific *casus belli* which brought Britain into the war, and the fate of Belgium was much cited in the early weeks of the war, especially following reports in late August of the German destruction of Louvain (including the university and its library). The plight of gallant *Catholic* little Belgium had especial resonance for Irish nationalists. 'The war,' asserted the *Cork Free Press*, 'is against military despotism and in defence of the integrity of small nations. "Louvain" and "Rheims" [also devastated by the Germans] alone are cries which would stir the blood of Catholic Irishmen.' An early army recruiting pamphlet exhorted Irishmen to 'Remember

Belgium! Enlist Now and Defend Yourselves.' 'What has happened in Belgium,' it declared, 'might by now be happening in Ireland but for the British fleet and the Allied armies.' In Ulster, too, Belgium's plight was linked to British self-defence. Evidently quoting from an English source, the Unionist *Newtownards Chronicle* published some verses including the following touching lines:

> Think, from our cliffs the eye can almost see
> Fair Belgian homes go up in smoke and flame.
> Unless you fight to keep your homeland free,
> She too must know that agony and shame.
> Then it may be, when Britain meets her fate
> Her laggards shall arise – Too late! Too late![25]

On 18 September the Irish Home Rule Bill finally became law and, though its operation was suspended for the duration of the war, this was enough to allow Redmond to commit Irish nationalists, not just to the defence of Ireland at home, but to serve abroad as well. Unfavourably comparing the way Germany and Britain had treated a small neighbouring country, in what became a famous speech at Woodenbridge, County Wicklow (though it was not very widely noticed at the time outside nationalist circles) on 20 September, he placed nationalist Ireland fully in support of the Allied war effort. The war, he declared, had been 'undertaken in defence of the highest principles of religion and morality and right'. Appealing to the (supposed) Irish military tradition, he said that it would be a 'disgrace' if young Irishmen shrank 'from the duty of proving on the field of battle that gallantry and courage which has distinguished our race all through its history'.[26]

A typical nationalist response came from a local government meeting in Navan, County Meath, a few days later where a resolution was passed congratulating Redmond and his party for the position they had taken on the war. The chairman of the local Board of Guardians said they backed Redmond in hoping that young Irish men 'would realise the duty that devolved on them of joining the British Army and fighting in Belgium and on the fields of France, so that when this war was over we would not get the contemptible name of having idly looked on, but they would have done something which would merit for them, in conjunction with gallant little Belgium, the admiration of the civilised world'.[27] But while most nationalists followed Redmond, a small minority rejected his conflation of Ireland, Belgium and the British decision to go to war. Keeping the title 'Irish Volunteers' (with perhaps 10,000 adherents), they broke away, and, as their leader Eoin MacNeill declared, stayed 'pledged to the cause of Ireland, of all Ireland, and of Ireland only', in no way 'bound to serve the Imperial Government in defence of the British Empire'.[28]

Unionist support for the war was naturally much more immediately forthcoming, and on 7 September the Ulster Unionist leader Sir Edward Carson affirmed that his party did 'not seek to purchase terms by selling our patriotism'. Deftly alluding to the traditional opinion of militant and separatist Irish nationalists, that 'England's difficulty is Ireland's opportunity', he declared that 'England's difficulty is our difficulty'.[29] There was, nevertheless, a little delay in forming actual units while the Ulstermen negotiated with the British secretary of state for war, Lord Kitchener, to ensure that there should be a specifically 'Ulster' Division. Redmond, for his part, was very keen for there to be a definitively Irish formation, ideally one which drew on the Irish Volunteers as fully as the Ulster Division did on the UVF. In the event, he had to make do with two 'Irish' divisions, the 10th (Irish) and the 16th (Irish), to go along with the 36th (Ulster) Division. And, although Redmond and his colleagues pressed hard for Irish Volunteer officers to be given British Army commissions, he met with only partial success, as few of the Volunteers had much military experience. The situation was rather different in the Ulster Division, since a much higher proportion of UVF officers had previous military service and were thus able to transfer into the army much more easily.

But there was a political cost to the differential treatment by the British authorities of the two Volunteer organisations. Although the British attitude was ostensibly based on military considerations, to nationalist observers especially it looked as though the Unionists were being particularly favoured. Redmond's hope that war enthusiasm, a firm belief in the war's moral purpose (reinforced by the achievement of Home Rule), and Irish patriotic ardour could be combined in the

raising of an 'Irish army' was never quite achieved. Despite the unexpectedly wide support for the war across the entire Irish political
spectrum, with the exception (in 1914) of a tiny minority of extreme
separatists, the nationalist commitment proved to be more fragile than
that of the Unionists. In all the belligerent countries, what war enthusiasm there had been at the start of the war soon ebbed away, to be
replaced in some places with a less overtly demonstrative but perhaps
steadier resolve to 'see it through'. This was especially so in countries
where a high degree of common purpose existed between populations
and their governments – the *union sacrée* in France being a good
example – or where national territory was occupied by enemy forces,
such as in Belgium and Serbia. But elsewhere, as in Ireland, the longer
the war continued more conditional loyalties were put seriously and
increasingly to the test.

The response in Ireland, nevertheless, was very considerable indeed.
Although it is impossible to establish the precise numbers of Irish
recruits (do we include all Irish-born? – in which case significant, but
difficult to count, numbers of volunteers in Great Britain and overseas
will have to be added), between August 1914 and November 1918
something over 200,000 Irish served in armed forces engaged in the
First World War. They fall into three main categories. In the first place
a fair number were serving soldiers at the start of the conflict. For
example in August 1914 there were 28,000 Irish-born regular soldiers
and 30,000 reservists in the British Army who were immediately called
back to the colours. Secondly, there were what were known as
'Kitchener's men', people who responded to the urgent call for volunteers made by Lord Kitchener after he was appointed secretary of state
for war in August 1914. Between August 1914 and February 1916 (just
before the Easter Rising) about 95,000 men joined up. Thirdly, there
were those who enlisted during the rest of the war, after the initial
recruiting surge, up to November 1918. These men total about 45,000,
including nearly 10,000 recruits in the last three and a half months of
the war alone. To put the numbers into some sort of context, we can
relate the 200,000-odd recruits to the total number of young men living
in Ireland at the time. According to the 1911 census there were just
over 700,000 men between the ages of fifteen and thirty-five in Ireland.

The great majority of the recruits fell between those ages. We can say, therefore, that between a quarter and a third of the available young men in Ireland – a strikingly high proportion in the absence of conscription – served in the First World War.

Ireland's overall recruiting response, nevertheless, was poorer than other parts of the United Kingdom, or, indeed, white British populations in places like Canada or Australia.[30] There were socio-economic, as well as political, reasons for this. In Britain, industrial and urban areas provided many more men than rural, a pattern mirrored in Ireland, where only Ulster (which included the industrialised part of the island) and Dublin recruited particularly strongly. It is also well to remember that there were multiple reasons for joining up. No simplistic explanation, which ascribes enlistment to purely political factors (such as patriotism or a belief in the moral necessity of the war), or economic (after all, it was a job), or social (the power of collective enthusiasm; many groups of 'pals' joined together), or whatever else, will do. And as the war continued, apparently indefinitely by 1916, popular commitment began to wane, again for multiple causes: war-weariness, fear, alternative economic opportunities as war industries expanded, and so on. Throughout the United Kingdom there was a massive drop in enlistments after the first rush of recruits, which eventually prompted the government to introduce conscription for England, Scotland and Wales in March 1916. Although compulsion was threatened (especially in 1918), it was never applied to Ireland, yet even its possibility provoked much opposition from nationalist activists, arguing that, at the minimum, Ireland could only assent to conscription if Home Rule were operated.

Parallelling the military mobilisation in Ireland, as elsewhere in the United Kingdom and other belligerent states, was a domestic war effort. This was partly (and increasingly) government-run, with war legislation regulating and disciplining the population in all sorts of ways: restricting movement, controlling essential war production, directing labour, censoring newspapers. But there was much voluntary engagement, too, as women, especially, sought to 'do their bit', forming committees to help Belgian refugees and provide 'comforts' for soldiers at the front. By the end of the war, the Irish War Hospital Supply

Depot had 6,000 registered women volunteers in eight sub-depots across Ireland, manufacturing surgical and other hospital equipment. There were also expanded opportunities for female employment. While there was less substitution of female for male employment in Ireland than in Great Britain (where conscription sucked men out of the civilian workforce), increasing numbers of women found jobs in the textile and engineering factories of Ulster. And there was, inevitably, a huge increase in demand for nurses and medical auxiliary work, widely regarded as particularly suitable jobs for women.

The Irish war mobilisation was also echoed on the republican side. By 1916 the now devotedly separatist Irish Volunteers totalled about 15,000 men. As their numbers had grown since the autumn of 1914, they had held training camps and marches across the country. After the conscription of single men aged between eighteen and forty-one was introduced in Britain in January 1916, the organisation was reinforced by a number of fervent republicans living in Britain who returned home. One of these was Michael Collins – later an IRA commander in the 1919–21 Irish War of Independence – who gave up his job in London saying he was going to join up. On account of this his employers gave him an extra week's pay, which he donated to the Irish Republican Brotherhood. Women, too, enlisted and were especially active in the revolutionary socialist (though tiny, only about 200-strong) Irish Citizen Army. Backing up the Volunteers was a civilian women's association, Cumann na mBan (sixty of whom served during Easter Week), and after the Rising sympathetic republican women, led by Kathleen Clarke, widow of the executed leader Tom Clarke, helped raise money for the Irish National Aid and Volunteer Dependants' Fund.[31]

There was help from further afield, too. On Easter Monday afternoon two foreign sailors, a Swede and a Finn, offered their services at the General Post Office. Liam Tannam, who was commanding the defence of the building, asked them why they wanted to fight against the British. The Swede 'said: "Finland, a small country, Russia eat her up." Then he said: "Sweden, another small country, Russia eat her up too. Russia with the British, therefore, we against."' They proved to be a bit of a liability. After the Finn had accidentally fired his shotgun and brought down part of the ceiling, they were employed on bomb-making duties at the back of the main hall. They remained to the end and were detained for a time afterwards. Tannam reported that although the Finn (who spoke no English) was not a Catholic, 'before he left he was saying the Rosary in Irish'.[32]

Gallant little Belgium

And what of Belgium? Was there any validity to the parallel drawn by Irish nationalists between England's treatment of Ireland and Germany's of Belgium? Despite its obvious significance – especially for Britain – in the national decision-making of early August 1914, Belgium, in general, has been somewhat neglected in studies of the First World War. 'While featuring prominently as a *landscape* of war and as a symbol of wartime propaganda,' wrote Tammy Proctor in 2005, 'Belgium and its people are strangely absent from the military and social histories of this period in European history.' Sophie de Schaepdrijver has mordantly observed that Belgium's role in the histo-riography has been 'that of bystander to its own history'.[33] While this deficiency is being rectified (a process in which de Schaepdrijver's own work forms an important part), 'little' Belgium's war experience still remains comparatively little known.

By the late autumn of 1914 over ninety per cent of the country had been occupied by the Germans, leaving only a tiny corner of Flemish Belgium, with a twenty-mile front line. Six hundred thousand soldiers, officials and refugees eventually escaped from the occupied zone, and a 'government of national unity' under King Albert was established in the French port of Le Havre. Retaining its 'neutrality', Belgium never formally became one of the Allies, and Albert refused to commit his troops to what he regarded as over-costly offensives. The German-occupied portion of the country was administered in two parts. The area immediately behind the front line was controlled directly by the army; the remaining three-quarters or so came under a German governor-general and central administration, under which the existing Belgian local government structures continued to operate in what de Schaepdrijver describes as an 'uneasy routine'. Although numbers of courageous Belgians resisted in various ways – from grumbling non-cooperation and the wearing of patriotic badges, to running clandestine newspapers and doing active intelligence work for the Allies – there were few, if any, direct attacks on the occupying forces. Wartime occupied Belgium settled down into a regime of 'improvised if tense partnerships at odds with the image of an entire society risen against the invader'.[34]

The widespread dislocation and population movements of 1914 were followed by an extended food crisis in Belgium. Far from self-sufficient, the country depended on food imports and over the first winter of the war acute shortages resulted from the British sea blockade and the Germans' refusal to supply the occupied territories. Led by Herbert Hoover, an American businessman living in London (and later United States president), an international 'Commission for Relief in Belgium' was established which, treading a delicate diplomatic line between British and German war priorities, organised food supplies, mainly through the Netherlands, for distribution in occupied France and Luxemburg, as well as Belgium. The dislocation of the Belgian economy left half a million people unemployed, a reservoir including many skilled workers, which the Germans thought could be exploited as labour in mining and heavy industries whose own workforces had been stretched by military mobilisation. From mid-1915, a German organisation endeavoured to recruit Belgian volunteer workers but with only moderate results. By the late autumn of 1916 it had enlisted only 30,000 workers, far short of the numbers needed.[35]

During 1916 labour shortages prompted the occupation administration to consider forced labour. This was first introduced in occupied France at Easter 1916, when 20,000 people, principally women and girls, were conscripted in the Lille region for agricultural work. Humiliatingly, the females were subjected to intimate gynaecological examination in the process.[36] In Belgium the imposition of forced labour followed a change of command in Berlin, after the so-called military 'silent dictatorship' of Erich Ludendorff and Paul von Hindenburg took power in August 1916. The subsequent Hindenburg Programme brought an intensified exploitation of national resources and the enhanced use of labour both within Germany and from the occupied territories.[37]

In October, workers in the Belgian and French occupied zones were conscripted with the status of 'civilian prisoners', and deported in trains (under atrocious conditions; some in cattle trucks) to labour camps in western Germany. In all 60,000 Belgians were deported between 26 October 1916 and February 1917, provoking widespread protests in Belgium and abroad. Cardinal Mercier ('Primate Denounces to the World the Deportations from Belgium') declared that able-bodied men were being 'carried off pell-mell, penned up in trucks and deported to unknown destinations, like slave gangs . . . Thus thousands of Belgians are being reduced to slavery.' Henri Pirenne, the leading Belgian historian, who himself was interned in Germany from August 1916 to the end of the war, claimed that the deportations stimulated a unanimous and heroic national resistance which united the disparate elements of Belgian society: Flemings and Walloons; Catholics and Freemasons; conservatives and socialists.[38]

The Belgian government-in-exile ran a powerful campaign denouncing this fresh manifestation of 'Prussian militarism', particularly targeting opinion in the (as yet) neutral USA. In his admiring and sympathetic account of 'Belgium under German occupation', the United States' minister Brand Whitlock wrote of 'those terrible days of the autumn and winter of 1916, with their darkness and their cold and their hourly tale of horror'. He thought that 'the pitiless and insensate cruelty, the brutal indifference to all human rights and human dignity that characterized this restoration of human slavery in our time . . . made those days in many ways the saddest that Belgium had endured'. There were, he wrote, 'no words' for it then: 'I could only write to my Government that it was enough to cause one to despair of the future of the human race'. In fact in labour terms the scheme was a complete failure. The process of matching workers to industrial occupations was very inefficiently organised and German firms found the work of the reluctant Belgian conscripts quite unsatisfactory. Although some forced labour continued in the military areas close to the front line in Belgium and France, by June 1917 the system of deportations and forced labour in Germany was abolished.[39]

One form of war service was spying for the Allies. Anxious to play their part in the war effort, many individuals in occupied Belgium joined intelligence networks, passing information to the British and

French, mainly through the neutral Netherlands. From the beginning of the war, British secret intelligence in the Netherlands had been run by Richard Tinsley, an officer in the Royal Naval Reserve who had been based in Rotterdam for some years, most recently working as the local manager of a Canadian steamship company running cut-price emigrant ships across the Atlantic. While apparently able enough, he was not universally trusted. Ivone Kirkpatrick, who worked for British Army intelligence later in the war, described him as 'a liar and a first-class intriguer with few scruples'.[40] A postwar history of British intelligence in occupied territory reported that most of the work involved 'train watching'. Belgium had the most developed railway network in the world, and, with agents positioned at key points of the system logging trains, counting carriages and trucks and, so far as was possible, identifying their contents, information was gathered 'of vital importance in drawing up the enemy's order of battle'. This 'had a direct effect on the operations and movements of our own forces, and became therefore the first objective of our Secret Service system'. Subsidiary efforts were devoted to reports on defensive works; shipping movements from the Belgian ports of Zeebrugge and Ostend; 'technical details as to artillery, aviation, aerodromes and similar matters'; as well as 'the acquisition by theft or purchase of German military compilations, and all military information generally'. By mid-1918 it was calculated that Tinsley's operation accounted for some seventy per cent 'of the total intelligence obtained by all the Allied armies not only through the Netherlands but also through other neutral states'.[41]

One of the most important of the British networks was 'La Dame Blanche' established towards the end of 1916 by Walthère Dewé and Herman Chauvin, the former an electrical engineer who worked for the Belgian telephone company and the latter an academic. Dewé wanted especially to gain revenge for the execution in April 1916 by the Germans of his cousin, Dieudonné Lambrecht, who had been running an espionage organisation since the end of 1914. He chose the name 'Dame Blanche' as there was a legend that the destruction of the Hohenzollern dynasty – the German imperial house – would follow the appearance of a mystical female figure clothed in white. Regarding spying as an inherently dishonourable activity, Dewé and Chauvin insisted that they would not be employed as 'spies' but 'recognised as soldiers of the Allied armies'. Indeed, they so successfully pressed for public recognition after the war for the 800 brave men and women in their organisation, that it had the very unfortunate unintended consequence, when twenty years later Belgium was once again occupied by Germans, of correctly identifying them as likely British agents.[42]

Women played an important role in the intelligence networks of occupied Belgium: nearly thirty per cent of the people publicly rewarded by the British after the war were female. A 190-strong Dame Blanche unit centred on Brussels was led by Laure Tandel, an unmarried female schoolteacher in her forties, and the personnel included other female teachers, shop assistants, nuns and mostly middle-class women 'without profession'. (The men – labourers, civil servants, engineers and railway workers – demonstrated an equally diverse range of occupations.) One woman, Gabrielle Petit, gave her life for espionage work. A twenty-one year-old saleswoman at the beginning of the war, Petit initially volunteered for work with the Belgian Red Cross. During 1915 she escaped from German-occupied Belgium and offered her services to British military intelligence. After some training in Britain she returned to Belgium in August 1915 and organised a small network of agents to collect information about the German Sixth Army, getting information out through the Netherlands. But her network was infiltrated by the Germans and she was arrested in February 1916. Tried before a military court, she was condemned to death and executed by firing squad on 1 April.[43]

Conscious of the international storm of condemnation which followed the execution in October 1915 (also by firing squad) of the English nurse Edith Cavell, convicted of assisting Allied soldiers to escape from occupied Belgium through the Netherlands, the German authorities endeavoured to restrict publicity about Petit's execution. Although a despatch from Amsterdam in *The New York Times* on 8 April 1916 reported the 'assertion' in a Belgian newspaper that Petit had been executed after being convicted of treason, it was not until 17 May that *The Times* in London carried a report under the headline 'More German death sentences on women'. The Amsterdam newspaper, *De Telegraaf*, had reported that Gabrielle Petit had been sentenced to death for espionage on 12 March but this 'was not made known until much later'. The official report stated that 'the accused spied for good pay along the railways and for months had furnished information to the enemy'. *De Telegraaf* also reported that a Frenchwoman, Louise de Bettignies, had been condemned to death at Lille for war treason, but since she 'received no payment' her penalty had been commuted to 'hard labour for life'. De Bettignies, dubbed the 'Queen of Spies', ran an extensive network in the Lille region which, until her arrest in October 1915, both helped a sizeable number of Allied servicemen to escape and provided a steady supply of useful military intelligence. Spared the firing squad, she fell ill in a German prison and died in hospital in Cologne in September 1918.[44]

Reflecting the global reach of wartime espionage, Tinsley's organisation also kept a watch for enemy agents seeking to get to the United Kingdom, or travel further afield. Information from the Rotterdam station contributed to the detection of German agents in 1915 and 1916. In June 1916, Tinsley identified a German intelligence cover address in The Hague, from where a number of American journalists had been recruited by the Germans. On 29 September a letter from one of these journalists, George Vaux Bacon, who was working in Europe, was intercepted and opened – thereby putting the British security service MI5 on his trail. He was shadowed in the Netherlands and Britain, where MI5 reported that he had a 'loose' (i.e. promiscuous) lifestyle, but 'eluded his watchers' while visiting naval bases in Ireland. Arrested in December 1916, he was found to be carrying sufficient incriminating material to be charged with espionage (MI5 reported that 'two of his socks were found to produce invisible ink when soaked in water'.) Confronted with corroborative information from another American recruited by the Germans, Bacon confessed, was court-martialled and in March 1917 sentenced to be shot by firing squad in the Tower of London. This was later commuted to life imprisonment and, at the request of the American authorities, he was deported to the United States where he provided evidence leading to the conviction in New York of the network's two leaders.[45]

Belgium's wartime situation cannot fully be compared to Ireland's. Yet there are some broad similarities which make the parallels not as

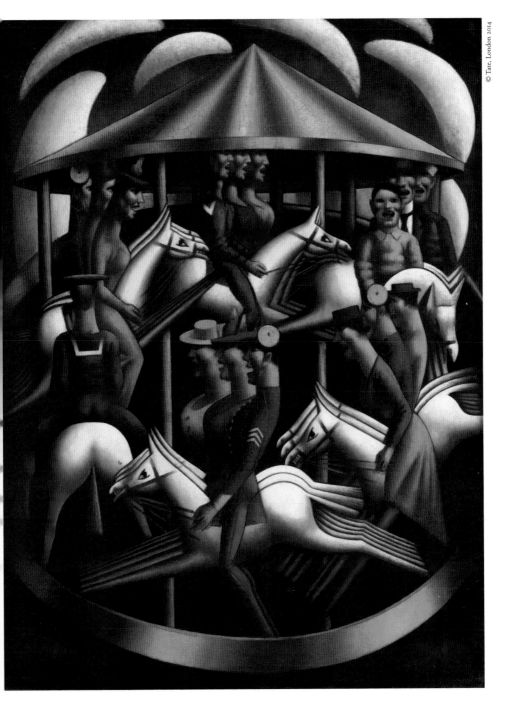

The Merry-Go-Round (1916), by the English artist Mark Gertler (1891–1939). Born into an Austrian-Jewish immigrant family, Gertler was a pacifist during the war and the painting embodies his bleak vision of a meaningless, never-ending conflict.

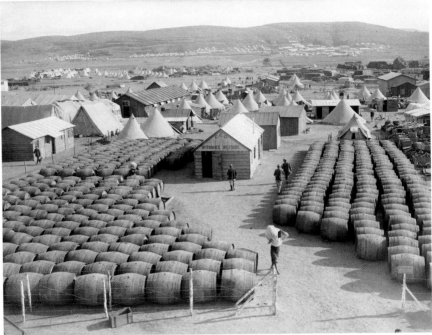

Wine stores assembled at the Greek port of Mudros for the French troops at Gallipoli confirm the conviction that an army must 'march on its stomach'. On the peninsula French wine and coffee proved to be useful barter for English jam and canned beef.

The execution of Cesare Battisti in his home town of Trento on 12 July 1916. Images like this distributed by the Habsburg authorities as propaganda backfired as they merely enhanced Battisti's status as a martyr to the cause of Italian freedom.

Images from Alan Hankinson, *Geoffrey Winthrop Young*

Photographs taken by volunteer ambulance-driver Geoffrey Winthrop Young on 8 August 1916 during the perilous crossing of the damaged bridge leading into Gorizia sixty feet above the Isonzo river.

A Mother of France (1916), by the Australian Hilda Rix Nicholas (1884–1961) reflects the patient suffering of women during the war. Nicholas's own husband was killed at the front in November 1916 just five weeks after they had been married in London.

The Trial of Sir Roger Casement, London, 1916, by John Lavery (1856–1941). Lavery, a Belfast-born Catholic with Irish nationalist sympathies, was very unusually invited to record the scene at Casement's appeal to his sentence of death for treason. This version of the picture includes the public gallery where Lavery depicted supporters of Casement, including Eva Gore-Booth, sister of Constance Markiewicz, who was then in prison for her part in the Easter Rising.

The perils of the trenches are not greater than those of a city like London. More deadly than the cold steel of the bayonet, the rattle of the machine gun, the bursting of shrapnel or the devastating effects of the high explosive shell is the attack of sin and temptation.

Concerns about the moral temptations facing soldiers on active service led organisations like the Young Men's Christian Association to produce pamphlets warning against the dangers of 'vice'.

The Englishwoman, Florence Farmborough, who had worked as a governess and tutor to Russian families before the war, served as a nurse with the imperial Russian army on the Galician and Romanian fronts. A talented photographer, she left a marvellous record of work and life on the Eastern Front.

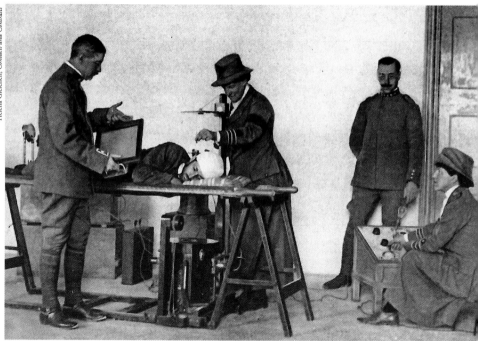

The intrepid feminists, Helena Gleichen and Nina Hollings, operating their portable X-Ray apparatus at Gorizia on the Italian front. Having been rejected by the British War Office, they successfully offered their services to the Italians.

Elements of the fabled Russian 'streamroller', the apparently inexhaustible supply of peasant soldiers – but only until 1916 – as photographed by Florence Farmborough.

Engineer Lieutenant Commander ~ Roberts by name ~ was wonderful ~
a shell. He died at his post also and was wonderful. My grief
at losing 2 such officers is very great; your boy was besides
the service such a pal to me. I feel a very great personal
loss. Please again accept my heartfelt sympathy and the
sympathy of the others here with me, and the "Nomad's" our
divisional mates (late "Tigress").

Yours very sincerely,

(Sd) Barry Bingham.

My father felt strongly that Capt Bingham (later awarded the V.C.) should have been the last to leave his ship & should have ordered Maurice to leave before him.

The bitter marginal note made by Maurice Bethell's grieving sister Agatha on a letter from Maurice's commanding officer, Barry Bingham, describing the events at Jutland when Maurice lost his life and Bingham survived.

The imperial German navy's First World War memorial at Laboe on the Baltic Sea in May 1936. Hitler deplored the structure, describing it as an 'unparalleled item of kitsch'.

Europe 1916, by Boardman Robinson (1876–1952). Profoundly anti-militarist, the Canadian-born Robinson toured east-central Europe and the Balkans with the American journalist John Reed during 1915. He returned to the USA to campaign against the war and published this cartoon in the socialist monthly *The Masses* in October 1916.

outrageous as might at first be thought. A steady intensification of government pressure and controls occurred in both places (as, of course, happened elsewhere). The threat of conscription in Ireland can be matched with the actual imposition of forced labour in Belgium. In both places this intensified national feeling and stimulated resistance to the ruling authorities. The possibility from 1916 onwards that conscription might be imposed on Ireland was a constant irritant for nationalists, who argued that such a measure could only be contemplated once Home Rule became operational and an Irish parliament could willingly assent. When in 1918 actual legislation for conscription in Ireland was introduced, although it was never implemented, it did much to create a 'pan-nationalist' opposition, markedly advancing the fortunes of the separatist Sinn Féin party which emerged after the war as the dominant nationalist political organisation. There were ambivalent responses in both countries to the wartime administration. In Ireland the loyalty of civil servants, local government officials, policemen, and so on, to the established order was increasingly criticised by advanced nationalists as a betrayal of their national obligations. In Belgium, where beyond the immediate battle zone the structures of local government at least initially remained in place, functionaries were similarly caught between the competing demands of civic and national duty.

In both places, among the most committed nationalists were individuals prepared to work with the enemy of the occupying power. These included the men of Casement's Irish Brigade, as well as the Dublin rebels who rose (as they thought) with German support. There was no internal uprising in Belgium against the German occupiers since a national army continued to exist which refugees and recruits from unoccupied Belgium could join. An estimated 30,000 volunteers also escaped through the Netherlands to enlist. Nevertheless, some who remained and served in occupied Belgium – women as well as men – did so at the cost of their lives.

Another possible similarity concerns the communal divisions in each country. There were deep ethnic-linguistic cleavages in both Ireland and Belgium. In Ireland the quarter of the population who were Protestant and very predominantly Unionist could be relied upon consistently to support the established government and the war effort. Despite the fact that their own leader, John Redmond, had refused to join a new coalition Cabinet in May 1915, Irish nationalists claimed that the inclusion of Sir Edward Carson indicated the British government's special favouritism towards Ulster Unionists and embodied a 'divide and rule' approach to controlling Ireland. In Belgium the Germans' 'Flamenpolitik' aimed to exploit Flemish linguistic grievances in order to promote pro-German attitudes. This involved a range of measures from Flemish-language roadsigns and the use of Flemish in school-teaching to the enforced 'Flemishisation' of the University of Ghent in October 1916. Although the policy certainly invigorated Flemish cultural organisations, it does not appear to have had much effect in actively enlisting Flemings to the German war effort.[46]

A final parallel lies in the impact which the wartime circumstances had on governmental attitudes to resistance. For the authorities in both Ireland and Belgium, this meant that any response to opposition and subversion was more draconian (and more militarised) than might otherwise have been the case. Execution by firing squad, for example, is not a conventional civilian procedure. The Irish cult of martyrdom which grew out of the 1916 executions has an echo in Belgium. Long after the war, Henry Landau, a British intelligence case officer in The Hague, reflected that 'valuable as his work had been during the eighteen months he had faithfully served the Allies', it was in death that Dieudonné Lambrecht 'exerted his greatest force. His example was an inspiration to others to carry on his work; his friends swore to avenge him, and out of the scattered remains of his espionage service emerged "The White Lady," the greatest spy organisation of the War.'[47]

'Changed, changed utterly'?

In one of his most famous poems, 'Easter 1916', William Butler Yeats provided his own response to the Rising and sketched out what became a very widely accepted vision of the impact which the Rising had on Irish nationalist public life and opinion generally. In the resonant last lines of the poem, he describes the executed leaders of the Rising as having been 'changed, changed utterly: a terrible beauty is born'.

Underpinning this observation was the notion that the executions caused a seismic shift in attitudes after which nothing could ever be the same again. Completed in September 1916, privately printed and distributed in 1917, but not published until 1921, it was an unusually political war poem from a writer who generally kept contemporary political references out of his work (and, famously, excluded 'war poetry' from his 1936 *Oxford Book of Modern Verse*). In 1923, St John Ervine improbably asserted that Yeats was 'the only English-speaking poet who did not write a poem about the war', ascribing this to Yeats's 'isolation from the common life of his time'. Ervine, who knew Yeats personally, said that he had 'never met anyone who seems so unaware of contemporary affairs', a state 'due, not to affectation, but to sheer lack of interest. He probably would not have known of the War at all had not the Germans dropped a bomb near his lodgings off the Euston Road.'[48] Like nearly everything Ervine wrote, this has to taken with a pinch of salt, and, in fact, Yeats did write war poems other than 'Easter 1916', including 'An Irish Airman Foresees His Death', and 'In memory of Major Robert Gregory' ('Soldier, scholar, horseman, he'; and the airman of the previous poem).

The Rising and the executions which followed certainly had a powerful impact on contemporary opinion. Writing some time after the events, Liam Roche reflected that 'we know not what forces have been unloosed. We are too near the event to judge in proper perspective . . . This much we can judge: never again can we get back to the conditions that existed before the storm burst; its effects will remain, either in the shaping of facts or the stimulation of inspirations. Ireland can not be the same.'[49] While 1916 itself was an important tipping point for many moderate nationalists, the sense of the events of that year forming a very definite watershed became only gradually apparent. In the immediate aftermath of the Rising it was by no means clear whether Ireland's political situation had changed irreversibly, or if the Rising and its impact, albeit hugely magnified by the wartime circumstances, was just another of the periodic eruptions of political violence with which Ireland had apparently been afflicted since time immemorial. As the Unionist *Irish Times* over-optimistically (as it turned out) predicted a week after the Rising had ended, 'the Dublin insurrection of 1916 will pass into history with the equally unsuccessful insurrections of the past'.[50]

After 1921, however, when three-quarters of Ireland had gained at least a qualified measure of independence, it might plausibly be argued that things had been changed, if not 'utterly' at least very greatly, and nationalists could begin to celebrate 1916 not as a 'glorious failure' but as a crucial moment in the journey to autonomy. The modest and limited achievement of Home Rule had now been replaced by what Michael Collins (himself one of the rebels of 1916) accurately predicted was 'not full freedom, but the freedom to achieve it'. As the state cut the remaining ties with the United Kingdom – finally declaring itself a republic in 1948 – 1916 could increasingly be commemorated as a founding moment in the emergence of the independent (though as yet incomplete) Irish state.

In a notably perceptive study of the Easter Rising, Fearghal McGarry has argued that one of the 'underlying weaknesses' of British rule in Ireland was its 'reliance on the pragmatic acquiescence – rather than affection or loyalty – of much of the nationalist population', and that the repression which followed the Rising 'would ultimately stretch this highly conditional acceptance of the legitimacy of British authority beyond breaking point'.[51] The intensity of that repression stemmed directly from the wartime circumstances. For Irish and British Unionists (and even some constitutional nationalists too – at least at the start of the Rising) the very violence of the rebels provoked an exemplary response. With, as some argued, British national survival at stake in the wider conflict, draconian measures were evidently justified to suppress dissent at home. In this way the situation in Ireland was very similar to that in other belligerents with grumbling national or sectional minorities, such as Austria-Hungary, Russia and the Ottoman Empire.

5

Jutland and the War at Sea

The battle of Jutland on 31 May–1 June 1916, called by the Germans the 'battle of the Skagerrak', was the greatest naval battle of the war, and an occasion when the most powerful and technologically advanced fighting machines of the age engaged in a distinctly old-fashioned way which would have been broadly familiar to Nelson a century before. Despite the availability of wireless communications and state-of-the-art (though as it turned out on the British side inadequate) fire-control systems, much of the action and direction depended on line-of-sight observation and visual signalling. Furthermore, since it involved only surface ships, it might be considered as the last great naval battle of the nineteenth century. Never again would there be a major naval engagement in which neither submarines nor air power (or both) were significantly deployed.[1]

Although the battle between the German High Seas Fleet and the British Grand Fleet – the most anticipated naval engagement of the war – occurred close to both countries in the North Sea, in terms of geographical reach the war at sea was the most undeniably global aspect of the First *World* War. This is demonstrated by the early naval battles in the Pacific, South Atlantic and Indian Oceans. In November 1914 British and German squadrons fought each other – with the Germans getting the better of it – at Coronel off the coast of Chile. The Germans, commanded by Admiral Graf von Spee, were then soundly defeated in the battle of the Falkland Islands on 8 December.

One German cruiser, the *Dresden*, escaped and survived until March 1915 when it was trapped by the British at the Chilean island of Juan Fernandez and was scuttled by its crew. A German light cruiser, the *Emden*, was briefly very successful commerce-raiding in the Indian Ocean. It also bombarded Madras (Chennai) in India, inflicting serious damage, and attacked Penang in Malaya, where it sank a Russian cruiser and a French destroyer, before itself being destroyed on 9 November 1914 at the Keeling Islands, south-west of Sumatra, by the Australian cruiser, HMAS *Sydney*.

REINHARD SCHEER AND THE BATTLE OF THE SKAGERRAK

Admiral Reinhard Scheer was appointed commander-in-chief of the German High Seas Fleet on 18 January 1916 in succession to Hugo von Pohl, who had shortly before retired through ill health. During his time in command from February 1915, Pohl had continued the essentially cautious policy adopted by the German navy since the start of the war. Because the German fleet was inferior in numbers to the British 'Grand Fleet' (though not, they thought, in technical specification and tactical expertise), the conundrum for them was balancing the terrible risk of naval defeat if they sought a major fleet action with the British, against the powerfully enticing prospect of winning a victory against the world's most powerful and celebrated navy. In effect, although the comparison is not exact since the naval war was inevitably more global than the military, what happened on the seas was the opposite of what happened on land, where the British debate turned on the balance between fully focusing on the chief theatre of the Western Front as opposed to dissipating resources on 'sideshows'.

At sea, apart from the single exception of Skagerrak/Jutland in 1916, 'sideshows' prevailed, as commanders on both sides hesitated to risk their most powerful formations in what might turn out to be one final, decisive engagement. If the war of attrition on the Western Front was a constant frustration for generals itching, like Sir Douglas Haig, for a great breakthrough, when movement could be restored and his beloved cavalry properly deployed, it was even worse for the admirals who commanded the great fleets of dreadnoughts which Britain, Germany and other martime powers had been building over the generation or so running up to the war. The most powerful, advanced and expensive war machines yet created were themselves so valuable that caution became the watchword in their employment. Taking on the enemy's main fleet was a very high-risk strategy. Sir John Jellicoe, the commander of the British Grand Fleet, was, after all, as Winston Churchill famously (if slightly inaccurately) observed, 'the only man on either side who could lose the war in an afternoon'.[2] Churchill, being in thrall to the 'Great Man' interpretation of history, inevitably tended to overstate and personalise the case. Nevertheless, the stakes were always going to be high in the maritime poker game played across the North Sea.

Scheer, however, was determined to be much more aggressive than his predecessor, and combine the full range of his weapons – surface ships, submarines, aircraft and mines – in attacking the enemy, and, if possible, enticing British formations into parts of the North Sea where German warships would lie in wait. The intensified operations began in the spring of 1916. Early in March the airship L.11, commanded by Captain Victor Schulze, accompanied by L.13 and L.14, was deployed from Nordholz naval air base near Cuxhaven across the North Sea to 'attack England in the north'. Setting off at noon on 5 March, the airships took almost eleven hours to reach the British coast, which they crossed between Flamborough Head and Spurn Head in Yorkshire. In bitterly cold conditions and a strengthening northerly wind, they turned away from 'the munitions factories at Middlesbrough' to target the port of Hull. Flying at between 4,000 and 6,000 feet, L.11 and L.14 both attacked the town. 'For twenty minutes following my instructions,' reported Schulze, 'bombs were dropped quite composedly on the harbour and docks and the effect of each bomb carefully watched.' Schulze claimed great accuracy for the bombing and 'people were seen through the telescope running hither and thither in the light of the flames'. When he was 'convinced of the excellent effect of the bombs dropped on Hull', Schulze moved on down the coast to Immingham where he dropped his last five bombs before reaching home twenty-six hours after they had departed.[3]

On 7 March, *The Times* reported that an air raid had occurred –
'A Yorkshire town attacked' – but left the location unnamed. Yet it
also carried a short despatch from Amsterdam: 'The Naval General
Staff, says a Berlin official telegram, announces:– "Some of our naval
airships last night heavily bombarded the naval base of Hull on the
Humber and the dock buildings there. Our airships were vigorously,
but unsuccessfully, fired at, and returned safely."' Under the headline
'Casualties in Yorkshire', *The Times* went on to report that during
the raid on a still unnamed 'town in Yorkshire' twenty-five explosive and an unknown number of incendiary bombs had been dropped
resulting in seventeen deaths, including at least five children and one
woman. 'No important buildings have been damaged,' continued the
report. 'No military advantage has been achieved by the raid. Not a
single soldier has been killed. The women and children who have been
sacrificed have been killed in ordinary terrace houses.[4]

The following month, Scheer launched a sea and air operation with
the primary purpose of luring British ships out, but also providing
German support for the planned Easter Rising in Ireland.[5] The plan
was to send a battlecruiser squadron to bombard Great Yarmouth and
Lowestoft on the East Anglian coast, while submarines and torpedo-
boats were deployed to attack any British ships which might attempt
to intercept the German formation. Over the night of 24/25 April –
Easter Monday and Tuesday – six airships bombed Norwich, Lincoln,
Harwich and Ipswich, and during the early morning of 25 April the
German battlecruisers attacked Great Yarmouth and Lowestoft as
planned. *The Times* of 25 April carried a report of the airship attack
on the same page as 'A Raid in Ireland . . . A German auxiliary and
submarine have made an attempt to land arms and ammunition in
Ireland.' The 'auxiliary' had sunk and 'a number of prisoners were
made, amongst whom was Sir Roger Casement'. As for the airships:
'Another Zeppelin raid on the Eastern Counties took place last night.'
Once again, the newspaper was circumspect about the precise location of the targets, merely adding that 'a few incendiary bombs were
dropped'. The following day, however, identifying the rising in Ireland,
the Zeppelin raid and a 'naval battle off Lowestoft' as 'all apparently
parts of a concerted German plan', *The Times* reported that a German

battlecruiser squadron had shelled Lowestoft, killing two men, one woman and a child, but had been chased off by British light cruisers and destroyers which had suffered only minor damage.[6]

Scheer planned next to mount a raid on Sunderland, which he thought was sufficiently far north to tempt out elements of the Royal Navy from their Scottish bases at Scapa Flow in the Orkneys, where most of Jellicoe's Grand Fleet was stationed, or Rosyth in the Firth of Forth, which harboured the Battlecruiser Fleet under Sir David Beatty.[7] As well as using surface vessels, Scheer's plan was to deploy submarines off Scapa and the Firth of Forth, as well as his 'Flanders Flotilla' of U-boats well to the south. In the event, because strong north-easterly winds prevented him from using airships for essential reconnaissance to warn of approaching enemy ships, Scheer abandoned the attack on Sunderland and substituted a plan to entice the British out by ostentatiously sending his battlecruiser squadron, under Admiral Franz Ritter von Hipper, into the western Skagerrak, the sea separating Norway from Denmark. At 2 a.m. on the morning of 31 May, therefore, Scheer despatched Hipper and the battlecruisers; two hours later the rest of his High Seas Fleet set sail.[8]

By this stage the British had already deployed their ships. As in the Second World War, when the work of the Bletchley Park codebreakers provided vital intelligence for Britain's naval war effort, in the Great War the Admiralty's signals intelligence branch, Room 40, were able to intercept and decipher some German naval signals. Already during the evening of 30 May the Admiralty had become convinced that major German fleet movements were under way and had issued instructions for Jellicoe and Beatty to put to sea – which shortly before midnight they both did. The following afternoon and evening (31 May), off the western coast of Denmark between about 4 and 10.30 p.m., the two fleets fought each other in a series of chaotic and destructive engagements, after which both sides claimed victory. Although sustaining considerable punishment, Hipper's squadron sank two of Beatty's battlecruisers in their first encounter. In the main battle fleet engagement after 6.30 p.m. another British battlecruiser and two heavy cruisers were sunk, while the German battlecruiser, *Lützow*, was crippled and later lost. The Germans also lost a pre-dreadnought battleship and four light cruisers. *Lützow* was the most powerful warship to be sunk in the battle, but many vessels on both sides suffered heavy damage. Late in the evening Scheer managed to evade the British and got his battered fleet to safety, after-wards claiming that by the time he anchored his flagship, the *Friedrich der Grosse*, at Wilhelmshaven, 'the crews on all our ships had attained full consciousness of the greatness of our successes against the superior enemy forces'.[9]

The inconclusive result of Skagerrak/Jutland was a great frustra-tion for both sides. Needing to be reassured that they had inflicted really serious damage on the Germans, the Admiralty deputed 'TR/16', Britain's single most successful First World War spy, to report on the state of the enemy ships. TR/16 was a naval engineer called Karl Krüger who had turned up at the British legation in The Hague in November 1914 offering his services as a spy. The secret service, to whom he was passed, were naturally very suspicious at first, but it emerged that he was reassuringly avaricious and held a strong grudge against both the German navy and the imperial royal family. Apparently, while serving in the navy some years before he had insulted a relative of the Kaiser, been court-martialled and cash-iered from the service. Claiming that he had ready access to German dockyards, he offered regular and up-to-date information about the German navy. Convinced of his commitment, he was taken on and run by Richard Tinsley in Rotterdam (hence 'TR': Tinsley-Rotterdam).[10]

In a file of sixty surviving intelligence reports, it is recorded that he 'made complete tours of the German shipyards approximately every month from May 1915 to January 1919' and that 'considerable value was attached to his information'. After Jutland the secret service was instructed to report on the damage to the German fleet and Krüger was put on the job. Between 3 and 20 June the agent visited ten German dockyards, including Kiel, Bremen, Rostock and Danzig, and on 27 June delivered a comprehensive five-page report which the Admiralty Director of Intelligence praised as '100%'. The most reas-suring aspect from the British point of view was confirmation that the Germans had sustained more serious damage than they had admitted. Krüger reported, for example, that eight capital ships would be out of service for at least three months. Rather suggesting (among other things) that German naval dockyard security was not very stringent, a second British agent, who operated out of Copenhagen – 'D.15' ('D' for Denmark) – also provided quite a detailed and accurate report of the post-Skagerrak state of affairs: '59 German ships took part in Naval battle, most of which are damaged,' he reported. 'Worst damage is KONIG, MARKGRAF, DERFFLINGER, SEYDLITZ.' He estimated the German casualties at 2,477 killed and 490 wounded (which, for intelligence gathered covertly and submitted nineteen days after the battle, compared well to the final official figures of 2,551 and 507 respectively).[11]

While the battle of the Skagerrak is credited with being a British victory on the grounds that it so rattled the Germans that they never again risked taking the High Seas Fleet to sea, this is not quite true since the German fleet came out twice more in 1916. Scheer was by no means intimidated by the result of the battle, and thought, with some justification, that the events had demonstrated technical superiority on the German side. 'We have,' he wrote, 'been able to prove to the world that the English Navy no longer possesses her boasted irresistibility.' The battle, moreover, 'proved that the organisation of our Navy as a High Sea Fleet was a step in the right direction'.[12] In August 1916, Scheer planned a fresh attack on Sunderland, again with the intention of enticing at least elements of the British fleet out. He devised new tactics for his submarines, deploying them in groups to defend his fleet from the north and south, as well as being ready to attack the British if the opportunity arose.

At 10 p.m. on 18 August, the High Seas Fleet set sail more or less due east from Wilhelmshaven, with eight airships providing long-range reconnaissance. The British, meanwhile, again from signals intelligence had advance warning of the German move, and had begun going to sea even before the Germans had left port. Scheer's U-boat screen performed well, sinking a light cruiser, HMS *Nottingham*, which was part of the advance guard to the Grand Fleet sailing south to intercept the Germans. It was not clear whether the *Nottingham* had been sunk by a submarine or a mine, which caused Jellicoe to hold back lest he should bring his ships into a minefield. Scheer's fleet, in turn, had been attacked by a British submarine, and at 5 a.m. his battleship *Westfalen* was sufficiently badly damaged by a torpedo for Scheer to send it back to harbour. The German airship reconnaissance was quite successful, though one report which mistook a smaller British squadron from Harwich for the Grand Fleet, led Scheer (providentially for him) to alter course away from vastly superior British forces coming from the north. By mid-afternoon on 19 August, he decided to bring his ships home, at about the same time as Admiral Jellicoe decided likewise. Scheer's submarines scored one more hit when another British light cruiser, HMS *Falmouth*, was torpedoed twice, crippled and then sank while being towed back to port. This was not quite the last High Seas Fleet venture into the North Sea. Two months later, Scheer took his ships out again, but was not able to repeat the productive combination of submarine and air reconnaissance he had managed in August, since from early October the naval staff in Berlin prohibited the use of submarines in combined North Sea operations as they were once more to be concentrated on commerce-raiding.[13]

Although he thought this policy was 'useless', Scheer had to acquiesce. He had consistently believed that the employment of U-boats 'was of fundamental importance for our warfare against England'. They could be used both against British maritime trade and British warships, though Scheer tended to favour the former as having the greater potential to damage the enemy. But this could only really be successful if their use was unrestricted, which, in turn, was a political decision. In February 1915 the Germans declared the seas around the British Isles to be a war zone in which enemy commercial shipping might be sunk on sight. But attacks on British ships carrying American passengers – in particular the liner *Lusitania*, sunk in May 1915 – provoked angry protests from Washington. In March 1916 a cross-Channel ferry, the *Sussex*, was badly damaged by a U-boat torpedo, killing the celebrated Spanish composer Enrique Granados and his wife and injuring a number of Americans. This produced another diplomatic storm and prompted Berlin in early May to abandon the policy, whereupon Scheer ceased commerce-raiding altogether and redeployed his submarines both in support of the surface fleet and also as mine-layers around the British coast. One 'important success', which he noted in his memoirs, resulted from mines laid by submarine west of the Orkney Islands at the end of May 1916. On 5 June the British cruiser HMS *Hampshire*, en route to Russia with the British minister of war Field Marshal Lord Kitchener on board, struck one of those mines and sank with the loss of Kitchener, his staff and most of the ship's company.[14]

In his memoirs, Scheer argued that 'the restricted form of U-boat warfare . . . adopted in the course of 1915', only targeting Allied mercantile ships, was 'extremely unsatisfactory'. Reporting to the Kaiser after the Skagerrak (which he asserted had been a clear-cut victory), he argued that 'even the most successful result from a high sea battle will not compel England to make peace'. Because of the 'disadvantages of our geographical position' and the 'enemy's vast material superiority', he believed that the only way to secure victory was 'by the crushing of English economic life through U-boat action against English commerce'. This, moreover, would have to be applied 'with the greatest severity', that is to say, without any restrictions. 'Full use must be made of the U-boat as a means of war, so as to grip England's vital nerve.'[15] Scheer recognised that there would be a political price to pay for such a policy, but reckoned on being able to bring Britain to its economic and political knees before the USA came into the war, or at least before its impact in the war could significantly be brought to bear. After February 1917, when he had finally succeeded in persuading Berlin to introduce unrestricted submarine warfare, it proved to be a disastrous decision. Although Allied shipping losses were at first extremely grave, new convoy protection techniques soon proved effective, and the policy was a major factor in finally bringing the USA into the war in April 1917.

BLOCKADE

In an interview with the London *Daily Chronicle* in July 1919, Reinhard Scheer asserted that 'the war at sea was the decisive factor', and that the hunger blockade was the cause of the German defeat'.[16] This analysis fitted the widely held belief in Germany that defeat in the war had essentially occurred on the home front; that Germany's armed forces had not been beaten in the field (or at sea); that domestic weaknesses had undermined Germany's capacity to fight; and even that brave and resilient German soldiers had suffered a 'Dolchstoss', or 'stab in the back', wielded by craven socialist politicians far from the battle front. 'In no way inferior to any nation on earth,' wrote one German naval officer in the aftermath of the war, 'we fought during four long years and stepped from victory to victory until we finally collapsed when men of our own race, essentially un-German, knocked the weapons out of our hands in the moment of betrayal.'[17] This convenient belief not only exonerated the German armed forces from any failures or particular responsibility for defeat, but it also reinforced assumptions on the British side about the utility of seapower which helped mitigate any sense that the Royal Navy had not fully lived up to expectations in the war. While the navy had failed to deliver a Nelsonian apotheosis through meeting and destroying its main foreign challenger, by intercepting supplies of food and essential raw materials, it had at least played a decisive role in undermining the enemy's capability to wage war.

There is much debate about the effectiveness of the Allied blockade strategy. Paul Kennedy has railed against what he calls 'the curious myth of the Allied naval blockade', arguing that what occurred in Germany was an 'internally induced food catastrophe', to which the blockade contributed little.[18] Yet the Allied preponderance in civil maritime shipping – the British alone commanded some forty-three per cent of the world's merchant shipping tonnage – and their ability to immobilise, if not also actually seize, German ships in foreign ports drastically reduced enemy imports of both food and strategically important raw materials. British dominance of international finance further curtailed the German ability to pay for goods in the first place. The blockade also had an important symbolic and psychological dimension, signalling to German communities across the world, their sympathisers and neutrals alike, how the global reach of British power could be deployed to threaten German economic interests and where possible extinguish German trade.

The British, and subsequently the Germans, proclaimed the North Sea and the English Channel as war zones where civilian and neutral shipping might be intercepted. From the beginning, however, the British encountered practical and legal difficulties in imposing any really effective blockade, and decisions had to be made about the allocation of naval resources to blockade duties (as opposed, for example, to engaging with the German navy). There were also problems of establishing what cargoes – especially foodstuffs – might legitimately be defined as war contraband, and how any policy could be enforced without dangerously alienating neutral countries, above all the USA, on whom the British themselves depended for food and other supplies. Nevertheless, by the beginning of 1915 a system had been set up whereby cordons of British warships between the Shetland Islands and Norway, and in the English Channel, were positioned to monitor traffic heading into the North Sea. An American or Dutch vessel heading, say, to Rotterdam (a key port for traffic to Germany) would be intercepted and diverted to the British ports of Kirkwall or Lerwick for inspection. But in order not to jeopardise diplomatic relations many vessels (especially American) were allowed to proceed, even though they appeared to be carrying contraband. So far as the British could tell, moreover, the overall impact of the blockade on Germany was slight.[19]

In February 1915 the Germans sought effectively to apply a blockade of their own by introducing unrestricted submarine warfare in the seas around the British Isles, rendering merchant vessels vulnerable to be attacked. The following month the British responded by tightening up their rules and asserting that enemy goods of any sort (even if carried on neutral vessels) could now be seized. With continuing diplomatic worries about the reaction of neutral states, however, this policy was not implemented at all rigorously. Throughout the year criticisms, first from the Royal Navy and subsequently from Parliament and the general public, about the ineffectiveness of the blockade chipped away at the Foreign Office's objections to a more stringent approach. These criticisms were sharpened by broader frustrations with the progress of the war and a widely held sense that the stalemate on the Western Front was in part the product of an insufficiently vigorous war policy generally. In February 1916 Major Rowland Hunt, the Unionist MP for Ludlow, told the House of Commons that the government had 'plainly shown that they are quite incapable of waging war' and were 'showing a very unreasonable fear of offending neutrals by allowing an enormous quantity of war material and food to go through neutral countries to Germany'. Hunt argued for a much more 'total' war, with fewer legalistic restraints such as had hamstrung the blockade. The government, moreover, should be 'turned out in order to give the people a chance of electing men who are not afraid to wage a strenuous war . . . who will give our gallant soldiers and sailors and those of our Allies a fair chance of winning this War, the greatest and most tremendous War that has ever been known in history'.[20]

Rowland Hunt was just one, rather obscure British parliamentarian, but his call to wage more of what he called a 'strenuous war' struck a powerful chord in Britain and also echoed similar views in the other belligerent powers. Such statements and the changing public and political opinion they represented, had varying though similar effects in different countries. Everywhere in 1916 there was a marked intensification of war policy, as well as the arrangements with which governments endeavoured to encourage and extract the maximum effort out of their populations. Sometimes, too, this was accompanied by actual changes in political and military leadership, leading either to a consolidation of military power, or, in some states, to a reassertion of civilian control.[21]

In Germany it was the former. By 1916 the balance of power shared between the Kaiser, the Chancellor (Theobald von Bethmann-Hollweg) and the military high command had begun to slip towards the armed forces, who certainly favoured a more strenuous war. In August 1916 the chief of staff, Erich von Falkenhayn, whose costly Verdun strategy had failed to bring any significant returns, was replaced by two military hard men, who had won victories on Germany's eastern front: Paul von Hindenburg, who succeeded Falkenhayn as chief of staff, and Erich Ludendorff as his deputy. Through the 'Hindenburg Programme' of 31 August 1916, they endeavoured, with limited success, to mobilise the German economy into expanded armaments manufacture. A Supreme War Office was created with power to regulate the whole economy and conscript all available civilians into war employment.

Similar developments occurred in other countries as they endeavoured to meet the challenges of an increasingly total war. In 1915 both France and Britain created dedicated government departments to oversee munitions production. Both were headed by radical politicians with noted demotic skills: the socialist Albert Thomas in France and the 'Welsh Wizard', David Lloyd George, in Britain, each of whom brought new urgency and coordination to the industrial war effort. As in Germany, the allocation of labour was a central concern. The British, alone among the major European belligerents not to have compulsory military service in peacetime, finally adopted conscription in January 1916, and followed it with various regulations directing the civilian workforce too. Increasing government intervention in the labour market, industrial organisation and the supply of commodities, especially foodstuffs, produced a kind of 'war socialism' in each of the major powers.

In Germany the establishment of a War Food Provisions Office in May 1916 was an attempt to coordinate policy centrally and ensure equal treatment across the nation. It was part of what George Yaney has called a 'snowball of hierarchical centralisation', which generated much regulation but failed in the end to produce a satisfactorily comprehensive system. The interventionist and progressive centralisation of policy, however, also provoked reactions from local government. In order to support war production in line with the Hindenburg programme, the army began supplying food directly to factories in Berlin for distribution to war workers. This cut across the city's existing, more equitable, rationing arrangements and resulted in a municipal 'rebellion' (Yaney's word) in the early summer of 1917. After a stand-off between the city and the Prussian central authorities, a settlement was reached whereby the Berliners retained the main responsibility for food distribution in their area.[22]

Whether or not primarily caused by the blockade, life was hard for civilians in wartime Germany. Marooned through the war in Leipzig, the mildly eccentric (at one stage she kept a pet crocodile named Cheops in her apartment), trombone-playing south Australian musician, Ethel Cooper, wrote regular letters to her younger sister Emmie in Adelaide, with vivid descriptions of living conditions and social attitudes. 'Coffee is running short,' she noted in January 1916, 'and the remainder has been taken by the government, to prevent the prices being driven up too much.' In February there was rationing: 'We have had butter-cards this month, limiting us to ¼ lb of butter a week – that was little enough, but this morning I see a new order in the paper, limiting it to ⅛ lb!' Cooper felt that they could 'get on well enough without it' and was more concerned about the supply of potatoes. It was not that they had run out, but the peasants in rural Saxony 'won't sell them for the price that has been fixed. Anyway for ten days there have been <u>none</u>.' The poor, who were surviving only on potatoes, were 'desperate'. Translating directly from German, on 13 February she said the 'food-usury' was getting worse: 'Potatoes are scarcely to be had, the people stand for hours in a queue <u>half a mile</u> long before the market, and then can only get 5lb at a time – that is, if they have luck. Bread has been cut down again, and cheese is <u>very</u> scarce.' While Cooper apologised for writing so much about food – 'it really is the one topic of general conversation' – there were some cultural compensations in wartime Leipzig. 'Presently,' she wrote, 'I am going to the Gewandhaus, where D'Albert [the Scottish-born and London-educated pianist] is playing this evening in the chamber-music concert.' Nevertheless, 'there are <u>so</u> few concerts this year, that one must not miss the little that there is'.

Food shortages were a constant theme in Cooper's letters. In the spring she went to stay with friends who owned a farm and 'when I saw eggs and bacon for breakfast . . . I nearly fell off my perch'. On the other hand, 'tea, coffee, cocoa and chicory are to be taken over by the Government,' she wrote on 2 April, 'and we are to have meat-cards next week'. Later the same month an article in the paper declared that crows, ravens and jackdaws 'were very good eating, if they were first well soaked in a thin camomile [*sic*] tea to rid them of the fishy taste. Well, it <u>may</u> be,' commented Cooper, 'and Leipzig is some way off the nearest battle-field, but it is still too near for me to care risking a diet of crow!' In August she reported 'an excellent new food – it is a tinned extract of soya beans, and is as good as meat, very nice in taste and very filling'. There was also smoked walrus which tasted 'rather like pickled beef – only that it is almost black and has a gamey flavour'. By

November she was eating whale, which was 'beastly', and tasted 'only of train-oil, but I daren't throw it away, so I am making a strongly flavoured mustard dressing to disguise it'.[23]

The food supply problems were exacerbated by a poor harvest in 1916. Although the harvests were good in both 1914 and 1915, from mid-August the following year it rained almost incessantly in Germany for three months. Potato growers, who left off harvesting in the autumn in the hope of profiting from higher prices in the spring, found their fields waterlogged and their crop blighted and rotten. This turned shortages into something much closer to famine, resulting in the so-called 'turnip-winter' (Kohlrübenwinter) of 1916/17. In Freiburg, near the frontier with Alsace in south-west Germany, potatoes were already being rationed from the summer of 1916. In the autumn there were disturbances 'as angry crowds gathered in front of stores in the old city in a futile hunt for eggs, butter, cheese, and potatoes'. Rationed foodstuffs, moreover, could be pretty meagre. In May 1916 the egg ration was set at three a week, and over the first three weeks of October 1916, Freiburgers were limited to only two eggs each. As Ethel Cooper appreciated, food supplies were more abundant in the nearby countryside, and, in Freiburg as in Leipzig, the 'Hamsterfahrt' (foraging trip) became a popular weekend activity as urban residents headed into the countryside in search of whatever food they could acquire. This also facilitated hoarding and black-marketeering. A census of Freiburg food supplies in May 1916 returned some eighty households and businesses with stores of over 500 eggs. Although most of these were legitimate, one pensioner had 5,000 eggs, a barber 1,500 and a priest had 700. The priest could claim charitable purposes, but the others seem to have been black-marketeers. 'Eggs, if properly stored,' as Roger Chickering notes in his classic and wonderfully observed study of wartime Freiburg, 'were – like other durables – a lucrative investment, a sure source of profit, and a reliable hedge against inflation.'[24]

Despite the evident privations of life in wartime Germany, there were pleasures too. Ethel Cooper spent one Sunday in June 1916 with an Englishwoman who was married to a German and some wealthy Americans playing golf on a country course near Leipzig. 'One could talk English without being insulted,' and supper in a country inn included 'eggs and milk and ham and strawberries'. In December she went to a performance (in German) of *Measure for Measure*. 'As a rule,' she commented, 'I don't like the way Shakespeare is given in Germany, but this was well done.' Despite the prevailing shortages, Cooper's bourgeois friends managed to assemble a decently lavish meal when required. On Christmas Eve, 'we had turtle soup, goose, and plum-pudding', with ample alcohol. Cooper's 'comical collection' of Christmas presents, nevertheless, reflected everyone's continued preoccupation with food and other necessities: 'Soap, mustard, curry powder, infant-food, coffee, jam, tinned fish, soup tablets, dried mushrooms, a packet of biscuits – invaluable things which will make life easier for weeks and weeks to come.'[25]

Around the Mediterranean blockades imposed by both sides had very serious effects. Operating out of Pola and Cattaro in the Adriatic, from late 1915 German submarines were particularly effective, and just over a quarter of the total 12 million tons of Allied shipping sunk in the war occurred in the Mediterranean. Indeed, the largest single vessel sunk during the conflict, the 53,000-ton British hospital ship *Britannic* (the Belfast-built sister ship of the *Titanic*) heading for Salonika, fell victim to a German mine off the Greek island of Kea on 21 November 1916. It was carrying 625 crew and 500 medical staff, but fortunately no wounded. Although it sank within an hour, only thirty people were drowned. One of the survivors, Nurse Violet Jessop, had also been on the *Titanic* when it was lost.

For the Germans, Mediterranean waters provided politically more attractive hunting grounds than elsewhere since, with fewer American interests than in the Atlantic, there was less likelihood of provoking diplomatic protests of the sort which followed the sinking of the *Lusitania* and the *Sussex*. In addition to their main business of 'Handelskrieg' (economic warfare) and the targeting of Allied shipping moving through the Aegean Sea bringing troops and supplies to the Salonika front, the Germans also used their submarines to supply Senussi forces in Libya who had rebelled against the Italian occupation of the territory imposed after 1911 and, encouraged by the Turkish leader Enver Pasha, offered to attack British-controlled Egypt from the west. Two Senussi campaigns were backed by Ottoman officers, money and supplies, carried by German submarines from Turkey. The first, along the coast, was launched in November 1915 and repelled by March 1916. That month the second campaign began inland, targeting oases in the desert of upper Egypt, but this, too, was checked and the Senussi driven out by February 1917.[26]

Both German and Austrian submarines operated in the Mediterranean (though the latter did not venture much beyond the Adriatic), but during the fifteen months between Italy declaring war on Austria in May 1915 and declaring war on Germany in August 1916, Berlin and Vienna colluded in a pretence that any submarine which sank an Italian vessel was Austrian. This meant, for example, that the Austrians had to field diplomatic complaints from the USA (and even agree to pay an indemnity) after the Italian liner *Ancona* was sunk by a German U-boat on 7 November 1915 with the loss of some twenty American citizens. Although the success of the German and Austrian submarines in the Mediterranean varied quite widely, during much of 1916 they were responsible for comfortably over fifty per cent of all the shipping losses anywhere. In June 1916 they sank forty-three ships totalling 67,000 tons, comprising seventy-seven per cent of the total for the month. In August the equivalent figures were seventy-seven ships, 129,000 tons and eighty-two per cent. Between 26 July and 20 August in the western Mediterranean, one German submarine, the U-35, brought off the single most successful cruise of the entire war, sinking fifty-four vessels, totalling over 90,000 tons. The chief of the German naval staff, Admiral Henning von Holtzendorff, boasted to the Kaiser that the submarine had sunk nearly 50,000 tons of coal, adding to the shortages and cost of coal in Italy and putting real pressure on the Italian economy.[27]

Neutral countries were affected too. German efforts to disrupt supplies from the British-owned Rio Tinto copper and sulphur mines in southern Spain targeted the mines themselves (where strikes were encouraged) as well the export traffic. Shipping restrictions cut imports of cotton and coal for Spanish industry, and in September 1916 the fruit carrier *Luis Vives* from Valencia (carrying, according to *The Times*, 'the eminently pacific cargo of melons and onions') was sunk by a German U-boat. The Spanish ambassador to Berlin complained that 'the prevention of the transport of the fruit harvest was a severe blow to Spain, and was ruining entire villages', but the Germans insisted that that the ship had been 'taking contraband foodstuffs to Liverpool'. Towards the end of December the Spanish press carried reports raising the possible complete cessation of trade with Great Britain, which had the potential to cause 'grave internal disturbances throughout Spain'. The maritime war, thus, though not specifically targeted on Spain, had a profound economic impact.[28]

The blockade of Ottoman territory in the eastern Mediterranean was mainly enforced by the French off Syria, where they had historic economic and political interests, and had grave consequences for the civilian population. In a study of Jerusalem in the First World War, Abigail Jacobson notes how the sea blockade seriously disrupted both Palestine's exports (of cotton, grain and citrus fruits), which caused an economic slump, as well as the importing of necessary food supplies. Wartime harvests, moreover, were poor and from the spring of 1915 Palestine was afflicted with infestations of locusts. To a limited extent grain shortages were met by supplies from eastern Jordan, while medical and food aid from Zionist groups in the USA (which was distributed to Christians and Muslims in Palestine as well as Jews) helped mitigate the worst of the suffering.[29]

'Greater Syria' (comprising modern Syria and Lebanon) was afflicted by a catastrophic famine during the second half of the war, causing perhaps half a million deaths. Linda Schatkowski Schilcher ascribes the outbreak of famine not only to the inadequacies of the Ottoman administration and supply systems, but more directly to the total Anglo-French blockade of the Syrian coast. This, she argues, 'was unmercifully constant throughout the war and must, therefore, be considered the primary cause of famine in the coastal regions'. Supplies of grain ran seriously short in Damascus in March 1916, provoking bread riots and other demonstrations. The Austrian consul reported that 'several hundred women of the lower classes and their children' had gathered at the building occupied by the provincial governor, Cemal Paşa, where they 'cried unceasingly: "Give us bread; we are starving"'. The outbreak of the Arab revolt in April 1916 exacerbated the problems by undermining support for the Ottoman government at the same time as it put more pressure on the army, which, furthermore, was given the task of purchasing and distributing supplies of grain. Lacking the required personnel, funds or transport, Cemal Paşa put the system in the hands of private contractors who themselves failed to cope in the face of escalating prices and suppliers who refused to deal with government representatives (or accept Ottoman paper money rather than gold). Inevitably those at the bottom of the social and political heap suffered the most. A poor harvest in 1917 and further administrative problems led to the 'total break-down of supply in the winter of 1917–1918'.[30]

By its nature Allied economic warfare was the most 'global' policy of all, and, combined with a focus on strategic war materials, it had an impact even in what Phillip Dehne has called the 'far western front'. 'Waging total war against global *Deutschtum*,' he argues, 'meant waging war in South America.'[31] In 1913, twenty per cent of the Dominican Republic's exports were to Germany, and eighteen per cent of its imports. By 1916 the figure for both was zero. Chile's nitrate exports (principally for agricultural fertilizers) fell by fifty per cent in the first two months of the war, as traditional markets in Germany and Belgium were cut off, though they recovered in 1915 as the United States took up some of the slack and Britain increased imports for explosives manufacture. The quantity and value of Argentina's three main agricultural exports, wheat, maize and linseed (which accounted for over forty per cent of its foreign earnings) dropped sharply between 1914 and 1917. The impact of wartime restrictions and loss of foreign markets was exacerbated by severe harvest failure brought on by a disastrous drought lasting from April to December 1916. Before the war German concerns had controlled up to sixty per cent of Argentina's grain trade and this became a particular target for British blockade-enforcers. On the other hand, the Argentina meat trade, overwhelmingly dominated by Britain companies, performed much better during the war. While wartime demand (temporarily) rescued Brazil's rubber industry (which had been in decline), the closing of European continental markets and shortages of shipping badly hit coffee sales, which fell by a third in 1914–15. As one historian dryly observed, 'coffee was not high on the Allies' list of shipping priorities, nor were they very much concerned whether the Brazilian economy might collapse for lack of spare parts and fuels'.[32]

One of the key economic war weapons which the British used was the 'Statutory Blacklist', published and enforced from early 1916. At the beginning of the war the British authorities used emergency legislation to impose all manner of controls and restrictions on the supply and movement of important commodities. Although fairly haphazard at the beginning, the arrangements were gradually systematised and from December 1915 British blockade policy was overseen by a government Foreign Trade Department which had to negotiate the delicate balance between waging effective economic war against enemy powers while not alienating neutral countries. The 'Statutory Blacklist', which was published in stages – European-based firms were named in February, and South American in March 1916 – embodied a sharp intensification of the campaign by listing specific companies and individuals with whom business was prohibited. The South American list, for example, included grain and coffee exporters, the 'German Coal Depot Company' in Buenos Aires and some shipping lines.[33] Names for the list were provided by local British Chambers of Commerce. Not only were they impelled by a patriotic desire to 'do their bit' for the war effort, but the businessmen concerned shrewdly reckoned that the economic war might enable British firms permanently to supplant German interests in the region. Some of the target companies scorned the blacklist. At the end of 1916 the German Coal Depot Company distributed greetings cards celebrating its tenth anniversary and claiming that 'in spite of all the intrigues, acts of coercion and reprisals with which our rivals have opposed us in their economic war, we pass this date with full prosperity and with the firmest confidence in the future'. Sir Reginald Tower, the British minister in Argentina, however reported to the Foreign Trade Department in London that intercepted telegrams between the company and its headquarters in Germany showed 'that the depot was actually just putting a brave face on a difficult climate for its business'.[34]

One consequence from the implementation of the Allied blockade in 1916 was the precipitation of Portugal into the war. Weak, poor, and overextended imperially, Portugal nevertheless toyed with coming in at the start. The British, however, realistically doubting the value of Portugal as an active ally, simply asked Lisbon to declare neither neutrality nor belligerence. For eighteen months (apart from January to May 1915 when there was a German-leaning government under General Pimenta de Castro), the Portuguese tentatively moved towards the Allied side. In November 1914, for example, they supplied fifty-six 75mm guns and some ammunition for use by the French. Twenty thousand rifles were sent to South Africa to help equip the forces deployed against the German African colonies. In June 1915, Lisbon offered the free use of its harbours (at home and overseas) to British ships. Meanwhile the government's financial position worsened as Portugal's maritime commerce suffered badly from the blockade and wartime disruption. The cocoa trade between Portuguese Guinea and Germany came to a standstill, while prices of food imports, including grain, rose sharply.

The war, meanwhile, came to Portugal, both in Africa, where Allied forces fought to conquer German South-West and East Africa (respectively adjacent to the Portuguese colonies of Angola and Mozambique), and in Portuguese ports where seventy-six German merchant vessels were stranded. In December 1914, for example, German and Portuguese forces clashed after German scouts had crossed into Angola from German South-West Africa. The incident, moreover, triggered a revolt among the local indigenous population, whom the Portuguese had inadequately being trying to 'pacify' over the previous ten years or so. After de Casto was overthrown in May 1915, the Portuguese, reckoning that they might boost their international status by participating in the war, became more amenable to British demands. London, keen to get hold of the German ships, let Lisbon know that, if the ships were requisitioned, loans totalling £3 million could be provided to the financially hard-pressed Portuguese government. This was enough to precipitate action and the stranded ships were seized, which in turn provoked the Germans into declaring war on Portugal on 9 March 1916.[35]

Portugal's ultimately very unhappy experience of the Great War reflected the hesitations and insecurities which accompanied its

decision to act. Their first military move was unashamedly imperial and in April 1916 they occupied a triangle of territory at the
mouth of the river Ruvuma on the Mozambique–German East
Africa border which the Germans had seized from them in 1894.
Anxious to participate in any Allied conquest of the German colony,
in July a 4,600-strong force under General José César Ferreira Gil
was despatched to Palma in northern Mozambique with instructions
to move up the coast into the German territory. The South African
General Jan Christian Smuts, who commanded the Allied forces in
East Africa, however, asked Gil to move inland to occupy the food
production centre of Newala. Inadequately equipped, indifferently led
and wracked with illness, Gil's force was reduced almost by half by
the start of September. They managed, nevertheless, to take Newala
on 26 October, but soon found themselves besieged by a smaller but
more effective German force which drove them raggle-taggle back
to Mozambique at the end of November. Far from strengthening the
Allied cause, Portuguese intervention in effect merely brought additional concerns for Smuts.

The Portuguese military contribution in Europe followed a similar
pattern, and more than fulfilled British apprehensions about their value
as an ally. A Portuguese Expeditionary Force of two divisions was sent
to the Western Front where they were deployed with the British, and
some artillery crews were provided for the French. The Portuguese
infantry did not, alas, prove to be very resilient. Consistently derided
by the British, they collapsed during the German spring offensive of
1918.[36]

Japan's maritime war

On 16 September 1916, George Barbour, one of G. M. Trevelyan's
ambulance unit drivers in north Italy, reported in his diary the
unlikely information that 'Japanese 15″ howitzers are now in action
against Monfalcone sector manned by Jap naval gun-crews of 15.
[Gerald] Barr travelled up with some from Mestre.' Barbour later
decided that Barr was an unreliable chap, 'a thorough shirker', who
had only 'joined our Unit the day before he was due to be called up
under the Derby scheme'.[37] Whether Barr had been winding up the

rather serious Barbour, or someone else was playing a joke on Barr, the story of Japanese naval gunners fighting on the Italian front was almost certainly untrue. Or at least untrue in the autumn of 1916 – for in 1917 and 1918 Japanese sailors on Japanese ships were deployed in the Mediterranean to help ease the Anglo-French burden of protecting vital supply convoys against (mostly) German U-boat attack.

Japan's involvement in the First World War stemmed from its prewar alliance with Britain, as well as national ambitions to expand its dominant regional position and confirm it internationally as a first-rank power. Under the 1902 Anglo-Japanese Alliance each partner had promised to aid the other if involved in war with more than one other power. Japan meanwhile was establishing itself as the most powerful state in East Asia. In 1895 it had acquired Taiwan, and, after defeating Russia in the Russo-Japanese War of 1904–05, it occupied Korea. Japan, too, sought to extend its economic and political influence in China, though here it came up against the existing interests of Western powers, principally Britain and the USA, both of whom worried about Japanese expansionism. Although Japan's initial intention in August 1914 was to remain neutral, the British, concerned about the threat to British trade from warships operating from the German naval base at Tsingtao (Qingdao) in the Shantung (Jiadong) Peninsula in north-east China, requested some limited naval assistance. This was enough to prompt a declaration of war by Japan on Germany. The Japanese navy and army separately saw it as an opportunity to expand their own influence, while everyone thought the conquest of Tsingtao would help consolidate Japan's position on the Asian mainland. By 23 August 1914, Japan and Germany were at war.[38]

Once at war the Japanese proceeded to occupy German Micronesia, comprising the Marshall, Caroline and Marianas Islands, together with Palaus and Yap, thus confirming their position as a leading Pacific power. They also completed the conquest of Tsingtao (which they had been planning for years) on 6 November 1914. Despite requests from the Allies for them to send troops to the Western Front and ships to serve in the Baltic, the Japanese army thereafter took no further part in land operations, and the navy declined to deploy any vessels in European waters. But they made a considerable contribution both in the Pacific and Indian Oceans, where Japanese ships helped the British expel Admiral Graf von Spee's German East Asiatic Squadron from the Pacific towards its eventual destruction in the battle of the Falkland Islands. The Japanese navy also provided escorts for troopships carrying Australian and New Zealand units to the Middle East, as well as French contingents from South-East Asia. Based in Singapore, they patrolled the South China Sea and Dutch East Indies. In February 1915, moreover, Japanese marines were landed at Singapore to help the local British authorities suppress a mutiny by Indian soldiers there.

Early in 1916, London asked Tokyo for more extensive aid to help counter an intensified threat from mines laid by German auxiliary cruisers. The Japanese responded by deploying a flotilla of destroyers to Singapore to secure the Malacca Straits and a cruiser division to guard against German commerce raiders in the Indian Ocean as far west as Mauritius and South Africa and north to the Red Sea. At the same time they stepped up patrols around the Philippine Islands and the South China Sea, while they continued to provide escorts for shipping from Australia and New Zealand.[39]

Despite this activity, there was concern in some British quarters that Japan was not doing all it could for the Allied cause. In December 1916, Sir John Jellicoe complained to Sir David Beatty that the Japanese attitude had not 'been entirely satisfactory'. Noting that the Japanese evidently had 'ideas of a greater Japan', which might include parts of China, the Dutch East Indies, as well as the British possessions of Singapore and the Malay States, Jellicoe worried about the threat which Japan generally posed to British imperial interests in Asia. The Japanese government, he wrote, had 'not shown that firmness in dealing with the Indian seditionists who have taken shelter in Japan which we might reasonably have expected from a good ally'. As a result, he claimed that the seditionists now evidently regarded Japan 'as a convenient and suitable base to work from'. This unsatisfactory attitude, moreover, meant that the Japanese navy was not as helpful as it might have been 'in searching shipping and other precautionary measures in connection with the Indian Sedition', and that the Royal Navy were obliged to deploy more scarce resources in Eastern waters than would otherwise have been the case.[40]

The British renewed their requests for assistance in late 1916 and early 1917, and the Japanese finally agreed to deploy ships in the European theatre. From April 1917 until the end of the war, the 2nd Special Squadron of the Imperial Japanese Navy, comprising a cruiser and fourteen destroyers (including two on loan from Britain), operated out of Malta and made a major contribution to the Allied naval effort in the Mediterranean. It was not without cost. In June 1917 a German U-boat torpedoed the Japanese destroyer *Sakaki*, blowing its bows off and killing sixty-eight sailors who had been concentrated forward for their midday meal. Describing the Japanese support as 'precious' in August 1917, the British commodore of the Malta base favourably compared them to the Italians and French. 'The net working rate of French navy is low comparing to British,' he reported, 'while the Italian navy is much lower than French. But the Japanese navy is different.' There was a diplomatic price to pay for this Japanese commitment. As a quid pro quo the British were obliged to guarantee support at the peace conference for the continued Japanese occupation of the Shantung Peninsula and the former German Pacific islands they had seized in 1914.[41] As the Japanese political and military leadership had hoped, therefore, participation in the First World War both helped consolidate Japan's regional status in the Pacific Basin and reinforced its aspirations to be a Great Power, equal in status to the USA and the old imperial powers of Europe.

BARRY BINGHAM'S MEMORIAL

At the battle of Jutland, 6,097 British and 2,551 German sailors were killed.[42] In the British postwar discussions about building memorials for the war dead, which resulted in those extraordinary battlefield cemeteries and monuments cared for by the Commonwealth (originally Imperial) War Graves Commission, the question of how best to commemorate casualties suffered at sea led to some debate. Clearly naval casualties could not be commemorated on the battlefield like those of the army. The Admiralty initially wanted to have nothing to do with the commission and advanced some unsuitable proposals.

One was that the Duke of York on his hundred-foot column in Carlton House Terrace by The Mall in London should be replaced with a statue of Britannia. Another suggestion was to appropriate the entire north side of Trafalgar Square (after all, Nelson already dominated the space), which would have entailed the removal of a statue of the Victorian imperial military hero, General Charles Gordon. Neither suggestion found much favour and eventually to mark the dead of the Royal Navy three identical obelisks were erected at the important 'manning ports' of Chatham, Portsmouth and Plymouth. With creditable sailor-like practicality, each monument was also intended to act as a waymark for shipping.[43]

The three British naval memorials were all completed and dedicated by the end of 1924. For perhaps obvious reasons, the commemoration process was less straightforward and took rather longer in Germany. It was only in 1926 when Wilhelm Lammertz, a former petty officer and president of a naval ex-servicemen's association in Duisburg, proposed the erection of a memorial. This, he thought, would not only commemorate the 34,836 German sailors who had lost their lives during the war, but could also look to the future and make the current young generation of Germans 'aware of the importance of re-creating a strong German navy'. A 280-foot tower, with a hall of remembrance, was erected at Laboe, close to the Baltic Sea entrance of the Kiel Canal. Laying the foundation stone in August 1927, Reinhold Scheer dedicated the memorial 'To German seamen's honour; to Germany's floating arms; May Both Return'. The monument was eventually inaugurated on 30 May 1936, on the twentieth anniversary of Skagerrak/ Jutland. General Admiral Erich Raeder, the commander-in-chief of the German navy, said that 'all the War-time animosities had been forgotten and that the Germans had always regarded the British as honourable and chivalrous opponents, of the same race and character as themselves. The British dead,' he added, 'were being commemorated as well as the Germans.' Adolf Hitler, who was present, did not make a speech, but afterwards described the tower as an 'unparalleled item of kitsch'.[44]

A Jutland-related memorial in Ward Park, Bangor, County Down, unexpectedly links the battle with Ireland and the Easter Rising.

It is close to Bangor Castle where Barry Bingham, son of the Irish peer Lord Clanmorris, was born. Bingham, captain of HMS *Nestor*, commanded the British 13th Destroyer Flotilla at Jutland and during the late afternoon of 31 May, in Arthur Marder's words, 'led with extraordinary *élan*' an attack on the destroyers screening Hipper's battlecruisers. One of Bingham's destroyers, HMS *Nomad*, was badly damaged by a German submarine, but shortly after, Bingham, along with HMS *Nicator*, launched an attack on the approaching main German battle fleet. Under overwhelming fire – *Nestor* was crippled and sinking when *Nicator* stood by to give assistance – Bingham ordered it to rejoin the flotilla. *Nomad* and *Nestor* were lost but the majority of their sailors were rescued by German torpedo boats. Bingham spent the rest of the conflict as a prisoner of war.[45]

One of Bingham's officers, Lieutenant Maurice Bethell (son of Admiral Sir Alexander Bethell), did not survive. Scarcely a week after the battle, Bingham wrote a letter of condolence to Bethell's mother from Mainz in Germany, including a dramatic account of the last moments of the *Nestor*:

In spite of my exhortations and persuasions he [Maurice] hung on & appeared disinclined to leave the ship until she was tipping up preparatory to plunging down perpendicularly stern first. Then he was seen to jump off the Fxle [Forecastle] but swim away from the men who were calling him from the boats – I did not see him because I was swimming at the time myself. He certainly jumped but whether he got sucked down with her or not or got a smack on the head from a splinter previously, I cannot say. After the men had all got into the boats I turned to him and said she's sinking we'll get clear of her – where shall we go meaning which boat should we go for. Maurice said We'll go to Heaven Sir! All right I said – and started down a rope's end hoping he was following me, but he didn't follow he was standing by a dying signalman. It was madness! Salvoe [*sic*] after Salvoe was hitting the ship. At last he was seen to jump by my cook's mate. . .

He [Maurice] was as cool under fire as if he'd done it all his life: he hoisted the boats out under shell fire absolutely unflinchingly and stayed by her to the bitter end, – wonderful bravery!

Bethell's stricken father, who had a keen sense of naval proprieties, was not, it seems, much comforted by Bingham's letter, as an annotation on it by Maurice's sister Agatha testifies: 'My father felt strongly that Capt Bingham (later awarded the VC) should have been the last to leave his ship & should have <u>ordered</u> Maurice to leave before him.' Bethell had another son, Edward, a soldier. He was killed in action in France in September 1918.[46]

Bingham's Victoria Cross was one of four given for service at Jutland, and the only one not awarded posthumously. After the war the Admiralty allotted a gun from a German submarine to his birthplace to commemorate the award. The weapon came from U-19, which had been deployed in the North Sea at the time of Jutland. It was, however, also the submarine from which Sir Roger Casement landed in Ireland on Good Friday 1916. So it is that in Unionist Northern Ireland there is a monument which unexpectedly turns out to commemorate both heroic service in the Royal Navy as well as Irish republican endeavour in 1916.

6

The Eastern Front

While the war in the east was much less static than that in the west, here, too, there was a degree of stalemate after the opening engagements.[1] There were no continuous lines of fixed trench systems along the thousand-mile front line, from the Baltic Sea to the Romanian frontier, and military movements back and forth of ten, twenty or even fifty miles, which would have astonished combatants on the Western Front, were commonplace. But the scale of the territory involved, above all the apparently limitless extent of the Russian empire, meant that on this front breakthrough attacks were rarely, if ever, decisive. There was a widely held assumption that the Russians, if able to do so in decent order, could almost indefinitely withdraw in the face of an advancing enemy, and, confident that their manpower reserves were greater than anyone else's, could exhaust their opponents through constant attrition, lengthening and increasingly difficult supply lines, and also even the climate itself (with those handy assistants, Generals Janvier and Février, who had so decisively helped to defeat Napoleon in 1812). What this notion did not take into account, however, was the extent to which the Russian imperial state itself had the political, social, economic and infrastructural capacity and resilience to survive to fight another day. As it turned out in this war, it did not.

The early battles on the Eastern Front in the autumn of 1914 largely set the pattern for what was to follow: German power, Austro-Hungarian frailty and Russian endeavour with sporadic achievement.

After a briefly successful Russian push into Germany's East Prussian salient (Russia was the only Allied power to occupy any significant part of the German empire in Europe during the war), the Germans decisively pushed them back, although the latter were able to hold on in Russian Poland. Further south the Russians had successes in Galicia, and by the spring of 1915 had penetrated to the Carpathian Mountains and begun to threaten Hungary. In March 1915 the great Habsburg fortress of Przemyśl in southern Poland fell to the Russians (an event which encouraged the Italians, believing the Habsburgs to be finished, to come in on the Allied side). Responding to Austrian appeals for help, the Germans moved eight divisions of battle-hardened troops from the Western Front, and in the battle of Gorlice-Tarnów (just east and south-east of Cracow), launched in early May, German and Austrian armies pushed the Russians well back into Russia itself. By November 1915 all of Poland and much of Lithuania and Latvia had been occupied by the Central Powers.

While badly battered, the Russians were not defeated and their armies managed a fighting retreat. But in 1915 alone (reflecting the enormous numbers of troops mobilised in the east) they had suffered approaching 2 million casualties. There was a crisis in the Russian high command and on 1 September 1915 Tsar Nicholas II himself assumed supreme control of the army. In practical terms this did not make much military difference – Nicholas II was no general – but it marked a continued commitment to the war and identified the imperial royal family more completely than ever with military success (or failure). As in other places, moreover, the huge national investment in the struggle, especially the losses sustained, served to commit the country more fully 'to fight to the finish, whatever its outcome'.[2] On the other side, the Central Powers' successes were good for morale in Vienna, stiffened Habsburg resistance and also encouraged them to fight on.

The proposal for a renewed Russian offensive in 1916 was born in the Allied conference at Chantilly in December 1915 which concluded that the Central Powers' successes of 1915 had been due to their interior lines of communication and consequent ability to deploy forces rapidly from front to front. To counter this, the Allies agreed that there should be a coordinated series of Russian, French and British offensives in 1916. The Somme, originally planned as a full Anglo-French enterprise, was to be the main offensive, with an Italian push on the Isonzo and a Russian effort to pin down German troops and prevent them being used as reinforcements in the West. Planning for this was upset by the German attack on Verdun in late February 1916, which prompted urgent appeals from the French which the Russians could not refuse. The first Russian response was an offensive at Lake Narocz (Narach, in modern-day Belarus) in March 1916 which was a complete disaster. Mistakenly placing their faith in strength of numbers and a preponderance of artillery (helpful enough but in the circumstances badly used), the Russian generals launched ill-coordinated assaults in desperately difficult winter conditions against well-dug-in and commanded Germans which were driven off at the cost of 100,000 casualties and a further sapping of Russian spirits. It was, concludes Norman Stone, 'one of the decisive battles of the First World War'. Although it 'paralysed much of the Russian army for the rest of the war', the 'emergence of a general whose common sense amounted to brilliance' – Alexei Brusilov – was yet in 1916 to give the Russian army one final 'great role'.[3]

In April 1916, Brusilov (who had commanded the Eighth Army with some success on the Russian south-west front) was appointed to replace General Nikolai Ivanov as overall commander of the armies in this sector. By Brusilov's own account of taking over the command, Ivanov appeared to have had a nervous breakdown. On his arrival at headquarters on 6 April he found him 'in a state of utter dejection'. He told Brusilov, 'amid sobs, that he could not understand why he had been relieved of his command' and that 'we were quite unfit to undertake any sort of offensive'. A glum dinner followed, presided over by the weeping Ivanov. Brusilov was 'diametrically opposed' to Ivanov's opinion and, despite the gloomy pessimism of his fellow generals, on 14 April, Brusilov got the Stavka (high command of the Russian army) to agree to his launching an offensive on his section of the front.[4] Thus came the last great Russian effort of the war, the Brusilov offensive. Launched on 4 June 1916, it began spectacularly well and effectively destroyed the Habsburgs' military capacity, though it simultaneously placed intolerable strains on the Russian empire. The initial success of the offensive additionally enticed Romania into the war on the Allied side, a reinforcement which flattered to deceive and in the end merely added to the Russians' manifold troubles, and thenceforward proved to be an unwelcome and tiresome burden for the Allies.

The Brusilov offensive

In under two months Brusilov prepared for his offensive more thoroughly and meticulously that any previous Russian operation.[5] Received wisdom (and established practice on the Western Front) had it that in order to break through enemy lines the best method was to focus on a carefully defined narrow front and commence with as heavy and sustained an artillery barrage as possible, aiming to pulverise the enemy defences and leave the way open for one's own troops to advance more or less at will. When costly experience demonstrated that deep lines of barbed wire and concrete emplacements were not so easily destroyed, the response was simply to increase and intensify the preliminary bombardment, as, for example, with the German assault on Verdun earlier in the year (though one of the lessons of that battle was that even a titanic barrage might not necessarily be sufficient). A further problem with the orthodox approach was the impossibility of concealing preparations for a concentrated assault from the enemy. One reason, indeed, for the failure at Lake Narocz in March was that the Germans had the likely point of attack spotted well before the Russians set off. Brusilov, by contrast, planned for surprise, with each of his four armies launching separate attacks (after only a short sharp bombardment) at different places along the whole of his 350-mile front. Thus, even after the offensive had begun, the enemy could be kept guessing as to which attack was the main one. Brusilov meanwhile could also be flexible as to where he could concentrate forces to exploit early success. All this, of course, was a calculated risk. To be successful, Brusilov had to spread his forces more or less evenly along the front, but this left only a few reserves readily available to capitalise on any breakthrough which occurred.

Brusilov also invested heavily in detailed preliminary training. There was close coordination of artillery and infantry; attack trenches were dug as near as possible to the Habsburg lines; reserves were marshalled just behind the front line in specially prepared deep dugouts with adequate communications trenches for moving forward. Careful maps – and some full-scale models – of Austrian trenches were prepared, based in part on extensive air photo-reconnaissance. The Russians also used classic deception techniques: false instructions were broadcast *en clair* over wireless while genuine orders were delivered personally. Bogus artillery batteries were also set up to deceive enemy air-spotters.

The offensive was launched on 4 June, a little earlier than Brusilov wished owing to urgent appeals for support from the Italians, who had been badly pushed back by the Habsburg offensive on the Asiago plateau launched on 15 May. Although Brusilov did not enjoy much of a superiority in terms of troop numbers – there were about 600,000 Russians against 500,000 on the Habsburg side – the surprise worked and the offensive was an immediate success, especially in the north-centre of Brusilov's front where the Eighth Army had advanced over forty miles by 16 June. Further south, too, Brusilov's forces moved forward strongly. Austrian losses of some 200,000 troops – many of whom simply surrendered – were irreplaceable and unsustainable. Faced with this critical situation, the Germans took control. Falkenhayn demanded of Conrad, the Habsburg commander (who had no option but to comply), that he divert troops from the Italian front to the east. A few German divisions were also sent to stiffen the Austrian resistance. The Turks helped too. In late August two divisions of Ottoman troops were deployed in eastern Galicia at the southern end of the front towards the Romanian frontier, where they performed very creditably indeed until they returned to Turkey in the following summer.[6] As the Russian offensive ran out of steam (mainly for lack of reserves) the battle line steadied. By September the front had closed down, with both sides together suffering casualties of over a million men.

The Russian success was not simply due to Brusilov's brilliance, and the valour of his troops, but also Habsburg weaknesses. Many of their units, in what had hitherto been a fairly quiet part of the front, seem to have settled into a rather complacent live-and-let-live attitude (an understandable state of affairs which soldiers adopted in other places too).[7] Conrad's focus on Italy, moreover, had led him to neglect the east and, discounting the continuing potential of the Russians, he had moved some of the best troops to his favoured Italian front. And then, of course, there was also the problem of Austria-Hungary's multi-ethnic army, especially in circumstances where Slav soldiers, for example, might find themselves facing fellow Slavs. The Russian advance certainly undermined the already fragile loyalties of minority units in the Habsburg armies. There were 'immediate mass defections by Czech and Ukrainian troops'. Other defections in June and July included a Croat unit, the 96th Karlovac regiment, one from Dalmatia – the 23rd (Landwehr) Regiment – and Slovene troops of the Pola 5th (Landwehr) Regiment.[8]

Among the more vivid press reports of the offensive reaching London were those of Stanley Washburn, *The Times*'s 'Special Correspondent with the Russian Forces'. In his late thirties, Washburn, the son of a Republican senator for Minnesota, had made a reputation for himself as a war correspondent reporting the 1904–05 Russo-Japanese War for the *Chicago Daily News*. On his return to North America he had taken up exploring and big-game hunting, which he recorded in *Trails, Trappers and Tenderfeet* (described as a 'delightful record by a true lover of the wilds') and *Two in the Wilderness: A Romance of North-West Canada* ('a fresh and inspiring story'). Washburn, as *The Times*'s official history dryly and a little condescendingly observed, 'wrote in the nervous and energetic style typical of the American Press of that period at its best'.[9] On the outbreak of the war, like many adventurous Americans, he headed for England. A journalist acquaintance, Harry Perry Robinson, was working for *The Times* and commissioned an article from him about American attitudes towards the war. This led to a meeting with Lord Northcliffe, the owner of the paper, who (as recollected by Washburn) immediately appointed him to report from Russia with a generous salary and an unlimited expense account.[10]

If Washburn's rather rococo memoirs are to be believed – they appear to have been written in the late 1930s (with the assistance of a diary and newspaper clippings) and were published thirty years after his death by his son as an act of filial devotion – his position as a representative of *The Times* gave him access to the highest diplomatic, military and political circles in Russia. 'The mere name of the paper,' he wrote, 'was an open sesame everywhere, as everybody wanted the publicity and the influence of the great London daily.' The memoir records many personal meetings with senior Russian leaders, including lunch with the tsar himself in October 1915. Within days of arriving at Petrograd in September 1914, for example, Washburn had spent two hours with the liberal-leaning Russian foreign minister, Sergei Sasonov, and got him to agree to Washburn drafting a statement to go out over Sasonov's name identifying the great commercial possibilities for Britain and the USA to take over Germany's £60 million-worth of trade with Russia. Time and again, Washburn claimed to have been taken into the confidence of Russian generals who, by his account, freely discussed strategy and tactics with him. Passing through London in November 1915 on his way back to the USA for a couple of months, he secured an interview with Lord Robert Cecil, a junior Foreign Office minister, on whom he urged the importance of improving British propaganda in Russia. The following March, back in London, he saw Sir Edward Grey, the foreign secretary, who improbably wanted to use him to communicate directly with Sasonov, bypassing the British ambassador in Russia, Sir George Buchanan.[11]

Despite the fact that Washburn features only occasionally in other people's memoirs, some of this can be corroborated. Three volumes of his reportage were published during the war. These contain edited (and sometimes amplified) versions of his newspaper articles. Although, unusually for *The Times* and an unwanted innovation imposed by Lord Northcliffe, he was given a personal by-line from May 1915, some earlier unsigned articles ('From our special correspondent') can safely be attributed to him, including the Sasonov statement of September 1914. There is, too, an official note of his meeting with Cecil, though no record appears to have survived of that with Grey (if it occurred at all).[12] Washburn did not pretend to objectivity, and claimed that he only took *The Times* assignment after Northcliffe reassured him that the paper's position, like Washburn's, was unequivocally behind the Allied cause. He wrote as an optimistic lover of Russia, relentlessly upbeat about the prospects for the Russian war effort, despite much evidence to the contrary. While he certainly reported from the battle zone, moreover, he was generally fairly comfortably billeted closer to corps headquarters than the actual front line, which he only rarely appears to have visited. Perhaps unusually for a war correspondent, during much of his time in Russia he was accompanied by his wife, Alice, to whom he dedicated his account of the Brusilov offensive, claiming that her 'presence with me in Warsaw and Russia during the campaigns of 1915 and 1916 has made my work possible'.[13]

Typical of Washburn's work is a report of a meeting with Brusilov himself, not long after the offensive had begun. With a by-line of 'Headquarters, South-Western Front, June 18', Washburn wrote that 'in an obscure corner of Southern Russia, from within the whitewashed walls of an old barracks', General Brusilov was 'to-day directing Russia's greatest and most successful offensive of the war'. After an hour-long private interview, Washburn quoted the Russian's assertion that the sweeping successes of his armies were 'not the product of chance, or of Austrian weakness, but represent the application of all the lessons which we have learnt in two years of bitter warfare against the Germans'. The 'main element' of their success, he claimed, had been 'the absolute coordination of all the armies involved . . . On our entire front the attack began at the same hour and it was impossible for the enemy to shift his troops from one quarter to another, as our attacks were being pressed equally at all points.'

Brusilov also commented on the wider war situation. The Germans, he thought, would not be able to send very large reinforcements to support the Austrians (as they had done the previous year) and he believed that the Russian capture of the important city of Czernovitz (Chernivtsi) to the south would 'create a profound effect in Romania and the Balkan States'. The general situation, moreover, had been 'further improved by the British Fleet's action [at Jutland], which was unquestionably a victory for our Allies, for the Germans were forced to retire to their base, abandoning whatever project prompted their manœuvre'.[14]

Washburn had a fine, journalist's knack for the human interest side of the war. In mid-August 1916 he reported from Lutsk, a fortified medieval town in north-west Ukraine on the river Styr, which he had last visited in June the previous year. A remote and peaceful place, before the war it had been 'as quiet and isolated as though it were on the banks of the Amur in far-off Siberia', and when Washburn had been there he had seen peasants 'digging trenches and laughing as they dug – for none believed the enemy would ever reach them'. But since then it had been occupied by Habsburg troops who in turn had been expelled by Russian forces (actually the 4th Finnish Guards Division) in the first week of the offensive. From his balcony on the main street Washburn watched a continuous stream of Russian units moving westwards behind the advance, yet he thought that the picture was not complete 'without your filling it in with the backwash from the battlefields, which day by day is crawling eastward ... When one knows the price that it costs to advance it dims the romance of conquest. Here we see the price, hour after hour, in cartload after cartload.' These wounded, he wrote, were 'patient, dirty, uncomplaining'; some 'sit with legs hanging over the ends of the cart chatting gaily of the victory'; some 'are crying softly to themselves, unable to endure the agony'; others 'lie as dead, with passionless faces looking straight up into the sky ... It seems terrible, but this is what war means.'[15]

In keeping with his focus on the individual human experience, Washburn had a special word for the Sisters of Mercy, who provided nursing care for the casualties: 'These devoted sisters! Surely nothing is too good for those who have left homes of luxury and comfort to serve the humble *mujik* soldier in the hour of his greatest sacrifice for his Emperor and Holy Russia.' Thus, he claimed, was 'the war bringing together closer than ever before the extremes in Russian life'. Perhaps so, but Stanley Washburn had a particular eye for upper-class women performing war service. At Lutsk, observing that 'the greatest need' was for more motor ambulances, he noted that an Englishwoman, 'Lady Muriel Paget has one on this front, which is doing heroic work and saving lives every day.' Paget, the daughter of the Earl of Winchelsea, was an indefatigable humanitarian activist who before the war had run soup kitchens in inner London. In 1915 she became organising secretary of the Anglo-Russian Hospital Committee, which funded a British-staffed military hospital in the Dmitri Palace on Petrograd's Nevsky Prospekt, as well as a field hospital near the battle front and a number of field ambulances. Harold Nicolson, who witnessed Paget lobbying for relief work in eastern Europe at the Paris peace conference, said that she was a woman whose 'energy is terrifying' and who sent 'Prime Ministers scuttling on her behests'.[16]

From early 1916 until after the Russian revolution in 1917, Paget spent much of her time in Russia working for the committee, both in Petrograd and elsewhere. In July 1916, Washburn encountered her at a field hospital at Rozhishche (Rozhyshche), north of Lutsk, where the Russian Imperial Guards had set up headquarters. Just five miles from the front line, the town was subject to what Stanley Washburn called 'a new and extremely unpleasant element' of modern warfare, 'namely, the enemy aeroplane'. He was bitterly scathing about the airmen who, he said, 'must have known' that the town was filled with wounded, their own as well as Russian . . . Again and again they came, sometimes five and six aeroplanes, and threw 'their explosives all over the town, and, not content with that, poured into the panic-stricken civil population veritable deluges of machine-gun bullets.' The British hospital, 'stuck out on a hill . . . with its Red Cross flags and white field tents was bombed almost every day'. Washburn reported that one evening he had visited the hospital and found Lady Muriel 'covered in blood', tending 'an unfortunate peasant woman' who had suffered a direct hit from an air raid while working in a nearby field, accompanied by her baby son and 'his three- or four-year-old sister'. The boy had been blown to bits; the mother grievously wounded and the little girl 'miraculously was uninjured'. As the mother lay dying, Washburn 'could not but wonder how the man who dropped the bomb would have felt had he stood beside me this evening'.[17]

Paget's version of what was evidently the same story was a little less highly coloured. In a letter to her husband, back in England, she reported that 'a woman with an abdominal wound from bomb was brought in'. Placed in the mess tent, 'a darling little girl of 3 called Ola was sitting quite unperturbed on her mother's stretcher'. Ola stayed

with Paget in her tent for two days: 'she didnt seem the least surprised
& was much more annoyed when I gave her a bath – *v* necessary & the
hair combing was not too pleasant'. Paget went on to note that a little
brother, about four years old, had been wounded by the same bomb,
'& we thought he had been killed & did not dare tell the mother, &
then we found him in another hospital – such joy . . . we hope he and
the mother may live'.[18]

The airplanes were German and Washburn shared the common
opinion that they were more ruthless opponents than the Austrians.
The dismissal of Germans as brutal 'Huns' was, of course, a powerful
and constant component of Allied propaganda. Whatever the truth of
the matter, Washburn concluded that the 'net result' of air raids which
targeted wounded soldiers and civilians was 'to increase the bitterness
daily against the enemy. People,' he observed, 'frequently express
surprise that so many Austrians are taken prisoners and so few
Germans. My own opinion is that it is largely because the Germans
have made themselves so hated by the Russians that, after a successful
attack, they are not in the mood to take any prisoners.'[19]

ROMANIA

Superficially, at least, Romania looked like a desirable prize which
could have opted for either side. Occupying a strategically valuable
position on the Black Sea across the mouth of the Danube, it was a
major producer of both grain and oil. It had, moreover, mobilised
800,000 troops at the start of the war, by no means a negligible total for
a small country with a population of 8 million.[20] Historically allied to
the Central Powers (through a secret treaty of 1883 with the Triple
Alliance of Germany, Austria-Hungary and Italy), by 1914 it was no
longer so clear that Romania's interests (like Italy's) lay with them.
While there were powerful pro-German elements in the country (the
royal family were a junior branch of the German Hohenzollern
dynasty), the Paris-educated prime minister, Ion Brătianu, leant
towards the Allies. Besides, an active alliance with the Habsburg
monarch was inconceivable, bearing in mind the 3 million ethnic
Romanians languishing under Hungarian rule (with a particular

concentration in Transylvania) over whom Romanian nationalists nursed powerful irredentist claims.

Like Italy, Romania saw the war as a welcome opportunity to advance some longstanding national objectives. Both countries, indeed, shared an interest, as Brătianu put it, to work together towards 'the liquidation of Austria-Hungary in their favour (if liquidation there must be)', and an agreement for consultation and possible joint action was signed between the two in September 1914. The following month Brătianu secured Russia's backing for irredentist Romanian claims in Austria-Hungary so long as Romania remained neutral towards Russia. This, among other things, led Bucharest to stop much-needed German munitions being carried to Turkey along Romanian railway lines. Over the summer of 1915 Brătianu came close to coming in on the Allied side, but the Central Powers' very successful offensive against Russia from the battle of Gorlice-Tarnów onwards made him stay his hand. In the end, any advantage which Romania might hope to secure from the war depended on Russia holding up well against the Central Powers. There was, after all, virtually nothing which Britain or France could practically offer.

After Bulgaria joined the Central Powers in October 1915, helping complete their occupation of Serbia, Brătianu softened his position and allowed the Germans and Austrians to purchase much-needed Romanian cereals and some oil. By the summer of 1916 over 2.5 million tons of grain had been exported. The Brusilov offensive, meanwhile, appeared to shift the balance of advantage back to the Allies and France, anxious for anything which might relieve the pressure at Verdun, began to promise generous political and military backing for Romania. Thus, after also securing promises of substantial support (both men and munitions) from the Russians and an Anglo-French push on their Salonika front to pin down the Bulgarians in the south, on 27 August 1916 Brătianu brought Romania into the war. Like Italy, Romania initially only declared against Austria-Hungary, but Germany declared war on them the next day and so Romania, a little reluctantly, found itself fully on the Allied side.[21]

Hopes were high, especially in France, that the Romanians could make a significant difference. The French commander Joffre even

asserted that 'no price' was 'too high to pay' for Romanian intervention. Poincaré thought that if the Romanians could crush the
Austro-Hungarians, 'we should compel Germany to make an additional effort which may well be beyond her immediate resources'. On
the Central Powers' side, the potential impact of Romania was, if
anything, judged even higher. Conrad thought it 'would decide [the
war] against us'. The Hungarian prime minister, Count Tisza, thought
it would be a 'catastrophe', and he favoured sacrificing Poland to the
Germans in the hope they would then help to defend Transylvania.
Even the Germans were apprehensive, and the news that Romania had
declared war 'fell like a bomb' at German supreme headquarters.
'William II completely lost his head, pronounced the war finally lost
and believed we must now ask for peace.' It also caused the Kaiser
finally to lose faith in Falkenhayn (who had assured him Romania
would remain neutral), after which he was replaced by Hindenburg as
chief of staff.[22]

Confirming Habsburg anxieties and illustrating how potentially
very destabilising the Romanian move could be right across the ethnic
mosaic of the imperial lands, was its impact on Joseph Gál's Hungarian
unit, which had been deployed on the Isonzo front since early in the
year. When they received the shattering news that Romania had come
into the war and invaded Transylvania, where their regiment had been
raised, they were 'indescribably dismayed . . . because really we are
Transylvanian boys and most of us are from the villages of the border
region . . . With aching hearts we think of our beloved homeland,
Transylvania's hills and valleys where since then war's bloody avalanche
has started.' The unit became seriously unsettled and they began to
'plan, by hook or by crook, that we will go home and we will protect
Transylvania'. Their commanders at first peremptorily rejected
requests for any such move, and even threatened them with exemplary
decimation if they refused to go back into the front line. Graphically
illustrating some of the endemic difficulties of mobilising the multi-
national Austro-Hungarian Empire for war on several fronts, the men
nevertheless resolved that they were now only prepared to fight for
their own homeland, and (as Gál recounted it twenty years later) they
prepared even to mutiny, reckoning that there was not very much to

choose between being shot by one's own side or by the Italians. But the high command relented and, to Gál's 'indescribable' joy, on 8 September orders were issued transferring the regiment to the Transylvanian front. A few days later they set off for Hungary, and beyond describing the happiness of arriving back home, Gál's bitter war memoir ceased there. It ended, as it had begun, in Transylvania.[23]

We do not know how Gál's unit fared when it got home (or nearly so), but the Romanians' main thrust into Transylvania began quite promisingly. Some 370,000 Romanian troops crossed into Hungary, ten times more than the defending Habsburg First Army, who provided scant resistance. The Romanians occupied south-west Transylvania, but proceeded no further, partly because their supply lines through the Carpathian Mountains proved grossly inadequate. Elsewhere things went less well. In the south, a force of four Bulgarian and two Ottoman divisions, with a few German and Austrian units, under the command of the very able German, Field Marshal August von Mackensen, on 2 September launched an unexpected offensive along the Black Sea coast into Dobruja. Here the Bulgarians had a recent score to settle since the Romanians had taken the province from them in 1913 after the Second Balkan War. The territory, moreover, contained a sizeable Bulgarian population. Here again (as so often in these disputed lands), the combination of an ethnic minority with irredentist passions powerfully sustained military endeavour. Although the Russians supplied three divisions to reinforce the single Romanian division in Dobruja, further afield the Allies had little to offer. The projected inter-Allied offensive (involving French, Serbian and British forces) against Bulgaria on the Salonika front, which the Romanians hoped would protect them from a Bulgarian attack, failed to materialise. The British high command was adamantly opposed to any large-scale operation in this 'sideshow' theatre and, to the great disappointment of the Romanians, the action was eventually restricted to what the French called 'une offensive affirmée', and was merely a limited holding operation which had little effect on the Bulgarians' offensive capacity against Romania.[24]

The Romanians' entry into the war rapidly turned into a disaster, and they found themselves fighting for their lives on three fronts.

Despite the hurried transfer of troops from Transylvania to the southern front, Mackesen's force steadily pushed forward, occupying Dobruja by the end of October. The movement of troops in turn left the weakened Romanian position in the north unable to resist the advance of a hastily assembled German and Habsburg force – under the demoted Falkenhayn's command – which had more or less expelled the Romanians from Transylvania by early October. A third German–Bulgarian–Turkish force, the 'Army of the Danube', moved in from the south-west, pushing towards Bucharest, and aiming to link up with Mackensen, whose troops were forcing the Romanians and their Russian allies back along the coast (they took the major port of Constanţa on 21 October). Another formation advanced north-west and combined with Falkenhayn's troops moving towards Bucharest, which the government evacuated on 25 November and which fell on 7 December. The remnants of the Romanian army – they had lost 73,000 men killed or wounded, 147,000 captured and 90,000 missing[25] – comprising about six effective divisions, retreated along with the Romanian government to Moldavia in the north. Here the front line steadied and, with Russian support, they held up the slackening Central Powers' advance.

Taking part in the retreat from Dobruja was a unit of the Scottish Women's Hospitals (SWH), which had been established in 1914 by Elsie Maud Inglis, with a band of like-minded practical feminists.[26] Inglis was a consultant physician and surgeon, lecturer at Edinburgh University and honorary secretary of the Scottish Federation of Women's Suffrage Societies. Determined to exploit the often unrealised potential of women, she and her colleagues collected money and personnel to equip and staff hospitals for war work. Rebuffed by both the British War Office (like Helena Gleichen's X-ray unit) and the Red Cross (who tended to toe the official line wherever they operated), they proceeded to organise independently. By the spring of 1915 there were Scottish Women's hospitals in France (at Royaumont, north of Paris) and Serbia, where Inglis herself took charge in May 1915. Some of the SWH volunteers got caught up in the Serbian 'Great Retreat' in the autumn and winter of 1915 when Central Powers' forces drove the Serbs over the Albanian mountains to the Adriatic Sea. A number, including Inglis, were taken prisoner, but were repatriated back to Britain in February 1916. In July the Serbs asked if a field hospital unit could be provided for the Serbian Division being assembled to fight with the Russians on the Eastern Front, and so, after an eventful journey by ship from Liverpool to Archangel in the far north, and then train right across Russia, the Russian unit of the Scottish Women's Hospitals found themselves at Odessa on the Black Sea. 'I don't quite know what we expected,' wrote Yvonne Fitzroy. 'Wolves, I suppose, and deep dark pine forests, with a Nihilist thrown in here and there as local colour. What we got was an attractive but unvarying country of birch and lime-wood.'[27]

At the end of September the unit was sent to Medgidia inland from Constanţa where they set up a hospital serving Russian as well as Serbian wounded. A letter from Ethel Moir, a hospital orderly, gives a sense of the atmosphere. The Russians, she wrote, were evidently hard-pressed and anxious for the hospital to keep going as long as possible: 'heavy fighting is going on very near here, wounded pouring in, and no arrangements made for them. They are terribly in need of Red Cross units; there are no hospitals to speak of, and oh, so many wounded.' Within twelve hours of getting the hospital set up, all the beds were full. 'We had,' wrote Moir, 'a frantically busy afternoon and night getting the patients washed; cleaning them was some job, as they were all simply filthy, caked with mud and crawling. The doctors then had to get the dressings done, and a lot of cases had to be operated on at once.' They were very close to the front line and Ysabel Birkbeck, one of the drivers, got caught in a series of air raids. 'We took the wounded to Medgidia;' she wrote in her diary, 'there was a bombardment going on there too. As we passed the Red Cross food place, a man was hit and blown to bits.' A little later on, she 'discovered I had a tyre down, and I got out and started to take the wheel off. Meanwhile my passengers [three male doctors] had jumped out of the car and run to hide in some rubble; I would have too if I had thought anything made any difference.' Afterwards she stopped at a café, when the enemy planes returned. The others tried to keep her inside but 'I could not bear the idea of a roof over my head, so went and sat on the steps of my beloved [Rolls] Royce . . . When I got up to crank the car, I found I had stopped her in a pool of blood.' Katherine Hodges, another ambulance driver, added a few details: Birkbeck 'had lots of shrapnel and stuff all over the car, but wasn't hurt. The Russian doctor she was driving was rather scared.' [28]

A fortnight after the Scottish women arrived at the front, the line broke and they joined in the retreat north to Galatz, Reni (on the Russian frontier) and beyond. Yvonne Fitzroy's party, threatened with being left behind, were fortunate to encounter Captain Charles Bryson, 'an Irishman from Belfast' who was serving with the Russian army (and after the war made a considerable name for himself writing detective novels under the pseudonym Charles Barry). Bryson had been appointed to liaise between them and the Russians. The women having been left without transport, the Ulsterman ('unshaven and very tired') pulled rank, backed it up with physical violence, and managed to commandeer a passing lorry and driver. 'We found ourselves,' wrote Fitzroy, 'at the mercy of an insane driver, who dashed along regardless of anybody, wrecked one refugees' cart, terrified the horses all along the road, and stopped for nothing and nobody.' There was some justification for the poor driver's behaviour. 'As Captain B. had had to knock him down twice before the poor man would consent to take us at all,' explained Fitzroy, 'he no doubt thought here was a great chance of getting his own back.' [29]

At Galatz, Yvonne Fitzroy reflected on the extraordinarily complex ethnic and national patchwork she encountered. 'Patriotism must be a difficult problem out here,' she wrote in December 1916. Their hosts, who had lived in Galatz for some time, were 'of Greek birth, but were for many years Turkish subjects, with interests in both Constantinople and Asia Minor'. One son had 'a Greek passport, and of his three brothers one is interned as a Turkish subject, another is in Bucharest with a Spanish passport, where the third was killed the other day in an air raid'. They had two sons-in-law: 'one is a Turkish subject exiled at Salonica; the other, also a Turkish subject, fought for the Russians through the siege of Port Arthur, and is now interned at Constantinople as a Russian officer'. [30]

The Scottish contingent – above all their transport section, nicknamed 'The Buffs' – were no-nonsense practical women who presented a rather different image to the more aristocratic Lady Bountiful-style of Lady Muriel Paget's Anglo-Russian Hospital. Paget's opinionated and socially conscious colleague, Lady Sybil Grey, was horrified at the appearance of two Scottish Women's Hospital volunteers who turned up in Petrograd from Romania in December 1916. 'One I *supposed* was a woman,' she wrote to her mother in England, 'and the other I literally thought was a man or at least a fat boy. They are all suffragettes, but it is *quite* unnecessary for them to look as they do. The girl,' she continued, 'was a chauffeur of an ambulance; she had on a cowboy hat over her short hair with a leather strap round her chin, a khaki coat like an officer's with a leather band round the middle . . . and puttees and boots.'[31]

France and Britain provided a little direct assistance to Romania. The French sent a military mission, led by General Henri Berthelot, a gourmandising optimist, who tried in vain to organise a last-ditch defence of Bucharest, but played a significant role in helping rebuild the Romanian army in 1917.[32] The British had a military mission, too, but of more significance was the expert demolition team they sent to deny the enemy as much as possible of Romania's precious grain and oil. The team was led by a professional engineer and adventurer called John Norton-Griffiths. An archetypal British imperial hero, he had been a soldier in the Boer War; a railway engineer in Africa and America; head of a successful engineering company; an enthusiast for empire emigration and (from 1910) a Unionist MP. On the outbreak of the war he had raised a unit, the 2nd King Edward's Horse, at his own expense, but was later taken on the staff of the army's Engineer-in-Chief to help organise the tunnelling companies on the Western Front which sapped forward to place explosive charges under the enemy lines. In his obituary in *The Times* he was credited with planning the great series of mines which destroyed the German front line at Messines in June 1917.[33]

In November 1916 the Director of Military Intelligence in London appointed Norton-Griffiths to be 'Chief of the British Mission for the destruction of cereals and oil'. On his arrival in Romania in late November, Norton-Griffiths divided his team into two: one group, under Captain J. Pitts, was to focus on 'grain and machinery', while his own was to concentrate on oil installations. Norton-Griffiths began work in the area north of Ploesti, the centre of the oil industry, where he came up against considerable resistance from the over-optimistic Romanians, who opposed complete destruction of drilling and refining machinery on the grounds that they would be able to hold back the advancing enemy (or, if not, soon recapture the territory), and wanted only oil stocks (but not infrastructure) to be destroyed.

Ignoring these pleas, Norton-Griffiths set about wrecking as much as he could. At Targoviste, his party destroyed four small refineries and set fire to the oil. 'All these fires,' he reported, 'lasted several days, the smoke hung heavily over the town and the flames, which at times rose to great heights, illuminated the neighbouring districts, thus allowing the enemy for the first time to become aware of our work.' The British demolition work was done just ahead of the enemy offensive. At Ploesti, Norton-Griffiths began work on 3 December, and the enemy arrived three days later. By then his men had superintended the destruction of thirteen refineries and (by his own estimate) nearly 400,000 tons of oil. Over the whole region, he estimated that perhaps twice that tonnage was destroyed.[34] Writing to his wife in January 1917, Norton-Griffiths claimed that 'the oil has been a complete success'. They had had to work 'night and day . . . riding roughshod over everybody in the pandemonium, generally raising hell in the absolute hell of terrific explosions, smoke, gas, the day as night once thousands of tons of oil were well under way . . . and always the uncertainty of the Boche cavalry cutting in behind us, which they did more than once'.[35]

A report by Captain John Scale (who had been posted to Romania from secret intelligence work in Petrograd) of the destruction of industrial installations at the Danube port of Braila in late December 1916 indicates the sort of scorched-earth policy that was applied beyond the oilfields. While a Romanian officer attached to the British unit, Captain Prince G. B. Bibesco, organised the evacuation of mill machinery, Scale was responsible for evacuating and destroying a cellulose factory and a rice factory, 'with one or two small works where shells were being manufactured'. He managed to get away about half of the 6,000 tons of cellulose stored at the factory before the rest was burnt. Then 'the factory including all engines and retorts (14 of which could have been utilised at once for the manufacture of asphyxiating gases) were destroyed by dynamite, and the factory itself fired'. It appeared, remarked Scale, 'to have belonged to an Austrian or German-owned firm'. After this, a cement factory was dynamited by a detachment of Russians under the instructions of Norton-Griffiths, who also wrecked the rice mill and engineering shops where shells had been made. The dock machinery and cranes were 'left to the tender mercies of the Russian detachment, who, while with us, carried out their work most thoroughly'.

Captain Pitts, detailed to destroy grain, had a particularly difficult time of it since 'the Romanian Government emphatically opposed all destruction'. The Romanians reluctantly agreed to allow the incineration of British-owned grain, of which there was a considerable quantity in the country. In order to deny it to the enemy and support the Romanian grain market, in 1915 the British government had bought some 430,000 tons of wheat, of which 100,000 tons had been given over to the Romanian army in August 1916. But the Bucharest authorities 'expressly forbade the firing of granges or farms, extended no help, and in fact placed obstacles in the way of any destruction'. Pitts did his best to limit the damage and in the end calculated that about 180,000 tons had been saved.

During December 1916 Pitts was assisted by men from an unusual British unit serving with the Russian Sixth Army: the Royal Naval Air Service (RNAS) Russian Armoured Car Division, a 500-strong formation raised by another maverick Unionist Member of Parliament, Oliver Locker-Lampson. Funded partly with Ulster Unionist money (originally collected to support Ulster's armed opposition to the prewar Liberal government's Irish Home Rule policy), the unit had been sent to Russia in December 1915 to demonstrate British solidarity with its eastern ally. It was posted to the Caucasian front where a Russian offensive had been pushing into Turkey since the beginning of the year. Here the unit was split up and underused, but Locker-Lampson's wish for deployment on a more active front was granted when they were sent to Moldavia as part of the hasty Russian reinforcements aiming to the plug the gap opened

up by the Romanian collapse. Continuously in action from the beginning of December, on the 16th they were posted to Braila, which is
where Norton-Griffiths found them and borrowed a party of one
officer and twenty-eight men 'to assist in the destruction of such
factories as were of military importance'. 'Their co-operation,'
reported Pitts, 'was indispensable.'[36] Later in the month British
Armoured Car men also helped the Scottish Women's Hospital
volunteers get their ambulances and transport waggons onto barges
to cross the Danube at Tulcea. 'It was so nice to have them here, and
hear English at street corners,' wrote Ysabel Birkbeck in her diary.
'They look so clean, so friendly, and,' she added a mite ambiguously,
'we are fearfully interested in each other. They congregate around
our cars to hear our adventures and tell of their own.'[37]

   While Norton-Griffiths evidently took much pride in reporting
the scale and completeness of the demolition he had been sent to do,
he also briefly reflected on the ambivalence with which local British
and American oil engineers had cooperated in the work. In early
negotiations, for example, E. J. Sadler of the Standard Oil Company
'felt keenly the possibility of destruction of an undertaking which he
had so ably developed since its inception'. 'Time alone,' wrote
Norton-Griffiths, 'can balance the gain as against the loss and devastation with which it has been the painful duty to lay waste the land.'
In a reflection which could as well apply to the whole war, he thought
it had 'been a revelation from the highest to the lowest that our
conception of obstructing the enemy means sacrificing the individual
and the fruits of the earth, at no matter what cost to either, to accomplish our ends'.[38]

   And did it? Alan Kramer asserts that 'the daring exploits of
Norton-Griffiths' constituted 'the greatest single act of economic
warfare in the war' – which may be overstating the case a little, as
does the claim by the official historians of Royal Dutch Shell (which
had substantial interests in Romania) that 'without the stocks and
sources captured in Romania, Germany would have collapsed two
years earlier'. The historian of Romania and oil, Maurice Pearton,
reckons that the 800,000 tons of oil which Norton-Griffiths estimated was destroyed, together with the wrecked oil wells and

refineries, 'effectively denied the oil industry to the Germans, at a crucial stage in the war, for about five months'. Yet, as the Germans had been a major force in the Romanian oil industry, there were abundant numbers of skilled technical personnel available for reconstruction. Indeed the Germans had planned ahead for the exploitation of the Romanian oil. Attached to Mackensen's headquarters was an economic staff, the 'Wirtschaftsstab', which included petroleum experts, and they were able to get production going fairly quickly and efficiently. In 1917 they managed an annual total of 461,491 tons, just over a quarter of that for 1915, but all – or the great majority – of which could be sent to Germany and Austria-Hungary. To this must be added the agricultural products which the Central Powers could also extract from Romania, which over the next year and a half amounted to 2 million tons of grain, 200,000 tons of timber, 100,000 head of cattle and 200,000 goats and pigs, in Norman Stone's opinion 'far more . . . than they could have done had [Romania] remained neutral'.[39]

Brusilov claimed in his memoirs that 'it came to us as a total surprise when the Rumanians displayed a complete ignorance of modern warfare',[40] a statement which principally testifies to the extremely poor quality of Russian military intelligence. Most commentators, then and subsequently, were dismissive of Romanian military capabilities. At the end of September 1916, Charles Bryson, the Russian liaison officer, told Margaret Fawcett of the Scottish Women's Hospital that 'the Roumanians had so far not done well; the only thing they could do properly was to run away'. Within a few days of arriving in Romania, John Norton-Griffiths had more charitably 'come to the conclusion (although much optimism prevailed) that the equipment of the Roumanian Army – their gunnery and machine-gun power in particular were such that the enemy, with his superior guns and tactics must – up to a point – and for a time, anyhow – have things, more or less, his own way'.[41]

The Romanian army 'entered the field pitiably equipped', wrote Charles Cruttwell after the war. 'The human material, 500,000 sturdy peasants was fairly good itself, but atrociously led. Eyewitnesses state that all through the campaign crowds of officers were strolling about

Bucharest with painted faces, soliciting prostitutes or one another.' Cosmetics are something of a leitmotiv. In December 1916 the nurse Ethel Moir reflected that while the ordinary Romanian soldiers could fight well if properly led, 'their officers are impossible, conceited, dressed-up fops, powdered and painted and dressed up to the nines. All they think of is their personal appearance.' Norman Stone noted an order on mobilisation that 'only officers above the rank of major had the right to use make-up'.[42] Whatever the personal proclivities of their officer class, the Romanians were actually in an impossible situation. The country itself was virtually indefensible. Apart from the sea coast, the only natural barrier to their territory was the Carpathians, and the main point of going to war was to occupy land beyond the mountains. Their own leaders (and, to be fair, some Allied observers) thought that mere numbers of troops would be enough to see them through, but the army turned out to be no match for well-led and mostly battle-hardened opposition. The stiffening which German commanders provided for the Central Powers' forces, combined with carefully organised supply lines, made the crucial difference.

SOLDIERS AND CIVILIANS IN THE EAST

While the numbers of troops engaged on the Eastern Front were rather smaller than those in the west (in 1915 there were 1.3 million Central Powers and 1.8 million Russian troops in the east as opposed to 1.9 million German and 2.45 million British and French in the west),[43] the numbers of non-combatants affected and displaced by the conflict in the east hugely exceeded those in the west. As Matthew Stibbe has observed, 'many more soldiers were taken prisoner and many more civilians were deported or forced to flee during the course of the fighting in eastern Europe, Italy and the Balkans than in France and Belgium'. By the beginning of 1917, the total number of displaced people in the Russian empire alone has been calculated at just over 6 million. Across Russia, there was, in Peter Gatrell's suggestive, resonant phrase, 'a whole empire walking'.[44]

The displacement of people in the east began with the Russian invasion of East Prussia when some 870,000 people – mostly ethnic

Germans – fled westwards. The Germans' successful counteroffensive, which took them into Poland (fifty miles short of Warsaw) and Lithuania by the end of 1914, had an equivalent impact, which was further exacerbated with the great German victories of 1915, after which they occupied all of Poland and much of the (then) Russian provinces in Lithuania and Latvia. With the steadying of the front line in the autumn of 1915 (in places 300 miles further east than the German-Russian border in 1914), Germany and Austria-Hungary established formal occupation regimes, dividing Poland between them.

Poland was a problem territory for the Central Powers. In the late eighteenth century it had been carved up between Prussia, Austria and Russia (which took the largest part, including the capital Warsaw), but a nationalist movement had developed, especially in the Russian portion, before the war. Seeking to exploit existing anti-Russian sentiment, the German administration tried, though without much success, to win Polish support by setting up a Polish school system (which had been banned by the Russians), allowing Polish-language instruction at Warsaw University and establishing a system of Polish local government. They also introduced greater civil liberties than hitherto for the sizeable Jewish population in Poland which had been persecuted under Russian rule. But the Germans were also anxious to secure their difficult eastern frontier and could never quite decide whether to treat Poland as a potential autonomous neighbour or simply as a vassal state. In July 1915, indeed, it was proposed that Germany should acquire a frontier strip of Poland, expel the existing Polish and Jewish population and settle the land with ethnic Germans. During 1916, Berlin abandoned this scheme and with the Austrians proposed to establish an 'independent' Polish kingdom, hoping (and, if necessary insisting) that grateful Poles would rally to the Central Powers' cause. Poland, too, had traditionally been a source of industrial labour for Germany, and by the spring of 1916 up to 120,000 Poles had been recruited to join the 300,000 already working in the Reich. In October 1916, following the introduction of the Hindenburg Programme in Germany, a forced labour ordinance was passed in Warsaw, though it was only patchily enforced and, unlike in Belgium, there were no deportations to Germany. In the end Berlin's blandishments, such as they were, failed to engage Polish nationalists in any significant numbers. The Russian revolutions of 1917 and the entry of the USA into the war, moreover, encouraged the Poles to think of greater freedoms than the Germans were prepared to offer, and led many nationalists to the conclusion (as was eventually to pass) that an Allied victory would be the best guarantee of an independent Polish state.[45]

Further east, the German occupation government in Lithuania and Latvia became known as the 'Ober Ost' (from the title of Paul von Hindenburg the Supreme Commander in the East, 'Oberbefehlshaber Ost'). It was, in the words of Vejas Gabriel Liulevicius, a combination of 'military utopia and administrative chaos', whereby the army sought to impose order, and establish a permanent administration and exploit the territory's resources to the greatest extent possible. The driving force behind the occupation regime was von Hindenburg's chief of staff, Erich Ludendorff, who imposed what was effectively a military colonisation on the occupied lands which were divided into three large military administrations (from north to south: Kurland, Lithuania and Bialystok-Grodno), then regions, which in turn were subdivided into districts, each headed by a district captain who 'wielded unlimited power over local natives, appointing mayors and official heads for communities'. Many of these individuals were disqualified for front-line service, and some could not cope with their new duties. One young administrator, who had been wounded on the Western Front, 'suddenly, probably because of the weight of his responsibilities, was seized by delusions, wandered through the forests during the nights and caused wild shoot-outs'. Inevitably there was much violence, and 'numerous complaints of German soldiers raping and mistreating girls and women, while men trying to defend them were beaten and threatened with death'.

Despite a superficial impression of complete, competent control, there were many overlapping responsibilities and sharp competition between different departments. Ambitions to strip the Ober Ost of natural resources went far. Great swathes of forest were felled to meet the insatiable timber demands of the Reich, and from Lithuania alone it was calculated after the war that 90,000 horses, 140,000 cattle and 767,000 pigs had been requisitioned. Prisoners of war and refugees

were drafted in to provide the labour needed for this exploitation, and
when in mid-1916 this proved insufficient, the 'Order of Rule' (which
declared that the Supreme Commander in the East exercised 'the
complete legislative, judicial and executive state power') imposed
forced labour on all adult men and women in the territory.[46]

The Germans believed that theirs was a civilising mission. Ludendorff
claimed, for example, that 'the German judge here in the poor, lice-
infested Lithuanian towns delivered legal judgments . . . with the same
objectivity and seriousness as in Berlin'. Partly inspired by the medieval Teutonic Knights who had sought (and failed) to dominate the
region in the Middle Ages, Ludendorff was the driving force behind an
ambitious programme to stamp German culture indelibly on the existing, though 'primitive', ethnicities of the region. Local German
newspapers were established and a translation section endeavoured to
link the local languages – Polish, Russian, Belarusian, Lithuanian,
Latvian and Yiddish – with a German vocabulary (for German was the
language of command) embodying 'coercive measures, bureaucratic
arbitrariness, and state power'.

Yiddish, with many German words, provided an unexpected
connection between the conquerors and their new Jewish subjects.
Since the Ober Ost administration aimed to be scrupulously impartial
towards all the subject population, it was welcomed by many Jews as
a distinct improvement on the previous frequently anti-Semitic regime.
Victor Klemperer, a journalist and literary scholar working in the Ober
Ost press section (who himself had a German-Jewish background),
observed that Jews 'are well disposed towards us and speak German,
or at least half-German'. While some of the Jewish community were
prepared to cooperate with the Ober Ost, there was also much anti-
Semitism, and any unexpected closeness between Jews and German
occupiers confirmed the suspicions (or appeared to do so) of some
other nationalities – especially Russians – that Jews could not be
trusted. In May 1916 a secret German report on the ethnic situation
asserted that it was 'a widely held misconception to consider the Jews
of Russia as special friends of Germany', as they had, in fact, 'no
national politics, but only economic interest'.[47] Damned if they did,
and damned if they didn't, was a familiarly dismal predicament for the

Jewish community, and where the Russians advanced again in the summer of 1916, Jews everywhere suffered persecution for consorting with the enemy, whether they had or not.

A 'DECISIVE TURNING POINT IN THE WAR'

Reflecting on the Brusilov offensive as a whole, Timothy Dowling rates it as 'a decisive turning point in the war'. This was true in three main aspects. First, the Russian offensive 'destroyed once and for all' Austria-Hungary as a military power. The Habsburg monarchy henceforth had to depend utterly on the Germans. Second, it brought Romania into the war, which briefly seemed to be a triumph for the Allies. But Romania's rapid collapse for the time being at least tipped the balance of advantage in the Balkans towards the Central Powers and sustained their war effort in the region for at least another year or so. Third, the prodigious effort invested by the Russians in the offensive (and in the support they had to give to Romania), together with the casualties suffered, critically impaired their capacity – in terms of both morale and materiel – for further fighting. The offensive, concludes Dowling, 'thus marked the height of Russia's wartime achievement, in June and July 1916, and at the same time set the Russian Army on the path to revolution'.[48] Thus, even what Norman Stone described as 'the most brilliant victory of the war',[49] had unforeseen and (for the Russians) decidedly unwelcome consequences. The boost that Romania's collapse gave the Central Powers, moreover, did much to moderate the intermittent notions raised in both Vienna and Berlin for a separate peace in the east (which might have spared imperial Russia from collapse and revolution). As Holger Afflerbach argues, 'the moment in which a compromise peace in the East was still in the air ended in October 1916'.[50] From then on, it was to be a fight to the finish.

The events of 1916 on the Eastern Front also crucially accelerated the political and social destabilisation of both the Russian and Habsburg empires, if not the German empire too. The deceptively stable frontiers between the three great empires of east-central Europe (well, for forty years at least) were decisively shattered by the ethnic and national

movements unleashed and accelerated by the circumstances of the
First World War. Reflecting on the imperialist ramifications of the
conflict, Joshua A. Sanborn has observed that 'with the exception of
the initial battles in East Prussia [and even this ignores the thirteenth-
century Teutonic conquest of the territory], all of the frontline areas
were located in the colonized spaces of eastern Europe, in places where
the population felt itself under the domination of a foreign power'.
The war (as, for example, in Ireland and elsewhere) encouraged
elements of the population to challenge the imperial status quo and
assert a right to 'national self-determination' (with much, if inevitably
imperfect, success in eastern Europe). This, as Sanborn has wryly
observed, has contemporary practical consequences. 'Eastern front
battlefield tourists today need hardly bother with visas to Russia,
Austria, Hungary, or Germany. Those sites now lie mainly in Poland,
Ukraine, Belarus, Lithuania, Latvia, Armenia, Georgia, Turkey, and
Romania.'[51]

7

Asia

The impact of the First World War in Asia reached far beyond the relatively limited zones of actual fighting, which included the conquest of Germany's north China possession of Tsingtao in 1914 and campaigns against the Ottoman Empire in the Middle East and Caucasus. In July 1916 a major revolt broke out in central Asia, sparked off by the imposition of conscription by the Russian imperial authorities on a recently colonised population. Not only did this reflect a general pattern of wartime challenge and response similar to other places, but since the colonised peoples were predominantly Muslim, it also echoed ethno-religious tensions in other war-affected parts of the world, such as the Balkans. Since the Ottoman sultan, as titular leader of the worldwide Islamic community, had issued a fatwa at the start of the war bidding Muslims to wage jihad (holy war) against the Russian, British and French infidels, there were concerns about the loyalty of Muslims in their territories. This was especially so for the British, the majority of whose some 60 million Muslims dwelt in Britain's Indian empire, which extended over an area larger than the entire continent of Europe (excluding Russia), and comprised territory covering the modern states of Bangladesh, India, Myanmar (formerly Burma) and Pakistan. From the very start, units of the British-run Indian Army were involved in fighting and throughout the war India proved to be a vast reservoir of manpower and material resources. Other parts of Asia were also exploited for the Allied war effort, including French

Indochina, the British possessions in Malaya, and China itself, which supplied many thousands of workers for non-combatant labour duties in Europe and elsewhere.

Revolt in Russian central Asia

The revolt in central Asia was triggered off by a decision made on 25 June 1916 by the Russian Stavka to impose labour conscription on the 'native' population of Caucasia and central Asia. After the imperial chief of staff, General Mikhail Vasiliyevich Alekseyev, announced that he needed half a million men a month to cover the army's losses (more than the minister of war could supply), it was agreed from 15 July to conscript 250,000 men from central Asia in the nineteen to forty-three age range as a labour levy to replace men who had been doing essential war work.[1] Although the indigenous population in central Asia had hitherto been exempted from military or much labour service, they had already been affected by the war in various ways. There were locally raised units in the Turkestan Corps, which fought with distinction against the Ottomans in the Caucasus. The men concerned were theoretically all volunteers, though a rough quota had been imposed on localities and many of the recruits had not gone particularly willingly. Increased wartime taxes were levied in the region and contributions in kind (such as yurts) were solicited for the war effort. The Kirghiz and Kazakh nomads, moreover, had been required to supply agricultural labourers in place of men from the Russian settler population who had gone to the front, especially from the Semirechie Oblast (province) along the Chinese frontier in what is now Kazakhstan.

The intensified enlistment of men across the Russian empire in the war was seen by some observers as a means of reinforcing imperial control. Ranald MacDonell, the British vice-consul in Baku during the first two years of the war, asserted (albeit long after the revolution and clearly with the benefit of hindsight) that 'mass mobilisation, and the calling up of millions of unwanted men, was the deliberate policy of the Tsarist government'. It was based on the belief that 'the peasant in uniform, even if he had no arms and ammunition, would be less fertile soil for subversive propaganda than if he were tilling the fields and supplying a less cumbersome army with food'. But 'it had exactly the reverse effect; for bodies of discontented men in barracks are more easily swayed than hard-worked individuals behind the plough'. By 1915, MacDonell noted troops beginning to resist being sent to the front. He recounted an occasion on which he and his wife went to the main railway station to see off a large contingent of troops. 'Their womenfolk lay on the line to prevent the train leaving; the soldiers refused to remove them, and they had to be removed more forcibly by Cossacks . . . It was a disgusting sight. We returned home,' he recalled in his memoirs, 'to read in our Reuters of the enthusiasm with which the Russian Steam Roller was steaming, or rolling, to the front.'[2]

Much of central Asia was fairly recently colonised territory. Analogous to the white conquest of the North American prairies, Russian imperial forces had been progressively conquering the 'borderlands' of central Asia since the late eighteenth century. Settlement followed, with Russian and Ukrainian farmers moving into the apparently empty territory hitherto populated only by nomadic peoples. The parallel with North America is striking, as, armed with the weapons and tools of modern 'civilisation' – firearms, agricultural machinery, telegraph lines, railways and the like – the settlers drove indigenous peoples off their lands and challenged the whole basis of their traditional existence.

There were also some significant differences. The indigenous population of central Asia was much greater than that of North America, and there was never any possibility of the Asians being driven near to extinction. Overwhelmingly Muslim, moreover, the peoples of Turkestan themselves shared strong religious affinities and were part of a wider transnational religious community. Although some official efforts were made to protect the local Kyrgyz nomads, the lure of rich agricultural land ripe for exploitation sustained an increasing flow of settlers, authorised and unauthorised, especially from the early 1890s onwards. Estimates of settler numbers vary. Sokol says that by the First World War there were 300,000 'Russians' (which includes ethnic Ukrainians) in Semirechye alone. A more recent study by Daniel

Brower quotes a 1911 estimate by the Tashkent administration that over 150,000 settlers were farming 'among the nearly one million Turkic nomads in Turkestan' as a whole. But some areas contained high concentrations of settlers. In the Semirechye districts of Pishpek and Przhevalsk (where the 1916 revolt was most intense) there were 80,000 settlers among an estimated 325,000 Kyrgyz.[3]

By 1914 Russian central Asia had become the richest and most productive cotton-growing region in the empire and to the outside eye it seemed unaffected by the war. Writing for *The New York Times* from Bukhara with a date-line of 6 May 1916, the American diplomat Montgomery Schuyler claimed that 'at last' he had 'discovered a country where the war is almost entirely unknown, where normal conditions reign, and where life is going on just as it has for the last 2,000 years, unmoved by what is passing over it'. Accompanied by his wife, he had travelled first to Tashkent, the regional administrative capital, and then towards the Chinese frontier on to Kokand and Andijan (where Muslim students were to demonstrate violently against conscription in July 1916). Here he noted a population composed both of settled agriculturalists working fertile and productive cotton fields as well as nomadic 'wandering Turcomans and Kirghez', herding sheep and 'making the woollen rugs known locally as "Tekke"'. In recent years the weavers had taken to using artificial dyes, resulting in luridly coloured carpets which were not to Schuyler's taste. But here he found an unexpected benefit arising from the war. 'One of the reasons for which lovers of art have to thank the war' (what other ones might there have been?), he wrote, 'is that all importation of the German dyes has now ceased and the rugmakers have been forced to stop using the cheap colors and to return to the soft vegetable tints which are so beautiful.'

Schuyler observed that there was 'a strong Russian military force in Turkestan, but so far as keeping order is concerned it has been quite unnecessary since the outbreak of the war'. The Kurdish community around the southern Caspian Sea had been expected to give trouble but 'with rare exceptions remained on their own side of the mountains in Persia [Iran] and have not tried to take advantage of war conditions'. In a chilling and ethnically loaded aside, Schuyler asserted that, in fact, the Kurds 'apparently had such a congenial and attractive occupation in killing Armenians that they have had scant leisure for other things'. Travelling west through Samarkand and Bukhara towards Krasnovodsk on the Caspian, he reported occasional sightings of Austrian prisoners of war in light blue uniforms, of whom 'many thousands' had been sent to the district. Housed in Russian army barracks, they were, he wrote, 'allowed a great deal of liberty, especially those of Slavonic race, and seem to go about without any restraint except for the presence of one Russian underofficer with each detachment of prisoners on the streets'. On the whole, however, the war scarcely intruded on the Schuylers' three-week stay in the region, or on his lyrical travelogue. One high point was a lavish dinner in a palace used by the Emir of Bukhara for official entertaining. 'The whole scene and surroundings,' he wrote, 'were irresistibly reminiscent of the *Arabian Nights* and it was hard to imagine one's self in the twentieth century and in the midst of a world war.'[4]

This was Schuyler's second visit to the region. A year earlier he had been sent by the American ambassador in Petrograd, George T. Mayre, to report on the conditions of Russian-held prisoners of war. At the start of hostilities the USA, as the largest and most respected neutral power, had undertaken to protect the interests of both Germany and Austria-Hungary in Russia. Among other things this involved monitoring the treatment of unprecedentedly large numbers of prisoners of war. Between August 1914 and September 1917, for example, the Russian authorities calculated (though these figures almost certainly underestimate the actual numbers) that they had captured over 1.9 million enemy soldiers, of whom 159,000 were Germans and 1.7 million Austro-Hungarians. Prisoners of war on all sides were used as labour (and were supposed to, but did not always, receive some payment). In the spring of 1917 the Russians estimated that just over a million prisoners were so employed, forty-three per cent in agriculture and twenty-seven per cent in mines and factories. They often worked in appalling conditions. In 1916 some 25,000 prisoners died constructing a railway to the Arctic port of Murmansk in north Russia. The Russians also discriminated between different ethnic groups, favouring (as Schuyler noted in May 1916) Slavs from the Austro-Hungarian forces, hoping in many cases to recruit them into fighting against their former Habsburg masters. Reporting to Mayre in April 1915, Schuyler observed that while 'Austrian subjects, especially Slavs' were 'treated as well as can be expected', Germans were 'being systematically annoyed and humiliated in many minor ways, as a protest against the treatment of Russian prisoners in Germany as reported in Russian newspapers'.[5] Russia's encouragement of ethnic dissent and difference within the Habsburg Empire (which had been sharpened by the war) could, of course, be a double-edged sword for an empire which itself contained a patchwork of ethnic minorities, especially along its peripheral regions.

While romantic, Schuyler's picture of the region in June 1916 was also hopelessly over-complacent. He certainly did not comprehend how existing pre-war economic grievances, social tensions and ethnic antagonisms were all exacerbated by the war and the progressively more onerous demands being made on the population in support of the imperial war effort. Increased wartime taxes and the requisitioning of goods for military use – horses, camels, yurts and various commodities, often paid for at unrealistically low fixed prices – bore heavily on the population, as did price inflation, especially of foodstuffs. By 1916, for example, grain was nearly 400 per cent more expensive than it had been in 1913. Widespread corruption among local officials, moreover, meant that payment for requisitioned goods was often less than the government prices, or even not paid at all.[6] Schuyler's views, nevertheless, were evidently shared by the local Russian administrators as they did not anticipate there being any great difficulty in imposing the labour conscription order. How wrong they were.

Meeting on 2–3 July 1916, a conference of administrators decided to implement the levy through district quotas, to be raised by local Russian and indigenous officials. This meant that these front-line officers would bear the brunt of any popular resentment, and, indeed, that they could manipulate the levy for their own personal advantage. Since the administration mostly worked through existing indigenous hierarchies, the better-off and more influential could evade the levy, leaving its full weight to fall inevitably on the poorest and most powerless part of the population. The timing of the measure was also particularly unfortunate, coming as it did when the harvest was in full swing. Although some allowance was made for the vital cotton crop – cotton-growing districts were given a smaller quota of men to meet – the heavier burden in other places caused increased resentment there. In a final miscalculation, the administration made no great attempt ahead of time to explain the new policy, or the precise purpose of the levy. In consequence, wild rumours began to spread – that it was actually military conscription, or that the labourers were to be deployed digging trenches in the very front line – which inflamed the feelings of an already apprehensive population.

On 4 July, four days before the official announcement of the levy, the first violence occurred at Khujand in Sughd province (today in Tajikistan) where a hostile crowd was dispersed by soldiers leaving two dead and thirty wounded. Over the next fortnight there were widespread disturbances with groups particularly targeting police barracks, seeking to destroy the prepared lists of conscripts. On 11 July several thousand protestors in Tashkent were beaten off at a cost of twelve killed. Two days later at Jizzakh (Uzbekistan), northeast of Samarkand, local religious leaders proclaimed a holy war not only to stop the conscription but also seeking independence from Russia, with aid (if possible) from Afghanistan and Germany. The Russian military commandant and police chief were killed, along with an interpreter and two policemen. The rebels moved on to destroy the railway station and telegraph lines. In the countryside bands of insurgents – attacking the physical sinews of the Russian colonial state – pulled up railway tracks and demolished bridges, killing sixteen Russian railway workers along the way. At Jizzakh, over eighty Russians were killed and seventy captured, 'mostly women and children, the majority of the women being raped'. Russian retaliation was swift and draconian. A substantial military force was despatched from Tashkent and Samarkand under the command of Colonel Pavel Ivanov (who in the aftermath of the Russian revolution gained notoriety as a hardline White commander in the civil war).

Ivanov was evidently determined to impose an exemplary lesson on the rebels. Within a week order had been restored and telegraph and railway communications repaired. All the Uzbek villages within a ten-mile radius of the town were destroyed; eighty-two leaders were summarily tried and sentenced to death, though many sentences were later commuted. But the greatest cost came with a scorched-earth policy imposed on the local population. According to one survivor, Ivanov 'gave the order to shoot, burn, confiscate household goods and agricultural implements'. His soldiers shot 'whomever they met . . . women were raped and other bestialities perpetrated'. In the countryside, 'they burned the growing crops while the ready grain was taken away'. The old, Uzbek section of Jizzakh was looted by the Russians and then burnt and levelled to the ground. Fritz Willfort, an Austrian prisoner of war who was confined in the town, estimated that a thousand locals were killed during the disturbances, though another source suggests that the number was 4,000.[7]

The most intense conflict occurred among the Kyrgyz population of east Semirechye province during August 1916. Here many thousands of rebels were mobilised, and mounted bands attacked Russian settlements across the region. Sent in October 1916 to report on the outbreak, Captain Iungmeister of the Imperial Gendarmerie noted that the 'pattern of attacks was everywhere almost identical – the Kirgiz [the generic term used at the time to denote Turkic nomads], armed with lances and a small number of rifles, fell upon the settlements, [and] massacred the men'. Elderly women and children were also killed and many prisoners taken. He confirmed reports of mass rape among the female prisoners. The settlers' livestock was seized, along with much other booty. 'Przhevalsk district, the richest area in Semirechie,' reported Iungmeister, 'is almost totally wiped out. Only the town of Przhevalsk and nearby settlements remain intact.'[8] Here, too, roads, bridges and telegraph lines were destroyed, as the rebels focused on any manifestation of the hated colonisers. The Russian casualty figures included fifty-two military and fourteen government employees killed, but these were dwarfed by the numbers of civilian settlers: 2,025 killed and 1,088 missing, the great majority of whom undoubtedly perished.[9]

As elsewhere, the Russians in Semirechye inflicted a terrifying retribution. The rebel bands were no match for the well-armed imperial

troops which were rapidly deployed to the region and by the beginning of September most resistance had ceased. In the meantime, the
Russian forces, in Edward Sokol's words, 'showed utmost cruelty.
Entire villages were levelled by artillery fire while against the insurgents themselves [General] Kuropatkin [who had been hurriedly
drafted in as governor of Turkestan on 21 July] gave the order "not to
spare the cartridges".' Bands of Russian settler vigilantes were organised into 'punitive detachments' and the military governor of
Semirechye, General M. A. Fold'dbaum, gave explicit orders to 'exterminate insurgent settlements to the last man, burn the nomadic camps,
and drive off livestock'. Kuropatkin's subordinates competed in the
killing of Kyrgyz and the destruction or looting of their possessions.
Captain Iungmeister concluded that Russian cruelty was 'equal to
that of the Kirgiz', and Alexander Kerensky (who was briefly prime
minister of Russia between the February and October revolutions),
sent to investigate the revolt and its aftermath by the Duma (parliament), reported that 'nursing babies were eliminated, as were old
women and old men'. In all, Kerensky thought that the indigenous
inhabitants had been 'exterminated, by the tens of thousands, in an
organised and systematic manner'. Many, however, escaped in a mass
exodus over the mountains into Chinese Turkestan, involving as many
as 300,000 people. As for the overall impact of the revolt, one Soviet
demographer calculated a fall of over 1.2 million (seventeen per cent
of the total) in the Turkestan population between 1914 and 1918, most
of which he ascribed to the disorders of 1916.[10]

Although General Kuropatkin was as draconian as anyone in
suppressing the rising, he also appreciated that repression alone could
not provide any sort of long-term solution. As well as touring the
province, aiming to calm both Russian settlers and potential rebels,
he worked to conciliate the indigenous population, emphasising the
benefits – peace, agricultural development, modern communications –
which he said Russian rule had brought to the territory. While stressing
that the Russians would always have a superior role to play, he set up
local committees to improve relations between the imperial administration and the local inhabitants. He insisted that the labour conscription
must go ahead, but conceded that it had been clumsily implemented

and promised that in the future it would be imposed more fairly, and would not fall disproportionately on the poorest section of the population. In mid-September, indeed, he was able to preside over the despatch from Tashkent of the first party of a thousand workers and by February 1917 over 100,000 men had been sent to European Russia. Even in Semirechye, according to Richard Pierce's account of the rising, Kuropatkin adopted a conciliatory and paternalistic approach, hoping that the displaced Kyrgyz could return and live at peace with the Russians.[11] Although many returned, the inter-ethnic antagonisms of 1916 coloured conflict in the region during the revolutionary period and civil war to come, and sustained those local nationalisms which emerged in force again when the Soviet Union collapsed in the late twentieth century.

Almost no news of the events in Russian central Asia got out. A four-line report in *The New York Times* from Berlin, dated 24 August, said without any explanation that 'the situation in Turkestan is growing worse'.[12] According to his memoirs, the *Manchester Guardian* correspondent Morgan Philips Price (later a Labour MP), who visited the Caucasus several times in 1916, had heard about the revolt 'because I happened to have some contact with the Moslem Refugee Society to whom the Turkestan refugees had made appeals'. He had heard rumours that it had been sparked off by the imperial conscription decree, that there had been 'sporadic fighting . . . between the Russian garrisons and Uzbeg peasants and Kirghiz nomads, [and] that considerable numbers of the latter had been killed and wounded'. He reported this to his editor (the famous C. P. Scott), but advised against publication until he had some more hard information, which was difficult to obtain as the whole thing had been 'hushed up'.

Scott was keen to cover the story. The liberal-leaning *Manchester Guardian* had a traditional sympathy for ill-treated minorities and since the beginning of the war had been somewhat ambivalent about the wartime alliance between the more democratic states of Britain and France with an imperial military autocracy like Russia. The central point of the war (from the *Guardian*'s perspective) being the defence of liberal democratic values against tyranny ('Prussian militarism'), whether Russia was reforming and turning itself into a democratic

state (as official British and French propaganda asserted) was a real
matter for investigation, and was one of the reasons Scott had sent
Philips Price to Russia in the first place. Now, as Philips Price had
discovered, 'the whole affair in Turkestan revealed in a flash that things
in the Tsar's empire were going from bad to worse'.[13]

It was six months before Price was able to begin to piece together
the full story of the revolt, by which time the February 1917 revolution seemed to have promised real, constitutional reform in Russia,
and it was a full year before he published the story, just at the time of
the October revolution, and before its consequences had become fully
apparent. In an account completed in May 1917, but not published (in
book form) until 1918, Price briefly referred to the revolt. 'Maddened
by repression,' the Kirghiz Tartars 'had taken the law into their own
hands, and had suffered an even more terrible penalty'. Price got the
causes of the uprising more or less right. The Kirghiz, having been
deprived of their lands by Russian emigrants, were driven to rebel by
the 'additional burden of military service, now suddenly imposed
without consulting their wishes'. The 'whole of the Moslem population of Semiretch,' he said, had annihilated Cossack garrisons 'and
carried 5,000 Russian colonists as prisoners into the mountains. The
rebellion,' he concluded, 'was of course suppressed with the custom-
ary ruthlessness.'

By the time this was published, he had covered the revolt in a newspaper article in November 1917, part of a series on 'Asiatic Russia and
the Revolution'. For the *Guardian* it was a great scoop: 'His is the first
news of this terrible affair which has appeared in the English press.'
The 'Kirghiz rebellion and slaughter, so far as we are aware,' had not
been mentioned in American or enemy papers, 'nor yet in the papers
published in China, which could have got hold of the story from the
Chinese end'. Philips Price, however, 'has been on the spot and has
learnt the facts there, so that the authenticity of his account cannot be
questioned'. Under a headline, 'A Rebellion in 1916: 500,000 Nomads
Massacred', the story in fact was covered in just six lines. Again, it was
even more sensational than the actuality: 'About 500,000 Kirghiz were
massacred, and something like a million fled into the confines of China
at the beginning of this year.' Reflecting over fifty years later on the

1916 revolt, Price thought it had demonstrated how the Russian empire 'was clearly cracking', though even for someone like him, on the spot in Russian Asia and also in Petrograd, the Russian revolution, when it occurred, still came as a great surprise.[14]

CHINA AND INDIA

The arrival of hundreds of thousands – if not perhaps as many as Philips Price's million – refugees from Semirechye into Sinkiang in western China between August and November 1916 demonstrates how almost nowhere, however remote, escaped the effects of the First World War. Harried by Russian forces, 'the difficult passes they encountered took a frightful toll of the large herds that they tried to drive with them'. The Chinese used the situation 'as an opportunity for expropriation on a colossal scale', and when surviving nomads began to straggle back to Turkestan from late November, 'those who finally reached home were literally almost naked'. The remaining refugees, also by now in a pitiable state, were repatriated in the spring of 1917. Their Russian prisoners, mostly women and children, similarly suffered terribly. Some were freed while crossing the Russo-Chinese frontier; others managed to escape and endeavoured to reach the Russian consulate in Kashgar.[15]

Reflecting on the 1916 rising a dozen or so years afterwards, Sir George Macartney, who had been British consul-general at Kashgar since the early 1890s, ascribed more agency to the Kyrgyz than had Philips Price. He asserted that they had been driven to breaking point by the Russian settlers and the oppressive tsarist regime. Taking advantage of the wartime reduction of the Russian garrison by drafts sent to the front, 'hordes of Kirghiz' had 'made a surprise attack on the Russians . . . plundered the Russian houses, and butchered every Russian man they saw'. They had carried off Russian women and children across the frontier, 'and then, with lightning speed, dispersed and lost themselves and their captives among the Chinese Kirghiz' in the Tien Shan mountains along the frontier. Writing in the late 1920s he remembered 'how later on a few Russian women, in rags and with shoes worn through, came into Kashgar, weary, emaciated, and diseased; they had been discarded by their captors, and had trudged on foot all the way from the mountains round about Uch Turfan, at last to find shelter in the Russian Consulate'.[16]

From the beginning of the war British representatives in far-flung places such as Kashgar had a watching brief to monitor the activities of enemy agents. Numbers of Turks and Germans passed through Sinkiang, prompting well-founded suspicions by Macartney and his Russian opposite number in Kashgar that the enemy was seeking to exploit pan-Islamic feeling against the Allies. One such agent was the German diplomat Werner Otto von Hentig who turned up in July 1916. Von Hentig was a Prussian career diplomat who had been an attaché in Beijing before the war and was an expert on Persia, where he had also served. In April 1915 he led a mission to Afghanistan, aiming to encourage anti-British elements there and in India. He was accompanied by a number of revolutionary Indian nationalists, including Mahendra Pratap, a left-leaning Rajput aristocrat, and Muhammad Barakatullah, a talented intellectual who had taught at universities in England, the USA and Japan. Barakatullah, indeed, had been one of the 'Indian seditionists' Sir John Jellicoe was undoubtedly thinking of when he had complained to Beatty in December 1916 about Japan's rather-too-accommodating attitude towards them. In 1915 a British report described him as embodying 'a sort of connecting link between three different movements, namely, the Pan-Islamic, Asian for the Asiatics, and the Indian sedition'.[17] For the British rulers of empire in Asia, a religio-nationalist-revolutionary combination like this was the stuff of their worst nightmares.

In fact, the power of Asian nationalism and pan-Islamism, for which Berlin had such high hopes, proved illusory. Although Barakatullah was named as prime minister of a 'Provisional Government of India' in exile in Kabul, in December 1915, there was little or no response in India to the calls for revolution. The Germans, too, failed to persuade the Emir of Afghanistan to enter the war on their side. A German effort to bring Persia into the war, moreover, also collapsed in late 1915 after the Russians threateningly moved forces into north Persia.[18] Frustrated in Afghanistan, von Hentig travelled north into Sinkiang, and stopped at Yarkland (120 miles from Kashgar), where his presence seriously rattled both Macartney and the Russian consul, Prince Mestchersky. In August a claim (which turned out to be false) from von Hentig that several hundred German troops had reached Afghanistan heightened their fears and they appealed to the Chinese authorities (who had their own worries about subversion among the predominantly Muslim population in Sinkiang) that he should be expelled. Reflecting the degree of hysteria, magnified by rumour, which the existence of von Hentig provoked, when he left Yarkland for Kashgar, accompanied by just three companions, the Chinese governor deployed all his forces to apprehend him, and later detained him with a hundred-strong guard. Macartney was eventually able to persuade the Chinese to send von Hentig on to Shanghai, from where, after stowing away on an American ship sailing to Honolulu and being interned in the USA, he eventually got back to Berlin. But the comic-opera over-reaction to the presence of a tiny German mission – as with other panicky suspicions about German-leaning Swedish missionaries in Kashgar, or the ominous arrival in September 1916 of two men claiming to be Norwegian mining engineers – reflects how acutely the British and Russian representatives feared the terrifying prospect of a Berlin-backed mass pan-Islamic rising against the Allied powers.[19]

Here, in central Asia, was a real-world replication of John Buchan's thriller, *Greenmantle*, first serialised in the monthly magazine, *Land and Water*, from the summer of 1916 and published in book form in October.[20] Buchan's fiction during the war was of a piece with his journalistic and propaganda work. Medically unfit for active service, he had been a war correspondent for *The Times* at the beginning of the war. For a time in mid-1916 he served on the intelligence staff of GHQ in France, and was appointed British Director of Information in February 1917. He set the novel in the context of near-contemporary events. Its hero, Richard Hannay (who had been the central character in Buchan's prewar bestseller, *The Thirty-Nine Steps*) is now a major in the British Army, recuperating in London having been wounded at the battle of Loos in September 1915. He is summoned to the Foreign Office where a senior official asks him to undertake a mission of the highest importance to discover and neutralise a German-inspired plan in the Middle East to galvanise the Muslim world and ignite a powerful 'Jehad' against the Allies. Islam, 'a fighting creed,' observes Hannay, 'is the only thing to knit up such a scattered empire'. And once such a 'hell' is let loose in the Ottoman Empire it may spread dangerously to Persia and India. Hannay and some old friends from his days prospecting and hunting in Southern Africa, along with an American, Blenkiron – a 'nootral' powerfully inclined towards the Allies – set off on an improbable escapade which takes them through enemy territory (Hannay, masquerading as a pro-German Boer, is at one point introduced to the Kaiser) to Constantinople and on east to the Turkish–Russian front in northeast Anatolia. Here they find a new prophet, 'Der Grüne Mantel' being groomed by a sinister and hypnotic German woman, Hilda von Einem, 'a devil, but she was also a queen'.

The main business of Hannay's adventure is the destruction of Greenmantle and von Einem's hideous scheme, and the novel comes to a climax in the Turco-Russian battlefield of the Caucasus in front of Erzerum. Out here Hannay, like his creator a deeply patriotic Anglo-Scot, felt lonely, 'fighting far away from my friends, far away from the true fronts of battle. It was a sideshow which, whatever its importance, had none of the exhilaration of the main effort.' It was, nevertheless, significant and titanic enough for the armies involved. In a neat subplot, Hannay steals German plans of Erzerum's defences, which he manages to communicate to the Russians, so enabling them to conquer the city (as they actually did in mid-February 1916).

The whole book is informed by Buchan's assumption that the war embodied a struggle between competing world systems, which could be mobilised for good by the Allies, or evil by the Germans – at the head of a 'monstrous bloody Juggernaut that was crushing the life out of the little heroic nations'. Buchan demonstrates in *Greenmantle* how a coalition of decent men – British, Afrikaner and American – could combine to defeat the enemy. Hannay and his colleagues, indeed, are so decent (as the *Times Literary Supplement* noted) that it never occurs to them 'even to consider the expediency of killing these dangerous national enemies [von Einem and company] when they were defenceless'. But Buchan's hero also realises 'the crazy folly of war' after being sheltered by a kindly German peasant woman in a remote south German forest. She was no 'Hun'. Hannay had 'thought we could never end the war properly without giving the Huns some of their own medicine', but now he realises that 'it was our business to thank God and keep our hands clean from the ugly blunders to which Germany's madness had driven her'.[21]

The loyalty of Muslim imperial subjects – Russian, French or British – was a constant concern for the Allies. In Russia the mufti of the state-controlled Orenburg Assembly, which had authority over most of the empire's Muslims, issued his own patriotic call for loyalty. 'The Russian state,' he proclaimed, 'is our fatherland, near and dear to our hearts, the hearts of Muslims, but also to the hearts of all peoples who live in it.' Over a million Muslims were mobilised in the Russian army, serving in mixed units against German, Habsburg and Ottoman forces. Mullahs were provided for chaplain duties, and although the tsar, Nicholas II, was himself devoted to the Orthodox Church, when visiting troops in 1914 'he visited mosques as well as Orthodox cathedrals to demonstrate his role as the "father" of a multiconfessional imperial family'.[22] When Montgomery Schuyler visited central Asia in the spring of 1916 he reported that at the beginning of the war the government had 'feared there might be trouble with the Mohemmedans on account of German propaganda carried on by active agents in Persia and the neighbouring countries against the cause of the Allies'. But it emerged that the local Muslims 'were fairly well contented with their lot and had no active desire for change'. His opinion on this was perhaps influenced by the Russian military authorities who had permitted his tour (and supplied a helpful officer to accompany him), but he ascribed it principally to the fact that in Turkestan the Russians' system of indirect rule allowed local communities 'very full liberty of local autonomy'. 'For ordinary business,' he asserted, there was 'practically no difference between the administration of the territory now and before the Russian rule'.[23] This happy situation (if, indeed, it obtained quite as unproblematically as Schuyler thought), of course, was precisely what was upset when the order for labour conscription was imposed in July 1916.

At the start of the war there were similar concerns in Britain about the loyalties of Muslims in British India. But, though sympathies were in some cases strained, the leaders (at least) of the Muslim community rallied behind the British war effort. On the outbreak of war the council of the Muslim League, the main communal representative body, passed a resolution of loyalty to the government, though some ulama – Islamic religious scholars and teachers – worked actively against the British. Nevertheless, concerns remained about the rank and file. Reviewing the position in March 1915, Sir Theodore Morison, an 'Old India Hand' and former principal of the Moslem College in Aligarh, warned that 'the Indian Moslems have a passionate sympathy for the Turks, and there is some danger that it may sweep all other considerations aside'. Muslim friends had told Morison 'that the anguish with which they see England attacking Turkey is the most terrible trial that they have experienced since the beginning of British rule in India'. Morison argued that the best outcome for Indian Muslims would be a separate peace settlement with Turkey, guaranteeing its territorial integrity and continuation as the 'bulwark of Islam'. A second-best would be the creation of a Muslim 'Arab kingdom' which, because Arabia itself was too poor and undeveloped even 'to maintain the civil and military administration of a fourth-rate power', would have to include not only Arabia but also Syria and Mesopotamia. 'These are the regions,' he asserted, 'in which European intrusion would be most keenly resented by Muhammedans everywhere,' but which comprised 'the very cradle of Islam and [were] intimately associated with the most glorious episodes in Moslem history'.[24]

While there was never any likelihood of a separate peace with Turkey, the British-sponsored Arab revolt from June 1916 specifically exploited local aspirations for an independent nation state. Although this further unsettled Muslim opinion in India, and while separatist Indian politicians such as Pratap and Barakatullah continued to work towards a nationalist revolution in India, during the war generally there was no fundamental challenge to British rule. India, indeed, continued to be the 'English barrack in the oriental seas' which Lord Salisbury had called it in the early 1880s.

From the start of the war the British-officered Indian Army had played an important role, supplying units for service on the Western Front, Egypt, East Africa and at the head of the Persian Gulf (initially to secure the Anglo-Persian Oil Company's installations in the region). During the war nearly 1.2 million Indians were recruited, in addition to the 240,000 troops already serving with the Indian Army. To this must be added money, equipment and supplies of war materials.[25] A celebratory account of 'India's contribution to the Great War', published in 1923, reported that between August 1914 and November 1918, 172,815 animals and 3,691,836 tons of stores had been despatched from Indian ports. The latter figure was illustrated with some striking statistics: 8,074,500 sand bags were supplied, 10,000,000 fathoms of cotton rope and 3,789,062 doses of cholera vaccine.[26] India's chief part was played in the Middle East. By the end of the war over half the troops in Mesopotamia (Iraq) were Indian and rather more than a third in Palestine. Throughout the war, too, India was exclusively responsible for providing all supplies and stores required by the troops, both British and Indian, in Mesopotamia.

It is often asserted that during the First World War India provided the largest volunteer army so far raised.[27] While technically this was true – conscription was not imposed in India – in practice, and, in common with the situation in other European colonies, where the enlistment of soldiers or labourers was often subcontracted to local agents and community leaders, the unforced readiness of individuals to join up was sometimes a little in question. As the demands for manpower increased through the war, so the recruiting methods became more interventionist and, in some cases, more coercive. Reflecting in 1920 on wartime recruiting, the secretary of state for India, Edwin Montagu, told his British Cabinet colleagues that Indian soldiers 'were persuaded, and to face the matter quite frankly, persuaded with great vigour, in certain places, particularly in the Punjab [where 136,000 Muslims had joined up], to join His Majesty's forces during the war'. Resentment in the Punjab, moreover, was also stimulated by the robust methods used to collect 'contributions' to war loans. In a review of wartime recruitment, Satyendra Dev Pradhan, drawing on an interview in 1972 with a Sikh veteran, delicately concluded that 'in the later period of the war, pressure was also applied to obtain recruits'. A more intensive recruiting system was introduced into the Punjab in

December 1916 (and later extended to other parts of India), using local civilian officials who were given enlistment quotas to meet and often resorted to 'threats and blandishments' to meet them. By 1918 the demands for recruits were so insistent that more draconian techniques were adopted, effectively amounting to press-gang methods in some places. In April 1918 the Punjab administration formally proposed introducing conscription, but the central government in Delhi vetoed the measure, fearing 'grave political consequences' and the possibility of widespread unrest.[28]

The Indian Army on the whole remained remarkably resilient, while individual soldiers and units faced the many challenges of modern, industrial war. An Indian Army corps of two infantry and two cavalry divisions was sent to the Western Front in September 1914 and spent a miserable (and costly) year there before the infantry were moved to the Middle East. The cavalry divisions, however, remained in France, where they served continuously until March 1918.

Evidence from mail-censorship reports reveals some of the unsettling circumstances Indian soldiers had to endure. In March 1916 a vegetarian Jat in a hospital in England complained that 'here they cook meat for both Hindus and Mahommedans in the same kitchen. And the men who cook the meat make my chapatties.' A Hindustani Hindu in Egypt accepted that he and fellow Hindus had to eat food even 'from the hands of sweepers' that they would have rejected at home. 'Had we not done so,' he remarked, 'there would have been no alternative but starvation.' In July, a Sikh cavalryman reported that in Paris he had often 'eaten food and drunk tea prepared by Musalmans', phlegmatically (and perhaps a little over-confidently) concluding that 'if you look at the condition of things in this country you cannot but see that all men here are considered equal in the sight of God'. But some soldiers stuck firmly to traditional practices. Despite the obvious dangers, it seems that many Sikhs refused to wear steel helmets, 'declining to give up their hallowed turban'. In June 1916 a Hindustani Muslim reported that French-style steel helmets had been issued to all regiments. 'The Sikhs,' he wrote, 'decline to wear them but the [Hindu] Jats and [the] Muslims are thinking over the matter.' By March 1917 helmet-wearing had generally been adopted. A Pathan cavalryman said a helmet provided good protection and suited 'robust-looking men very well, and is not unbecoming in the case of men with long hair . . . Uncle Jahan Khan,' he added, 'who is both fair and robust, looks splendid in a helmet and cannot be distinguished from a European at a distance.'[29]

The most worrying manifestation of Indian subversion was not in India itself, but in Singapore, where in February 1915 a badly led Indian regiment, the 5th Native Light Infantry, mutinied. The soldiers had been unsettled by the prospect of having to fight against fellow Muslims in the Middle East and the assurance from some interned German sailors they had been guarding that 'the English' were losing the war. On 15 February, while the colony was on holiday for the Chinese New Year, some 400 mutineers armed themselves and began attacking European officers and civilians. The outbreak lasted less than a week, during which over thirty people were killed. A combination of regular troops, British, Malay and Chinese volunteers, assisted by Russian, Japanese and French marines from visiting warships, restored order, after which forty-eight mutineers were executed mostly by firing squad. In one instance, twenty-two were shot in public at one time. The remnants of the 5th Light Infantry were deployed to Africa where they participated in the Cameroons campaign and served in German East Africa during 1916.[30]

Although officially neutral until August 1917 (and despite a chaotic domestic political situation), from autumn 1914 Chinese leaders sought to extract such advantage as they could from the conflict. The revolutionary democrat Sun Yat-sen saw the war as an opportunity for China while European powers were pre-occupied elsewhere. 'Europe will not have time to bother about the East . . . ,' he wrote. 'This is our chance to rise up and make our stand.' In August 1914, President Yuan Shikai offered 50,000 Chinese troops to the British minister in Beijing, the Ulsterman and Queen's Belfast graduate Sir John Jordan, to help conquer the German enclave at Tsingtao (Qingdao), but Jordan turned the offer down flat. In his study of China and the Great War, Xu Guoqi describes Yuan's sketchily documented offer as 'China's first offer to join the war', but it is safer to see it not so much as abandoning the neutrality China declared on 6 August 1914, as a national desire to participate in expelling the Germans from Chinese territory and ensure that Tsingtao was restored to China. Leaving the matter to the Japanese and the British would undermine China's own international status. The Japanese, themselves keen to seize any opportunity of expanding their influence on the Asian mainland, certainly opposed Chinese participation. Indeed, they only reluctantly accepted even British involvement in the operation. Jordan's rebuff, which deeply offended the Chinese, abundantly demonstrated how irrelevant the Great Powers involved in the war regarded any role China might play, and thus further reinforced the desire of Chinese leaders to exploit the war to enhance China's international status.[31]

The Japanese, of course, had very similar ambitions and in 1914–15 were themselves determined to take advantage of the wartime situation at China's expense. In January 1915 they presented 'the infamous Twenty-one Demands' (Xu Guoqi's words) to the Chinese government, which were aimed at reducing China to the status of a Japanese vassal state by consolidating existing Japanese influence in Shandung and Manchuria, and enforcing the appointment of Japanese 'advisers' to Chinese government departments and the police. Although disturbed by the severity of the demands, Britain and France could do little to help and on 9 May – 'a day of national shame' – China had in effect to comply. This public national humiliation, however, provoked a wide national reflection about China's position in the world and further reinforced the desire of Chinese leaders to use the wartime situation to national advantage. With broad agreement that China should join the war (if only to secure a seat at the peace conference when some of the Sino-Japanese issues might be up for discussion), there was some debate over which side, though the balance of advantage was always more with the Allies than the Germans. In November 1915 the Chinese formally told Britain that they were prepared to join the Allies if they were invited to do so by Britain, France and Russia, but the Japanese objected on the transparently specious grounds (among other things) that this might 'bring China to a state of disorder and devastation'. In February 1916, Sir John Jordan reported to London that China was 'willing to join with the Entente provided that

Japan and the other Allies accepted her as a partner on a footing of at least national equality', which was precisely what the Japanese refused to do.[32]

Faced with this Japanese veto, Liang Shiyi, one of President Yuan's closest advisers, devised a policy called 'yigong daibing' (using labourers as soldiers), through which China could begin to take part in the war (and, by extension, participate in the international system) by offering to supply non-combatant personnel for service with the belligerent powers. It was rather like the position taken by Ze'ev Jabotinsky and his associates with the Zion Mule Corps which served at Gallipoli. While not quite full participation, it was a plausible means to a clear and desirable political end. Although Liang first sounded out the British in mid-1915 about the possibility of their recruiting Chinese labourers, it was a year before anything much happened.

By the beginning of 1916 the British were beginning to experience serious manpower shortages both for the army and domestic war work. One policy response in Great Britain was the introduction of conscription in January. The great Somme offensive from the beginning of July further exacerbated the situation, and in August, Lloyd George, recently made British war minister after Lord Kitchener had died on his way to Russia, agreed that Chinese labour could be used in France and other places so that British men could be released for work at home in agriculture or the munitions industry. A recruiting organisation was formed and in November 1916, Thomas J. Bourne, a railway engineer with long experience in Asia, arrived at the British possession of Wei Hai Wei in north-east China. Canton, near Hong Kong, had been considered as a recruitment base, but, rather as the inhabitants of northern India were regarded as better soldiers than men from the hotter south (where the enervating climate was supposed to produce torpid and jaded people), it was decided that men from northern China would make the best workers. Recruitment began slowly, but by the end of 1917, 35,000 men had gone to Europe, and by the end of the war some 100,000 men had been raised by the British.[33]

Smaller numbers of labourers – though this is only in comparative terms as there were 40,000 of them – were recruited by the French from January 1916. In order to run the scheme at the Chinese end, but also preserve the fiction of Chinese neutrality, an ostensibly private concern, the Huimin Company, was formed by a director of the Chinese Industrial Bank and Liang Shiyi. They dealt with Georges Trupil, a retired French army colonel, who arrived in Beijing with cover as a private businessman, but was actually an official representative of the French government. This private enterprise cover enabled the Chinese authorities to dismiss the reasonable complaints of the German legation in Beijing that, by releasing French (and British) men for more military duties, the scheme violated Chinese neutrality. French-recruited labourers began to arrive in Europe in August 1916. Most of the workers – both French and British – were taken by ship across to Pacific to Canada, overland to Halifax, and thence by ship to Europe. This was hazardous enough. Xu Guoqi has calculated that at least 700 men lost their lives before they even got to France, mostly in ships sunk by German submarines.[34]

As with other non-European workers, the Chinese were carefully supervised when they reached Europe, though this differed as to whether they were under French or British control. Those recruited by the French were better treated and paid, and (according to Xu Guoqi) 'racism was less pronounced in the French camps'. An American report in 1918 on the Chinese workers concluded that 'in the British service they are under strict discipline, but under the French are very free, practically having no restrictions placed upon them out of working hours'. Both the British and French, however, subjected the workers to military regulation; the men wore uniforms; and they were generally accommodated in barracks. They performed a wide range of work, from dock labour, factory work, road-mending and general infrastructure repairs, to handling munitions. The Chinese were reportedly more suited to working in the battle zone than some other nationalities, and though the British had promised that they should not take part in military operations, many were used close to the front line and often came under shellfire or enemy air attack. There are no reliable figures for Chinese casualties, but Xu Guoqi estimates that 'around 3,000 Chinese lost their lives in Europe or on their way there due to enemy fire, disease or injury'.[35] Nearly 2,000 members of the Chinese Labour Corps are commemorated in Commonwealth War Graves Commission cemeteries in France (1,864), Belgium (85) and England (20). Although commemorated by name, and with their

unit numbers, nothing else is known of these men, such as their next of
kin, or even their ages.[36]

China was not the only source of non-European labour behind the
Western Front. By the end of the war, the British Labour Directorate
alone had nearly 200,000 labourers on its books, comprising almost
96,000 Chinese; 48,000 Indians; 22,000 South Africans, and smaller
numbers of Egyptians, West Indians, Maltese and other nationalities.[37]
A perennial concern of both metropolitan and colonial administrators was the potentially unsettling effect military or labour service
abroad might have on the individuals concerned. In May 1916 the
French postal censor in Marseilles cited the concerns of a Frenchman
in Tonkin about the recruitment of 'Annamite volunteers'. He thought
that 'nothing good' would result from this. It would 'eventually create
malcontents and revolutionaries, as well as the upsetting of our beautiful colony. They will no longer feel like planting rice in their fields
after they have seen in France a number of things that one must not
let them see or hear.' Among the dangerously subversive sights in
France was that of white women in inferior situations, quite unlike
anything encountered overseas. 'Would you believe that white
women,' wrote a Malagasy worker in Toulouse, 'who at home love to
have us serve them, here work as much as men. They are very numerous in the workshops and labour with the same ardour as men.' There
was also the danger of colonial workers getting 'above themselves'. In
August 1916 a French official in the Dordogne was disturbed to see
Indochinese workers drinking together with French colleagues in
local bars, raising the disturbing prospect that they might become
infected with democratic European attitudes and levels of labour
activism.[38]

MESOPOTAMIA AND THE CAUCASUS

The deployment of British and Indian forces at the head of the Persian
Gulf in the autumn of 1914 developed into the Indian Army's single
largest commitment.[39] Basra had been occupied on 25 November 1914
and Qurna, at the confluence of the Tigris and Euphrates rivers, a
fortnight later. In a classic case of mission creep (or what Cyril Falls

called 'the insidious policy of another step forward'[40]), the comparative ease with which the expeditionary force had established itself
encouraged both the local commanders and their masters in India to
contemplate greater conquests in the region. In April 1915 a 9,000-
strong column was sent from Basra to Ahwaz in Persia to secure the
eighty-mile pipeline from the oil wells to Abadan on the Gulf. At the
end of May the 6th Indian Division (comprising 3,500 British and
8,600 Indian soldiers), under the command of Major General Charles
Townshend, began to push north up the Tigris from Qurna towards
Amara, which fell on 3 June. A third column advanced up the
Euphrates and against stiff opposition in stifling heat captured
Nasiriyeh on 25 July, thus establishing British control over the whole
Basrah vilayet (province).

Over the summer the Viceroy in India proposed 'as a matter of strategic necessity' an advance to Kut-el-Amara (Al-Kūt), 120 miles
further north on the Tigris. Townshend, after a break in India to
recover from fever and diarrhoea (which was becoming endemic in the
command), was again put in charge. Again he reached his objective –
this time with a deft use of deception – and defeated the Turks just
short of Kut, capturing the town on 28 September. This victory raised
spirits in India and Whitehall. By the autumn of 1915 any success
against the Turks was most welcome, especially since the Gallipoli
campaign had effectively ground to a halt. The momentum of the
offensive raised the heady prospect of a further advance on Baghdad,
another hundred miles upstream, the capture of which would be a
striking success and help restore British prestige in the East. Despite
Townshend's own misgivings about inadequate resources and stretching supply lines, he pushed on to Aziziyah, about halfway between
Kut and Baghdad. Pressed, if a little cautiously, by London and more
vigorously by the ambitious overall commander in Mesopotamia, Sir
John Nixon, Townshend, after a pause for resupply, was prevailed
upon to advance upstream. He got as far as Ctesiphon, twenty miles
short of Baghdad, where his force was soundly beaten off by well-
dug-in Turkish troops. Townshend withdrew back to Kut, where,
expecting to be reinforced and with sufficient food supplies for two
months, he dug his force in to hold off the advancing Turks.

The siege of Kut which followed (and lasted from 7 December 1915 until 29 April 1916 when Townshend surrendered) was one of the great set-pieces of the war in the Middle East. Townshend had something over 3,000 British and 8,000 Indian troops under his command, along with 3,500 non-combatant Indian camp followers, including labourers, cooks and orderlies. There was also the town population of about 6,000 Arab civilians. Some of the Indian units were under strength, and at Ctesiphon the Turks had inflicted heavy casualties on the officers of the division. Of 317 British officers, 131 were killed, wounded or missing; and of 255 Indian officers the equivalent figure was 111.[41] This aggravated a general problem suffered by the Indian Army during the war. With battlefield attrition the prewar cadre of experienced officers was a wasting asset. Replacements, however enthusiastic, frequently lacked the expertise or linguistic skills required to command non-European units effectively, a factor compounded by casualties among the precious subaltern Indian officers who provided the crucial link with the rank and file. This, in turn, had an impact on morale, which suffered increasingly as the siege continued.

British commanders in Mesopotamia (as elsewhere) worried about straining the loyalties of Indian troops. In February 1916 over 400 men of the Muslim 15th Lancers refused to march from Basra to the Tigris front on account of their 'very strong religious scruples against fighting in the vicinity of the holy places of Baghdad and Kerbela'. In his study of the Indian Army, David Omissi argues that the issue was purely religious and there was no 'broader political content'. The men accepted their oath of allegiance, but pleaded that 'they were willing to fight any enemy, including Arabs or Turks, in any other place except Arabistan, which they considered from their religion as holy ground'.[42] Similar religio-cultural factors affected the troops at Kut, where food shortages became acute and the lack of fresh vegetables and ready supplies of protein seriously undermined the men's health. By the end of January stocks of fresh and preserved meat had been virtually exhausted and the garrison began to consume its pack animals. British troops, albeit reluctantly at first, survived on rations of horsemeat, which the great majority of Indians refused to eat. Believing that the

Indian Mutiny (or Rebellion) of 1857 had been sparked off in part at least by breaking food taboos, Townshend was at first reluctant to compel his Indian soldiers to take horsemeat. By the time he did so (in April 1916, when barley, the principal available grain, was rationed to seven ounces daily per head), the men were nearly past helping. Indeed many were so weak that they could not digest meat.[43]

While Townshend's force fought off a couple of Turkish assaults in December 1915, British efforts to break the siege with a relief column from Basra – the last in early April 1916 – came tantalisingly close to success but the Turks held them off. Why were the Ottoman forces, who had generally proved such feeble opponents up to the end of 1915, so much more formidable in 1916? Partly it was the result of a change in their ethnic composition. The core fighting strength of the Ottoman army was composed of Anatolian Turks, who (as at Gallipoli) proved to be tough and resolute soldiers, fiercely loyal to their Turkish officers. At the start of the war the majority of the Ottoman forces in Mesopotamia were composed of reluctant Arab levies, haphazardly trained and badly led, who proved a poor match for the Anglo-Indian forces set against them. For much of 1915 the Ottomans were fully engaged fighting the Russians in north-east Anatolia and, from April, the British and French at Gallipoli, but towards the end of 1915 they were able to move more Turkish units to the Mesopotamian theatre. In December 1915 the veteran German general Colmar von der Golz, who had been an adviser to the Ottoman army before the war, was put in command of the Turkish Sixth Army in place of the allegedly more timid Nurettin Paşa. In 1916, moreover, the Allied withdrawal from Gallipoli released Ottoman troops for service elsewhere. Golz, who died of cholera on 19 April, in fact left the day-to-day command at Kut to Colonel Halil Bey who held steady until Townshend's force was starved into submission. Lord Kitchener considered that Townshend's surrender at Kut on 29 April 1916 was a catastrophe to be compared with the British capitulation at Yorktown in 1781. By contrast, and especially following their victory at Gallipoli, it was (in Edward Erickson's words) 'a magnificent achievement for Turkish arms'.[44]

During the siege there were tantalising reports of Russian advances in Persia, which it was hoped might divert Turkish forces away from

Kut. With a weak central government and inadequate military forces of its own, Persia was fair game for the belligerent powers, as the British had demonstrated when occupying Abadan in 1914. In December 1914 the Turks had ambitiously invaded Persian Azerbaijan with an under-strength division, hoping to turn the Russian flank and encourage rebellion among the Turkic peoples in Russian-ruled Caucasia. They were expelled by a Russian force which invaded Persia in turn, aiming particularly to suppress the activities of Turco-German agents who were believed to be trying to bring Persia into the war. By the end of 1915 the Russians had occupied much of north-east Persia, and in March 1916 reached Karind, 130 miles from Baghdad, where they stayed put to gather strength before a further advance in June towards Khanikin on the frontier with Mesopotamia. They were never really in a position to help the British at Kut, but, even after it had fallen, observers in London nursed hopes that Russian and Anglo-Indian forces could link up against the Turks. In May 1916 an intrepid patrol of over a hundred Russian Cossacks, having travelled 200 miles through mountainous territory, reached the British garrison at Ali Gharbi, sixty-five miles downstream from Kut.

This caused great excitement in England. 'Russians Win Through to British in Tigris', trumpeted a full-page headline in the *Daily Mirror*. The Russians remained in Mesopotamia for a fortnight, during which King George V ordered that each of their officers should be awarded the Military Cross, 'in recognition of this exploit and [recalling Anglo-Russian endeavours in the wars against Napoleon] of this the first meeting of British and Russian troops, as allies in the field, for one hundred years'. But the possibilities of any significant joint Anglo-Russian operations in the theatre were more apparent to amateur strategists working with small-scale maps in London than to the troops on the ground. After the fall of Kut the Turks were able to concentrate their forces and when the Russians did advance they were sharply repulsed and forced to retreat beyond Hamadan, halfway to Teheran. With the contending forces mostly living off the land, the local Persian population suffered terribly, by one account leaving the region 'utterly desolate' at the end of 1916.[45]

The Turks were not able to capitalise much on their success at Kut, as they were hard-pressed by the Russians in the Caucasus. The war on this front had begun well for the Russians who consolidated their position in 1915.[46] In January 1916 the Russian commander, Nikolai Yudenitch, launched a major offensive which carried his forces deep into Turkey. Erzurum fell on 16 February and the important Black Sea port of Trebizond (Trabzon) on 18 April. On 27 July, Yudenitch took Erzincan, described by Cyril Falls then as an 'ancient and beautiful little city' (but no longer so having been rebuilt following an earthquake in 1939),[47] destroying the Ottoman Third Army in the process. The Ottoman Second Army responded in August with an offensive on the southern end of the front. In one sector a corps strengthened with Gallipoli veterans and led by Mustafa Kemal had some success, but little was achieved overall and the defeat cost the Ottomans 30,000 killed and wounded out of a total effective strength approaching 100,000 men. The historians of Caucasian battles, William Allen and Paul Muratoff, likened the Turkish strategy here to that of the French general Nivelle in the Aisne offensive in the spring of 1917 (though the point could be expanded to many other battles on the Western Front). 'In both cases,' they wrote, 'there was the same underlying lack of elasticity in the planning of a big offensive, and the same blind lack of imagination in the infinite capacity of the staffs concerned to ignore the known difficulties in front of them.' As was unfortunately so often the case, moreover, the decisions of the generals (on whatever front) resulted in the launching of 'a desperate and hopeless adventure'.[48]

A tragic by-product of this local war in Caucasia was the vicious treatment of the Armenian population by the Ottomans. Here, as in other places, the war provided opportunities for both the contending powers and oppressed national minorities to exploit the possibilities of nationalism. Ethnic and religious tensions were exacerbated everywhere and from early in the war localised communal violence broke out in many places. For Armenian nationalists the Ottoman Empire's extremity was Armenia's opportunity. Many young Armenian men fled to Russia where they were welcomed into the army. With nationalist aspirations being encouraged by the Russians, moreover, the authorities in Constantinople readily came to regard the Armenians as a whole with the deepest of suspicions. What apparently began with a radical plan forcibly to remove the Armenian population to camps in Mesopotamia and Syria turned into widespread massacres and violent displacement. 'At the beginning of 1915,' reported *The Times* in July 1916, 'the Ottoman Armenians numbered more than 2,000,000. By the end of the year, two-thirds of their number had either been massacred in their native towns and villages or "deported" to destinations which more than half of them never reached.'[49] As during the wider war itself, the extent of the violence seems utterly out of proportion to the issues at stake, though the Turkish participants themselves quite evidently believed that the killings, expropriations and expulsions were fully justified.

Allen and Muratoff calculate that the Ottomans lost some 400,000 troops (half the total strength of the army) between November 1915 and March 1917. Three-quarters of these casualties (which include prisoners and losses from epidemics and desertion) occurred in operations against the Russians. The result was that, even though the Russians dropped out of the war in 1917, Ottoman strength was so reduced that they were unable very effectively to resist the renewed British offensives of 1917 and 1918.[50] Despite the reverse of Kut, therefore, 1916 proved a turning point for the British. By the end of the year sufficient manpower, organisation, leadership and supplies were being put in place which would sustain an almost continuous advance for the rest of the war. Baghdad was captured in March 1917, and while the main effort in 1917–18 was focused on Palestine, by late 1918 Mosul had been occupied and a bewildering collection of semi-independent British and Indian forces had pushed forward from Mesopotamia to carry British control into North Persia, Transcaspia and the Caucasus, in the long term (though as it turned out vain) hope of permanently securing British interests in the Middle East, central Asia and India.[51]

A 'CRISIS OF IMPERIAL GLOBALISATION'?

Tim Harper has argued that 'the Asian aspect of the 1914–18 War was a struggle for the intertwined futures of the imperial regimes that spanned the continent: Russia, the Ottomans, the Qing, and the great arc of the British Raj from Cairo to Kowloon'. The war provoked 'a crisis of imperial globalisation', for the first time raising among European rulers across Asia general anxieties about the long-term resilience of their colonial rule. The apparently insatiable needs of total war made unprecedented demands on colonial societies and economies; administrations became more interventionist, stretching the loyalties of imperial subjects further than ever before. At the same time many Europeans volunteered to serve in the war and returned home. In Malaya, for example, a fifth of the colonial civil servants departed, leaving their remaining colleagues to pick up the slack, but the 'resultant overstretch exposed the underlying vulnerabilities of the system'.[52]

There was a similar situation even in the neutral Dutch East Indies, where war-magnified rumours helped encourage anti-Dutch nationalist elements. The withdrawal of Dutch troops from the Celebes for the defence of Java at the beginning of the war prompted a rumour that the Dutch were going to abandon the island altogether. In August 1916 anti-Dutch violence broke out across Sumatra. In Jambi it was sustained by a story circulating through the Muslim population that the Turks had recognised the rebellion and were sending troops to assist. There was also widespread opposition in Java to the raising of a conscript native militia, which the Dutch administration had proposed in order to bolster the colony's defence in the hazardous wartime circumstances. By 1916, moreover, export restrictions imposed by the Allied blockade had caused social and economic distress through sharp falls in the prices of tropical products, such as coffee, rubber and tobacco, on which the colony's economy depended. Wartime circumstances paradoxically both isolated and integrated the Dutch East Indies to the wider world. The Allied blockade and the restriction of all sorts of communications cut the colony off from the metropolitan Netherlands, undermined the economy and left the local colonial administration to cope as best it could. But it was faced with an increasingly restless population, in which political and social grievances were progressively intensified by the imposition of wartime regulation and sustained by the generally unsettling sense of revolutionary potential and change which the war provoked.[53]

The circumstances of the war and the rhetoric (on both sides) of national rights, freedom and even democracy, raised expectations and provided opportunities for nationalists across Asia, as elsewhere. One manifestation of the unsettled times was the uprisings and revolts which occurred in places as far distant as central Asia, Indochina and Singapore. For Edward Sokol the 1916 revolt in Turkestan was a harbinger of what was to come. It affected 'in one form or another the 11 million native peoples of Russian Central Asia and sounded the first rumble of the oncoming disaster' of the February and October 1917 revolutions. 'The Revolt of 1916,' he wrote, was both 'the prelude to the Revolution in Russia proper' and a 'catalytic agent' which hastened the alignment of forces in the region, committing people more definitely 'to one camp or another than would have been the case had no revolt occurred'.[54]

A propaganda piece by an old China hand, Edward Manico Gull, musing on the provision of Chinese labour for the Western Front and published in 1918, asserted that the 'emigration from the shores of Shantung' would 'take its place in history certainly as one of the most picturesque and interesting, possibly as one of the most important aspects of the great European War. For never before has the East provided the West with manpower on anything approaching the same elaborate scale.'[55] Allowing for a touch of hyperbole, and Gull's evident exclusion of manpower from both British India as coming from 'the East' (or perhaps he thought that predominantly military recruits were something different) and French Indochina, the raising and deployment in Europe and the Middle East of hundreds of thousands of men from Asia to support European military endeavours, in both combatant and non-combatant roles, is a further illustration of the First World War's extraordinary global reach. That tens of thousands of them died in the process adds a tragic dimension to the whole affair and left unnumbered families in Asia bereaved and mourning for sons, husbands and fathers caught up in what for many of them was a completely inexplicable catastrophe.

8

The War in Africa

Africa was pitched into the First World War not so much for its own sake but as a consequence of the imperial control which European powers exercised over much of the continent. In 1914–18, as for most of the nineteenth century, Africa was, at one level, merely a location where the European rivalries and global ambitions of the so-called Great Powers were played out, albeit invariably at the cost of indigenous African liberties and indigenous African lives. By 1914 the partition of Africa had left only two independent states: Ethiopia and Liberia; the rest of the continent had been divided out between the European powers of France, Britain, Portugal, Belgium, Germany, Italy and Spain. In North Africa, the Ottoman Empire retained nominal sovereignty over Egypt. During the war the imperial rivalries of the nineteenth century were revived. There was fighting in Africa the whole way through the war, from August 1914 until November 1918, and, wearing what Brian Digre has called 'imperialism's new clothes', the victorious Great Powers secured the 'repartition of tropical Africa', carving up the former German colonies between them.[1]

The forces released by the war simultaneously stiffened imperial rule in Africa (and Asia) and provoked resistance among indigenous peoples. Viewed globally, as John Iliffe, the historian of Tanganyika (Tanzania), has observed, 'the First World War was both the culmination of European imperialism and the beginning of its decline'. In order to secure victory, 'colonial powers tightened control over subject peoples and increased demands upon them', but 'at the same time the demands and opportunities of war stimulated political awareness and organisation amongst subject peoples'.[2]

Morogoro

During the afternoon of Saturday 26 August 1916 the 2nd Rhodesia Regiment (raised from white settlers in what is now Zimbabwe) and two companies of an Indian unit, the 130th Baluchi Regiment, captured the town of Morogoro in central German East Africa. General Jan Smuts, the British commander-in-chief in East Africa, along with his general headquarters, arrived the next day. Morogoro, which had been the German colonial seat of government since December 1914 (when it had moved from the vulnerable coastal city of Dar es Salaam) and was on the central railway line from the coast to Kigoma on Lake Tanganyika, was an important conquest. 'Mrogoro [*sic*],' announced *The Times* on 4 September, '"the great boma [enclosure]," as the captured Askaris call it, the strong-hold in which Colonel von Lettow-Vorbeck, the commander of the German troops in the Colony, was to have fought to a finish for the last remnant of Germany's Colonial Empire, is in our hands.' Citing a report from Reuters news agency, *The Times* described Morogoro as 'a town of splendid avenues, squalid buildings, and long, shadowy streets, over-arched with flamboyant jacaranda, pine, plane, and palm. The German women and children [there was no mention of any non-white inhabitants], descending fearfully from their lofty refuges in the [surrounding] mountains, were pleasantly surprised by the cheerful courtesy of the British and Indian soldiers and the perfect discipline of the troops.'[3]

Others were less impressed with the place. Bertie Cranworth, a Trinity Cambridge man who had spent some time farming in Kenya in the early 1900s and who was serving with an artillery unit, thought it 'really an insignificant little town', but as it was the first town they had seen 'for three hundred miles', they found it 'most exciting'. Approaching Morogoro it was clear that the Germans were trying to make the railway unusable. In his breezy memoirs written in the late 1930s Cranworth recollected lying in the pouring rain some six miles short of the town where they 'heard the crashes and saw the flames as the Germans ran their engines and rolling stock from both sides of a destroyed bridge over a deep gorge'. John Crowe, the British artillery commander, who rode in with Smuts, found signs everywhere of the 'haste with which the enemy had retired'. The station store houses were still burning and 'at the goods station the platforms were deep in coffee, which they had not had time to destroy, and which hundreds of native women were now carrying off in baskets and sacks'. Large sections of the railway track had been destroyed, though a sizeable community of Indians (mostly from the Punjab), brought in by the Germans to work on the railway, were left behind. 'They were delighted at our arrival,' wrote Crowe, 'or at all events professed to be.'⁴

Cranworth described the town as consisting of 'a few decent bungalows, a barracks and the old Government house'. Here he came across what he called 'a curious side of German mentality, local, I trust. The troops had left under pressure in a great hurry, but they had had time to issue the evacuation orders [sic] and on every piece of furniture was laid an exhibit of human excreta.' Cranworth thought that 'this example of frightfulness apparently pleased them', but it 'certainly didn't hurt us', yet struck him 'as a curious example of Kultur'. This, it seems, was one of the 'many proofs of the precipitate flight and demoralised condition of the enemy forces' which Smuts in his official report of operations said he found at the town.⁵

On 29 August, Sergeant Dan Fewster, an English gunner whose unit had left Britain in February 1916, reached Morogoro, 'the largest town we have struck since leaving Mombasa' (where they had landed in Kenya five months before). In his diary he noted the wide, tree-lined streets. 'The shops and bazaars are mostly kept by Indians,' he wrote, 'though there seems to be a good number of Greeks and Portuguese about.' In the main square he found a large crowd had gathered: 'It appears that a native had been caught looting. He had been condemned to death and after having dug his own grave, he had been brought here to be shot.' The provost marshal 'had his crime and sentence read out in the English, German, Dutch and native languages. The firing party was selected from a battalion of the King's African Rifles. The culprit stood against a wall. After the volley was fired, he stood long enough for me to think that the whole party had missed him. Then his knees crumpled and he slowly collapsed. I thought this rather peculiar. I had seen men hit but if it was serious they went down in a hurry. Apparently it is not so in all cases.'

The British forces' own looting was a different matter. With no apparent irony, immediately following his account of this execution, Fewster went on to record that South African drivers attached to his unit 'had "found" a great heap of German tobacco, sufficient to fill a Ford car. This was a godsend to us, for we have had no tobacco for weeks...' Embodying, too, a different sense of British moral superiority, Fewster described the treatment of the (white) civilian population of the town. 'The German ladies are walking about as if nothing has happened,' he wrote. 'No one molests them in any way. I think this speaks volumes for the good conduct of our troops, considering we had not seen a white woman for nearly four months. But of course, ours is not German "Kultur".'6

The British established their own headquarters at Morogoro and settled down to replace German municipal discipline with a more relaxed (or so they imagined) British regime. Commandeering a printing press left undamaged by the retreating Germans, an enterprising team based of Rhodesians started up the first English-language newspaper in German East Africa, the *Morogoro News*. Although short-lived – it survived for only five editions – it combined local and war news with more light-hearted articles of a sort which would have been familiar to readers of the 'trench newspapers' which were popular on the Western Front. The war news, which covered the battles of the Somme and Verdun, the Russian front, the 'Allies in the Balkans', Italy and 'Roumania and the War', reminded readers in their East African fastness that they were part of a worldwide enterprise. An article on 'The occupation of Morogoro' took an unusually long historical perspective, beginning with the Fall of Troy and asserting that in general 'blood, fire, and rapine, have followed the fall of conquered cities'. Anticipating such a fate, many of the German inhabitants of Morogoro had fled to the surrounding hills, only, happily, to return when 'in fact the defeated were treated much in the same spirit as the unsuccessful opponents in a football or cricket match . . . In place of the bullying swagger of the German Military caste, the deferential courtesy of British Officers, commissioned and otherwise, is too good to be realised.'

The last page (of four) of the newspaper's first edition carried the jokes, though the humour was ponderous enough, such as 'Notice: The valuable shooting rights in the Morogoro district are now To Let . . . The late tenant, Herr Hun, had excellent sport during the last season and reports having bagged many brace of snipe(rs), also a number of bulls of the "John" variety.' There was also a short piece about 'Private Stiggins', serving in East Africa but dreaming of home, assuming 'the war couldn't last for ever' and thinking of 'the missus and the kids and the money they'd saved'. Mrs Siggins, meanwhile, 'was at this moment imbibing her tenth gin in a not very fashionable pub in Hoxton [East London]' and 'wondering if an ounce more separation allowance could be squeezed out of her husband, and if the new baby would resemble him sufficiently to prevent the neighbours talking'.[7]

The circumstances of the capture of Morogoro were typical of the East African campaign. Afterwards the British put a brave face on it, unambiguously claiming it as a victory. Lieutenant Commander William Whittall, who commanded a Royal Naval Air Service company of Rolls-Royce armoured cars in both the South-West and East African campaigns, said that 'it had been confidently expected that the foe would make a really determined stand at Morogoro . . . But once more, by prompt resort to wide turning movements, the Germans were hustled out.'[8] Whittall's account, first published in 1917, was one of sustained British advance and continuous German retreat. The reality was more complex. To be sure, the Germans were on the run, but deftly managing to evade British attempts to pin them down, they provided troublesome opposition to greatly superior forces until the very end of the war.

The troops which occupied Morogoro exemplified the range of British imperial (and other) troops involved in the theatre. Reflecting on the East African campaign as a whole, Bertie Cranworth thought that one of the factors working to the Germans' advantage was their unity of command as against the spectacularly varied nature of the Allied forces. 'Possibly no more heterogeneous forces ever took the field,' he thought; 'drawn from all quarters of the globe, speaking different languages, eating different food, fighting in different fashions and under different commands.' Listing 'a few of the nationalities that our troops consisted of', he managed: 'British regulars and irregulars; African troops from Kenya, Uganda, Nyasaland, the Gold Coast [now Ghana], Nigeria and the Belgian Congo; British, Dutch and Cape "boys" [mixed-race Cape Colony Coloured troops] from South Africa; Rhodesians, Belgians, Indians of many tribes and races, regular and irregular, West Indians and Portuguese.'[9] Volunteers from the British Caribbean territories were perhaps among the most unusual of these. In July 1916 a draft of 500 officers and men from the first three battalions of the British West India Regiment, which had been posted to Egypt, was sent to join the East African Expeditionary Force, ostensibly on the grounds that they would be better able to survive the tropical climate than white troops. Although mostly relegated to labouring duties (as were detachments in France as well as Egypt), Richard Smith concludes that when they were 'deployed in the front line they performed as well as other units in the British Army'.[10]

THE CONQUEST OF GERMAN COLONIES

When Germany went to war in August 1914, so, in effect, did its four African colonies of Togoland, the Cameroons, German South-West Africa and German East Africa. This was a boon for France and Britain (and subsequently for Belgium, if not Portugal too) since it raised the attractive possibility of eliminating the German colonial presence in the continent and themselves acquiring some additional territory. Indeed, in Africa as elsewhere, the war, as Jack Gallagher remarks, provided 'a vast bargain basement for empire builders'.[11] Tiny Togoland, sandwiched precariously between the British Gold Coast and the French possession of Dahomey, was never going to survive for very long. By 12 August, Lome, the capital of the German colony, had been occupied by two companies (fewer than 500 men) of the locally raised British Gold Coast Regiment. The principal objective in Togo was Germany's 'single most important overseas wireless station', at Kamina, a hundred miles inland. Reflecting how, by the time of the First World War, technology had shrunk the world, the station provided a vital communications link from Berlin to all of its African colonies and South America, as well as with German naval units and merchant shipping in the South Atlantic Ocean. With British forces closing in on Kamina from the south and west, and a French column from the east, the Germans destroyed the wireless station and capitulated on 26 August.[12]

German South-West Africa (now Namibia) took longer to subdue. Here there was no question of French participation as, apart from the Portuguese colony of Angola to the north, South-West Africa was surrounded by British-controlled territory, including to the south the recently established Union of South Africa. The South Africans, indeed, undertook the major part in the conquest of the territory. As with Togo, the fundamental objectives were strategic: the seizure of the colony's two main harbours (Swakopmund and Lüderitz) and the destruction of wireless stations at Swakopmund and the inland capital Windhoek. South Africa's commitment to the war, however, was not total. Many Afrikaners, defeated in the Boer War of 1899–1902, remained unreconciled to British supremacy in the region. Some had removed themselves from the Union altogether and settled in South-West Africa. As in some other parts of the empire – such as Ireland and Quebec – with conditional loyalties, the effusions of imperial solidarity which accompanied the declaration of war in August 1914 actually stimulated opposition, with protestations, for example, that 'Afrikaner blood should not be shed . . . in an imperialistic war between Germany and Britain'.[13]

In South Africa this opposition initially went further than elsewhere, and in October 1914, S. G. 'Manie' Maritz, the commander of one of the three South African Defence Force columns deployed to conquer South-West Africa, rebelled. In a precursor of Dublin 1916 the original intention had been to proclaim 'independence' and set up a Provisional Republican Government, but the ill-organised planning was disrupted when one of the leaders was shot dead at a police checkpoint set up in the hunt for a band of armed criminals. After Maritz rebelled, several thousand Boer commandos joined in under the overall leadership of General Christiaan de Wet, but the uncoordinated rebels were no match for over 30,000 government troops, the majority of whom were Afrikaner loyalists, and by January 1915 the rebellion was over and Maritz had fled to join the Germans in South-West Africa.

Afrikaner republican discontent grumbled on through the war, and found inspiration with other anti-British imperialists. One of the rebel generals, Jan Kemp, likened their action not only to a 'national' uprising almost 'Irish in its spirit', but also to the Ulster Unionists' paramilitary resistance to the British government during the Irish Home Rule crisis of 1912–14 (a parallel which would not at all have pleased the Ulstermen after August 1914). The 1914–15 Afrikaner rebellion, moreover, has been seen 'as a warm weather version of the 1916 Easter Rising' (Bill Nasson's felicitous phrase). Certainly, Irish republicans were inspired by the events in South Africa. Roger Casement welcomed the rebellion and some Irish volunteers of Easter 1916 styled themselves 'De Wets', and ostentatiously adopted Boer commando cocked hats. But Nasson also notes how comparatively leniently the Afrikaner rebels were treated 'for their treasonous offence'.[14] In marked contrast to the treatment of Irish rebels in 1916, the absence of any systematic executions after the rebellion meant that the defeated Afrikaners did not (in the way as happened in Ireland) become 'martyrs' and powerful symbols sustaining future political opposition.

With de Wet's rebellion crushed, the South African government (itself led by Afrikaner loyalists, though both the prime minister, Louis Botha, and defence minister Jan Smuts, had fought *against* the British in 1899–1902) could renew the offensive against German South-West Africa. Backed by British naval units, South African forces took Lüderitz in September 1914, and in mid-January 1915, Swakopmund was occupied by a force assembled in the adjacent British enclave of Walvis Bay. Thereafter columns from Swakopmund (under Botha) and from the south (under Smuts), along with a third invading from the east, pursued the Germans into the interior. The fighting in this theatre was, on both sides, deliberately restricted to white men. With a total strength of scarcely 5,000 soldiers – all white, and mostly locally raised paramilitary Schütztruppen – the principal German strategy was to avoid any full-scale confrontation with the increasing numbers of Allied troops. By early 1915 the South Africans had over 40,000 men in the field, and, although their advance was impeded by supply problems (especially water) they inexorably moved forward, capturing Windhoek on 13 May. The intention of the German governor of South-West Africa, Dr Theodor Seitz, was simply to tie down as many enemy troops as possible and retain a semblance of German authority in the colony for as long as he could.

Having paused at Windhoek to organise his forces for a final push, Botha began his advance northwards on 18 June, and forced Seitz to agree terms, signing an armistice on 9 July 1915. The Germans mounted no climacteric 'last stand' and Seitz emerged with his force substantially intact. The German reservists were permitted to return to their homes and the German civil administration of the colony continued, though now under overall South African control. The terms of the armistice reflected the extent to which the combatants on both sides still desired to maintain the fiction that the war was purely a white man's affair. While Botha and his colleagues might try to be fastidious about the employment of non-whites, there was in fact no way that they could actually be excluded, since the whole structure of white control in Southern Africa depended on the wholesale exploitation of the black community. During the war in Africa, for example, for every individual white soldier there were often two or three non-combatant black Africans, mostly serving as 'carriers' and in other support roles. Black Africans, therefore, were involved, whether white people admitted it or not.

Unlike the campaign for South-West Africa, black African troops participated from the start in the Allied conquest of the remaining two German colonies, the Cameroons and German East Africa. The Cameroons was a large triangular-shaped territory with the British colony of Nigeria to the north-west and French Equatorial Africa on the other two sides. Just to the south east was the Belgian Congo, so all four western European belligerents had interests in the area. The situation was complicated by the existence of Spanish Guinea, or Muni, a small neutral enclave in the south-west corner of the Cameroons. Here the main British objective was to capture the coastal harbours (especially Douala) to prevent their use by German cruisers. This was quickly achieved by the beginning of October 1914, but operations further inland met with mixed success. Along the Nigerian border, the Germans repulsed units of the British West African Frontier Force, while French columns advanced into the colony from the east and south. Those in the east fared better than the southern forces, one of which suffered a sharp defeat close to Muni, leaving the Germans with a precious lifeline to the outside world through which supplies continued to move until at least early 1915.

The Cameroons campaign stuttered on into 1915, handicapped by a marked lack of coordination between the British and French (and the Belgians). The inhospitable tropical conditions contributed to sickness and supply problems which produced a high rate of attrition among the Allied troops and their labour units. Despite the Germans' own supply problems (they were critically short of ammunition), their strategic situation improved as they withdrew into the interior; their lines of communication shortened while those of their adversaries became stretched. They also proved to be stubborn opponents and rattled the British with a thrust into Nigeria in April 1915 which forced the Emir of Yola and his local administration to flee. By the late summer of 1915, however, the weight of numbers on the Allied side had begun to tell, though the French failed to cut off the Germans' possible line of retreat to neutral Spanish Muni. Scattered German garrisons in the north, running short of all sorts of supplies, began to surrender. One commander reported that they had been reduced to subsisting on 'African food' and in order to survive had been forced to eat all their 'horses, donkeys and camels'. In the south the Anglo-French forces were unable to deliver any coup de grâce to the main German body of 15,000 soldiers, porters and followers, who managed to achieve a fighting withdrawal into Muni on 15 February 1916. Later removed to the Spanish island of Fernando Po, just off the Cameroons coast, they were interned there for the rest of the war.[15]

Having conquered the Cameroons, the British and French then proceeded provisionally to divide it up between them, pending any postwar peace settlement. Taking advantage of the presence in London

of a French mission led by the diplomat François Georges-Picot, decisions about the territory were made at a meeting on 23 February 1916.
Since Picot had just negotiated a draft of the famous Sykes–Picot
Agreement, dividing parts of the Middle East between the French and
the British, this was to be his second significant cartographic intervention in the imperial history of the war. The British negotiating position
reflected the extent to which African territory was often used simply
as a bargaining counter between the imperial powers. Although the
Admiralty made a bid for Douala and its harbour, the British went into
the meeting more or less prepared to accept anything the French
demanded. By making concessions in West Africa, it was hoped that
the French could be kept out of East and Central Africa where Britain
had more pressing strategic and political interests. Working on a
1:2,000,000 scale map (thirty-two miles to the inch), Picot picked a
point west of Douala (keeping it in the French zone) and another to
the north-east, on the river Benue near Yola (just across the border
with Nigeria). According to the British record, he then 'began to join
these two points in a casual way with a blue pencil'. While Picot knew
little about West Africa, one of the British team, Charles Strachey, was
familiar with the region and endeavoured to get the line drawn so that
the only road in the east of the Cameroons running north–south would
fall within the British zone.

In postwar negotiations the British were able to acquire some territory in northern Cameroons which helped consolidate the position of
Islamic rulers, such as the Shehu of Borno and the Lamido of Fombina,
upon whom they depended for control over northern Nigeria, and
who had supported the British war effort. Otherwise this arrangement
became the basis of the partition agreed after the war (though, better
informed in 1919 than they had been in 1916, the French managed to
claw back the north–south road). Thus Picot's pencil line, casually
drawn one day in London in February 1916, and owing more to imperial and metropolitan considerations than any concern whatsoever for
the territory or peoples of the Cameroons themselves, became for
forty years an international frontier between French and British territory in West Africa. Only at independence in 1961 did the local
inhabitants of the British Cameroons finally get a say with a plebiscite.

The southern population voted to rejoin the newly independent Cameroon, while the Muslims of the north narrowly opted for union with Nigeria.[16]

VON LETTOW-VORBECK AND GERMAN EAST AFRICA

After the conquest of South-West Africa and the Cameroons, the British could focus on the subjugation of German East Africa.[17] Here the war had begun quite well for the Germans. Aware that the main British concern was the protection of their shipping in the Indian Ocean and that their principal targets (as in the other German colonies) would therefore be harbours, the German defence plan was to abandon the coast and concentrate inland. The newly appointed military commander, Colonel Paul von Lettow-Vorbeck, nevertheless, was determined to take the initiative. With an eye to the wider strategic situation (and as he asserted perhaps a little disingenuously with the benefit of hindsight in his postwar memoirs) he hoped to pin down as many British troops as possible and prevent them from being used elsewhere.[18] On 15 August 1914 his forces crossed into British East Africa (now Kenya), to the north and captured the town of Taveta just inside the border. A German light cruiser, the *Königsberg*, stationed at Dar es Salaam, put to sea and on 6 August inflicted the British Empire's first merchant-shipping loss of the war by sinking the 6,000-ton cargo steamer *City of Winchester* in the Gulf of Aden. The *Königsberg* evaded the British blockade for almost a year before being detected and sunk in July 1915. The Germans also took the war to the Belgian Congo which abutted their territory to the west. By the beginning of October a German gunboat had sunk the only Belgian steamer on Lake Tanganyika and thus (for the meantime) secured German control of the lake.

The British had their own plans and hastily assembled an 8,000-strong expeditionary force in India to conquer German East Africa, beginning with an amphibious landing at Tanga on the north coast of the colony. Inadequately organised, wracked by sickness during the voyage from India, and with dangerously over-confident commanders, on 3/4 November two brigades got safely ashore but were beaten back by the Germans, taking heavy casualties in the process and leaving behind them some precious military supplies, including eight machine guns, over 450 rifles and half a million rounds of ammunition. After the defeat at Tanga the British remained on the defensive in East Africa until early 1916, when South African troops became available following the conquest of German South-West Africa. In the meantime von Lettow-Vorbeck spent the time systematically organising supplies for his forces, improving communications and concentrating stores of food and munitions across the territory. By the end of 1915 he had nearly 3,000 European troops and just over 11,000 askari (locally raised soldiers) under his command. German morale was raised when a blockade-busting cargo ship, the *Rubens*, reached the colony in March 1915, and a second, the *Marie*, arrived a year later, both carrying weapons, ammunition and medical supplies, which helped to sustain the German effort through much of the rest of the war.[19]

In February 1916, Jan Smuts was appointed to command the British imperial forces being assembled to conquer German East Africa. The British officer originally chosen for the job, Sir Horace Smith-Dorrien, having fallen ill, Smuts's appointment was as much political as military. London needed all the help it could get from South Africa, and Botha, having seen off an Afrikaner nationalist political challenge in a general election in October 1915, was prepared to raise troops for the campaign, not least in order to bolster South Africa's own territorial ambitions in the region.[20] Smuts's intention was to assemble a predominantly South African force and subdue the Germans in a quick and efficient campaign during 1916. But he failed in this optimistic plan. Numbers were not the problem. To counter von Lettow-Vorbeck's 3,000 European and 11,000 African soldiers, by March 1916 Smuts had 28,000 British and South African troops, 14,000 Indians, 7,000 King's African Rifles askaris (raised in East and Central Africa), as well as 600 Europeans and 14,000 Africans of the Belgian Congo Force Publique which he could call on. Although Smuts achieved some limited success, his forces were insufficiently prepared, and the Germans too resourceful and elusive, for any outright victory.

The campaign began badly. Scarcely a month after reaching British East Africa, and before Smuts had himself arrived in the territory, the

2nd South African Brigade were pitched into battle. On 12 February 1916 they were ordered to attack the well-defended German strong-point of Sailita, south-west of Kilimanjaro, just across the German East African border and which they had occupied since early in the war. Three battalions of South Africans who came under punishing German fire were forced to retire, and were saved from complete disaster by William Whittall's armoured cars and a couple of battle-hardened battalions from the 1st East African Brigade: the British regular 2nd Loyal North Lancashire Regiment, and the Indian 130th Baluchis, the latter of which repulsed an enemy counterattack, including a determined German bayonet charge. Edward Paice describes this humiliating experience as 'the South Africans' Tanga', their '"welcome to East Africa" from von Lettow-Vorbeck'.[21] The 138 South African casualties from this single engagement equalled about a third of their total for the whole campaign in South-West Africa.

Smuts's broad strategy was for forces to advance into German territory from British East Africa and Uganda in the north, the Belgian Congo in the west and Northern Rhodesia (now Zambia) in the south-west. From May 1916 the northern columns began a steady push towards the central railway, reaching Dodomo (inland from Morogoro) by the end of July and Morogoro a month later. From December 1915, with the assistance of two forty-foot armed motor boats brought *Fitzcarraldo*-like overland the 2,400 miles from Cape Town, the British had begun to wrest control of Lake Tanganyika from the Germans. North of the lake a Belgian force under General Charles-Henri Tombeur launched an offensive into Ruanda and Urundi in late April 1916 and advanced towards Tabora on the central railway. The Belgians (just like the British and French) were keen to use the opportunity of the war to consolidate, if not also expand, their imperial interests in Africa. 'One of the aims of our military effort in Africa,' the Belgian colonial minister, Jules Renkin, told Tombeur in March 1916, 'is, as you know, to assure our possession of a German territory as a pawn.' Beyond the acquisition of bargaining chips for the peace conference, they wanted actual territory too. A Belgian memorandum in October 1916 noted the attractiveness of 'lands such as Ruanda, fertile, rich in cattle and suitable for white settlement'.[22]

The unit from the south-west – the Nyasa-Rhodesia Field Force – was commanded by General Edward Northey, one of the few British commanders in East Africa whom the Germans thought was any good. Northey turned a heterogeneous collection of men from the King's African Rifles (the only regular soldiers he had), two battalions of the South African Rifles (many from the campaign in South-West Africa) and men of the Northern Rhodesia Police and the British South Africa Police (from Southern Rhodesia), into a small but effective force. Beginning his advance in May 1916, Northey took Iringa, 120 miles south-west of Morogoro, at the end of August, aiming to cut off the enemy retreat. Although Northey's relentless pressure helped keep them on the run, the Germans escaped into the south-east corner of the territory where they were able to hold out well into the following year.

Writing in April 1916 to a friend in South Africa, Captain A. J. Molloy – who was serving with the 5th South African Infantry, which had experienced the surprise defeat at Sailita in February 1916 – made some shrewd observations about the quality of the contending forces and of the various groups involved. It had struck Molloy 'most forcibly' that they had 'a lot to learn in the way of bush fighting from our black enemies, and that in spite of all talk to the contrary, we have found them an enemy to be fully reckoned with'. Although the askari were 'resourceful, brave and well trained for this kind of fighting', as was common in European accounts of the conflict in Africa, Molloy also observed a 'savage' dimension to their fighting. The African, he added 'is however a brute and does not hesitate to mutilate and kill all wounded or prisoners'. At Sailita, in fact, the fate of some wounded on the British side resulted, at least in part, from poor organisation. Grossly underprovided with stretchers and medical facilities, the 7th South African Infantry had had to leave thirty casualties on the field, none of whom appear to have survived. Molloy observed that the Germans were not to be underestimated and that they 'can teach us something in the art of concealment and defence'. The campaign in East Africa, moreover, 'had been an eye opener' to the veterans of the fighting in South-West Africa: 'They have seen more here in one day than occurred in the whole G.S.W. campaign.'

Bearing in mind how dismissive many South African soldiers had been of the existing imperial troops in East Africa, adversely comparing their own swift and successful conquest of South-West Africa with the muddle and stalemate further north, but also no doubt remembering that an Indian battalion, the 130th Baluchis, had helped prevent a South African retreat at Sailita from becoming a rout, Molloy had praise for other British imperial troops. 'India,' he wrote, 'can produce soldiers worthy of that name, who have maintained the best traditions of the British Army,' and 'the King's African Rifles, a native regiment, have proved themselves to be excellent soldiers'. Molloy finally asserted that the South African troops had not been properly prepared ('with trained troops, we would not have suffered one half of the casualties we did'), and that they had suffered from 'a deficiency of maxim guns and how to use them'.[23] In sum, then, Molloy noted the unpreparedness of the South African units in training and equipment, their dependence on other British imperial troops and the capabilities of the German enemy, in terms both of fighting quality as well as their mastery of the African terrain ('the art of concealment and defence'). This last factor was, above all, to be the secret of von Lettow-Vorbeck's survival until the end of the war.

In William Whittall's admiring (and somewhat complacent) account of the campaign, the occupation of Dar es Salaam on 4 September 1916, the Anglo-Belgian capture of Tabora on 19 September and the seizure of the whole central railway marked the end of 'the decisive phases of the campaign'. By the end of September, 'therefore, the essential part of Smuts's task had been satisfactorily accomplished'; the possession of the German colony was 'un fait accompli'. Subsequent operations, he claimed, were 'of only subsidiary interest'.[24] Written in late 1916 or early 1917 (the book concludes with a quotation from a Smuts's despatch of 27 October 1916), this was absurdly optimistic. Smuts, in any case, had had enough, and with the formal proceedings apparently concluded, he departed in January 1917 and left the 'mopping up' to others. It was rather as Lord Roberts had done in the Boer War a decade and a half earlier, when, having (as he thought) defeated the Afrikaners in the field and captured Pretoria, he left the remaining business to Sir Herbert Kitchener. Smuts, whose guerrilla commandos had held out to the bitter end then, no doubt appreciated how unrewarding and long drawn-out the end game in East Africa might be. Besides, he had other political fish to fry in London where, in part based on a largely undeserved reputation as a military commander, he was admitted to the highest levels of imperial decision-making as a member of Lloyd George's Imperial War Cabinet from June 1917.

Smuts's plan to defeat von Lettow-Vorbeck by enveloping him was frustrated by the latter's sensible refusal to stand and fight, coupled with his remarkable ability to maintain his forces while keeping on the move. From 1917 onwards, moreover, constantly keeping one step (or more) ahead of the pursuing British, von Lettow-Vorbeck retreated south deep into Portuguese East Africa (now Mozambique), then north again and west into Northern Rhodesia, holding out until after the armistice agreed in Europe on 11 November 1918. He formally surrendered at Abercorn (now Mbala), just south-west of Lake Tanganyika, on 25 November. He still had in his force thirty European officers and 125 other ranks, 1,168 askari and 1,522 carriers, as well as 1,726 other followers (including 427 women). The *Bulawayo Chronicle* sympathetically described a 'long motley column [of] Europeans and askari, all veterans of a hundred fights', with 'women who had stuck to their husbands through all these years of hardship, carrying huge loads, some with children born through the campaign, [and] carriers coming in singing with undisguised joy at the thought that their labours were ended at last'.[25] The Germans and some others were taken by boat to Kigoma and thence by train on the central railway to Dar es Salaam. On the way they stopped at Morogoro where von Lettow-Vorbeck recalled they 'once more found the German women whom we had left behind us . . . two years before'. Evidently having survived conquest by the British in good order, they had prepared tea and coffee, 'arranged tables and baked plenty of rolls and cakes'. It was a comforting domestic touch of traditional German hospitality to help sustain them on their slow journey back to Europe.[26]

Inevitably the war in East Africa had an impact on neighbouring territories, including the Belgian Congo (now the Democratic Republic of the Congo) to the west, and the British Protectorate of Nyasaland (now Malawi) and Portuguese East Africa to the south. The mobilisation of Belgian forces was accompanied by some defensiveness about Belgian imperialism in general. From the 1890s the exploitation of the so-called Congo Free State, a personal fiefdom of King Leopold II of the Belgians, had become an international scandal. The British radical journalist, E. D. Morel, backed up by an official British report by Roger Casement, had exposed the atrocious conditions of workers in the rubber industry, so much so that in 1908 the Free State was abolished and the Belgian parliament took direct responsibility for the territory. In 1917 one wartime apologist for the reformed Belgian administration, Charles Stiénon, described at length the benevolent conditions which now obtained in the Congo in order to refute the calumnies on the Belgian people made by 'le traitre Casement et M. Morel'. During the campaign, asserted Stiénon, 'not one woman was outraged' and compensation was paid for any animals requisitioned, so much so that the local Tutsi people readily supported the Allied cause rather than that of their former German masters. Matthew Stannard argues, indeed, that the sufferings of Belgium in Europe, and its subsidiary involvement in fighting Germans in Africa, helped reshape 'Belgian imperialism by lifting the albatross of the Leopoldian past', so much so that Belgium could eventually take a place 'among the righteous imperial powers' at the 1919 peace conference.[27]

For Nyasaland Africans, already struggling under the burden of European domination, the 'intensity and persistence [of the war] were almost beyond belief'. Reflecting their principal experience of the conflict, they called it 'the war of *thangata*', a Chichewa word meaning 'help', which in the colonial situation had come 'to signify not "help" but unwarranted demands by Europeans for African service'. Initially these were for troops to join the local British King's African Rifles. A study by Melvin Page reveals that the motivations for enlistment were just as varied and plural as elsewhere. As in Europe, for example, 'Big Words' were used by both colonial and community leaders to persuade individuals to join up. It was claimed that if they were not stopped, the Germans would 'come into Nyasaland, take away the land, and enslave or kill the African population'. Some enlisted simply 'in deference to their traditional leaders'. But there were other factors. It seems that for all young men, wherever they were, the lure of military adventure was a powerful inducement. One former askari told Page in 1972 that 'we joined the war because we were men'. And, of course, there were also attractive financial rewards. 'What I needed was money,' another veteran recalled, 'so I ran in haste to enrol my name as a soldier.'[28]

Recruitment for labour duties, which during the war far exceeded that for soldiering, was rather different. There was little, if any, of the martial glamour which people (frequently over-romantically) associated with being in the army, and from the start the Nyasaland authorities had difficulties in recruiting men for the highly unpopular 'porterage' work, so much so that in December 1914 they were given powers to impose compulsory military service. The wartime manpower demands provoked resistance, including an unsuccessful rebellion led by John Chilembwe in 1915. The coordinated East African offensive in 1916 intensified labour recruitment, which was compared by some Europeans to the press gang. One witness said: 'They used to chase people as if they were chasing chickens,' and Africans likened it to the slave-raiding which British colonial rule was supposed to have ended. Over the whole war an estimated two hundred thousand men served as soldiers and labourers, representing over two-thirds of Nyasaland's adult male population, massively disrupting social and economic life, and intensifying resentment with the political circumstances which had led to this predicament. Melvin Page argues that in Nyasaland the war made two of the great features of colonial rule, tax and *thangata*, 'more a reality than ever before', and that 'Nyasaland's Africans gained, for the first time, a collective appreciation of the full power, as well as the vulnerabilities, of their European overlords'. The war, he adds, was an important watershed in Nayasaland's history, which contributed to the ultimate destruction of European rule in the territory.[29]

French recruitment techniques in Senegal were very similar, and the analogy with tax-collecting held true there too. For what was called the new 'tax in blood', French auxiliary forces ran man hunts and local agents were well paid for each recruit they delivered, frequently bound and linked with 'ropes around their necks', in a manner distressingly reminiscent of slave-trading. As Joe Lunn puts it, the Senegalese responded with a mixture of 'flight, desertion and occasional armed resistance'.[30]

While white men (with or without the assistance of non-whites) were fighting for control in Africa during the Great War, some indigenous African groups seized the opportunity to assert their position and carve out territory for themselves. Like the Senussi in Libya who rebelled against the Italians in 1915–17, they often got caught up in the wider conflict. In the context of a continuing worldwide war, moreover, any challenge, for example to the Allied imperial powers in Africa, tended to be seen not just as a local matter but also potentially as part of a coordinated enemy offensive. Since local rebellious groups were generally happy to accept help from the 'enemies of their enemies' (thus the Senussi accepted arms and money from the Germans and Turks), this became a self-fulfilling perception, and influenced the severity of the response. As with the Rising in Dublin at Easter 1916, which seemed to the British authorities to be not so much a 'little local difficulty' as part of an attack inspired and funded from Berlin (or wherever), this perception was likely to intensify the severity of the official response to the challenge.

Naturally, both sides looked to pick up allies wherever they could. During 1915 Turkish agents were reported to be working in Darfur, in the western Sudan, hoping to encourage the sultan, Dinar, to come into the war against Britain. Suspicions were raised after a letter from Ali Dinar to a fellow Muslim leader calling for a jihad against the infidel British regime was intercepted. Before the war, Ali Dinar, sandwiched between the French in Chad and the British in the Sudan, had managed to retain a fair degree of independence, while conceding a theoretical sovereignty to the British at Khartoum. With the outbreak of war, Khartoum began to worry that anti-British religious propaganda might stir up Islamic groups and sought to enforce its control over the region more fully than hitherto. Sir Reginald Wingate, the governor-general of the Sudan, worried that the dangerous infection of defiance might spread beyond Darfur. In July 1915 he told London that there was 'no doubt whatever' that Ali Dinar

had 'absorbed the Turco-German poison' and had 'entirely repudiated all allegiance to the Sudan'. While Wingate hoped to avoid 'actual
hostilities', he was concerned about the destabilising effects Ali
Dinar's continued defiance would have on 'our own tribes on the
Darfur frontier'.[31]

Robert Savile, the British governor of Kordofan, adjacent to Darfur,
was keen to use force to depose Ali Dinar swiftly, but Wingate
(evidently thinking of the troubled history of hasty British expedi-
tions to the Sudan) was anxious about sending 'a relatively small force
under Christian leaders into a little known country against a population inclined to bouts of fanaticism (which might spread eastwards if
the military operation were immediately successful) and of whose
attitude towards an invading force we cannot be certain'. The British
authorities in Egypt, and in London, opposed too adventurous and
potentially costly a policy in the region. But further evidence of Turco-
Senussi collaboration in Libya, adjoining Darfur, towards the end of
1915 gave the hawks in Khartoum the evidence they needed and an
expedition into Darfur was launched in March 1916. After capturing a
couple of towns just across the border, the expedition was held up in
the light of French concerns transmitted through London. Already
worried by pockets of resistance in their north African possessions in
response to the conscription of soldiers and 'carriers', the French were
afraid that a British advance against Ali Dinar would drive him west
and unsettle their territory. Eventually the French were persuaded to
deploy troops blocking a retreat and Wingate launched a final attack.
Ali Dinar's army was routed on 2 May and the next day the British
captured his capital of El Fasher. Ali Dinar escaped into the remote
desert in the south-west of Sudan, but was tracked down and killed on
6 November 1916.

The expedition against Ali Dinar was a complete success, but it was
followed by an argument as to who should pay the costs. Even in
wartime, when blank cheques were promiscuously issued on all sides,
bureaucrats could still be found keeping careful watch on expenditure.
Wingate argued that Britain should pay on the grounds that 'the
campaign had been a direct consequence and part of the world war'.
The War Office in London flatly asserted that the Sudan should pay.

In the end a decision was found from December 1915 that expenditure in the Sudan 'attributable to the existence of a state of war' should be billed to Egypt (on the grounds that the Sudan was technically a condominium jointly ruled by Egypt and the United Kingdom) when the British Treasury found 'no sufficient reason why assistance should be sought from the Imperial Exchequer in preference to Egyptian funds'. On such convenient rulings were Britain's imperial costs kept under control (at least until local administrations began seriously to object from the 1920s onwards). So Cairo footed the bill. As Martin Daly mordantly observes: 'Egypt paid the piper, and London called the tune.'[32]

From a British imperial perspective, Darfur in 1916 is a good example of a wider wartime phenomenon: a territory with a fairly relaxed prewar relationship to a greater power distantly asserting ultimate political rule, which, with the onset of war, in order to secure the territory or to extract resources for the war effort endeavoured to exert greater control than before. This, in turn, could stimulate opposition in the subject territory. A pattern, then, of challenge and response might be established which could easily escalate into violent conflict.

Another example of this was the Volta-Bani Anti-Colonial War, a revolt against French military conscription which occurred in what is now the Republic of Burkina Faso in West Africa. The withdrawal of European administrators and indigenous tirailleurs in 1914 for service in France persuaded some of the local population that the French empire was in trouble and that it might be a propitious time to challenge the authority of the colonial state. France's extremity, thus, was an opportunity for anti-colonialists. French demands for conscripts in 1915, moreover, looked like desperate measures to some. Reflecting on the causes of the rising after it had been largely suppressed, the lieutenant governor of Senegal, Raphaël Antonetti, thought that the unprecedented recruitment campaign appeared to the locals 'as another proof that we no longer had any soldiers' and that 'our force was broken'. In this, the largest African resistance movement during the war, anti-colonialists mustered between 15,000 and 20,000 men between February and June 1916. The 5,000 French troops deployed to suppress the rising inflicted an estimated 30,000 African casualties. In one single engagement, at Bobo-Dioulasso on 6 May, approximately 3,000 Africans (men, women and children) perished (as opposed to ten killed and seventy wounded on the colonial side). French 'pacification' was severe indeed, as indicated by the military commander's directive, though it did not lose sight of the necessary maintenance of productive economic activity in the colony. 'Submission,' he wrote, 'entails complete disarmament of the rebels, imprisonment or death of the leaders, destruction of the fortified walls, repossession of houses, and return to agricultural work.' To bring rebels to heel, moreover, in some places their elders and women were taken hostage and only returned to them after they had complied with orders.[33] So it was that the 'Great War for Civilisation' bore down on the people of the Volta region in West Africa.

FORCES NOIRES

The ambitious French notions of a 'force noire', whereby Africa could provide a virtually inexhaustible supply of fighting manpower for use in any theatre of operations, were not on the whole shared by the British who were much more hesitant both about employing indigenous Africans outside the African continent itself and also using Africans in combatant roles. During 1916, however, the continuing drain on manpower led some British policymakers to consider the recruiting potential of Britain's African territories for service elsewhere. When the matter was raised in London in June 1916 there was no thought of using non-white personnel as combatants. If they were to be used at all, black Africans would only be employed in labour battalions and the like. From the start of the war white South Africans had been adamantly against using non-whites as troops. When a leading black politician, Walter Benson Rubusana, offered to raise a 5,000-strong unit to fight in the war, the secretary of defence replied that the government did 'not desire to avail itself of the services in a combatant capacity of citizens not of European descent in the present hostilities'. Since 'the present war' had its origins 'among the white peoples of Europe', the government was 'anxious to avoid the employment of coloured citizens in warfare against whites'. Underlying this refusal were clear worries that black African involvement might raise African political expectations and upset the prevailing racial hierarchy in southern Africa.[34]

White South Africans had already been alarmed by the British intention to use Indian troops in the war. 'If the Indians are used against the Germans,' argued the *East Rand Express* in 1914, they would 'return to India disabused of the respect they should bear for the white race'. The British Empire, it asserted, 'must uphold the principle that a coloured man must not raise his hand against a white man if there is to be any law and order in either India, Africa, or any part of the Empire where the white man rules over a large concourse of coloured people'. With heavy sarcasm Solomon Plaatje (a founder member in 1912 of what became the African National Congress) mused that perhaps 'the South African Government is so deeply in love with the Natives that they are scrupulously careful lest the Natives should singe so much as a hair in the present struggle, and that white men alone may shoot and kill one another'.[35]

In fact, during the first two years of the war, over 50,000 non-white South Africans were employed as non-combatants in German South-West Africa and in East Africa, but in 1916 it was proposed to extend this to service in Europe. Since the cost was to be borne by London, the South African prime minister Louis Botha did not have to refer the matter to the South African parliament (where it would have met with considerable opposition). Recruitment began in September 1916 for what became known as the South African Native Labour Contingent. The scheme was widely supported by the educated black elite who, despite being rejected for military service, still saw it as an opportunity for advancing the political interests of their community. In October 1916 a correspondent to the Zulu newspaper, *Ilanga lase Natal*, argued that white opposition to the raising of the Contingent provided a 'great chance to acquire a just and recognized status as loyal subjects of the crown'. In the end (as was the case with any voluntary enlistment during the war anywhere) individuals joined up for a variety of reasons – economic, social and emotional, as well as political. From 1917, however, as Brian P. Willan has argued, 'the South African government seems to have exercised a strong degree of compulsion through the agency of the [African] chiefs'.[36]

The first two Labour Contingent battalions arrived in France in November 1916. In all 25,000 black South Africans enlisted and 21,000 left South Africa, not all of whom reached Europe safely. In February 1917 the transport SS *Mendi* sank after a collision off the English coast with the loss of over 600 African lives, the commemoration of which eighty years afterwards drew public attention to the role of black South Africans in the First World War. In France the men were housed in compounds, both for convenience and also to insulate them from any possible corrupting influence of other war workers unfamiliar with the racially defined restrictions of the South African social and political system. But the fearful predictions raised at the start by opponents of black African recruitment could not entirely be prevented. Many black South Africans found themselves working alongside whites and one later political activist, Jason Jingoes, remembered his service in France with some affection as 'it was our first experience of living in a society without a colour bar'. There were a number of incidents when Labour Contingent men protested against their living and working conditions, including one in which thirteen Africans died after being fired upon by white officers and NCOs.

Although in January 1917 London asked that the Contingent numbers be increased to 50,000, the South African government decided in January 1918 (according to General Botha 'for reasons of a purely military nature') to bring the 'experiment' to an end, and most of the men had been repatriated by May. Illustrating how any dangerous notion that racial equality, as had been experienced in Europe, might have been transferable to South Africa was sharply cut short is an anecdote which Jason Jingoes told of an incident at Rouen docks on their way back home. In a canteen run by French women volunteers, an Afrikaner colonel was offended by 'the nasty fact that Africans were served tea before him . . . [and] that they used the same cups'. Another white officer – not an Afrikaner – remonstrated with him, arguing that 'Black and White were created by one God; their only difference lies in the colour of their skin'. Not at all, asserted the colonel, turning to the black Africans present: 'When you people get back to South Africa,' he declared, 'don't start thinking you are whites, just because this place has spoiled you. You are black, and you will stay black.'[37]

It was in Africa itself, however, that there was almost unlimited mobilisation of indigenous manpower. Many accounts of the First World War in Africa stress its marginality. Of the many 'sideshows' in the war, the African campaigns are characterised as among the most peripheral of all. The conquest of a handful of German possessions, none of which had any compelling strategic value, involving relatively small numbers of fighting soldiers, can be seen at best as a kind of historical curiosity, a white man's war (as many European imperialists imagined) exotically located among essentially uncomprehending and uninvolved indigenous peoples, suitable perhaps more for comic fictional treatment (such as William Boyd's excellent An Ice-Cream War[38]) as any serious historical analysis. In their turn, both popular and more serious historical accounts of the war in Africa routinely emphasise its peripherality by describing it as 'untold' or 'forgotten'.[39] From a European perspective this may perhaps be the case, but surely not in Africa itself, where (as much recent historical scholarship concerning the topic has revealed) mass mobilisation of the civilian population occurred as strikingly as in any part of Europe.

Supporting and sustaining the fighting formations were toiling multitudes of non-combatant personnel in staggering numbers. Geoffrey Hodges has estimated that something over 989,000 Africans served with just the British forces in East Africa *alone*. Of these 57,000 were troops and over 930,000 were 'followers': gun porters, medical staff, 'carriers etc.', and casual labour. While conceding that it is impossible to arrive at any precise figure, David Killingray, who says the First World War saw 'the largest mass mobilisation of labour ever seen in Africa', puts the figure for East Africa higher, at over a million men. Elsewhere similarly large numbers were raised by the British. In Egypt 327,000 men were recruited for military labour service, three-quarters of whom were conscripts.[40] The French raised proportionately greater numbers than the British for combat roles. In French West

Africa, for example, 171,000 men were enlisted as tirailleurs, many 'by coercive methods reminiscent of the repudiated era of the slave trade'.[41] In the absence of any precise figure of the total numbers of Africans mobilised in the war, we are left with Hew Strachan's cautious approximation that 'over 2 million Africans served in the First World War as soldiers and labourers, and upwards of 200,000 of them died or were killed in action'.[42]

The British mobilisation of African manpower, although eventually very extensive, was not ambitious enough for some commentators, who compared British attitudes most unfavourably with French. In October 1916, Major De Brézé Darnley-Stuart-Stephens, an Irish-born veteran soldier with experience in West Africa and the Cape Colony forces, enthusiastically asserted that a 'Million Black Army' could be raised in British Africa from the 'great warrior nations' of the Zulus, the Basutos, the Matabele – in southern Africa – and the West African Ashanti, who were all 'formidable foes of the past' who had fought against the British. Systematically exploiting their 'unlimited recruiting ground in West Africa', he argued, the French had already mobilised 30,000 African soldiers to fight in France and elsewhere. Darnley-Stuart-Stephens was mystified as to why Britain had neglected this valuable human resource, particularly 'at a time when annihilation [of Germany] is the only course by which we can arrive at a peace which will endure'. Annihilation, he added, was only possible 'by flinging into the scale overwhelming numbers'. Darnley-Stuart-Stephens reckoned he himself could raise 20,000 troops in West Africa: 'Hausas, Yorubas, and Fullini'. He had, too, a cheerful faith in the potential of these soldiers, who would, he claimed, not need much training in the techniques of modern warfare. As success on the Western Front mainly depended 'on fighting at close quarters, and as accuracy of shooting will not be of first account, the natural instinct of these savages from West Central Africa for the use of the bayonet would go far to make up for their want of marksmanship'. Darnley-Stuart-Stephens boldly asserted that 'a couple of hundred thousand' African soldiers (carefully led by white officers of course) 'could, after six months' training, be usefully employed in daredevil charges into German trenches'.[43] They were, it seems, indeed to be cannon fodder.

Writing at about the same time, William Whittall, who had fought in both South-West and East Africa, also extolled the virtues of 'the native soldier; whether he be Kings' African Rifleman or German Askari, he is as good a fighting man as you would ask to have beside you in a tight corner, or as worthy an enemy as the veriest fire-eater could desire as an opponent'. With an imperturbable (and clearly racially defined) confidence in the manly and warlike qualities of the askari, Whittall said that while the African soldier was 'not much of a shot', he was 'a magnificent bayonet fighter, as might be expected when it is remembered that he is almost born with a spear in his hand'. Whittall exemplified the deeply paternalistic attitudes so characteristic of the time. These brave men, he asserted, also had a 'child-like' mentality and required 'understanding and thinking for all the time'. They needed to be managed carefully, and so the claims that there was unlimited black African manpower at the disposal of European powers was in practical terms an illusion. 'There has been much irresponsible talk,' he wrote, 'of letting loose millions of black men to swamp the Germans by sheer weight of numbers. Well and good, if only it were possible, but it is not.' The problem, he said, was not the supply of men, but that of suitable – white – officers. Even if they were available, and had the requisite language skills, it would take 'two years to get a new formation into anything like working efficiency'.[44]

In one contemporary account of German East Africa, John Henry Briggs, a veteran Church of England missionary who had been interned in the colony for much of the war, asserted that 'the requisitioning of vast numbers of natives, even including women, for transport and other work, the forcible enlistment of thousands into their native army, and the arbitrary and brutal way in which it was all carried out, practically reduced the country to a state of slavery'. He lamented the treatment of non-German 'Europeans – planters, miners, traders, or missionaries – both men and women', who had (like himself) been 'interned in concentration-camps . . . while the indignities heaped upon them by the German guards and the native soldiers were such as will very seriously lower the prestige of the white man in East Africa'. Briggs further thought that the 'most disastrous results of the war' would be 'seen in its moral effect on the native races'. At least 50,000 men had been recruited 'and trained in arms and taught to kill white men'. They had, moreover, 'also seen white men eagerly seeking by every device in their power to kill other white men . . . The prestige of the whole white race,' he concluded, 'has been most seriously lowered in German East Africa.'[45]

Briggs's views demonstrate the extent to which, as Michael Pesek has asserted, the colonial order had been 'turned upside down' by the war. In a study of British and Germans in East African prisoner of war camps, Pesek describes how white British prisoners – who included many missionaries and their families – were humiliated by being paraded as captives in front of the local population. One missionary reported afterwards that on the way to an internment camp at Bagamoyo on the coast north of Dar es Salaam, 'the streets were lined by excited crowds collected to look at the prisoners'. The captives were 'drawn up on exhibition for half an hour . . . surrounded by a crowd of natives and Arabs, who were left free to amuse themselves by a competition in insult and invective'. Once incarcerated, although many of the prisoners were initially allowed to retain their African servants and cooks, they were also forced not only to do physical work, but to perform it under the orders of Africans.

Ernest Holtom, a Royal Navy doctor taken prisoner in November 1914, indignantly complained that white men had been employed as unskilled labour in the construction of a guard house at Tabora. 'Native masons,' he wrote, 'did the actual building, and our men had to carry stone and water for them – in fact, to do *coolie* [his emphasis] labour.' Other prisoners had to carry their own water supplies, collect firewood for cooking and, perhaps most degrading and humiliating of all, clean their latrines themselves, 'even though their Askari guards also used them'. A missionary priest, Ernest Spanton, himself spared menial work on the grounds that clergy were ranked as officers, reported that the cleaning of latrines by white men was 'calculated, and deliberately calculated, to degrade them in the eyes of the natives'. After British and Belgian forces had captured Tabora in central German East Africa in September 1916 and released most of the European prisoners of war held by the Germans, the tables were turned on their former captors. Now German prisoners were paraded in front of Africans and they, too, had to carry their own water and firewood, as well as cleaning the latrines.[46]

'AND 102 ASKARI. . .'

Overlooking the Zambian side of the Victoria Falls on the river Zambezi is the First World War memorial for what was then Northern Rhodesia. It is dedicated: 'In memory of Northern Rhodesians who gave their lives for the Empire in the Great War 1914–1918.' On it are listed three dozen or so names of white men, below which are the lines: 'Also 102 Askari whose names are recorded on the N.R. [Northern Rhodesian] Police Memorial at Livingstone. Also many other natives of the territory of whose names no complete record exists.' So it is that indigenous Africans who died in the Great War are relegated to a kind of monumental footnote.

The Commonwealth War Graves Commission register for what is known as the Livingstone Camp Memorial at least names the 102 individuals mentioned on the Victoria Falls memorial. This is quite unusual as the vast majority of the Africans who died are not recorded by name. Explanatory text on the commission's website explains that 'Northern Rhodesian native carriers who fell in the Great War and whose names and graves are alike unknown', are collectively commemorated on this and two other memorials, in Harare and Mbala.[47] Elsewhere, after the war, statues were erected depicting carriers as well as askari in Mombasa and Nairobi in Kenya, in Lagos in Nigeria (since dismantled) and Dar es Salaam (Tanzania). In Mombasa, as elsewhere, there is an inscription composed by Rudyard Kipling, founder member of the Imperial War Graves Commission: 'This is to the memory of the Arab and native African troops who fought; to the carriers who were the feet and hands of the army; and to all other men who served and died for their king and country in Eastern Africa in the Great War 1914–1918. If you fight for your country, even if you die, your sons will remember your name.'[48]

In Africa there is what might be called a remembrance deficit. Kipling was evidently well aware that not all the names of those who served and died would be recorded. All he could offer in his carefully worded inscription was an assurance that in the end the certain remembering of the fallen would be left, as ever, to their families. In Europe (and elsewhere) the War Graves Commission controversially (at the time) applied the admirable and much-praised principle of equality, that the British Empire's war dead would be commemorated individually by name, and equally treated, regardless of rank, or race or creed. Hence those achingly beautiful war cemeteries with their matching headstones, which differ only by unit badge and some details of individual inscriptions. Those for whom there is no known grave are listed by name on the great 'monuments to the missing' at, for example, Thiepval on the Somme or the Menin Gate at Ypres.[49]

But in Africa it was different. Here the Commission applied a dismayingly familiar racial hierarchy in the commemoration of the empire's dead. The Commission's general rule, established by the mid-1920s, was that all Europeans would be commemorated, with individual headstones or by being named on permanent memorials, but that African 'natives' would not. In November 1925, the principal assistant secretary of the commission, Lord Arthur Browne (an Irishman who later succeeded as the 8th Marquess of Sligo), laid down that even if identified Africans were buried in particular cemeteries, their names would not be included in the specific cemetery register, since by doing so 'we should be unnecessarily drawing attention to the fact that we have neglected to commemorate by a headstone'. The graves of Africans, whether soldiers or carriers, indeed, were not to be maintained but allowed to 'revert to nature' and the dead recorded (if at all) simply as 'missing'.[50]

Despite the Imperial War Graves Commission's refusal in general to give equal treatment to the indigenous African casualties, some individual carriers and soldiers do have their own graves. In the British cemetery at Morogoro lie Jacob Tro Tlhotlhalemaye, a 'follower' who served with the Cape Coloured Labour Regiment, along with some thirty of his fellow labourers. Here, too, is Private Kraft Ogin of the Nigeria Regiment; 'George', 'Harry', 'Kametini' and 'Aaron', all drivers with the East African Transport Corps; and Be Sala Efun, a private with the Gold Coast Regiment, who died on 29 November 1916. For him, very unusually, there is a supplementary piece of

9

The Somme

For the British the battle of the Somme is perhaps the single most iconic engagement of the First World War. It began on 24 June 1916, with an artillery bombardment which lasted seven days before the infantry assault was launched on 1 July, and continued for four and a half months, until 18 November. From the beginning the cost was horrific, and over the whole battle British and French formations fought along a twenty-mile stretch near the river Somme, sustaining some 623,000 casualties, of whom 420,000 were British. The Germans suffered something between 500,000 and 580,000 casualties.[1] During the battle the Allies advanced no more than ten miles, and the Somme has come above all to exemplify a perception of the fighting on the Western Front as unremittingly costly and essentially futile.

The Western Front was frequently compared unfavourably with Gallipoli. In September 1916 General Sir Andrew Russell, who had served with the Anzacs at Gallipoli and was by now commander of the New Zealand Division, wrote to Sir Ian Hamilton from the Somme. The campaign at Gallipoli, he said, would always be the one to which his division would 'look back with the greatest interest'. It was, he claimed, like the French proverb: 'On revient toujours à ses premiers amours.' 'In truth,' he added, 'this fighting on the Western Front, is but a dull affair in comparison: a sordid history punctuated with 5.9s and Minnenwerfers. Certainly lacking the romance attached to our life last year.'[2]

The trajectory of the war from Gallipoli to the Somme, moreover, carries one from a First World War campaign where there still seemed to be an element of romantic high endeavour to one where the sheer, all-encompassing intensity of the slaughter had drained the smallest scintilla of romance from the experience. By 1916 on the Western Front, too, there was a widespread sense that the war would go on for ever. In March 1916, a Bavarian soldier, Josef Kohler, remarked, 'we absolutely no longer believe that [the war] will ever come to an end; it appears that we are all condemned for life'. Three months later, after his first experience of the front line, what Geoffrey Donaldson, a captain with the Royal Warwickshire Regiment, felt most strongly was 'the hopelessness of it all'. Writing to his mother on 2 June 1916, he felt 'that fighting will never end the war'.³ The casualties in France and Flanders were greater than at the Dardanelles. Noting that while the 120,000 British Empire losses at Gallipoli represented a ratio of two casualties for every nine men in the theatre, Jenny Macleod has observed that on the Western Front the figure was five out of every nine. And during the first month of the Somme *alone*, the losses totalled 196,000. The Somme, she concludes, 'was a watershed: it tainted all that came after it. Conversely, the battles that came before – particularly Gallipoli – retain something of the sense of romance and excitement that characterised the earliest days of the First World War.'⁴

One reason why the Somme is so prominent in the British 'memory' of the First World War is that it was the first major battle in which Lord Kitchener's New Armies were deployed. These divisions were composed of the men who had joined up in the first heady few months of the war; volunteer civilian soldiers who constituted a British nation in arms. As Catriona Pennell has demonstrated, moreover, the so-called 'spirit of 1914', in which populations across Europe appeared enthusiastically to welcome the war, was neither so hysterical nor simplistic as is sometimes thought and war enthusiasm (such as it was) was clearly tempered with an apprehensive sense that the struggle might be both long and costly.⁵ These apprehensions were more than met in the summer of 1916.

On the first day of the infantry assault on the Somme the British Army suffered its heaviest ever casualties in a single day. The official returns showed a total of 57,470 casualties, of whom 19,240 were killed.[6] A fair proportion of the 2,152 listed as missing must also have been killed, and many of the wounded did not long survive either. One of the conundrums we have about the Somme, a century later, is that even after that terrible first day British and French commanders continued with the offensive, not just in the days immediately following, which is understandable in terms of pressing on with the push in the hope of securing the much-desired breakthrough, but for months longer, which requires rather more explanation. The easy categorisation of the British Army simply being 'lions led by donkeys', propounded by Alan Clark among others,[7] cannot survive close scrutiny. The fact is that experienced and intelligent officers (as well as stupid ones, of course), at all levels of command, continued to engage in the often atrocious warfare of the Western Front. The rank and file, too, for the most part and for most of the war, also served steadily in the most terrifying and horrific of circumstances. That there were alternatives is demonstrated, for example, by large-scale mutinies in the French and Russian armies in 1917, as well as in Habsburg and German units in 1918, but many of these occurred not on the battlefield but at home. This was certainly the case in Russia where the most extreme collapse of military forces accompanied a comprehensive breakdown in the state itself.

By beginning with a consideration of the mid-point of the Somme battle, in September 1916, we might find some clues both to the rationality of the tactics adopted (at least in the eyes of the generals concerned) and the resilience of the front-line troops who took the greatest risks of all in the pursuit of those tactics.

GUILLEMONT, GINCHY AND FLERS-COURCELETTE

One of the myths punctured in Catriona Pennell's book is that there was a uniquely poor recruiting response in nationalist Ireland to Kitchener's call. Irish Catholics and nationalists (though the terms are not invariably synonymous) enlisted in Lord Kitchener's New Armies in substantial numbers and formed a clear majority of the 16th (Irish) Division, which drew recruits from all over Ireland; Ulstermen, too, as it included many Catholic nationalists from west Belfast.[8] Nicknamed by some 'Redmond's pets', it was the beginning (as the nationalist leader John Redmond hoped) of a fully fledged Irish Army Corps, to match the famous Canadian Corps or the Anzacs. But this was not to be and the formation of an 'Irish army' was to be left to the separatist wing of Irish nationalism. The 16th Division, nevertheless, carved out a fine reputation for itself in some stiff fighting on the Western Front. They reached France in December 1915 and to accustom them to trench warfare were deployed in small units in the front line over the next three months. Having served their apprenticeship, at the end of March they were given a section of the front line to hold opposite Hulluch near Loos. They had their first real test at the end of April (during the same week as the Easter Rising in Dublin) when they came under gas attack and shellfire on 27 and 29 April, suffering 1,162 casualties, including 353 killed.[9]

The division stayed in the Loos sector until the end of August (by which time they had incurred over 6,000 casualties) when they were moved up to the Somme for a push towards Guillemont, a fortified village about two and a half miles from the start line on 1 July, which the British had been trying to take since 30 July. On 3 September the division's 47th Brigade was given the task of taking the village. Even getting just to the front line, over ground which had been fought over for more than a month, was a nightmare. Lieutenant Blake O'Sullivan of the 6th Connaught Rangers wrote to his mother after the battle describing the nauseating 'stench from bloated carcases' along the approach to the jump-off point: 'We waded slowly through the cold sludge, tripping and tangling in the wire, and stumbled over a dead man. Lying on his back with arms and legs stretched out like an X. He was actually half afloat in the mud and nodded his head solemnly as each of us sloshed by.'[10]

Lessons had been learned from the lengthy but inadequate bombardment before 1 July. There was a four-hour artillery barrage before zero hour at noon. Unfortunately some of the British guns fired short, hitting the Connaughts who lost 200 men before they had even started. The barrage, however, was more intense and focused than had been the case on 1 July, and, having begun advancing just before the shelling lifted beyond the enemy line, the Connaughts caught the Germans by surprise and reached their objectives. The battalion commander, Lieutenant Colonel 'Jack' Lenox-Conyngham, a much-loved Protestant commander of a largely Catholic unit, was killed in the process. The other assault battalion, the 7th Leinster Regiment, advanced on the dot in parade-ground order and also captured their first objectives. 'What does it feel like to go "Up and over?"' wrote Max Staniforth of the Leinsters to his wife on 12 September. 'I don't know. I concentrated my thoughts on keeping my pipe alight. It seemed to be the most important thing at the moment, somehow.' He said that there was 'none of the "wild, cheering rush" one imagines,' but he remembered 'noticing that the air was just one loud noise – like moving in a kind of sound-box'. The machine-gun bullets 'snapped about your head rather like a swarm of angry hornets: all hissing and crackling; it was rather curious. I don't know quite how to describe it.'¹¹ The other two battalions in the brigade, the 8th Royal Munster Fusiliers and 6th Royal Irish Regiment – the latter going over the parapet 'with their pipes playing' and in 'excellent order' – passed through them and took the second objectives. Guillemont (or what was left of it) was captured in a well-planned and executed, neat, but limited, operation.

Six days later the whole division was involved in the capture of Ginchy, half a mile further on, where the Germans had repelled a series of British attacks from the west. The Irish were given the job of attacking from the south. On 9 September two brigades from the division had sharply contrasting experiences. Ordered to hold back for two minutes, until 4.47 p.m., to allow a final bombardment of the enemy, the 47th Brigade found that the British barrage had not destroyed the German front line and they suffered very heavy casualties. The 48th Brigade, on the other hand, did not receive the delaying order and thus moved up slightly ahead of the British barrage, incurring some casualties from this, but it gave them the edge against the Germans, and they had occupied the village within an hour of starting. The Irish soldiers, though quite tired and with understrength battalions, also seem to have integrated the use of trench mortars and Lewis guns successfully with their advance. The cost, however, was high. Over the first ten days of September, the 16th Division lost 240 officers and 4,090 men out of 432 and 10,410 who had started. Over a thousand men were killed.

It was here that Lieutenant Thomas Kettle fell, leading a company of the 9th Royal Dublin Fusiliers just ahead of Lieutenant Emmet Dalton – who won a Military Cross in the engagement, acquired the nickname 'Ginchy', later became IRA Director of Munitions, and was to reach the rank of general in the army of independent Ireland. Kettle was a former Irish nationalist MP and Professor of National Economics at University College Dublin, who had been in Belgium at the beginning of the war buying guns for the nationalist Irish Volunteers. He joined up believing that the war had a just cause, being fought on behalf of small nations such as Belgium, Serbia and Ireland too. But he had been dispirited by the Easter Rising in Dublin. While he had no sympathy with the rebels, he correctly predicted how posterity might view him vis-à-vis the 1916 leaders. 'These men,' he wrote, 'will go down in history as heroes and martyrs, and I will go down – if I go down at all – as a bloody British officer.'[12] Kettle was not the only prominent Irish nationalist on the Western Front. Willie Redmond MP, the younger brother of the nationalist leader John Redmond, also served with the 16th Division, though on account of his age (he was fifty-four) the divisional commander kept him away from front-line service in September 1916. Redmond greatly resented this and, having talked his way back to the front line, was killed in action near Mesen (Messines) in June 1917.

Not all the 16th Division's casualties in September 1916 were inflicted on the battlefield. Private Joseph Carey, a Dubliner with the 8th Royal Irish Fusiliers, was executed by firing squad on 15 September, having been convicted by court martial of desertion. Carey was one of the 300 British soldiers 'shot at dawn' during the war for desertion and other offences. His is a particularly distressing case. Aged thirty-five when he enlisted in April 1915, he was in the line during the attack at Hulluch in April 1916. On 4 May he went absent without leave, was quickly apprehended and given Field Punishment No. 1 – that is, being tied to a cartwheel or stake for two hours each day. He twice absconded in June, but was found behind the lines on each occasion and subsequently charged with two counts of desertion. Carey pleaded not guilty at a court martial on 21 August and told the court: 'I lose my head in the trenches. I do not know what I am doing at all.' He told them there was a history of mental instability in his family and that both his father and brother had committed suicide. He was nevertheless found guilty and sentenced to death, though the court recommended the sentence be commuted 'on the grounds of Carey's "defective intellect"' (despite the fact that a medical board had pronounced him 'of sound mind' before the trial).

The practice in the British Army was that capital sentences had to be confirmed up the chain of command to the commander-in-chief himself, Field Marshal Sir Douglas Haig. Carey's brigadier recommended that the sentence be carried out, partly because the battalion concerned had a poor disciplinary record. The divisional commander, General William Hickie, was more compassionate and recommended 'that the sentence be commuted and the prisoner be given a chance to redeem his character in the near future'. But Hickie's advice was rejected. Both the army commander and, on 12 September, Haig, confirmed the sentence, which was carried out three days later. The exemplary requirements of military discipline overruled the mitigation recommended by the court martial and General Hickie, which in both instances appeared to demonstrate some appreciation that Carey's actions were affected by his mental health.[13] In other times much more account would have been taken of the impact of traumatic stress in such cases. So unsettling, indeed, was the British Army's record in this matter during the war that a widely supported public campaign in 2006 successfully persuaded the government posthumously to pardon 306 soldiers executed during the First World War for cowardice or desertion.

On the same day that Joseph Carey was executed, 15 September, the battle of Flers-Courcelette began. Here, for the first time, tanks were used in action. It was an attempt to break the stalemate of the trenches with the assistance of new technology and a harbinger of future warfare. The British began developing tanks, or 'landships' – armoured vehicles using caterpillar tracks – during 1915. Production of the Mark I model began early in 1916 and under conditions of the greatest possible secrecy the first tanks reached France in August 1916.[14] In February 1916 King George V was given a demonstration and noted in his diary that he had seen 'the Caterpillar, which is an armoured motor which goes over trenches and through wire and with which we hope to attack the Germans'. Although the proponents of tanks in England feared that the element of surprise would be lost if they were used in 'driblets', and argued that they should first be deployed only in large numbers, Haig insisted that if 'valuable results' could be achieved 'by the use of even a few tanks', then that should be done. In the end he got fifty tanks, fewer than he wanted, of which thirty-six survived mechanical failure to be used in the battle, parcelled out in small numbers across the line of attack.

These early tanks were very cumbersome. Eight feet high and fourteen feet wide they weighed up to twenty-eight tons, and had a crew of eight or nine men. They were by no means perfect. They moved at an average speed of about two miles an hour, more slowly than a walking infantryman, were prone to mechanical failure and vulnerable to enemy shellfire. But they did offer a real chance to tip the balance a little away from the defending side on the Western Front and, although their record was mixed on their debut on 15 September, they did more than enough to justify their deployment and, indeed, their further development by the British. With eleven British divisions involved (there had been fourteen on 1 July), the Flers-Courcelette push was the second heaviest effort in the whole Somme battle. While Haig inevitably hoped for a breakthrough, there was a general belief, as William Philpott notes, 'that the battle was reaching its climax after two and a half months of wearing down the enemy's reserves and morale'.[15] The three-day artillery bombardment was twice as heavy as on 1 July. In some places it worked well and British air-spotting helped the accuracy of the firing, adding another innovative technological dimension to the occasion. On the left of the British line the initial bombardment was followed by a well-executed creeping shrapnel barrage (an important technique developed through the Somme campaign) which enabled the 2nd Canadian Division to reach its first objective, a sugar factory south of Courcelette village, within an hour of starting. The six tanks allocated to the Canadians – which were given the names of French drinks beginning with 'C', such as Chablis and Cognac – were deployed in support of the infantry for mopping-up purposes, though two did not get beyond the starting line and two others got irredeemably stuck while advancing.

In other sectors the tanks were deployed ahead of the infantry advance. In order to protect them from the British creeping barrage, gaps about a hundred yards wide were left for them. Since the tanks were specifically intended to be used against enemy strongpoints, this meant that those positions would also be spared British shellfire at the moment of the infantry attack. The 14th Division, with three tanks, were given the task of reducing a particularly well-fortified German post named the Quadrilateral. Deficient targeting meant that the strongpoint escaped serious damage even in the preliminary barrage. On the morning of the infantry assault, two of the tanks broke down before the start line, but the third reached the Quadrilateral, and took heavy punishment, including armour-piercing bullets, which forced it to retire. The infantry, left to advance without the protection of either tanks or a creeping barrage, were driven off with heavy casualties.

Yet there was success, too. The 41st Division which was to attack northwards from Longueval towards Flers was supported with ten tanks, only four of which survived to reach the village. But they achieved precisely what had been intended, one tank crushing wire at the entrance to the village and providing covering fire for the accompanying foot soldiers. 'The scene in Flers was without precedent in war,' recorded the British official history, perhaps embroidering the tale a little. 'Firing as it went, the tank lurched up the main street followed by parties of cheering infantry.' The tank commander, Lieutenant Stuart Hastie, afterwards recalled going up the main street 'during which my gunners had shots at various people who were underneath the eaves in some cases, or in the windows of some of the cottages'. Later, looking round, he 'could see no signs of the British Army coming up behind me'.[16] Yet, if the infantry were not precisely out in the open cheering, they were certainly clearing the wrecked buildings on each side of the street and the village was taken by 10 a.m.

The elite Guards Division, who fought at Flers-Courcelette, pushing north of Ginchy, east of the 14th Division, also had ten tanks in support. Unfortunately only two of them survived long enough to be of any assistance. Here, in the absence of the tanks themselves, the gaps left open for them to advance merely left the enemy defences unscathed, allowing their machine-gunners to inflict heavy losses on the advancing guardsmen. Among the fallen here was the prime minister's son, Lieutenant Raymond Asquith, serving with the Grenadier Guards. Three future Conservative MPs and government ministers, all Old Etonians, were also with the Grenadiers. In the chaotic advance Harold Macmillan (the future prime minister), was first wounded in the knee and then shot in the left buttock. He sheltered in a shell hole, dosed himself with morphine and claimed afterwards to have passed the time reading Aeschylus's *Prometheus* in the original Greek before he was rescued. Harry Crookshank (Minister of Health and Lord Privy Seal 1951–55), was less fortunate. A shrapnel wound in the groin castrated him. Oliver Lyttelton (Minister of Production 1942–45 and colonial secretary 1951–54), survived without injury, but wrote later about the confused horror of it all. 'I have only a blurred image of slaughter,' he recalled. 'I saw about ten Germans writhing like trout in a creel at the bottom of a shell hole and our fellows firing at them from the hip. One or two red bayonets.' Yet he also expressed the intoxication of the miraculously unscathed. 'The 15th was the most wonderful day of my life,' he told his mother. 'I drank every emotion to the dregs and was drunk. It was superbly exhilarating.'[17]

It is sometimes forgotten in Britain that the Somme was a Franco-British battle from the start. Originally it was to have been primarily a French affair with British support, but Verdun changed all that.[18] Yet, while the French took the junior part, they were in some places more successful than the British. At the very start of the battle on the southern end of the front the French Sixth Army under General Emile Fayolle did very well. With exemplary preparation and furious concentration the French artillery managed to destroy the German defences in a way the British generally failed to do (at least on 1 July). At this end of the battle General Sir Walter Congreve's British XIII Corps did best of all the British formations on the first day, partly through their innovative use of a creeping barrage. But however successful adjacent French and British units might be, there was little genuine coordination. Indeed the French and British fought the battle of the Somme more in parallel than as any sort of joint endeavour, as illustrated when the British push beginning on 22 July was a shambles and un-coordinated with a simultaneously unrewarding French effort.

In early September a French push was timed to coincide with the British Fourth Army's attack towards Guillemont. French and French colonial formations athwart the river Somme achieved some local progress, at one point penetrating nearly two miles into the German lines. The French counter-battery fire was particularly effective, and a sophisticated system of battlefield communications, involving signal pennants, Roman candles, telephones and runners, enabled commanders on the ground to control the creeping barrage. The advance was sufficient to allow the overall French commander, Ferdinand Foch, briefly to consider the possibility of a cavalry breakthrough. South of the river the French Tenth Army under General Joseph Micheler had what Philpott calls a 'muted success', an all-too-usual modest advance at heavy cost. Micheler had fewer gunners than Fayolle and they were less precise in their targeting. Here, again, the impact of Verdun was felt. Not only did demands there restrict the numbers of guns available, but a significant proportion of Micheler's troops had only recently been transferred from that front and had had little time to recuperate or get much training for the attack.

The British planning for the Flers-Courcelette push in mid-September assumed that the French on their right flank would attack in support. But Fayolle began a major offensive towards Combles with five divisions on 12 September, three days before the British moved. The attack began well. The French reached the German third line, and in some places beyond, but it was on a fairly narrow front – about 2,000 yards wide – which left their flanks exposed to enemy fire. After three days of heavy fighting the offensive ground to a halt, just as the British push began. In order to support their ally, Foch insisted that Fayolle continue the offensive even though he reasonably claimed it had been a 'wasted day for me with useless casualties'. But Fayolle did notice the deployment of tanks (while overestimating their impact). 'The British take Martinpuich and Flers,' he wrote on 15 September.

'The new war machines are doing wonders, it appears. At last they make a concerted attack, with long preparation and fresh troops, and of course it succeeds.'[19]

William Philpott, who runs against the popular tide by calling the Somme a victory, describes September 1916 as the 'tipping point'. One reason for this was the success of French attacks during the month, an achievement sometimes neglected by Anglophone accounts of the battle, and one which by expanding the battle (especially to the south of the Somme river) 'increased the pressure on a defence already weakened by two months of attrition'. The French effort during September, 'more and larger than those of the British, is', he argues, 'a vital missing piece of the Somme jigsaw puzzle'. Yet they did not actually produce victory, and he concedes that 'strategic victory in a battle of attrition was undoubtedly a chimera – hoped for, planned for, even on occasion imminent, but unrealisable'. And, even though the battle had 'relieved the pressure on Verdun, restored the initiative of the allies, worn down the enemy's manpower and morale and, as part of the General Allied Offensive, stretched German resources dangerously thin', the offensive ultimately proved to be 'abortive'.[20] Considering the casualties, moreover, if victory there was, it was decidedly pyrrhic.

SITES OF IMPERIAL MEMORY

In his wise and important book exploring the European cultural dimension of the Great War, and borrowing the French historian Pierre Nora's concept of 'lieux de mémoire', Jay Winter has observed that the battlefields of 1914–18 are populated by multinational 'sites of memory . . . and mourning'.[21] For the British and British imperial world nowhere is this more true than on the Somme, where battle sites, cemeteries and memorials exist for almost every part of the 'white' British Empire, and some parts of the non-white empire too. Serre, Beaumont-Hamel, Thiepval, Delville Wood, Pozières, and Longueval all have a special resonance in different parts of the world. Across the battlefield the carefully tended Commonwealth War Graves cemeteries contain imperial as well as British and Irish dead, and at intervals there are poignant 'memorials to the missing', listing those many tens of thousands who have no known grave.

At Serre, Beaumont-Hamel and Thiepval, graves and monuments mark the losses during the first terrible days of the infantry assault. All three villages were in German hands, were heavily defended and were objectives to be taken on 1 July. The hill-top village of Serre was at the north end of the push, the so-called 'battle of Albert', named after the French town just to the rear of the British front line. Among the British troops assembled here for the offensive was the 11th Battalion of the East Lancashire Regiment, colloquially known as the Accrington Pals. Although they were undoubtedly 'Kitchener men', the chronology of the unit's formation is revealing.[22] Reflecting the fact that not everyone joined up right at the very start of the war, it was not until early September 1914 that the mayor of Accrington, Captain John Harwood, offered to raise a local unit. Recruitment only started on 14 September, but the battalion reached full strength of 1,100 men in under a fortnight, drawing in men, not only from Accrington, but also the nearby Lancashire towns of Burnley, Chorley and Blackburn.

Pals battalions, units raised by local authorities, employers or committees of private citizens and drawn from a particular district, were an important component of the New Armies. Nearly forty per cent of the battalions formed between August 1914 and June 1916 were locally raised. They were especially characteristic of recruiting in the great cities of Britain, and they gave individual army units a greater social and geographical cohesion than ever before. Civic pride and loyalties were believed to infuse a special spirit in the units concerned. Aiming to enlist a 'Manchester Clerks' and Warehousemen's Battalion' in late August 1914 and faced with initial reluctance from the army authorities, Herbert Dixon, chairman of a Manchester trade association, complained that the local recruiting officer 'seemed hardly able to grasp the main idea, namely, the better spirit obtained by those acquainted with one another working together'. In London, as Peter Simkins has noted, some Pals battalions were 'unashamedly elitist'. There was a Sportsman's Battalion (which became the 23rd Royal Fusiliers), which included 'authors, artists, clergymen, engineers, actors, archaeologists, big-game hunters, footballers, cricketers and oarsmen'. The Belfast-born painter John Lavery (who was later to be appointed an official war artist), at the age of fifty-eight joined the Artists' Rifles (the 28th Battalion, Country of London Territorial Regiment) and found himself drilling in the quadrangle of Burlington House with 'rather a scrubby lot of painters, sculptors, actors, musicians, hairdressers, scene-shifters, etc., of all ages'. He arrived late for drill one day and overheard bemused spectators discussing this motley crowd. 'Who are they?' one asked. 'Don't you know? Why they're German prisoners. Aren't they awful?'[23]

In these units, men joined together, trained together, served together and many died together. After they were formed, the Accrington Pals spent four months or so stationed close to home before in March 1915 being concentrated with other units to form part of the 31st Division, which was full of Pals battalions. The Accrington Pals were part of the 94th Brigade, which also included Pals battalions from Sheffield and Barnsley. They remained in England until mid-December, when they were hurriedly sent to Egypt to reinforce the garrison there against a feared Ottoman attack. By the time they arrived the threat had receded and, having spent less than two months training and labouring on the Suez Canal defences, they embarked for France on 2 March 1916, arriving at Marseilles six days later. Sent north to the Somme sector, the Accrington Pals were first deployed on the front line near Serre during the afternoon of 28 April. At 11.30 p.m. the following evening, they sustained their first fatal casualty, when twenty-year-old Private Jack Clark of Burnley was killed by artillery fire.

The battalion's first taste of the front line lasted nine days, during which two men were killed and one died of wounds. Then they had fourteen days' respite before another ten days in the line, when they suffered two further fatal casualties. From 31 May to 18 June they spent eighteen days behind the lines engaged in some 'special training' for the coming battle, going over ground where the German positions had been marked out with flags and tapes. There followed five days at the front, where things had hotted up somewhat and during which twelve men were killed, followed by six days in the rear area before they were assembled on 30 June for the advance. This pattern of spending about one-third of the time in the front line (and two-thirds out of it), and the rather sporadic casualties incurred, was fairly typical of the everyday British experience on the Western Front. Before late June 1916, indeed, the Somme sector had been generally a quiet part of the front. Regular roulement in and out of the line (rather like the French at Verdun), helps to explain how units and men could survive and retain resilience as fighting forces.[24] Spells in the front line, however, even if supplemented with 'special training', could, of course, only partially prepare men for the intense horrors of a real 'push'.

Popular mythology has it that, when the whistles blew to start the infantry assault on the Somme at 7.30 a.m. on 1 July 1916, British soldiers left their trenches and headed – some accounts say they were ordered to do so at walking pace – for the German lines. The Germans, meanwhile, their defensive positions *not* having been destroyed in the week-long Allied artillery bombardment, had time to emerge, set up their machine guns and inflict terrible casualties among the steadily advancing British soldiers. This, as Robin Prior and Trevor Wilson observe in their forensic investigation of the battle, is the 'dominant paradigm' of 1 July. But while it happened like this in some places, the variety of experience is so varied that it is impossible to generalise about the day as a whole. Prior and Wilson's careful analysis finds that of the eighty battalions which went into action in the first attack, '53 crept out into no-man's land close to the German wire before zero . . . while ten others rushed the line from their own parapet'. Of the other seventeen, twelve 'advanced at a steady pace', and there is insufficient evidence for the remaining five. Some of the ones who advanced steadily did so because they were following a creeping barrage, and were among the most successful units of the day. But despite the variation in the tactics used, Prior and Wilson conclude that 'the pattern of death in prohibitive numbers applied to most of the front'. They add that 'the reason is plain. As long as most German machine-gunners and artillerymen survived the British bombardment, the slaughter of the attacking infantry would occur *whatever* infantry tactics were adopted.'[25]

This conclusion reminds us of the importance of the artillery bombardment with which the battle began on 24 June. In this industrialised, mechanised, technically advanced new kind of warfare, artillery was central to victory. It has been calculated that artillery caused sixty-seven per cent of all casualties during the Great War, and up to 1916 at least it was generally assumed that the way to win a breakthrough on the Western Front was simply to increase the size, duration and intensity of the artillery bombardment until the enemy lines were so pulverised that little or no opposition was possible. A focus on cutting the German wire and destroying trench defences, however, downplayed the crucial importance also of counter-battery fire, to subdue the enemy artillery. The neglect of this in some places proved to be extremely costly. The type of shells used was also a factor. The majority of shells used in the barrage before 1 July were shrapnel, good for killing soldiers in the open, but less effective for cutting wire or destroying concrete emplacements.[26]

The almost slavish concentration on 1 July to the exclusion of the broader context, and the actual beginning of the offensive almost a week earlier, seriously distorts any proper understanding of the battle. There are very good reasons for the privileging or 'foregrounding' of the 1 July attack, both at the time and in the subsequent literature (especially the non-specialist literature). The desperate heroics and the catastrophic casualties of that day make a rightly irresistible human story. Ironically, as the fulcrum of modern warfare moves away from the intimate physical engagement of soldier against soldier, the compulsion remains to focus on the human narrative of the central battlefield. There is less 'romance' (if there is any at all), and certainly less 'human interest' in stories of gun crews sweating away at their repetitive task miles behind the front line, impersonally doling out death and destruction to unseen targets and opponents. We seem to need to stay with the utterly compelling experiences of those men in the trenches waiting as zero hour approached for what we know, with the benefit of hindsight, is to be a terrible fate. There is an echo here in the mordant words of Rudyard Kipling, writing (after the war) of the battle of Loos in September 1915 in which his only son, John, perished. 'It does not seem to have occurred to any one,' he wrote, 'to suggest that direct Infantry attacks, after ninety-minute bombardments, on works begotten out of a generation of thought and prevision, scientifically built up by immense labour and applied science, and developed against all contingencies through nine months, are not likely to find a fortunate issue.'[27]

At the Somme, 'ninety-minute bombardments' were replaced with something much more serious and extended. And yet it was still not enough. Despite the fact that the Somme saw the heaviest Allied bombardment of the war so far, it was spread far too thinly and was quite insufficient to destroy the German defences. The British, too, generally gave a low priority to counter-battery fire – attacking the enemy artillery – which left the German guns largely unscathed to concentrate on well-identified British positions, particularly the front line and reserve trenches. The result of these deficiencies, combined with errors in timing the attack, was all too grimly demonstrated at Serre. The Accrington Pals and the Sheffield City Battalion were committed as attack battalions for the 94th Brigade, with sections of the Barnsley Pals battalions in reserve. The lead battalions carefully moved into no-man's-land ten minutes before zero (7.30 a.m.) and lay down a hundred yards ahead of the British trenches. But when they got up to advance they found to their horror that since the British barrage (following corps instructions) had moved beyond the enemy front line ten minutes early, the German machine-gunners had had time to emerge and set up their weapons. Many were killed before zero and the battle was effectively over within the first half-hour. Of 720 Accrington Pals who took part in the attack, seventy-seven were killed, 463 wounded and eighty-one missing at the end of the day.[28] To make matters worse, the back-up battalions suffered heavy casualties from German artillery targeting the British front line and rear trenches where they were assembling ready to advance.

If you visit the original British line at Serre today, you can find the remains of a front-line trench at the edge of Railway Hollow Wood at the Sheffield Memorial Park where an Accrington Pals memorial was erected in 1991. Looking up the gentle slope into what was no-man's-land about a hundred yards away, is a small Commonwealth War Graves Cemetery, which is as far as many of the pals got.

Less than a mile to the south is Beaumont-Hamel where the 29th Division, who had been at Gallipoli to the very end, were deployed on 1 July. The division included the only British Empire troops to fight that day, 'a Newfoundland battalion drawn from the hard-bitten fishermen of that iron coast'.[29] As elsewhere, the attacking troops seem to have been both optimistic as well as naturally apprehensive. On the eve of the battle the Newfoundlander, Lieutenant Owen Steele, wrote in his diary: 'we were busy all day getting ready to go off to the firing line tonight to commence the greatest attack in the world's history ... It is surprising to see how happy and light-hearted everyone is,' he continued, 'and yet this is undoubtedly the last day for a good many.'[30] The Newfoundlanders and the 1st Battalion the Essex Regiment were readied to back up an initial assault by the division's 87th Brigade and were sent forward after over-optimistic and tragically erroneous reports had reached divisional headquarters that some troops had penetrated the German lines. The Essex battalion were slowed down by the 'complete congestion of the trenches with the bodies of dead and dying', which left the Newfoundlanders to advance alone over open ground. 'The majority of men,' reported the British official historian, 'were hit before they had gone much beyond the British wire.'[31]

On 30 June the Newfoundland Regiment had mustered twenty-five officers and 776 non-commissioned officers and men. Only sixty-eight men responded to the roll call at the end of 1 July. The final official casualty figures, which were among the very worst for any single unit on the first day of the Somme, were 234 killed, 386 wounded and ninety-one missing. Since the battalion effectively represented the entire Newfoundland army, as William Philpott has observed, 'alongside the many local tragedies of 1 July 1916, here was a national disaster'. Owen Steele, in fact, did not go over the top that day. He was held back as part of a mandatory ten per cent reserve. But on 7 July he was struck by a stray German shell behind the front line and died the following day.[32]

Despite its devastating losses, the Newfoundland Regiment recovered and with fresh drafts from home at the end of July was posted with the 29th Division to the Ypres salient in Belgium where they remained until early October. Then they returned to the Somme where they scored a rare success at Gueudecourt near Bapaume on 12 October. In a limited operation under a well-planned creeping barrage, they took and held their objective, albeit at the loss of 120 fatal casualties. The regiment went on to fight at Arras and Masnières (near Ypres) in 1917, and Courtrai in Belgium in 1918. There are Newfoundland memorials at all these places, but the principal one is at Beaumont-Hamel, where a great bronze caribou, the emblem of the regiment, stands on the highest point overlooking the slope where so many Newfoundlanders perished. Since Newfoundland was absorbed into Canada in 1949, this is now so much of a Canadian memorial that there is little to remind the visitor of the British lives also lost there on the first day of the Somme.

Another mile south-east at Thiepval there is further sacred territory and the unmistakable Ulster Tower, which in Scottish baronial style commemorates the exploits of the 36th (Ulster) Division. Here on 1 July the division achieved some striking, if temporary, success. While on the left the 108th Brigade failed to capture the village of St Pierre Divion, the 109th on the right managed to capture the important German strongpoint of the Schwaben Redoubt. The 109th Brigade were helped by the fact that here there was effective artillery fire which had done serious damage to the German defences. Stokes mortars fired smoke shells which helped screen the infantry who had sensibly crawled into no-man's-land before the barrage lifted. The 9th Royal Inniskilling Fusiliers found that the bombardment had successfully cut the German wire and the leading waves were able to move forward without great loss. The Ulstermen here advanced further than any other formation on 1 July, but since to the south 32nd Division's attack on Thiepval had failed, the men of the 109th Brigade were left terribly exposed to German fire on both flanks. By late morning there were about a thousand soldiers holding a salient a thousand yards deep and just 200 yards wide. Their problems were compounded by the fact that the reserve 107th Brigade coming forward got ahead of a British artillery barrage and caught in the open were badly cut up both by 'friendly fire', and enfilading German machine guns. By the early afternoon the advanced position of the Ulster Division troops was probably irredeemable. They were short of ammunition and supplies of all sorts; nothing could get through the German barrage behind them. Small remnants held on until 3 July but by then the line which the division held was not much more than 500 yards from where they had started. On the first two days of the Somme, the Ulster Division lost 5,500 all ranks, killed, wounded or missing, out of a total of about 15,000 men.[33]

The 36th Division, representing as it did the Ulster Protestant community, was a 'pals' formation writ large. It was supposed (though erroneously so) to be drawn almost entirely from the pre-war paramilitary and anti-nationalist Ulster Volunteer Force. John Buchan praised them as 'splendid troops, drawn from those volunteers who had banded themselves together for another cause, [and] now shed their blood like water for the liberty of the world'.[34] After the war, nevertheless, the sacrifice of Ulster lives on the Somme became part of the creation narrative of the new northern Unionist state when Ireland was partitioned in 1921. In Ireland as a whole there was a progressive identification of the Somme, and, indeed, the whole war, with just the Protestant-Unionist community. Even the date of the battle seemed especially significant, since 1 July had been the actual date (by the defunct Julian calendar) of the battle of the Boyne in 1690, a crucial victory of the Protestant King William III over the Catholic King James II. Unionists' selective memory of the war, which for many years erased the considerable Catholic and nationalist participation, was cast in materials more enduring than bronze, and was firmly incorporated into the Unionist-Orange mind. The Somme was conflated with the Boyne, and annual ceremonies on 1 July and 11 November, which embodied explicitly Protestant rituals, were used to recall Ulster's ungrudging sacrifice in the war and confirm its continuing loyalty to the United Kingdom and (while it existed) the British Empire.

In the years after 1918, however, Ulster Unionism's professions of loyalty to the empire were as much a product of weakness and anxiety as anything else. In the years immediately following the war especially, something of this was no doubt part of the similar manifestations of British imperial solidarity associated with dominion commemorations of the Somme, but unlike Ulster these monuments and their accompanying rituals have increasingly been used as sites of autonomous and distinctive nationality. The South African memorial at Delville Wood is a prime example. In August 1915 a 6,000-strong 1st South African Infantry Brigade, overwhelmingly composed of Anglo-South African volunteers, left for Britain. At the end of 1915 the brigade was posted to the Middle East where they saw action against the Senussi in western Egypt. In April 1916 they were drafted to France with the 9th (Scottish) Division, and deployed on the Somme in July. Here they took part in an initially quite successful operation at Longueval on 14 July when, in a well-managed surprise attack, supported by a more intensive but much shorter artillery bombardment than that before 1 July, four British divisions reached and captured the German second line of trenches. There was even a moment when the breakthrough seemed sufficient to deploy cavalry as mounted infantry, able to seize ground rapidly. Lancers of the 20th Deccan Horse, serving with the 2nd (Indian) Cavalry Division, were sent in and cleared some enemy positions to the west of Delville Wood, spearing some sixteen Germans, surely among the oddest and unluckiest Western Front casualties.[35] Eleven of the cavalrymen were killed, including Yasin Khan from Hyderabad, Abbas Ali Khan from Poona (Pune) and Didar Singh from the Punjab.[36]

But here, too, the fighting turned into a savage attritional contest. On 15 July the South Africans had been ordered to take Delville Wood 'at all costs'. This they managed, save for a sector in the northwest of the wood. But the Germans responded with a counterattack and for five costly days the South Africans grimly hung on. 'In spite of terrible losses,' wrote James Edmonds, 'they had steadfastly endured the ordeal of the German bombardment, which seldom slackened and never ceased, and had faced with great courage and resolution repeated counter-attacks delivered by fresh troops.' While at the beginning of the battle the South Africans had been 3,150 strong, they emerged from the wood having lost over 750 killed and 1,500 wounded. But they inflicted casualties too. The German official history of the fighting recorded that their opponents 'partly of British, partly of Dutch ancestry' had cost their attackers 'a lot of the best blood'. Bill Nasson has observed that Delville Wood provided an ideal heroic narrative 'for the Union of South Africa's war chart . . . The Brigade's powers of endurance personified an idealised image of gritty South African dependability in the very face of annihilation,' and one which powerfully contributed to a 'mythic code of selfless war sacrifice'.[37]

After the war Delville Wood became the favoured site for a South African national war memorial. The driving force behind the scheme was the flamboyant and wealthy entrepreneur Sir Percy FitzPatrick, who had lost one of his sons in the fighting in France in 1917. FitzPatrick is credited with initiating the two minutes silence which began during the war as a daily 'noon pause' in South Africa, but was later adopted in Britain for 11 a.m. on Armistice Day, 11 November. Delville Wood as a whole – 'sacred' and 'imperishable' South African ground – was purchased and an elaborate memorial designed by Sir Herbert Baker (whose architectural métier was the physical expression of orotund imperialism) was dedicated in October 1926. The project was politically sensitive as Afrikaner nationalists (rightly) accused some of its supporters of wishing to use it to privilege the British imperial connexion. One Afrikaner MP, Tielman Roos, told the Union parliament in 1920 that Baker was principally interested in 'British grandeur, for which so many lives from here were quite uselessly sacrificed'. At the unveiling of the memorial FitzPatrick declared that 'South Africa might be the home of those who fought, but England was to them the Mother Country of the Empire.' The South African prime minister, General J. B. M. Hertzog, had to tread a difficult line at the ceremony. His party had announced in advance that he would represent the 'Hollandse-Afrikaner' nation at 'Delville Bos', where he would honour 'the innocent Afrikaners who fell in the World War'. Hertzog said nothing of the empire or England, instead he invoked a wider and higher inspiration. South Africans, he asserted, had responded 'to the far-off call of a world in distress imploring aid in the name of mankind, of national freedom, and of world peace'.[38]

After the Second World War, when South African forces again served in British imperial formations, the Delville Wood memorial was appropriated by apartheid-era South African governments in ways which followed Hertzog's rhetoric to commemorate South Africa's steadfast dedication to Western Cold War values of democracy and freedom, as well as a more specifically white South African commitment to Christian 'civilisation' against supposed African 'barbarism'. In the mid-1980s, with the backing of state president P. W. Botha, the Delville Wood Commemorative Museum was completed for the seventieth anniversary of the battle of the Somme. The museum's explicit purpose was to present 'South Africa's united resolve to fight, to sacrifice, and to die for civilised traditions of the Free World'. In keeping with new political sensibilities, space was found for Black Africans in the displays, with (as Bill Nasson puts it) 'recognition as courageous camp followers of the Springboks of 1916, in saintly tribute to faithful duty in auxiliary roles as medical orderlies, stretcher-bearers, guards and drivers'.[39] So, even in the late years of apartheid South Africa, there was some recognition of that wider participation which was so characteristic everywhere in the First World War.

There are two important Australian sites of memory close to and on the Somme: at Fromelles and at Pozières, on the dead straight road that runs north-west from Albert, behind the British lines, to Bapaume, which the Germans held. The Anzacs were deployed on the Western Front from the spring of 1916. On 19 July the Australian 5th Division was used in a disastrous attack at Fromelles near Lille with the aim of pinning down German units which might otherwise have been used as reinforcements on the Somme a little further south. This battle site, where the Australians suffered very heavy casualties, was commemorated with an Australian government-sponsored memorial park, inaugurated in 1998 for the eightieth anniversary of the end of the war. Reflecting the ways in which individual endurance and compassion have often come to dominate modern conceptions of the war, at the centre of the park is a statue – 'Cobbers' – of one soldier carrying a wounded comrade, perfectly embodying Charles Bean's Anzac ideal of mateship. Fromelles was further embedded into Australian collective memory after a mass grave containing 250 unidentified bodies (203 Australian) was uncovered in 2008. Accompanied by much public ceremony the 'missing of Fromelles' were reburied in 2010 in a specially created new Commonwealth War Graves Cemetery. With modern DNA-matching techniques, moreover, some 144 of the Australian dead of 1916 had been reported identified by May 2014.[40]

Pozières at the Somme has a longer commemorative history. Three Australian divisions, the 1st, 2nd and 4th, fought here in late July and early August 1916 in a series of costly advances with modest gains.

During the rest of August the divisions endeavoured in vain to take the German strongpoint of Mouquet Farm beyond Pozières, until they were taken out of the line exhausted on 5 September. Charles Bean maintained that the fighting in the summer of 1916 'was in some respects the heaviest they [the Australians] ever experienced'. The casualties on the Somme totalled 23,000 officers and men. When the 5,500 losses at Fromelles are added, 'the Australian force in France had in less than seven weeks suffered more than 28,000 casualties'. This compared to 26,000 casualties over eight months at Gallipoli the previous year.[41]

Visiting Pozières in 1917, Charles Bean predicted that the 'small square mile', which was 'one great Australian burying ground to-day', would 'be the goal of eternal pilgrimages tomorrow'. It has not quite turned out as he thought. Gallipoli has become the single most important pilgrimage site for Australians wishing to visit a First World War battlefield, though many Australians do visit the Western Font. In 1919 the 1st Australian Division erected an austere obelisk as a memorial at Pozières and the site of the 'Windmill', a grassy mound at the highest point on the Pozières ridge, which the 2nd Division captured on 5 August 1916, was purchased for preservation by the Australians in 1935. Although in recent years the main Australian National War Memorial at Villers-Bretonneux, to the south of the Somme battlefield, has been the scene of most official ceremonies, soil from Pozières was scattered in the tomb of the Australian Unknown Soldier interred in Canberra in November 1993. Pozières, thus, as Joan Beaumont observes, remains 'at the heart of Australian national commemoration'.[42]

Although, as with Australia, Gallipoli remains the single most important Great War site, the Somme also has a central place in New Zealand commemoration, for the New Zealand Unknown Warrior was exhumed from Longueval where the 2nd New Zealand Division fought in September 1916, suffering 7,000 casualties, over 1,500 of whom were killed. A memorial obelisk, one of three in similar style on the Western Front – the other two are near Ieper (Ypres) and Mesen (Messines) – stands here on the site of Switch Trench, the division's initial objective, and was dedicated on 8 October 1922.[43] Reminding observers of how very far the Kiwi soldiers had come to fight and die, each of the three New Zealand battlefield memorials carries the same painful inscription: 'From the uttermost ends of the earth.'

GERMANS ON THE SOMME

Leutnant Ernst Jünger, of the 73rd Fusilier regiment, whose unflinching memoir *Storm of Steel*, first published in 1920, became a classic participant's account of trench warfare, was among the German defenders of Guillemont in September 1916. Posted to the front line during the night, the scene that greeted them in the morning was of a pulverised wasteland. 'The country around, so far as the eye could see, had been completely ploughed by heavy shells. Not a single blade of grass showed itself,' he wrote. 'This churned-up field was gruesome. In among the living defenders lay the dead. When we dug foxholes, we realized that they were stacked in layers.' Guillemont village 'seemed to have disappeared without trace; just a whitish stain on the cratered field indicated where one of the limestone houses had been pulverized'. The village railway station was 'crumpled like a child's toy; further to the rear the woods of Delville Wood, ripped to splinters'. To Jünger's mind an incident two days later illustrated how stretched the German defence was. At midday one of his men had him 'come over and look in the direction of Guillemont station, from behind a torn-off British leg'. There Jünger saw that 'hundreds of British soldiers [who may have been men of the 16th (Irish) Division] were running forward through a flat communication trench, little troubled by the weak gunfire we were able to direct at them'. This, he thought, showed 'the inequality of the resources with which we had to fight. Had we essayed the same thing, our units would have been shot to pieces in a matter of minutes.'[44]

In his detailed and revealing account of the German army on the Somme, Jack Sheldon notes how the Germans took the loss of Guillemont particularly badly as they had been defending it hard all through August. Reserve Vizefeldwebel Heinrich Warnecke of Ernst Jünger's regiment recalled that he had been on many battlefields during the war, 'but never did a place of battle leave so moving an impression on me as that of Guillemont on 3 September 1916. I, too, belonged to the 1st battalion that shed its lifeblood here.' The defenders took appalling casualties. When after the battle the survivors of the 5th Company of 2nd Battalion Infantry Regiment 76, originally about 200 strong, reached the rear assembly point and posed for a photograph, there were five left. The 3rd Company of Fusilier Regiment 73 were completely wiped out, so that in the regimental history the relevant page was left blank, apart from a bleak statement by the historian. 'Nobody,' he wrote, 'from 3rd Company can provide a report – all the men were killed, as was every officer.'[45]

At the British attack at Flers-Courcelette on 15 September, Rittmeister von Krosijk of the 2nd battalion Field Artillery reported 'a report from one of the batteries that an extraordinary vehicle was advancing'. Initially, he said, 'it was thought that it might have been an ambulance, because it was thought that a Red Cross flag had been seen, but that was not certain'. But they were disabused of this idea when an adjacent battery reported coming under machine-gun fire from the vehicle. Krosijk's battery managed to knock out the tank, and 'the British soldiers, who emerged from the vehicle, were all shot down by the machine-gun fire of our infantry'. Further to the west, where the British 150th Brigade advanced with two tanks, Gustav Ebelshauser of the 17th Bavarian Regiment recorded that 'the monsters' motors hummed and droned louder as they crawled increasingly nearer. They advanced relentlessly . . . Holes, hills, rocks, even barbed wire meant nothing.' Ebelshauser also remarked on British air power, and the integration of air power with artillery. 'Not only did the mechanical birds fly low with machine-guns shooting at any moving body in sight,' he wrote, 'but they dropped signals – star shells of different colors – which were immediately picked up by the batteries.'[46]

One of those tanks named after an alcoholic drink – Crème de Menthe – which reached the sugar factory at Courcelette had a terrifying impact on some of the defending Germans. 'A man came running from the left,' recalled Feldwebel Weinert of the 211th Prussian Infantry Regiment, 'shouting "There is a crocodile crawling into our lines!" The poor wretch was off his head. He had seen a tank for the first time and had imagined this giant of a machine, rearing up and dipping down as it came, to be a monster.' A cooler description of his

first encounter with the new machines comes from Leutnant Braunhofer
of the 5th Bavarian Infantry Division, albeit three months after the
battle, but he conveys the impressive power of the new weapon well.
Defending the village of Flers, 'a tank appeared on the left front of my
company position which I immediately attacked with machine gun
and rifle fire and also, as it came in closer, with hand grenades. These
unfortunately caused no real damage because the tank only turned
slightly to the left but otherwise just carried on.' The tank moved on
'without my men being able to do anything against it', and later positioned itself close to the exit from the village and 'placed the whole
length of this road under continuous machine-gun fire'.[47]

There is evidence from the German side to support the argument
that during September 1916 the attritional pressure was beginning to
cause real strain. The incremental impact of the piecemeal British
advance since early July took its toll. 'It is true that the loss of one
piece of ground after another,' wrote General Max von Gallwitz, who
was appointed overall German commander on the Somme in mid-July,
'does not amount to much in itself, but the repetition serves to
strengthen the enemy and weaken us. Think of all those "missing!" If
this game goes on any longer, we will be unable to supply the necessary replacements in men and equipment.'[48] We can see how in
Germany the Somme became a shorthand for intolerable pressure, and
a portent of what must be avoided. When considering the possible
introduction of unrestricted submarine warfare the German arguments focused mainly on the restriction of the imported food supplies
upon which Britain depended. Price rises and food shortages would
provoke riots as British domestic morale collapsed. Ludendorff also
thought it would help reduce munitions supplies to the Western Front.
'We must,' he asserted, 'spare the troops a second Somme.'[49]

For all its sustained horror the Somme also saw moments of human
decency. An account by Erzatzreservist Tebbe of the 164th Infantry
Regiment tells how just before the assault on Guillemont on
3 September, a British soldier who appeared in no-man's-land was
wounded and taken prisoner by the Germans on the front line.
Although he had been shot through the chest, he was conscious and
after having been bandaged up 'was quite cheerful'. Half an hour later

the British attacked in great numbers, overwhelming the neighbouring German blockhouses in which 'the British grenades caused a dreadful bloodbath, from which very few Germans escaped'. The British moved on towards where Tebbe and a comrade were sheltering in a dugout with a mass of wounded men, 'huddled together as deep as possible, helpless before the hand grenades'. But 'then the wounded British soldier, who was down below in the dugout, became our saviour'. He climbed the steps and shouted to the advancing troops that 'there was nobody in the dugout who was capable of fighting. Protectively, he stood in front of the Germans who had earlier treated him in a knightly manner.' The Germans were spared and led off to captivity. 'In a sunken road we halted. British medical orderlies treated our wounds and gave us tea and cigarettes.'[50]

From the other side, Alexander Aitken recounted a successful New Zealand attack at Goose Alley in front of Fricourt on 25 September 1916. 'A handful of prisoners, Bavarians, surrendered and were sent to the rear; several others, including a company officer, had been badly wounded.' The officer, 'dignified, distinguished, was bleeding from a grave wound in the upper part of the leg'. They bandaged him up as best they could, but felt that he was surely dying. 'Deadly white and in grievous pain,' remembered Aitken, 'he made no complaint and thanked me in French. One can have no quarrel with such a man.'[51]

ECHOES OF THE BATTLE

In the south-east Belfast inner suburb of Cregagh there is a veterans' 'colony' of houses – homes fit for heroes – built for ex-servicemen by the Irish Sailors' and Soldiers' Land Trust in the 1920s. In this estate Picardy and Bapaume Avenues join Thiepval Avenue, which is crossed by Hamel Drive, Albert Drive and Somme Drive. What is remarkable about these battlefield place names is the way in which terrible sites of death and destruction are commemorated in what have become prosaic home addresses. The French have a word for it: banalisation. It is difficult to translate precisely, but it conveys the sense of rendering something ordinary, and in this particular case it is making something frightful and extraordinary quite mundane and commonplace. But, all the same, one wonders how it was for those veterans returning from the horrors of the war to be thus reminded of the trenches and the slaughter every day. That place where people died had become a mere address, a place where people live. Perhaps that is as it should be. Yet there remains, to turn a phrase, a corner or two of a Northern Irish field which are forever France.

10

The Eastern Mediterranean and the Balkans

On 18 October 1916, *The Times* of London announced that two days earlier two Allied ships had landed a thousand French and Italian sailors at the Greek port of Piraeus, and that they had occupied both the town hall and the railway stations of Athens and Piraeus. One hundred and fifty sailors 'with two machine guns' had been posted at the Athens municipal theatre. The city was reported quiet. Although the official explanation for this landing of Allied troops in a neutral state was that they had been deployed to assist the Greek police and 'put an end to the demonstrations which have threatened to cause trouble',[1] the underlying impetus came from a French-led effort to force Greece into the war on the Allied side. Greece, in fact, could scarcely avoid being drawn into a wider Balkan conflict – in part an extension of the Balkan Wars of 1912–13 – fuelled by the very instability and rivalries which had contributed to the outbreak of war in 1914. Balkan ethnic and sectarian passions and antagonisms in turn exacerbated relations with the declining Ottoman Empire, which had ruled the region for 400 years up to the late nineteenth century. For some Balkan leaders, indeed, the Great War seemed to provide an opportunity finally to extinguish Ottoman power (and, of course, secure treasured national objectives). During the war this situation was increasingly mirrored by that in the Middle East and the Arabian peninsula, still ruled by the Ottomans, where proto-nationalist and restive Arab subjects also saw Constantinople's wartime extremity as providing a political opportunity for them.

GREEK SCHISMS AND GREEK MEMORIES

The Allied landing at Athens in October 1916 was one of a series of interventions which brought Greece to the brink of civil war. Although it remained neutral at the start of the war, there were deep differences between the progressive, reforming and intensely nationalistic prime minister Eleutherios Venizelos, who favoured intervention on the Allied side, and the Prussian-military-academy-educated King Constantine, who was married to Kaiser Wilhelm's sister and was strongly inclined towards the Central Powers. Venizelos, prime minister since 1910, had presided over the massive accretion of Greek territory (at Turkey's expense) following the Balkan Wars and believed that defeat for the Central Powers would open up the possibility of recreating the Byzantine Empire. Greece would expand further to take in Constantinople, the Aegean islands and even territory in Anatolia where there was a sizeable Greek population.[2]

While an uneasy domestic peace was maintained over the first year or so of the war, Venizelos sought to extract what advantages he could from the situation. Meanwhile the Allies were anxious to support Serbia, threatened as it was by Austro-Hungarian aggression from the north. In London, Lloyd George proposed sending an army to the region 'in order to bring all the Balkan states into the war on our side and settle Austria'. In January 1915 Britain offered Greece concessions in Asia Minor if they would come into the war on Serbia's side. Venizelos responded by saying that he would do so if either Bulgaria or Romania (still both neutral at this stage) could be persuaded to help or, failing that, the British and French landed two army corps (approximately 80,000 men) at Salonika (Thessaloniki) in northwest Greece, the nearest convenient port from which Serbia could be helped. Politicians in Paris and London were attracted to the apparent possibilities opened up by a new front in the east – Lloyd George, for example, spoke of how '80,000 men from the W[est]' could bring in

'800,000 in the E[ast] – which would, they thought, help break the deadlock on the Western Front.[3]

This, of course, was also the thinking behind the Gallipoli campaign, which overtook the Salonika plans after neither Bulgaria – which was in any case leaning towards the Central Powers – nor Romania showed much interest in coming in with Greece on the Allied side. Offering slices of enemy territory to potential allies – which could only be honoured after victory had been secured – meanwhile remained on both sides' agendas. A significant factor, for example, bringing Bulgaria in on the Central Powers' side in September 1915 was the promise of Greek Macedonia, including Salonika. The Bulgarians had long wished to acquire this Mediterranean port and had hoped to seize it from the Ottomans in the Balkan War of 1912, but had been narrowly beaten to it by the Greeks. Late in 1915 the British tried to tempt the Greeks with Cyprus (unusually offering territory the British already possessed), though this was insufficient inducement at the time.

The Gallipoli campaign brought with it the beginning of a piecemeal Allied occupation of Greek territory, albeit with the acquiescence of the Venizelos government (not that they could have done much to stop it). In February 1915 the main advanced Allied base was established on the island of Lemnos, where the Greeks withdrew their artillery garrison from the fine natural harbour of Mudros, just sixty miles west of the Dardanelles. Other Aegean islands, which had been acquired by the Greeks in the Balkan Wars, including Tenedos (Bozcaada) and Imbros (Gökçeada), were also occupied by the British and French. In January 1916, moreover, the French occupied Mytilene on Lesbos and Castellorizzo (Megisti) off the Turkish coast. Since the Turks had not formally accepted the Greek claim to the islands, technically the Allied occupation did not violate their neutrality.

For many Allied soldiers these eastern Mediterranean islands provided idyllic oases of calm after the horrors of Gallipoli. At Christmas 1915 Clement Attlee found himself on Mudros, where he and the South Lancashires combined some light training with 'topping hot baths at Therma where there is a natural flow of water and marble baths, relics of classical times. We needed them badly as we were most of us more or less infested with insects.' The Greek bath-keeper served them 'omelettes, sweet biscuits and sardines'. Ivan Heald, the Irish journalist who had served with the Royal Naval Division on the peninsula, also landed up on Mudros. 'Meanwhile life is jolly here,' he wrote. 'If the sun shines one can bathe in the sea, and every night there is a whole night's sleep.' A fortnight later he was on Tenedos, some twenty miles south of the Dardanelles and five miles off the Turkish coast. 'These are great days for us here,' he told his mother on 3 February. 'I can hardly believe it is only a month since we were being knocked about by howitzer shell. Here soldiering is as it should be.' That week Heald's company were on guard duty with 'sentinels very picturesque on the skyline' deployed along the coast. 'I go on daily tours to see them away over the hills and through the vineyards,' he wrote. 'The only soldiers besides ourselves are a few jolly old Zouaves in red fezzes and baggy trousers. We *entente* in a little canteen kept by a Serbian, and they sing the songs of the Foreign Legion.' A fortnight later he reported an eight-day visit with a fellow officer to Mytilene, seven hours' passage south by motor launch. As the 'only British officers', they 'made quite a stir': 'we had tea with the consul's wife, and were entertained on a battleship by the midshipmen, and sang songs with French officers, and were rich young English milords. One night, a Greek stole [the] other officer's handkerchief in a café, and the next morning my courier brought the man up to my hotel and beat him in my presence.'[4]

In April 1915, Venizelos had offered Greek troops for Gallipoli, but King Constantine objected and the prime minister resigned. Having won a majority in the ensuing parliamentary election, he returned to power in August. When the Bulgars joined the Central Powers the following month Venizelos argued that Greece had to honour the terms of a mutual defence alliance signed with Serbia in 1913 and was now finally obliged to come into the war. With the king's reluctant approval, Venizelos mobilised the Greek army and invited the Allies to send forces to Salonika. On 5 October the first French and British troops began to arrive, sparking off a renewed lively debate in Greece between the Venizelists and royalists who remained unconvinced about the necessity for Greece to fight. Although he narrowly won a vote of confidence in the Greek parliament, Venizelos was forced to resign again when the king refused to abandon neutrality.

After yet another general election in December (from which Venizelos abstained) a so-called 'government of national unity' was formed under the veteran politician Stephanos Skouloudis, who adopted what he called a policy of 'very benevolent neutrality' towards the Allies. For about a year, while domestic Greek politics were paralysed by this 'national schism' ('ethnikos dikhasmos'), and, despite Skouloudis's apparent benevolence towards the Allies (though in fact his government could do little to prevent the French and British building up their forces in Salonika), pro-German elements remained powerful, while the Allies and the Central Powers shadow-boxed across the theoretically neutral Greek political landscape.

Observing, and participating, in this was the thirty-two-year-old Scottish writer Compton Mackenzie. Due to age and medical circumstances (persistent sciatica), combined with a congenital inability to take military discipline very seriously, at the start of the war Mackenzie was thought unsuitable for active military service. Very keen to participate, however, he exploited his own excellent social contacts and wangled a posting to the staff of Sir Ian Hamilton, the British commander-in-chief at Gallipoli.[5] By May 1915 he was an intelligence officer in Hamilton's headquarters at Imbros. Here he stayed until August when he was sent on sick leave (having acquired dysentery and cystitis to accompany his sciatica) to Athens where he ended up working for Major Rhys Sansom, who with cover as assistant military attaché was running a combined espionage and counter-espionage operation, reporting to 'M.I.1(c)', the British Secret Service Bureau in London. Sansom's organisation gathered economic and blockade intelligence and he had also been obtaining information about the Turks under the guise of running a relief fund for refugees from Turkey and Asia Minor. But his main purpose was to track and, if possible, counter enemy intrigues in Greece.

Continued Greek neutrality, even if biased towards the Allies, meant that the Central Powers still had diplomatic representation in the country, as well as droves of spies. Cyril Falls, the British official historian of the Salonika campaign, noted that when the Allied forces arrived at Salonika the 'German Consul's agents had stood on the quay counting troops and boxes of shell as they were landed'. The presence at the port of consulates of all four hostile powers was 'intolerable. The most exact and detailed information about the numbers and dispositions of the Allies was known to be telegraphed regularly to Berlin, Vienna, Sofia, and Constantinople. The city was swarming with spies.' But once Salonika had been transformed into an Allied armed camp the military authorities could sort this out. Despite Greek protests, during the afternoon of 30 December, the French organised an operation to arrest the four enemy consuls (they were afterwards deported) and as many of their agents as could be found.[6]

The option of rounding up enemy agents was not open to the British in Athens where, from mid-October 1915, Mackenzie, comfortably billeted in the British School of Archaeology and with the codename 'Z', was given the task of running British counter-intelligence. This kept him very busy and by the end of 1916 his office – described as a 'Bureau of Information attached to the British Legation' – had built up a card index of 12,000 suspects. Early in 1916 he was also appointed Military Control Officer and given the job of monitoring the traffic and issuing visas for intending travellers.

Mackenzie liaised with a much larger and better-appointed French 'Bureau de Renseignements' which was set up in December 1915 and located in the French archaeological school. The British enviously regarded their plans for 'a photographic studio, a chemical laboratory, half a dozen automobiles and unlimited funds'. They also had a 'service de contre-espionage' whose director, Engineer-Captain Ricaud, was astonished to discover the tiny extent of Mackenzie's much more modestly funded operation. Ricaud proved to be an exemplary colleague, but Mackenzie could not secure a British war medal for him (though he was himself awarded a Légion d'Honneur by the French). In his memoirs published fifty years later he still resented 'the failure of the British Government to accord him any recognition by decorating him with one of those strips of ribbon that were showered like confetti at a wedding on so many onlookers during the war'.

The British and French divided some of the counter-intelligence work between them, but Mackenzie was careful to keep the German legation for himself as he had already bought the services of the legation's Greek porter, whom he called 'Davy Jones'. 'As soon as I met him,' recalled Mackenzie, 'I recognised in him the authentic spy, the spy by nature, with his very pale blue eyes filmed with suspicion and furtiveness almost as if by a visible cataract.' Jones was Mackenzie's 'master agent', though he was quite difficult to run. Agents, reflected Mackenzie, 'respond like fortune-tellers to what they think their clients want'. This being so, a case officer had to avoid asking any sort of leading questions. Mackenzie's policy, therefore, was never to let Jones see 'that I was more interested in one scrap of his information than in another'. For six months Jones provided copious amounts of information, much of which Mackenzie was able to trade with the French and make 'our ill-equipped, ill-defined sub-Bureau indispensable to the grand new French Bureau'.[7]

The French, both at Salonika and in Athens, were inclined to force the pace in Greece. Although the Allies together clearly backed Venizelos and wanted to bring the Greeks into the war (a line which Mackenzie enthusiastically supported), the proactive policy of the French unsettled the more cautious British and seemed to embody wider regional ambitions. Compton Mackenzie was convinced that Admiral de Roquefeuil, head of the French naval mission, backed by the French Minister of the Marine, 'did not care a button about either Mr. Venizelos or King Constantine', but was 'filled with an ambition to establish the predominance of his own country in the Near East'. Over the summer of 1916, the French became increasingly concerned about the equivocal loyalties of the Greek armed forces, especially after the Athens government in May had ordered the surrender of the important stronghold of Fort Rupel in eastern Macedonia, northeast of Salonika, to a mixed Bulgarian and German force. On French initiative a partial Allied blockade was imposed along the Greek coast and the Allied governments demanded that the Greek army be demobilised and returned to a peace footing. While the Greeks complied, there were anti-Allied demonstrations in Athens. Meanwhile in

August, Venizelist soldiers in Salonika launched a revolt against the royalist government. Venizelos himself agreed to form a provisional republican government and on 26 September, under French protection, he and his closest supporters left Athens and established their rival government in Venizelos's native Crete. Here he announced that Greece would enter the war on the Allied side, as eventually happened in June 1917 after King Constantine had abdicated in favour of his son, Alexander.[8]

The Venizelist revolt of September 1916 threw Athens into turmoil, and precipitated the Allied landing at Piraeus on 16 October. King Constantine was outraged and compared Venizelos to the Irish republican Roger Casement (who had been executed for high treason on 3 August). He told Sir Francis Eliot, the British minister, 'that, if he caught him, he would treat his former prime minister in the same fashion as Britain had treated the Irish rebel'. Following clashes between royalist and Venizelist troops, in mid-November the Allies imposed a neutral zone south-east of Salonika beyond which the king agreed to withdraw units loyal to him. But when the French demanded that the Greeks surrender munitions, which they claimed were no longer needed as they had demobilised their forces, the king flatly refused, and on 1 December parties of French sailors, three companies of British marines and a small Italian detachment were landed at Piraeus and moved in to occupy positions around Athens. After some sharp fighting, which resulted in 191 French and twenty-one British casualties, and a brief French naval bombardment, hostilities ceased when the king agreed to give up some munitions and the Allied troops were withdrawn.[9]

There was extensive rioting in Athens as royalists took the opportunity to attack Venizelists and hostile crowds gathered outside the Allied legations. The French began to evacuate their staff. Compton Mackenzie and his colleagues, along with 200 or so Venizelists seeking sanctuary, and two French agents who had been arrested and released by the Greeks, found themselves besieged in the annexe to the legation where his office was, with sounds of gunfire around the city and periodic reports of Allied diplomats' and Venizelist houses being looted. Mackenzie was less surprised at this than some of his colleagues and a month later told his chief in London, Mansfield Cumming, how he would always remember the military attaché 'on December 1st marching into the Chancery and saying – all is now perfectly tranquil – and just as he finished his sentence a tremendous battle breaking out right under the windows of the Legation'.

The British were trapped for two days and nights, but matters were enlivened during the first afternoon by 'what seemed a fantastic apparition' of a Greek wedding party, complete with priest who arrived at the legation. It appeared that some days before 'two young Greeks had lured a girl to a lonely house on the outskirts of Athens where one of them had violated her'. The girl's mother had come to Mackenzie's office to seek 'the help of the famous "Anglo-French Secret Police" [evidently Mackenzie's outfit was not particularly covert] to avenge her daughter's honour'. A band of locally employed staff 'had seized the ravisher, brought him to the Annexe, and thrashed him', following which the guilty party had 'expressed a strong desire to marry the girl as soon as possible, and protested that he should never have violated her if they had not already been betrothed and if her mother had not been tiresome about the furniture'. The mother thereupon had insisted that the wedding should take place at the annexe, and so it came to pass, after which the wedding party left the building 'during a quiet interval between two fusillades'. Mackenzie was presented with several boxes of sugared almonds which came in handy as 'except for some olives, and a little bread and cheese they were all we had to eat for a couple of days'.[10]

It was decided that Athens had become too dangerous for Mackenzie's operation and on 5 December he and a hundred members of his staff (including agents), along with 150 Venizelist refugees, relocated to the island of Syra (Syros), eighty miles southeast of Athens. Here Mackenzie occupied the former Austrian and Turkish consulates and spent what appears to have been a very enjoyable (and productive) eight months running the Aegean Intelligence Service, which combined a general intelligence-gathering operation with British counter-intelligence throughout the region. In contrast to the parsimonious conditions of Athens, and partly because of the

increasingly valuable intelligence he was supplying, this was agree-
ably well resourced, with a budget of £5,000 per month (equivalent to
something over £200,000 today).[11]

Mackenzie drew on his Athens experiences for a gently satirical
novel, *Extremes Meet*, published in 1928, whose central character,
Roger Waterlow, is head of British intelligence in wartime Greece,
endeavouring to gather information about Turkey and enemy intrigues,
while constantly plagued by 'idiotic questions from Malta, Cairo, and
Marseilles'. One of his agents, codenamed 'Keats', a man with 'very
pale blue eyes', is the porter at the German legation, and an 'infernally
efficient' spy. Waterlow believed that the best agents brought optimistic intelligence. 'A good agent,' he told his obese assistant, 'tells you
that a lack of coffee and contraceptives among the Turks will make
them sue for peace in less than a month. The fighting arms, fat boy,
are always thirsting for an intellectual tonic. That is what the secret
service is intended to provide.' Waterlow was also languidly sceptical
about British policy towards the Greeks. Why, he reflected, should
the locals 'be heckled into going to war for the sake of a lot of money-
grubbing Frenchmen and football-mad Englishmen'?[12]

While this sort of thing may not have endeared Mackenzie to his
former colleagues in the secret service, there was little they could
do about a fictionalised account. But Mackenzie, who never wasted
a word he wrote, unwisely (as it turned out) plundered his official
wartime correspondence for three volumes of memoirs which were
published in the early 1930s. In the second of these, *First Athenian
Memories*, he covered his intelligence work in Athens in 1915, and,
although he did not provide very many specific details of the organisation he was employed by, he was cheerfully irreverent about the work,
as illustrated by the title of one chapter: 'Early absurdities of secret-
service'. But his third volume of memoirs, *Greek Memories*, proved to
be the last straw for his former colleagues. This book dealt extensively
with his intelligence work in Athens and Syra, and named both the
wartime chief of the secret service, Mansfield Cumming (and his use
of the single initial 'C' in correspondence), as well as many of his local
staff. Mackenzie also added verisimilitude by including numerous
transcripts of letters and telegrams. Inevitably, *Greek Memories* was

published with great publicity about its revelations. 'Mystery Chief of the Secret Service', announced the *Daily Telegraph*, 'Capt "C's" identity disclosed'.[13]

The current Chief of the Secret Intelligence Service, Admiral Hugh Sinclair, immediately took steps to have the book banned. It was, he told the Foreign Office, full of material 'considered objectionable from the point of view of the national interest'. He complained that it blew both the wartime and current cover of the service, and named not just serving members but past ones who might be re-employed in the future and thus needed to keep their association with intelligence work secret. The book also established 'a very dangerous precedent for present employees on leaving the Service, and also for journalists' who might consider publishing memoirs and the like. Mackenzie was prosecuted under the Official Secrets Act, which prohibited the unauthorised disclosure of official information obtained while in government service. Since he readily admitted that he had based large portions of the book on his official correspondence, he had no option but to plead guilty. The committal and subsequent trial, nevertheless, had an opéra bouffe quality (especially as recounted by Mackenzie in his later memoirs). At the committal, an MI5 officer on the stand was embarrassed by revelations that among the list of secret service officers they had identified in Mackenzie's book, one, Clifford Heathcote-Smith, the British consul-general in Alexandria, listed 'Intelligence Officer in the Aegean 1915–18' in his *Who's Who* entry; another, Alan Wace, a professional archaeologist, had never been a member of the secret service at all; and a third, Captain Christmas, was dead and thus presumably not available for future employment.[14]

At the trial, much of which was held in camera, General Sir Ian Hamilton, his old chief from Gallipoli, and Admiral William Sells, who had been naval attaché in Athens, both provided Mackenzie with superb character references. Sells told the judge not only that Mackenzie was 'in every sense of the word a man of honour and a loyal subject', but that his wartime work had been 'considered of great value'. Although he could have been jailed for the offence, the judge imposed a nominal fine of £100 and ordered Mackenzie to pay a further £100 towards the costs of the prosecution. Slight though the punishment was, he also incurred the considerable costs of his own defence and it put him off making further revelations in his final volume of wartime memoirs, published in 1940. In it he said he had 'suppressed a certain amount of interesting material about espionage because, although the publication of it twenty-two years later could do no harm to anybody or anything, I could not be bothered with any more arguments about intelligence work'.[15]

SERBIA AND SALONIKA

Serbia, regarded by Austria-Hungary as the villainous power behind the assassination of Franz Ferdinand in June 1914, had been the first target of the Habsburg armies, but their invasion in the autumn of 1914 was unexpectedly repulsed by the Serbs and the two sides had fought themselves to a standstill by mid-December. These early battles came at great cost, not only to the armies involved but also to the civilian population and the countryside itself, which, still recovering from the hardships of the Balkan wars of 1912–13, was left devastated by the impact of modern, industrialised warfare, itself intensified by the myriad ethnic and religious antagonisms of the region. The Serbian victories of 1914, combined with those of 1912–13, when the old Ottoman enemy had been defeated, however, powerfully boosted Serbian national self-confidence. But the 1914 campaign came at a high price. It cost the Serbs 164,000 casualties out of its 250,000 combatants, and they inflicted 273,000 casualties on the 450,000 enemy troops. In all some 69,000 men died on the battle-field of wounds or disease.[16] Atrocities committed against civilians by the invading Habsburg forces – akin to those of the Germans in Belgium – were widely reported. While these repeated excesses experienced in the Balkan wars, they also marked a wider escalation of the practice of war in which it increasingly came to be assumed that civilians and non-combatants might themselves be legitimate targets for military action.

During 1915 the left-wing American journalist John Reed toured east-central Europe and the Balkans with the Canadian-born illus-trator Boardman Robinson, both hoping to witness some 'grand

dramatic climaxes' of the world war. With a slight air of disappointment, however, he noted afterwards that 'it was our luck everywhere
to arrive during a comparative lull in the hostilities'. Making the best
of it, he said that this left them 'better able to observe the more normal
life of the Eastern nations, under the steady strain of long-drawn-out
warfare'. This was a revealing observation considering that, when he
wrote the introduction to his book in March 1916, the war had then
lasted for scarcely eighteen months. But it was of a piece with the
increasingly general sense of permanence which the war had engen-
dered. Men, wrote Reed, 'had settled down to war as a business, had
begun to adjust themselves to this new way of life'.[17]

Reed visited Serbia twice during his tour, in the spring and autumn
of 1915. The chapter titles of two of the articles he wrote on his first
visit – 'The country of death' and 'A nation exterminated' – neatly
sum up the desperate circumstances he encountered. The campaign
of 1914 had been followed by a serious cholera and typhus epidemic
which it was calculated killed 350,000 people (out of a total 4.4 million
population). Reed found it a country of 'hollow-cheeked . . . filthy and
starved-looking' soldiers, remnants of an army which had suffered a
'fearful struggle with the greatest military power on earth' (this was
gilding the lily a bit, since the invaders had been entirely Habsburg),
with 'a devastating plague on top of that'.[18]

When in September 1915 Reed briefly visited Serbia again, he travelled from Sofia where there had been strong rumours that Bulgaria
would soon come into the war on the side of the Central Powers. At
Pirot, just across the frontier, the Serbians were full of confidence.
'Is Bulgaria going to war?' asked the Serbian customs officer. 'She'd
better not – we'll march to Sofia in two days!' But, asked Reed, what
if Serbia were attacked by Austria and Germany? 'Pooh, they tried
it once! Let them all come! Serbia can whip the world! . . .'[19] Sadly,
for the Serbians, this was not to be the case. Serbia's resources were
stretched very thin in 1915, by which stage over 700,000 men had been
mobilised for military service, over a sixth of the total population,
and the country was dangerously short of food and military materiel.
After the Allied landings at Gallipoli in April 1915, Berlin had begun
to worry about sustaining their Ottoman ally and began to make

plans for a renewed offensive against Serbia through which the most effective communications to Turkey ran. Bulgaria was tempted to join the Central Powers with the promise of Serbian as well as Greek territory, and also part of Romania, should it come in against the Allies. It was at this point, aiming to support the Serbs and encourage Greece to join the Allies, the French (followed by the British) began to land forces at Salonika, but this deployment was far too little and far too late to be of any help to the Serbs.

On 5 October 1915 the Bulgarians launched an attack into eastern Serbia. Two days later German and Austro-Hungarian forces invaded from the north. Despite some desperate defence, the Serbs were quickly driven back by the overwhelming forces massed against them. The Bulgarian advance in the south cut off any possibility of Allied assistance from Salonika and by the end of November the military position was hopeless. But rather than capitulating, in an attempt to preserve their army as a fighting force, the Serbian high command decided to retreat west to the Adriatic coast where they hoped the Allies could provide some practical assistance.

This retreat – Serbia's 'Golgotha' – in the appalling winter conditions of December 1915 through the inhospitable mountains of Albania and Montenegro, was one of the most astounding exploits of the First World War. Out of perhaps 250,000 soldiers and civilian refugees who started the march, an estimated 70,000 perished. An unknown number of civilians accompanied the army, and one postwar calculation hazarded that 140,000 civilians were killed or died during 'la retrait d'Albanie, à l'aller et au retour'.[20] An English journalist, Gordon Gordon-Smith, reported on the horrifying conditions of the march. At Lioum-Koula (near Prizren in south-western Serbia), where the unit he was with paused for a day, 'I went out for a walk five miles along the road. Every five hundred yards or so I came on dead bodies of men who had succumbed to cold or exhaustion.' Gordon-Smith, in an admiring propagandist account, compared the retreat over the Albanian mountains with Napoleon's crossing of the Alps, except that Napoleon had done so 'after long and careful preparation' while 'the unfortunate Serbs began theirs when their army was in the last stages of destitution, without food, with uniforms in rags, and with utterly inadequate means of transport'. The final stages of the march were the hardest, 'as fodder for the animals and food for the men was practically unprocurable'. In the mountains near Puka (modern Pukë), Gordon-Smith found places where wolves had torn apart the carcasses of dead horses. Having survived arctic conditions in the mountains, they then had to march the last twenty miles or so to Scutari (Shkodër) close to the Adriatic Sea through 'mud of the deepest and most tenacious kind'. From there they continued south to Durazzo (Durrës) and Volonë on the coast.[21]

Also accompanying the Serbian army, though a little further south, was the resourceful and unusual Flora Sandes, who was serving as a nurse with the Serbian 2nd Regiment of infantry. The daughter of an Irish family, Sandes had been brought up able to ride, shoot and drive a car, and claimed in her autobiography that when she was a small child, she 'used to pray every night that I might wake up in the morning and find myself a boy. Fate,' she continued, 'plays funny tricks sometimes', and during the war she had found herself 'suddenly pitchforked into the Serbian Army, and for seven years lived practically a man's life'. In August 1914, aged thirty-nine, having been rejected by the British War Office, she went to Serbia as a nurse (like Elsie Inglis) in one of the many Allied and American humanitarian missions organised to bring assistance to the country. By November 1915 she was in south-western Serbia where the Serbian forces 'were constantly being edged back' by the advancing Bulgarians who outnumbered them 'by more than four to one'. 'We were,' she wrote, 'fighting a rear-guard action practically all the time for the next six weeks – a mere handful of troops, worn out by weeks of incessant fighting, hungry, sick, and with no big guns to back them up.'[22]

During the retreat Sandes, who embraced the ideals and dress of masculine militarism, was sworn into the Serbian army as a regular soldier. 'Looking back,' she recalled, 'I seem to have just naturally drifted, by successive stages, from a nurse into a soldier.' She reported that there was 'nothing particularly strange about a woman joining up', as 'Serbian peasant girls' occasionally served in the army; indeed, there was one in her own regiment. But Sandes was hardly a conventional soldier, nor was she treated quite like one, since the regiment's commanding officer gave her a horse to ride, she had an orderly to look after her needs, and she slept on her own camp bed. Almost immediately, nevertheless, she was in action, shooting at the pursuing Bulgarians: 'sometimes we just sniped as we liked, and sometimes fired by volley as the platoon sergeant gave the order . . . I had luckily always been used to a rifle, so could do it with the others all right.' Travelling through Toulon in August 1916 after two months' leave in London, her story was picked up by the French newspaper *Le Matin*. Under the headlines 'An Irishwoman in the Serbian army/Engaged as an ordinary soldier, she has heroically won her sergeant's stripes', it described how she had gone out to Serbia to nurse but had become a soldier during the 'tough retreat to Durazzo'.[23]

The withdrawal of the Serbian army left Montenegro, which had entered the war against the Central Powers in August 1914, painfully exposed. In January 1916, badly outnumbered and outgunned, Montenegro surrendered in the face of a strong Austro-Hungarian offensive. The Montenegrin resistance in the first fortnight of 1916, however, helped to shield the Serbians who had reached the Adriatic coast in December 1915. On 11 January 1916, to Greek protests and with the very reluctant acquiescence of the British and the Italians (who wanted it for themselves), the French began occupying the Greek island of Corfu to use it as a sanctuary for the Serbian army. In order to justify yet another Allied infraction of Greek neutrality the French falsely claimed that the island had been used as a station for supplying Austrian submarines. By the end of February some 135,000 Serbs had been evacuated to the island, and another 10,000 refugees to Bizerta in the French North African colony of Tunisia. Once the Serbs had recovered and been resupplied the plan was to deploy them on the Salonika front. In March 1916 an Allied scheme to move them to the Greek mainland and thence by train to Salonika was categorically vetoed by the Greek government, anxious still to retain some semblance of neutrality, and in the end they were moved by ship directly. By July over 150,000 Serbs had been concentrated at Salonika.[24]

Serbia and Montenegro had a very tough time of it under enemy occupation in 1916–18 (as had already been the case after the initial

Habsburg advance in 1914). Especially from the summer of 1916, however, here more so than, for example, in occupied Belgium and France, armed nationalist groups, able to concentrate in remote mountain districts, began to plan violent resistance against the occupying forces. Rumours that the Bulgarian authorities in eastern Serbia were going to conscript Serbs into their army merely drove more young men deep into the countryside. In September 1916 the German consul in Belgrade reported to Berlin that Romania's entry into the war at the end of August had injected 'fresh hope' among the Serbs and also that a Serbian Orthodox priest who had been preaching resistance had been hanged by the Austro-Hungarian authorities. Sporadic fighting was reported at the same time in the Bulgarian-ruled territory around Niš. Late the same month in an operation which prefigured resistance in occupied Europe during the Second World War, a Serbian officer, Lieutenant Kosta Milovanović-Pećanac, was landed by plane from Salonika south-west of Niš to contact local guerrilla groups, tell them that an Allied offensive into Serbia was planned, ready them for 'Chetnik action', and attack railway lines and bridges. Pećanac prepared a proclamation (to be issued when the Allied offensive was due) declaring that 'after a year of slavery the moment has come for liberation from the German-Bulgarian yoke, as our valiant warriors are heading towards us'.

On 15 December Serbian comitadji (partisans) attacked a patrol of Austro-Hungarian gendarmes near Blaževo (east of Niš), killing eight of them. This provoked a military sweep across the district. Houses were searched, some fifty destroyed, and in nearby Brus thirty men suspected of being partisans were summarily executed. At Kosovska Mitrovica, north-east of Prishtina, over the turn of the New Year, the occupation authorities became alarmed at the possibility of a large-scale insurrection, especially after a copy of Pećanac's proclamation was discovered in one suspect's home. 'If we do not manage to stifle attempts at an uprising now,' reported the local military commander on 11 January, 'we will have to reckon with an incomparably more powerful *comitadji* movement in the spring.' Draconian measures were therefore applied. One hundred suspects were arrested, half of whom were subjected to a variety of punishments. Twenty-nine of them were sentenced to death, of whom thirteen were executed.[25] This pattern of attack and reprisal was to continue for the rest of the war in the occupied territories, leaving the country devastated, perhaps as much morally as physically, and bequeathing a legacy of antagonism and resentment which boded ill for future communal relations in the region.

Serbian forces, meanwhile, had been committed to the Allied effort at Salonika. In his study of Britain and France in the Balkans during the First World War, David Dutton observed that 'the Salonika campaign seems to defy rational comprehension'.[26] Having failed in its original purpose of saving Serbia from comprehensive defeat over the winter of 1915/16, an Allied force which at times numbered over a half a million men was left to languish with no apparent military purpose, engaged in warfare almost as static as anything on the Western Front, much of it based in malarial swamps where the medical casualties far exceeded those from actual fighting. Strategically and militarily suspect, the Salonika commitment owed much to French concerns and ambitions in the region. While the French participation at Gallipoli had been prompted as much as anything else by a desire not to leave the field clear to the British, at Salonika the opposite was the case. Here it was primarily a French adventure, with the British reluctantly taking part lest they should find themselves excluded from any regional spoils of victory. In terms of participation on the Allied side, indeed, from 1915 to 1918 Salonika was one of the most fully representative theatres of all during the Great War, with fighting units from France, Britain, Italy, Russia, Serbia, Montenegro and (eventually) Greece, contending, at one time or another, against Central Powers' forces from Germany, Austria-Hungary, Bulgaria and the Ottoman Empire. As elsewhere, to support the fighting forces considerable numbers of non-combatants were recruited, of whom only scanty records survive. The British alone reported that by January 1918 there were more than 16,000 Greeks, nearly 2,400 Turks, 2,000 women (of unspecified nationality) and 2,000 Maltese. Twenty-four Macedonian Labour Battalions contained 'Greeks, Serbs, Turks, Bulgarians and Jews'.[27]

The first Allied troops to arrive at Salonika in October 1915 were the French 156th Division and the 10th (Irish) Division of the British

Army. That both had been withdrawn from Gallipoli signalled the declining confidence which the Allied high command had in the Dardanelles. Men from the 10th Division were not greatly enamoured of the place, though the attractions of a cosmopolitan port city were considerable after months in military camps and on the battlefield. On first arrival Sergeant John McIlwain noted that the local inhabitants were 'quiet and undemonstrative', but they soon recognised opportunities for making money, 'with our fellows making fools of themselves buying Koniak [sic] and kindred spirit from hawkers who in hundreds follow us up'. Another soldier recalled that the 'natives' had been hostile from the first 'and several men of the Division found eternal rest via a knife thrust in the ribs! In one way,' he mused, 'this was hardly to be wondered at, as prior to 1912, Salonika was Turkish territory, and the Turks formed a goodly percentage of the population.'[28]

The French first moved units north from Salonika up the river Vardar valley across the Serbian frontier where they soon came into contact with elements of the invading Bulgarian Second Army.[29] The 10th Division had been left very weak from its time at Gallipoli but, after a brief pause for training and resupply, by the end of November it too was deployed just over the frontier. Suffering badly from bitter winter weather (for which many of the soldiers were quite unprepared) the Franco-British force checked a powerful Bulgarian push in the battle of Kosturino on 6–8 December, but were forced to withdraw back over the frontier, which the Bulgarians would not at this stage cross, and eventually concentrated once more around Salonika. 'The Bulgars came on like flies,' wrote the Irish poet Francis Ledwidge, serving with the 10th Division, 'and though we mowed down line after line, they persisted with awful doggedness and finally gave us a bayonet charge which secured their victory'.[30]

The Allies remained in Salonika in the Armée d'Orient, which by the end of 1915 comprised five British and three French divisions, the latter including a significant proportion of colonial African soldiers, with some smaller contingents (including 3,000 Serbians), amounting to approximately 150,000 troops in all. During 1916 the forces at Salonika were further increased – by December there were twenty

Allied divisions, including Italians, two Russian brigades and two regiments of the Greek National (Venizelist) Force – as the city was transformed into an entrenched camp nicknamed the 'Birdcage' against a possible Bulgarian attack, with elaborate barbed-wire defences around a seventy-mile perimeter.

In fact, as the British official historian Cyril Falls recounted, during the early months of 1916, 'life at Salonika was uneventful, but not without its interesting and even its amusing side . . . The only inconvenience was an occasional air raid.' The local inhabitants, he asserted, were delighted at the profits to be made provisioning the garrison – 'the shopkeepers reaped a golden harvest' – and the suppliers of food, drink and entertainment 'had their full share of the spoils'. Falls was dismissive and patronising about the city in general. 'In its tawdry fashion,' he wrote, 'Salonika undoubtedly was gay, but the tawdriness was more notable than the gaiety; the very women of pleasure were the last reserves of the Army of Aphrodite.'[31] The refusal of the Central Powers to attack the Salonika base, especially in early 1916 before the defences had been built up, was a puzzle to some postwar commentators. It was one of the many 'lost opportunities' which (with the powerful benefit of hindsight) the German General Max Hoffmann identified. The existence of an Allied force at Salonika, he argued, pinned down Bulgarian (and other Central Powers) forces in Macedonia, which could have been deployed more usefully elsewhere on the Eastern Front, and might have encouraged Romania to join the Central Powers, or at least remain neutral. Salonika, moreover, had become the key base for the Allied defeat of Bulgaria in 1918.[32]

During the first quarter of 1916, General Maurice Sarrail, the French commander at Salonika, chafed at the bit to launch an offensive. The British were not at all keen, however, believing that the force, large as it was, required reinforcement before a push could be contemplated. But no troops were available: the French needed all they had at Verdun, and there were in any case no troopships to spare, since they were all being used to move forces from the Middle East to France and Serbians from Corfu to Salonika. At an Allied conference in Chantilly on 12 March 1916, the British Chief of the Imperial General Staff, Sir William Robertson, offered a further objection which neatly further demonstrated the worldwide reach of the war. To be mobile, the British divisions at Salonika, he said, needed mules, but the prevailing short-age of shipping prevented their importation from South America. The senior British general at Salonika, Sir Bryan Mahon, had calculated that each division would need 1,676 pack animals more than they already had and 1,232 drivers (these included volunteers from Malta and Cyprus, as well as locally hired men). The Chantilly conference, nevertheless, agreed that there should be a general offensive in the summer of 1916 and Sarrail was allowed to move his forces out of the entrenched camp into more forward positions north up the Vardar and north-east into the Struma Valley.[33]

The Greek surrender of Fort Rupel to the Bulgarians in May 1916 put the Salonika command on the alert for a further advance and forces were moved out to protect the city. The 10th Division were deployed in the Struma early in June. Having suffered from the cold the previ-ous December, they were now hit by torrid early summer weather. 'A bloody march, hot as hell,' wrote Lieutenant David Campbell of the Royal Irish Fusiliers, 'a fearful time getting men along. 27 of ours fell out, 60 of the Leinsters, 80 of the Connaught Rangers, 119 of the Hampshires.' Once positioned in the malarial marshy valley, they were also plagued with mosquitoes. 'The tortures we suffered that summer,' said Campbell, 'are beyond description.' Inspecting an outpost one morning, he found his men 'so swollen and red . . . that I could scarcely recognise them. They had been attacked by mosquitoes during the night and almost eaten alive.' Despite extensive anti-malaria precautions – mosquito nets (though in short supply), gloves and quinine were distributed – the division suffered badly. Between July and October 1916 nearly 20,000 cases of malaria were reported, many of them repeat attacks, causing 296 deaths. Malaria was endemic in the region and a major cause of the glum fact that there were twenty times as many non-battlefield casualties as battlefield ones over the whole Salonika campaign. Of the 481,262 non-battlefield casualties, 162,517 resulted from malaria.[34]

At the beginning of August, by which time some 150,000 Serbs had arrived, General Sarrail began preparing a Franco-Serbian offensive north-west towards Monastir (Bitola) in Serbia. But the Bulgarians opposite him began crossing the Greek frontier on 5 August, and launched a major push of their own on the 17th. After some stiff fighting over the next fortnight – the Bulgarians proving to be determined adversaries – the Allies stopped their advance. With British forces pinning down Bulgarian and German units in the Struma Valley, Sarrail began his offensive on 12 September. The chief burden was taken by the Serbs, buoyed up by the prospect of once more setting foot on their homeland, which they reached on 30 September. Although the Germans rushed reinforcements to the front, the Allies pushed on during late October. On 19 November, Serbian and French cavalry entered Monastir, closely followed by French and Russian infantry. Running out of steam and with extended supply lines, the Allied forces could go no further and the front stabilised just north of Monastir, where it remained for almost two years. But the offensive had been costly, the Serbians losing some 27,000 men, the French 14,000 and the enemy perhaps 45,000.

For the British further east, they incurred 5,000 casualties during supporting operations in the Struma valley. Here, too, after the autumn of 1916 the front remained largely static until late 1918 when the British made some modest advances into Bulgaria, alongside much more impressive Serbian, French and Greek victories which led the Bulgarians to capitulate on 30 September 1918 and with which Serbian troops triumphantly liberated their own country and Montenegro from enemy occupation, laying the basis for a new 'South Slav' state of Yugoslavia.

The defence of Suez and the Arab revolt

Mobilising ideologies in support of war aims was widely adopted during the Great War. Both the Central Powers and the Allies sought to exploit ethnic, national and religious convictions as a weapon against the enemy in specific places, or even more generally as a force multiplier. And it worked the other way round, too. The Great Powers' extremity seemed to be everyone's opportunity. Just as some existing states plied for international hire, usually for territorial reward, nationalities and other interest groups saw advantages to be secured in offering their services to one side or the other. To be sure, not all of this bargaining and jockeying for position was based merely on cynical calculations of material advantage. Many of the individuals involved were idealists, simply trying to negotiate the tricky waters of wartime international politics without too egregiously compromising their principles. This was demonstrably so in the Middle East where both sides believed that Muslim loyalties could be engaged, and where the British, especially, thought that Arab aspirations for autonomy from their Ottoman rulers could be mobilised for Allied benefit.

The Middle East also had to be fitted into wider considerations of European imperial and national interests. From a western and northern European perspective, the region seemed, as A. P. Thornton remarked of the mid-nineteenth century, to be no more than 'a chequer board for European diplomacy'.[35] As in other parts of the non-European world, the Great Powers tended to carve up territory (usually working on fairly small-scale maps) along lines dictated by metropolitan considerations rather than any concern for the interests of the local inhabitants. So it was to be in the Middle East in 1914–18, with the partial qualification that, because of the wartime circumstances, some indigenous pressure groups also aimed to secure advantages, though in the cruel postwar world their achievements turned out in many cases to be more apparent than real.

Britain's chief interests in the Middle East were the defence of India and the line of vital imperial communications which ran through the Suez Canal. Britain had effectively ruled Egypt since 1882, though until the beginning of the war the Sultan of Turkey had retained nominal suzerainty. From November 1914, however, Britain took full control and Egypt became a vast military base for Allied operations against the Ottoman Empire. After they came into the war, the Turks nursed hopes of reconquering Egypt, if not also the territories lost to Italy in the war of 1912: Libya, Cyrenaica and Tripolitania. The Germans, meanwhile, thought about encouraging Egyptian nationalists to rise up against the British. Though rather less keen on any sort of Egyptian independence, the Turks nevertheless welcomed Arab volunteers into their armies, hoping also to foment unrest among the Muslim soldiers in the Indian and Egyptian army units along the canal. In February 1915 an under-strength Turkish force, 19,000-strong and depending on perilously stretched supply lines, reached the canal with an impressive hundred-mile march across the Sinai desert, but were beaten off by superior numbers of British and Indian troops. The Turks, particularly discouraged by the absence of any sign of a nationalist uprising in Egypt (upon which they had been depending), retreated back across the Palestine frontier. For the rest of 1915, when, after April, the British and Turks were focused on Gallipoli, there were no further operations in this theatre, apart from a few small-scale Turkish raids towards the canal.[36]

After their victory at Gallipoli the Ottoman high command turned again to the possibility of attacking Suez. During 1915 the transport infrastructure in Palestine had been improved. By November the Turkish railhead had reached Beersheba, just thirty miles from the frontier. There the commander of the Ottoman Fourth Army in Palestine, Cemal Paşa, created a desert force headquarters, headed by the German Colonel Kress von Kressenstein. In April 1916, Kress led a raiding party across the Sinai which destroyed a British outpost at Katia about twenty miles from the canal. In early August he launched a more substantial attack on Bir Romani, west of Katia, with a 12,000-strong force, including German and Austro-Hungarian artillery, but this was beaten off by British and Anzac troops. Turkish losses, described as 'light', totalled 'about a thousand killed or wounded'.[37]

After this, the initiative swung to the British, who spent much of 1916 painstakingly preparing for an advance into Palestine, building a railway and laying down a water supply pipeline eastwards from the canal. By October 1916 there were 150,000 British and 6,000 Indian troops in Egypt. As in other theatres, the fighting forces were backed up with droves of non-combatants. In addition to thousands of locally employed casual workers, the British garrison was also supported by a 13,000-strong Egyptian Labour Corps, many of whom had already served at Gallipoli. The auxiliary units were boosted in January 1915 by the creation of a Camel Transport Corps, which by the end of war totalled 25,000 drivers and 30,000 camels.[38] Right at the end of 1916 a British force, including the Australian and New Zealand Mounted Division, captured Magdhaba, the last significant Turkish position in

Sinai, and left the British well positioned for their slow advance into Palestine during 1917.

Cemal Paşa's caution about undertaking offensive operations was partly influenced by concerns over the domestic security situation in his area. At the start of the war the Arab population in 'Greater Syria' (Syria, Lebanon, Palestine and Jordan) showed little evidence of disloyalty to their Ottoman rulers. Since the Ottoman army was organised regionally, moreover, a majority of the units in Cemal's command at the end of 1914 comprised Arab soldiers from Syria and Iraq who by and large supported the Ottoman cause. Apart from anything else, as Rashid Khaldidi has observed, this was underpinned by 'four centuries of loyalty to the greatest Islamic state by the majority Muslim population'.[39] While there was some support among more advanced nationalists for political decentralisation and local self-government, as well as the assertion of cultural rights (such as education in Arabic rather than Turkish), the general attitude was that communal rights and aspirations could be accommodated within a gradually reforming imperial political system. In the Ottoman Empire (as elsewhere), however, the war put conditional loyalties under strain, sometimes to breaking point. The actual decision for war had been made by the mildly modernising but Turkish-run Committee of Union and Progress, which had been a powerful influence in Ottoman politics and government in the pre-war years. Together with the emergence of a 'Young Turk' movement, the union was inclined towards Turkish nationalism and the 'Turkification' of the empire. Once the empire had joined the war, the mobilisation of imperial resources further intensified Turkishness and Turkish national sentiment in the empire and its administration.

This can be seen in Cemal Paşa's policies in Syria. The French had traditional interests in the region and the French consul-general in Beirut from March 1914, François Georges-Picot, had been quietly raising the possibility with Maronite Christian leaders of a French-backed armed uprising against Turkish rule. After Turkey had entered the war and Picot had been expelled, the Turkish authorities discovered documents in the consulate relating to this and also implicating some Arab leaders with foreign intrigues. From November

1914, too, both the French and British had been making contacts in Syria, aiming to foment anti-Turkish unrest. This was enough for Cemal, who used the captured documents in a series of treason trials of dozens of Lebanese, Syrian and Palestinian leaders, including politicians, journalists, lawyers and soldiers. A Francophile Lebanese Maronite priest, Yusuf Hayek, was publicly hanged in Damascus on 22 March 1915. On 21 August eleven more victims – ten Muslim and one Christian – were hanged together, again in public, in the central square in Beirut. A further series of public executions occurred in 1916. On 5 April, a Christian Beiruti, Joseph Hani, was hanged, and on 6 May twenty-one more were executed, seven in Damascus and fourteen in Beirut, among whom was a senator, three parliamentary deputies, a magistrate, an army officer and a newspaper proprietor. Seventeen of these men were Muslim, the remainder Christian. As well as the public executions, punitive taxes were levied on the local population and many hundreds of further suspects were imprisoned or exiled. Concerned at the high level of desertion from his forces, in 1916 Cemal Paşa had a Muslim, a Christian and a Jewish deserter executed together in Jaffa as an exemplary warning to others. He also gradually posted Arab army units away from his command in exchange for more reliable (as he believed) Anatolian ones.[40]

Both before and during the early part of the war many Palestinian Jews joined the Ottoman army with the deliberate political objective of securing their place in the empire. Before the war, non-Ottomans had been able to retain their foreign citizenship and under a longstanding capitulation and indemnity system stay under the protection of foreign consulates – Russian for many of the Jewish immigrants who had come to Palestine in increasing numbers from the late nineteenth century. The Young Turk constitution of 1909, however, had provided for civil and religious freedoms and opened the army to non-Muslim recruits. After Turkey joined the Central Powers, the capitulation system lapsed and male settlers were faced with a stark choice between 'Ottomanisation' – taking Ottoman citizenship (and becoming liable for compulsory military service) – or deportation. For women, the decision was optional, though some political activists with their male colleagues welcomed the opportunity to become 'new Ottomans'.

They were, wrote Baruch Ben-Yehuda, a leader of the Jewish Young Generation Association who graduated from the pioneer Hebrew Gymnasium in Jaffa in 1914, 'enthusiasts of Ottomanisation in theory and practice'.[41]

The realities of enlistment were far from inspiring. When the war was pronounced to be a jihad, many non-Muslim recruits were posted to amele taburlari (labour units). One such was Alexander Aaronsohn, who joined up in August 1914 with twenty Jewish comrades, and initially served in a regular infantry regiment. After the declaration of jihad, however, all the Jews and Christians in the regiment were ignominiously transferred to a labour battalion. 'I shall never forget the humiliation of that day,' he wrote, 'when we, who, after all, were the best-disciplined troops of the lot, were first herded to our work of pushing wheelbarrows and handling spades, by grinning Arabs, rifle on shoulder.' This treatment naturally alienated the recruits concerned and propelled Jews like Aaronsohn towards the Allied side. Aaronsohn managed to buy himself out of the Ottoman army. Equipped with a false neutral passport and accompanied by his 'wife' (actually his sister Rivka), he eventually escaped on a United States warship taking refugees from Beirut in July 1915. He became part of a wider Jewish intelligence network led by his brother Aaron, which operated quite productively in Palestine before being violently broken up by the Turkish authorities in the autumn of 1917.[42]

Cemal Paşa's repression in Syria, which was both the result of and sharpened by the wartime circumstances, created martyrs for the nascent Arab nationalist cause and powerfully contributed to the alienation of moderate Arab opinion from Ottoman rule. There was also much discontent in the Hijaz (the western part of the Arabian peninsula) where the Allied blockade had interrupted food supplies and all but destroyed the pilgrimage to the Islamic holy places on which the economy of the region depended. All this was grist to the Allied mill in their endeavours to foment revolt. From the summer of 1915, Sir Henry McMahon, the British high commissioner in Egypt, corresponded with Husayn ibn 'Ali, Sharif of Mecca and head of the Hashemite clan, offering British support for Arab self-government in exchange for an uprising against the Turks. In September the British were emboldened by the arrival in Cairo of Lieutenant Muhammad Sharif al-Faruqi, a Mosul-born Arab infantry officer who had deserted from his unit in Gallipoli. Faruqi claimed to have been part of an Arab officers' society which had encouraged disaffection in the Ottoman Fourth Army, before his unit had been posted to the Dardanelles, and he presented to the British the inviting prospect of a powerful and widely spread organisation which could have a great impact if mobilised for the Allied side. McMahon, then, was encouraged to offer assurances to Husayn that in exchange for the latter leading a revolt against the Ottomans, Great Britain would 'recognise and uphold' Arab independence in the Arabian peninsula and also in parts of Palestine and Syria.[43]

McMahon was deliberately vague about the precise territory involved and also qualified his offer with the phrase 'in so far as England is free to act without detriment to the interests of her present Allies'. This particularly meant France and Russia. France's interests were addressed in a series of negotiations from November 1915 to May 1916 which resulted in the Sykes–Picot Agreement, which more than any other single development in the war defined the political shape of the modern Middle East.[44] The agreement was a straightforward exercise of pure great power diplomacy which took no account of any opinions the local populations might have had. Although the French were anxious to protect their regional interests, most of their energies were naturally focused on their titanic struggle with Germany. It is an indication of how low in policy priorities the Middle East came, indeed, that Picot, who was an especially enthusiastic French imperialist but a relatively junior diplomat, was not only nominated to argue the French case, but was also allowed to write his own brief for the purpose. Picot consequently instructed himself to seek as much territory as possible, asserting that France's interests in Greater Syria extended east to Mosul and south-west to the Egyptian frontier.

The French government were in fact much less expansive than Picot and were actually reluctant to take on territory in the Syrian interior. This allowed Picot, as the negotiations proceeded, magnanimously to moderate his claims to the Mediterranean coast of Lebanon and Syria, as well as Cilicia in south-eastern Anatolia, which was what

Paris actually wanted as a minimum. The chief British negotiator, Sir Mark Sykes, a Conservative MP with a slightly overblown reputation as a Middle Eastern expert based on a series of travel books he had written about the region, was determined, however, to insure Britain's position in Egypt and in the Persian Gulf.

Sykes and Picot got on well personally and over the turn of the year 1916 they drafted a colour-coded agreement partitioning the Middle East. France was allocated a 'Blue Zone', including the Lebanese and Syrian coastline, Cilicia, and the Mosul vilayet in northern Mesopotamia, which Sykes conceded in order to leave a buffer between Russian interests further north and British to the south. Picot agreed to the British 'Red Zone' encompassing central and southern Mesopotamia, southern Palestine along the Egyptian frontier, and the ports of Acre and Haifa on the Mediterranean. The Syrian and Jordanian interior was to be assigned to an 'independent Arab state or confederation of states', divided into zones where France and Britain would respectively have exclusive rights to appoint political and economic advisers. The only part they could not agree on was central Palestine, which they parked in a 'Brown Zone', with an unspecified international administration to be sorted out at a future date.

This draft was subject to two conditions. The first (on British insistence) was that it would not come into force until an Arab revolt had been proclaimed. The second was that the two powers had to get the consent of their Russian ally. Sykes and Picot therefore went to Petrograd, where after a bit more moving about of other people's territory (the Russians offered France a share of Turkish Armenia in exchange for land on the Persian frontier) and Russian consent to the special position of Palestine (while secretly assuring the French that they would back their claims for the territory), the agreement was approved. It was formally ratified by an exchange of letters on 15–16 May 1916.

Sharif Husayn was not informed about Sykes–Picot. Had he known about it he would surely never have agreed to support a British-backed Arab revolt. The British and French understanding of how autonomous an 'independent Arab state' might be, moreover, was always going to be much more limited than anything to which the Arabs aspired. In the meantime the Arabs could only base their hopes on the McMahon assurances. The revolt itself was launched by Husayn's son Faisal on 5 June 1916 at Medina in the Hijaz, about 250 miles north of Mecca. There were also attacks on Mecca and the Red Sea port of Jeddah. These were both captured but the successes of the revolt in 1916 were more sporadic than sustained. Faisal, for example, was never able to take Medina, which remained in Turkish hands right until the end of the war.

British support for the revolt was mostly in the form of munitions and money, and a British military mission was despatched to the Hijaz in October 1916, including a charismatic young Arabist, T. E. Lawrence, who was to play a major liaison role with the Arabs for the rest of the war. But the political significance of the revolt, marking an Arab withdrawal of allegiance from the Ottoman Empire, was always greater than its military effectiveness. Despite some further successes from 1917 onwards, in the end the defeat of the Ottomans in Palestine depended more on conventional British, Indian and imperial forces than the massed irregulars intermittently assembled by Husayn and his fellow leaders. Indeed, in the mid-1930s one retired Turkish general, Mehemed Jemal Pasha, told George Antonius that British political warfare had been more effective than the Arab revolt. 'In his view,' he said, 'the disaffection spread in Syria by the Anglo-Arab propaganda turned out to have been even more detrimental to the Turkish hold on the country than the military losses caused directly by the entry of the Arabs into the War.'[45]

SYKES–PICOT AND THE MODERN MIDDLE EAST

The Sykes–Picot agreement was just one of a series of incompatible undertakings which the Allies in general (and the British in particular) made concerning the Middle East and the future of the Ottoman Empire. Besides the Treaty of London of April 1915, by which Russia, France and Britain promised that if the Ottoman Empire was partitioned, they would support Italian claims to territory on the Mediterranean coast of southern Turkey, and the McMahon–Husayn correspondence, there was also the Balfour Declaration of

October 1917 in which Britain agreed to support the establishment of a 'national home' for the Jews in Palestine, though neither the precise status of this 'home' (was it to be an autonomous state, or what?), nor its geographical extent was spelled out. The ambiguities of these commitments – in turn perhaps creative, cynical or even necessary for the purposes of international diplomacy – stimulated much political dispute and horse-trading in the troubled postwar years. For a time revolution removed Russia as a direct player which meant that Allied agreements involving the old regime could be set aside. The realities of power politics in Asia Minor, particularly the emergence of a strongly nationalist Turkish republic under the hero of Gallipoli, Mustafa Kemal, effectively nullified arrangements with Italy (and later Greece) concerning the distribution of ex-Ottoman territory. This left dispositions in the Middle East to be competed over primarily between France and Britain, with the desperately concerned Arabs and Jews largely relegated to a role as spectators.

Sykes–Picot was renegotiated in 1919, giving the British the Mosul vilayet in exchange for allowing the French a share in the exploitation of its oil reserves and giving them a free hand in Syria.[46] After a suggestion that Palestine might be taken on by the USA was turned down flat by Washington, the British bid successfully for it on the ostensible strategic grounds that it was necessary for the defence of Egypt and the Suez Canal, though the actual reasons were more to do with national prestige and keeping the French out. The only independent Arab state to emerge after the war was Arabia, though even here the British assumed that they would remain the paramount international power in the region. The wider Arab aspirations for national freedom were frustrated by the Franco-British carve-up which left France with Syria (including Lebanon) and Britain with Iraq, Trans-Jordan and Palestine, making permanent the frontiers originally delineated by Sykes and Picot in May 1916, and which still define the political map of the modern Middle East. Technically, France and Britain were granted these territories as mandates under the supervision of the League of Nations, with a responsibility to develop each country to a point where it could become fully independent. Husayn's sons Faisal and Abdullah were installed as kings of Iraq and Jordan respectively, but in practice all the indigenous regimes set up under the mandates were treated very like colonies and had little autonomy. The aspiration for 'Arab independence', which had been such a powerful factor in stimulating the Arab revolt of 1916, was not achieved in most of the region until after the Second World War, and, in the case of Palestine/Israel not at all.

Satia Priya has persuasively argued that for the British (as also for the French) the deserts of Arabia and the Arabian world constituted an 'empty space' in which all sorts of schemes and stratagems could flourish. It was a location, moreover, where idiosyncratic European policy entrepreneurs, such as Henry McMahon, Georges Picot, Mark Sykes and later T. E. Lawrence, could flourish and peddle their own favoured strategies.[47] But it was a space, too, with its own inhabitants and dynamics, which were fundamentally affected by the imperial conflicts of 1914–18 and after. The indefensible political boundaries and conflicting sectional aspirations with which the belligerents of the First World War filled up that space, moreover, have left a doleful legacy of bitter antagonisms and unrealised ambitions which bedevils the region to this day.

The USA

Woodrow Wilson, the Democratic candidate, was returned as president for a second term in the election held on Tuesday 7 November 1916. While his campaign slogan was 'He kept us out of war', the global reach of the war had already involved the USA in a variety of ways. By the autumn of 1916 American industries were supplying prodigious amounts of war materiel to the Allied side, much of which was financed by American banks. Many individual Americans, moreover, had themselves already chosen to get involved, both in humanitarian endeavours and also as active participants, mostly fighting on the Allied side. The North American continent was not so isolated from the 'European war' as many observers seemed to think, and no-one much remarked on the fact that the USA's northern neighbour (with whom they shared an undefended frontier) was a belligerent power from the beginning. The war came to the American homeland, too. German secret agents ran a violent sabotage campaign against the supply of munitions for the Allies, while both British and German agents mounted propaganda campaigns to garner support for their respective causes. The neutral space of the USA also provided opportunities, and sympathisers, for anti-British activists for whom Britain's involvement in the war appeared to offer fresh possibilities for action. Irish republican groups had long flourished in the USA and, especially after the 1916 Easter Rising in Dublin, they aimed to attack the British and pro-British elements in America with renewed vigour. Indian subversives, too, linked to the Ghadar ('Revolt') Party which wanted to overthrow British rule in India, posed a particular threat, particularly on the west coast of the USA.

WOODROW WILSON'S 1916 ELECTION

In 1916 Woodrow Wilson won a comfortable majority in both the popular vote – he had 9.1 million votes to his opponent's 8.5 million – and the Electoral College (277 votes to 254), but, due to the peculiarities of the United States presidential election system, he actually scraped in with a razor-thin majority in California. If his rival, Charles Evans Hughes, had gained only 3,774 more votes of the nearly one million votes cast in the state, Wilson would have lost the election. While domestic matters had an influence (and Wilson's progressive credentials which had helped him win the 1912 contest were still important) his handling of war issues dominated both his re-nomination and the election campaign in general.

The United States responded to the outbreak of war in 1914 with a mixture of shock, sympathy and an element of sanctimoniousness. It had been widely believed that war was impossible between the advanced and 'civilised' states of Western Europe. Voicing a common opinion, *Harper's Weekly* argued that it was one thing 'if civilized Europe were holding back India, for example', in which case war 'would be comprehensible'. But, on the other, for Germany and France, 'with a whole complex and delicate civilization in common, to be using huge death engines to mow down men and cities is so unthinkable that we go about in a daze, hoping to awake from the most horrid of nightmares'.[1] But a sense of relief at not being involved seems to have been among the strongest emotions. 'Peace-loving citizens of this country will now rise up,' declared the *Chicago Herald*, 'and tender a hearty vote of thanks to Columbus for having discovered America.' The *Wabash Plain Dealer* 'never appreciated so keenly as now the foresight exercised by our forefathers in emigrating from Europe'.[2]

Wilson was a son of a Presbyterian manse and was president of Princeton University before he had successively been elected governor of New Jersey and then president of the United States in 1912. He himself ascribed his mixture of emotional engagement with detached rationality to his own Scots–Irish ethnic background. His private secretary from 1911 to 1921, Joseph Tumelty, recalled a conversation in which Wilson said that 'on the one side there is the Irish in me, quick, generous, impulsive, passionate, anxious always to help and to sympathize with those in distress', while, on the other, 'there is the Scotch – canny, tenacious, cold, and perhaps a little exclusive'.[3] In his response to the war Wilson drew on his religious and academic background, combining a cool sense of rightness with a rational appreciation of the USA's best interests, as well as a keen understanding of the American people's deep-seated desire not to become involved in the European conflagration. Reeling from the death, on 6 August 1914, of his beloved first wife Ellen, it was nearly a fortnight before he was able to compose a considered 'appeal to the American people' in which he called for strict impartiality towards both sides and asserted the USA's potential role as a mediator. America, he wrote – blithely relegating the Ottoman Empire and Italy (neither of which were yet in the war), as well as China, to the second division – was 'the one great nation at peace, the one people holding itself ready to play a part of impartial mediation and speak the counsels of peace and accommodation, not as a partisan, but as a friend'. Wilson, however, was also sharply aware of the dangers in his country's emigrant society of partisanship at home, and he worried about the divided sympathies of American citizens 'drawn from many nations, and chiefly from the nations now at war'.[4]

According to the US census of 1910, out of a total 92 million population, Germany provided the largest number of foreign-born people at 2.5 million, followed by 'Russia and Finland' at 1.7 million; Ireland and Italy with about 1.3 million each and Austria-Hungary with 1.2 million. These figures, which reflect the preponderance of emigrants from central, eastern and southern Europe over the turn of the twentieth century, do not represent the total size of 'hyphenated' communities (the Irish-American population in 1914, for example, was estimated at 4.5 million), but they do suggest the potential for traditional allegiances to colour responses to the war. State origin, of course, was not the only consideration. The American Jewish community, for example, numbering some 4 million, included many who had left Russia to escape persecution and were strongly anti-Russian.

As the experience of Chicago demonstrates, the outbreak of war stimulated atavistic national loyalties in some unexpected ways. One Irish-American patriot recruited a thousand Irishmen into two regiments and a medical corps, prepared to serve against England as soon as the call came from Dublin. Serbian demonstrators picked fights with Germans in south Chicago and at the beginning of September the Superintendant of Chicago Schools, Mrs Ella Fagg, had to issue an order prohibiting fighting between children of warring nationalities in the city's school playgrounds. Even the Chicago Symphony Orchestra was affected. At a summer concert in Ravinia Park on the North Lake Shore, the orchestra found itself divided over a scheduled programme which, in an effort to be even-handed, included various national melodies. While the majority of the orchestra were of German origin, their French, Belgian and Russian colleagues objected to playing 'The Watch on the Rhine' and the Germans, in turn, played discordant notes during the French anthem, 'La Marseillaise'. In the end, the players agreed not to play any patriotic tunes at all.[5]

Although Wilson remained studiously neutral, elite American opinion leaned strongly towards the Allied side. This was fuelled by shared cultural values, a political system which owed much to British precedent, top universities modelled on Oxbridge, and close and abundant economic relationships, especially with the United Kingdom. This latter factor was reinforced by the Allied blockade and domination of maritime trade. By the end of 1914 American trade with the Central Powers had virtually been extinguished, but the slack had more than been replaced by incessant and increasing trade with the Allied states. Exports to Britain and France from the United States rose from $750 million in 1914 to $2.75 billion in 1916. The British were careful not to alienate the Americans whenever possible. When the French wanted to place cotton (upon which the prosperity of the southern states depended) on the contraband list, the British agreed to purchase any surplus in order to maintain the price.[6] The 'freedom of the seas' – or rather, the freedom of Americans to voyage and trade at will and unscathed across the seas – became the most important single issue of neutrality. This is why the German policy of unrestricted submarine warfare became so inflammatory.

Public opinion in general, meanwhile, remained strongly opposed to involvement. One vivid illustration of this was the runaway best-selling popular song of 1915, 'I Didn't Raise My Boy to be a Soldier', which Susan Zieger argues 'became both an icon of popular antiwar sentiment and a lightning rod for promilitarist criticism of the peace movement'. 'Ten million soldiers to the war have gone,/who may never return again,' went the song. 'Ten million mothers' hearts must break/for the ones who died in vain.' In the chorus a mother takes up the refrain, deploring the enlistment of sons to the war and asserting that the universal power of motherhood could be mobilised behind an alternative way of settling national differences:

> I didn't raise my boy to be a soldier,
> I brought him up to be my pride and joy.
> Who dares to place a musket on his shoulder,
> To shoot some other mother's darling boy?
> Let nations arbitrate their future troubles,
> It's time to lay the gun and sword away.
> There'd be no war today,
> If mothers all would say,
> 'I didn't raise my boy to be a soldier'.

Reflecting the aspirations of an active women's peace movement in the United States – founded in January 1915, the Women's Peace Party had 40,000 members by February 1916 – the song also spawned parodies, such as 'I Did Not Raise My Boy to be a Coward', but the song yet illustrates that deep, and natural, vein of humane concern which Wilson's anti-war policy tapped into.[7]

The loss of the *Lusitania*, torpedoed by a German U-boat on the afternoon of 7 May 1915, provoked a very strong reaction in the USA, shocked by the scale of the tragedy. Out of nearly 2,000 passengers and crew, 1,200 were lost, of whom 128 were American. Wilson, typically, did not immediately react, but pondered on the problem for a few days. On 10 May he delivered a scheduled speech to newly naturalised American citizens in Philadelphia and used the occasion to reflect on

American ideals. 'The example of America,' he said, 'must be a special example' – an example 'not merely of peace because it will not fight, but of peace because peace is the healing and elevating influence of the world and strife is not'. He continued with a resonant phrase that was for many above all to define his position on the war: 'There is such a thing as a man being too proud to fight. There is such a thing as a nation being so right that it does not need to convince others by force that it is right.' Wilson was clearly aiming here for the moral high ground, and expressing a conviction based on his own Christian beliefs that might was *not* right and that forbearance in the face of violence was the noblest path. For some less sympathetic observers (especially in Britain), however, the phrase 'too proud to fight' seemed to be both pusillanimous and conceited, suggesting that the USA was morally superior to the warring nations of Europe.[8]

Wilson formally responded to the sinking of the *Lusitania* with a series of 'Notes' to the German government. The first, on 13 May, condemned the use of submarines against commerce and demanded that they disavow actions against unarmed merchant vessels, make reparations (unspecified) for the damage done and take steps to prevent a recurrence. The Germans replied by asserting (correctly) that the *Lusitania* had been carrying munitions and was therefore a legitimate target. Wilson dismissed this and reiterated his demands in a second note on 7 June. In private the Germans modified their submarine policy by warning commanders not to attack neutral ships or large liners and in public they proposed to instruct their submarines not to attack American liners with special markings and neutral liners flying the American flag. On 28 June, moreover, a German submarine had sunk a British merchantman, the *Armenian*, carrying 1,400 mules, off Cornwall, after a warning had been issued (as provided for in the so-called 'cruiser rules' regulating attacks on merchant shipping). Even though a reported twenty Americans went down with the ship, the fact of the prior warning was enough for Wilson to moderate his position.

In a third note on 21 July the president observed that 'the events of the past two months' had demonstrated that a submarine campaign could be conducted 'in substantial accord with the accepted practices of regulated warfare'. Hoping that the German government would now disavow its action against the *Lusitania*, Wilson stated that a repetition of similar actions would be regarded by the United States as 'deliberately unfriendly'.⁹ The Germans, rattled by the possibility of alienating the USA to the point that they might enter the war against them, agreed in September to suspend unrestricted submarine warfare, thus apparently vindicating Wilson's policy and reinforcing his claim to be able to keep the USA out of the war without sacrificing its honour. 'Without mobilizing a regiment or assembling a fleet,' announced the *New York Evening Post*, 'by sheer dogged, unswerving persistence in advocating the right, he has compelled the surrender of most arrogant, the best-armed of nations, and he has done so in complete self-abnegation, but in fullest, most patriotic devotion to American ideals.'¹⁰

During 1915 Wilson began to review the USA's own defences. Apart from the war there were problems with Mexico, which since 1910 had suffered almost constant revolutionary turmoil, threatening United States interests and provoking an actual intervention at Veracruz in 1914. By the end of 1915 a more or less stable government had been established under Venustiano Carranza, but radical forces under the command of Pancho Villa continued to operate in the north of the country. Concerned that the USA should be strong enough to be taken seriously in international affairs, over the summer of 1915 Wilson had the Secretaries of War and the Navy prepare expansion schemes for the armed services. These were announced in the autumn and laid before Congress in December. A massive naval building programme was proposed, of sixteen capital ships over five years, and a forty per cent increase in the army (to 140,000 men) with the creation of a 400,000-strong reserve force.

This provoked much opposition from the isolationists. The arch-neutralist William Jennings Bryan, who had resigned as secretary of state over the second *Lusitania* note, declared that 'this nation does not need burglars' tools unless it intends to make burglary its business'. In early 1916, therefore, Wilson embarked on a campaign of speeches across several states arguing the necessity of 'preparedness'. The country, he told an audience in Pittsburgh, 'should prepare herself,

)og Tired (1916) by Christopher R. W. Nevinson (1889–1946). Nevinson, a pioneer Futurist who believed 1at modern art was the only way to depict the war, served with the Belgian Red Cross on the Western ront in 1914–15 and was appointed an official British War Artist in 1917.

A British imperial nightmare: the Turkish Captain Kasim Bey (*first from left*), Indian revolutionaries Mahendra Pratap and Muhammed Barakatullah (*third and fifth from left*) and the German agents Werner Otto von Hentig and Oskar Niedermayer (*second and fourth from left*) photographed in Kabul in May 1916. From here the Germans hoped to set off a massive Muslim jihad against their British and French enemies.

Images of African soldiers serving under the command of the able German Colonel Paul von Lettow Vorbeck who remained fighting against the British from the start of the war until 25 November 1918

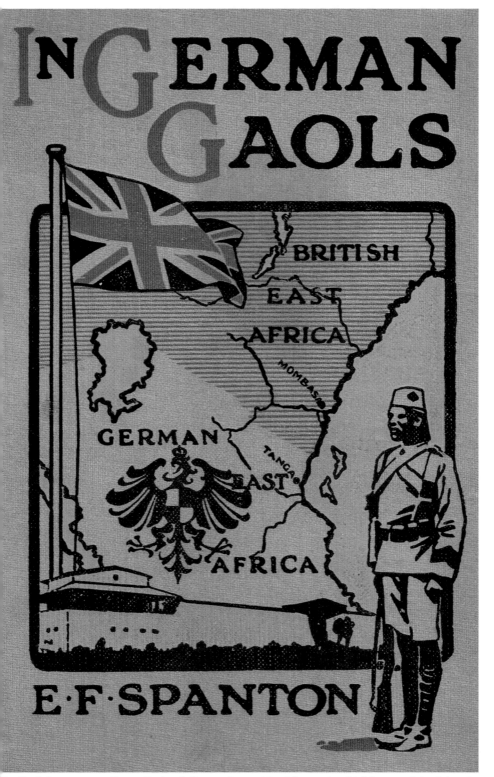

IN GERMAN GAOLS

E·F·SPANTON

The English missionary Ernest Frederick Spanton's memoir of the war in which he complained that the Germans deliberately degraded their prisoners by making them clean their own latrines.

The British commander, Sir Douglas Haig and the French General Joseph Joffre (*second and third from left*) appearing to resist the civilian political control of David Lloyd George, the British Minister of Munitions (and later Prime Minister), with Albert Stanley his French equivalent (*first left*), visiting the Front on 12 September 1916. Other soldiers look on sceptically.

View from the Old British Trenches, 1917, by William Orpen (1878–1931). The Dublin-born Orpen painted this scene from the Somme battlefield in the summer of 1917 after he had been appointed an official British War Artist. This peaceful sunlit landscape recalls the moments before the battle started more than the conflict itself.

Sergeant Flora Sandes, English-born of an Irish family, who served first as a nurse and then as a soldier with the Serbian army during Serbia's 'Golgotha' – the appalling retreat to the Albanian Adriatic coast during the winter of 1915.

American pilots depicted in James McConnell's memoir, *Flying for France*. Demonstrating the high attrition rate the pilots suffered, three of the nine were noted as 'killed', and by the time the book was published in 1917 McConnell himself (*on the extreme right*) had also perished.

Anti-war sentiment in the USA (as well as the new medium of recorded popular music) was reflected in the phenomenal success of the 1916 hit song, *I didn't raise My Boy to be a Soldier*.

Woodrow Wilson, 28th United States President, a Scots-Irish moralist determined to keep his country out of the war if possible. He claimed that the Irish in him – 'quick, generous, impulsive, passionate, anxious always to help and to sympathize with those in distress' – was combined with Scottish traits: 'canny, tenacious, cold, and perhaps a little exclusive'.

The telegram which conveyed the first news of Rasputin's assassination to Britain, sent by Samuel Hoare in Petrograd to 'C' (Mansfield Cumming), the head of the British Secret Service.

Urgent

DECODE OF TELEGRAM.

Sheet No.

No. of Sheets

(a) Handed in at ... { PLACE / DATE / TIME

(b) Rec'd in P'GRAD { DATE / TIME

(c) Decoded by   Dec 19/31

(d) Passed to Typist Section at   CTG

REMARKS.

Urgent. news   Private for C : ——
News correct that Rasputin was killed in
Petrograd in private house out early morning
of Dec. 17 30

816

The great Douaumont Ossuary at Verdun which contains 130,000 remains recovered from the battlefield. Completed in 1932, it has now become a site of reconciliation. The French President and the West German Chancellor met here for a 'day of reconciliation' on 22 September 1994. In February 2014 the name of a German soldier was for the first time inscribed in the monument, though not without some controversy.

not for war, not for anything that smacks in the least of aggression, but for adequate national defense'. In a speech at the Auditorium in Chicago on 31 January 1916 he argued that while 'a year ago, it did seem as if America might rest secure without very great anxiety and take it for granted that she would not be drawn into this terrible maelstrom . . . now no man can confidently say whether the United States will be drawn into the struggle or not'. Wilson warned an audience in Cleveland that a time might come when it would be impossible to maintain what he called the 'double obligation', which on the one hand was 'to keep us out of the war', and, on the other, 'to keep the honor of the nation unstained'. In Topeka he said that the latter, indeed, might involve using 'the force of the United States to vindicate the right of American citizens everywhere to enjoy the protection of international law'.[11]

Wilson's promotion of preparedness went some way towards meeting the criticism of interventionists, such as Teddy Roosevelt, who claimed that without strong and credible armed forces the USA would be dangerously exposed in an increasingly perilous world. Women, too, were determined to be prepared. Early in 1916 a group of prominent suffragists in Maine formed a 'Women's Defense Club, to instruct American women to shoot, and shoot straight'. *The New York Times* reported that the intention was that if they were 'ever called upon to defend their homes, their children, and themselves', they would not be 'helpless as were the Belgian women'. The club's founder, Lurana Sheldon Ferris, asserted that, rather than wait to be raped or killed by 'madmen', she and her colleagues would be 'prepared to kill' if 'necessity' required. Reportedly also 'stirred by atrocity tales' from Belgium, the American Women's League for Self-Defense organised rifle training and other military drills in New York. By April 1916 they had 300 recruits, including 'dentists, lawyers, surgeons, heads of departments, teachers, private secretaries, and stenographers'.[12]

While defending the country's 'honor', and stiffening its defences, Wilson simultaneously explored ways in which the USA could facilitate an end to the war. Although his closest political adviser, Colonel Edward House, was notably pro-Ally (and believed that America's participation in the war was inevitable), he also wanted the USA to help establish a better world order. Wilson, moreover, used him as an emissary to sound out opinion in Europe on the possibilities of mediation. In exchanges between Colonel House and the British foreign secretary Edward Grey in 1915, the idea was raised by Grey of a 'League of Nations' which could help resolve international quarrels. House developed a scheme by which the USA (having first privately got the Allies to agree) would propose that peace negotiations should begin 'upon the broad basis of both military and naval disarmament', and the establishment of an international body including the USA.[13] The Allies, as pre-arranged, would accept the call, leaving the Central Powers either to participate (and accept reasonable terms) or to face the possibility of the USA joining the war against them. Although House travelled to Europe early in 1916 to discuss the possibilities in London, Paris and Berlin, he found little practical enthusiasm anywhere for peace negotiations, especially since Wilson refused to commit the USA to any specific territorial adjustments – what he dismissed as 'local settlements', but which the French, for example, concerning the restoration of their 'lost provinces' of Alsace and Lorraine, considered to be non-negotiable preconditions for any peace agreement. Going rather beyond his instructions, however, House agreed a memorandum with Grey on 22 February outlining the plan and noting his own support for Allied territorial demands, including the restoration of Belgium and the transfer of the two provinces to France. But Grey, for his part, said he could not commit the British government to the scheme, adding that in any case nothing could be done without the agreement of the Allies, observing furthermore that 'the Cabinet would probably feel that the present situation would not justify them in approaching the Allies on this subject at the present moment'.[14] It was, in effect, a cool brush-off to the American approach.

Wilson, meanwhile, was increasingly taken with the idea of a possible postwar international organisation and resolved to combine a public call for a peace conference with a proposal that the USA should take the lead in setting up such an organisation. A chance for this came with an invitation to address a meeting on 27 May in New York of the League to Enforce Peace, which had been established by ex-President William Howard Taft in 1915 to campaign for the creation of a league of all the Great Powers to act in concert for the resolution of international disputes through conciliation if possible, but with the use of sanctions if necessary. The fact that the league was supported by Taft and many prominent pro-Ally Republicans made the occasion an attractive opportunity for Wilson to reach the middle ground of voters he would need for re-election in the November election. Wilson's speech, in Patrick Devlin's words, was 'epoch-making' in that it broke with the USA's long-held policy of international non-involvement. Wilson argued that the sheer scale and reach of the war meant that the country could not remain uninvolved. 'Our own rights as a nation, the liberties, the privileges, and the property of our people have been profoundly affected,' he said. 'We are not mere disconnected lookers-on . . . We are participants, whether we would or not, in the life of the world.' He argued that 'the nations of the world must in some way band themselves together to see that the right prevails as against any sort of selfish aggression', and he pledged that the United States was 'willing to become a partner in any feasible association of nations' dedicated to the sovereign freedom of all nations and the security of 'small states'. The world, he asserted, 'has a right to be free from every disturbance of its peace that has its origin in aggression and disregard of the rights of peoples and nations'.[15]

Wilson's mixture of preparedness, high principle and peace served him well in the 1916 election campaign, as did a commitment to progressive measures on such matters as rural credits, workmen's compensation and child labour. In August, faced with a threatened national railroad strike, he dramatically forced through legislation to establish an eight-hour day, which defused the dispute and reinforced his progressive credentials. At the Democratic convention in St Louis in mid-June, Senator Ollie James of Kentucky lit up the audience with a barnstorming defence of the president. 'Without orphaning a single American child, without widowing a single American mother,' he declared, 'without firing a single gun, without the shedding of a single drop of blood', Wilson had 'wrung from the most militant spirit that ever brooded above a battlefield an acknowledgement of America rights and an agreement to American demands'.[16] His Republican opponent, Charles Evans Hughes, had no difficulty in seeing off a potential challenge for his nomination from ex-President Theodore Roosevelt, who was hawkish on defence and explicitly interventionist, but Hughes's campaign was hamstrung by a lack of focus. His appeals to the German-American and Irish-American communities (the latter inflamed by the draconian British suppression of the Easter Rising) worked against him as Wilson countered with a robust defence of undifferentiated loyalty to America alone. When Jeremiah O'Leary, the fiercely Irish-American president of the American Truth Society, accused Wilson of being pro-British, the president sharply replied that he 'would feel deeply mortified to have you or anybody like you vote for me. Since you have access to many disloyal Americans and I have not I will ask you to convey this message to them.'[17]

Wilson could certainly give as good as he got, and his firm defence of American rights and American neutrality saw him safely (if narrowly) into the White House for a second term. In the end, however, the former counted for more than the latter and Germany's disastrous decision in January 1917 to resume unrestricted submarine warfare, with the threat this posed to the rights of the USA and its people to trade and travel at will, was fundamental in eventually propelling the country into the war on the Allied side the following April. In the meantime the successful election re-invigorated Wilson's desire to mediate between the warring states and before the year was out he was to launch another peace initiative.

AMERICANS AT WAR

At the beginning of the war American political opinion across the board was against any sort of involvement. Even Teddy Roosevelt, later an ardent interventionist, supported Wilson's declaration of neutrality. Nevertheless many Americans were keen to participate. For some emigrants, still perhaps citizens of the warring powers (and even second- or third-generation migrants), it was simply their patriotic duty. When US volunteer Carroll Dana Winslow reported to join the French Air Service in the spring of 1916, he was greatly surprised to be addressed in perfect English by a French guard. It turned out he had 'lived in New York for twelve years, but on the outbreak of war had returned at once to serve'.[18] Others were inspired by the issues at stake: freedom, democracy, self-determination, and so on. Not just for soldiers of fortune, for whom the war provided a grand opportunity to ply their trade, but for many others too the war provided employment and economic opportunities in all sorts of trades and professions. Inevitably medical and para-medical employment was enormously boosted by the war. No doubt, too, for many young men and women the excitement of war itself was a powerful incentive. Not everyone wanted to fight; quite the contrary. For a significant group of people the motivation to serve was humanitarian more than anything else. And some were just curious. In a story about a Paris barber who had specialised in cutting the hair of American men, Ellen La Motte (who had herself lived in Paris before the war) remarked that there were 'rather foolhardy, adventurous heads, curious sensation hunting heads, who had remained in Paris to see the war, or as much of it as they could, in order to enrich their own experience'. Piatt Andrew, who founded the American Field Service, the most important volunteer ambulance organisation, wrote of 1914 that 'many young Americans were already stirring with the desire to participate in the great world drama'.[19]

Among the earliest to participate were Americans already in Europe. One such was Miss Norman Derr, daughter of a retired navy doctor in Atlanta who, aged twenty-four, had gone in 1910 to study art in Paris and Rome. In August 1914 she happened to be in Lucerne where she remarked on the different responses of English and Americans to the war. While the English were 'all calm and confident that they would be safe', the Americans were 'frenzied almost in their apprehension and strife'. Resolved to help, she found a position first at a French hospital on the Riviera and then at an English one at Menton. Having gained a Red Cross qualification she was enlisted into the French military nursing service with the rank of lieutenant. In 1916, to raise money for the American Fund for French Wounded, friends in Atlanta published a series of letters written to her aunt in which Derr recounted her experiences at a hospital at Vitry in the Marne valley near Paris from September 1915, where she became known as 'Mademoiselle Miss'. A sense of high adventure accompanied her arrival in this terrible New World. 'But oh,' she wrote, 'I can't express what it means to hear the guns for the first time! It is a sensation so vast and lonely and crowded and cosmic all at once that one seems born into a new phase of existence where the old ways of feeling things do not answer any longer.' Derr assisted in the operating theatre, and despite fourteen-hour days and sometimes thirty-plus operations a day, she described it as 'a marvellous life', and, writing in October, 'like a weird dream, laughter (for they laugh well, the soldiers) and blood and death and funny episodes, and sublime also, all under the autumn stars'.[20]

Derr recounted how French imperial soldiers passed through her hospital. There was a North African Arab, a 'poor wild child of the desert', who was inconsolable when drafted away from the hospital; another, 'a pearl fisher – a good Catholic and a brave fighter – had come from the sunny shores of Guadeloupe, to die for France'. Mortally wounded, a French priest administered the Last Rites, during which 'a marvellous change passed over his face as if it had grown white and luminous'. Derr, the well-heeled white woman from Atlanta, Georgia, held the black soldier's hand as he died. '"Mama," he murmured, "Louis," then fainter and sweeter – "*O mon bon Dieu*," and it was over, and nothing remained but a radiating smile.' 'And if I ever doubted how to die,' she wrote, 'my black pearl fisher from Guadeloupe has shown me the way.' This poignant, almost melodramatic, scene is one of only three such deathbed tableaux in the book. In each case, moreover, Derr describes a peaceful end. A telling line, however, in an October 1915 letter – 'a record day without a death' – reminds us that death was a constant presence, and it seems clear that in her letters to America, Derr was very selective about some of the grimmer realities of field hospital work in France.[21]

Ellen La Motte's angry and uncompromisingly candid book, *The Backwash of War*, is very different. Her subtitle told it all: *The Human Wreckage of the Battlefield as Witnessed by an American Hospital Nurse*. La Motte, a professional tuberculosis nurse in St Louis and Baltimore before the war, had moved to Paris in 1913 and, having been introduced to the writer and medical volunteer Mary Borden by her friend Gertrude Stein, came to work at Borden's Rousbrugge field hospital, north-east of Ypres.²² The book, dedicated 'To Mary Borden Turner, "The Little Boss", to whom I owe my experience in the zone of the armies', was published in New York in 1916, though after the USA came into the war the following year it was suppressed by the official censor. Comprising a series of thirteen 'sketches' dated between 18 December 1915 and 27 June 1916, the book's tone was set by the first story, entitled 'Heroes', which opens with a soldier who had attempted suicide (having 'fired a revolver through the roof of his mouth') being brought into the hospital. He was a deserter who 'had to be nursed back to health, until he was well enough to be stood up against a wall and shot. This is War,' observed La Motte sardonically. 'Things like this also happen in peace time, but not so obviously.' In another story a terribly wounded poilu called Marius took three noisy and smelly (urine, faeces and gas gangrene) days to die. There are no peaceful, transcendent deaths in La Motte's volume. In one sketch, from May 1916, La Motte reflected on 'women and wives'. 'You know,' she wrote, 'they won't let wives come to the Front. Women can come into the War Zone, on various pretexts, but wives cannot. Wives, it appears, are bad for the morale of the Army.' She noted that the staff at the hospital, most of whom were married, had relationships with local women. 'Arnand, the orderly', and 'Simon, the young surgeon', both visited girls in the village; 'the *Gestionnaire*, the little fat man in khaki, who is purveyor to the hospital', drove twelve miles into the country 'to sleep with a woman'; and 'the old doctor – he is sixty-four and has grandchildren – he goes down to the village for a little girl of fourteen. He was,' added La Motte, 'decorated with the Legion of Honour the other day.'²³

La Motte's account is complemented by that written a decade after the war by her boss at Rousbrugge, Mary Borden. Borden was a novelist (initially under the pseudonym Bridget Maclaglan) from an extremely wealthy Chicago family, who, after an unsuccessful marriage to a missionary in India, settled in London in 1913. Here she moved in radical and artistic circles and had an affair with the English Vorticist writer and painter Wyndham Lewis. On the outbreak of the war, at her own expense, she fitted out the field hospital in Rousbrugge, and later one on the Somme. She herself worked in them as a nurse from 1915 to the end of the war. She described her 1929 episodic memoir-with-poems, *The Forbidden Zone*, as 'fragments of a great confusion', in which she had 'blurred the bare horror of facts and softened the reality in spite of myself, not because I wished to do so, but because I was incapable of a nearer approach to the truth'. She too tells the story of a suicide victim brought into the hospital. 'But why suicide?' she asks the surgeon. '"Panic," answered Monsieur briefly. "Fear – he tried to kill himself from fear of being killed. They do sometimes."' She asked if he would live. '"Perhaps," replied the doctor.' 'And what then?' 'He'll be court-martialled and shot, Madame, for attempted suicide.' Borden went to the general to plead for the man's life, but he told her they had 'epidemics of suicide in the trenches. Panic seizes the men. They blow their brains out in a panic.' The threat of capital punishment was necessary to stop this sort of thing, otherwise, he said, 'we'd find ourselves going over the top with battalions of dead men'.[24]

As the story of the suicide shows, both La Motte and Borden well appreciated the irony that their caring mission was devoted to healing men so that they might again face death. 'Everything is arranged,' wrote Borden. 'It is arranged that men should be broken and that they should be mended. Just as you send your clothes to the laundry and mend them when they come back, so we send our men to the trenches and mend them when they come back again.' As with socks and shirts, this continues 'just as many times as they will stand it. And then you throw them away.' Borden mused on the decisions she alone had to make as to whether a soldier would be passed on for treatment or not: 'It was my business to know which of the wounded could wait and which could not.' Often men were held back because there was no hope for them. Borden ran her triage by temperature and claimed she could tell the difference between living and dying men. 'They were all half-frozen when they arrived, but the chill of their icy flesh wasn't the same as the cold inside them when life was almost ebbed away. My hand could instantly tell the difference between the cold of the harsh bitter night and the stealthy cold of death.' And sometimes the staff conspired even to end life. Faced with a terribly injured and blinded casualty, the chief surgeon told Borden: '"Give him morphine," he said, "a double dose. As much as you like." He pulled a cigarette out of his pocket. "In cases like this, if I am not about, give morphine; enough, you understand." Then he vanished like a ghost.'[25]

The reasons why these women served undoubtedly mirrored those of their male compatriots. Before the USA came into the war, patriotism was scarcely a factor. Their public explanations were often high blown. Norman Derr told the *Atlanta Constitution* in October 1916 that admiration for French culture had been a key factor: the 'knowledge of what France had done for civilization in art in every branch, in literature, painting and the drama'. Derr had been 'thrilled with her [France's] spirit of her nobility from the moment war was declared'. She went on, however, to describe the emotional rewards of helping the 'brave men' of France: 'It is to serve these that the nurse finds her supreme compensation' and 'when one gets into the work the spirit of heroism of the French makes every man or woman with a heart, who comes into contact with them feel that no sacrifice is too great to make in their aid'.[26]

Many of the wounded at Norman Derr's field hospital were brought in by 'American autos' of the American Ambulance Field Service.[27] The American Field Service (AFS), as it became, at its peak comprised over 2,000 volunteers. It was essentially the brainchild of Piatt Andrew, a graduate of both Princeton and Harvard, who had gone on to study economics in Germany and France. Between 1910 and 1912 he had been assistant secretary of the Treasury in President Taft's Republican administration. On the outbreak of war (and at the time unemployed) he resolved to go to France, telling his parents that what motivated him was the 'possibility of having even an infinitesimal part in one of the greatest events in all history – the possibility of being of some service in the midst of so much distress . . . and above all the chance of doing the little all that one can for France'.[28] The Field Service began when volunteers 'who wanted to do something to help' gathered at the existing American Hospital at Neuilly in the Paris suburbs. During the battle of the Marne in the autumn of 1914 the Americans were kept busy carrying wounded in makeshift ambulances to the Neuilly hospital and others in the area. After the battle line had settled down into the trenches of the Western Front, they found themselves relegated to ferrying injured soldiers between British and French hospitals well away from the war zone. This work, wrote Andrew, 'was not of a character to appeal to enthusiastic and ardent young Americans, who were physically able and morally eager to share more of war's hardships and dangers'.[29]

After negotiations with the French authorities, Andrew and his colleagues secured agreement in April 1915 for their outfit to be incorporated into the French forces and deployed 'in the French army zone as part and parcel of the French army'. As the French were concerned about the loyalties of the volunteers, as citizens of a neutral country, the American Field Service vouched that men would only be accepted if they had at least three reliable references 'testifying to their character and unquestioned loyalty to the Allied cause'. These Americans were themselves clearly *not* neutral. They agreed, moreover, to be 'subject to French military discipline', despite Andrew's view that this was 'probably unenforceable', as a volunteer could always appeal to the United States government for protection if necessary. 'Fortunately,' recorded Andrew, 'it was never put to the test. During our three years of service there was never a question of espionage or disloyalty among our volunteers, nor were there any cases of serious infraction of military discipline.' The volunteers themselves were nearly all college boys, generally drawn from a narrow, upper-class social range. The largest college representation came from Harvard (325), followed by Yale (187) and Princeton (181). Before the end of 1915 the AFS had formed four complete sections with up to thirty volunteers and twenty ambulances, each contingent being 'sufficient to handle all of the sanitary transport of four French divisions'.[30]

The use of motor transport brought with it significant changes in the care of battlefield casualties. Before the First World War both the French and United States armies had staffed slow-moving, horse-drawn ambulances with trained medical personnel, who were able to administer treatment en route. In 1914, however, the French found that the enhanced speed of motor ambulances, together with the relatively good road communications near the front line, meant that the key requirement was to get casualties moved as quickly and comfortably as possible to the field hospitals, where they could 'receive proper treatment under advantageous conditions'. The ambulances, they claimed, did not need medical but technical expertise – drivers, mechanics and so on. The French thought 'it was as illogical to expect doctors and surgeons to accomplish this work as it would be to ask automobile experts to do surgical and medical work in the dressing-stations and hospitals'.[31]

A number of AFS sections were posted to Verdun in 1916, and the service history contains accounts of individual experiences culled from diaries, memoirs and letters home. Harvard-man Henry Beston Sheahan (later to be well known as a writer and naturalist) was there at the start, based first at a hospital where 'pasty-faced, tired attendants unloaded mud, cloth, bandages, and blood that turned out to be human beings', and averaging runs of 200 miles a day during the first week of the offensive. The 'voice of war,' he wrote, 'is the voice of the shell. You hear a perfectly horrible sound as if the sky were made of cloth and the Devil were tearing it apart, a screaming undulating sound followed by an explosion of fearful violence.' Sheahan also reflected on the meaning of the war itself. 'What in Heaven's name is to be the end of all this?' he asked. 'What is the world to be like which will some day follow this cruel welter of savagery and pain?' He was not a pacifist – 'because I see war as part of the web of life'. It was 'competition distilled to its ultimate essence, and will not be done away with' – and here there was an echo of the Wilsonian vision – 'until international competition is under some rigorous and centralized control. Yet how can such a despotism of power be established, and by whom?' War, he thought realistically, could not be 'eliminated from the mechanism of civilization by a folding of hands and a general promise to be good'.[32]

Over 150 members of the American Field Service were killed in the war. William de Ford Bigelow recounted the funeral of Edward Kelley, killed on 25 September 1916 by shellfire in Marre, eight miles north-west of Verdun. The French inspector in overall charge of the ambulance work, M. Gouzin, gave a eulogy which concluded: '*Adieu, Kelley, reposez en paix dans cette terre sanctifiée par votre sang: votre mort est un symbole et un exemple, votre souvenir ne périra pas!*' ('Farewell, Kelley, rest in peace in this earth sanctified by your blood: your death is a symbol and example, your memory will last for ever.')

Kelley's comrades then each 'tossed some earth onto the coffin in its resting-place and turned away, eyes dry, throats queerly tight – turned away to the scurrying tasks of the day's service'.

Deployment to Verdun was particularly challenging. William Bueller Seabrook from Atlanta, Georgia, who after the war achieved notoriety as an occult writer and self-confessed cannibal, said 'three weeks is about the limit of human endurance' in this sector. 'It is hard to write about – this Verdun service. Those of us who used to laugh at danger have stopped laughing.' Writing to his mother from Verdun in June 1916, Malbone Hunter Birckhead, an Episcopal minister and Harvard graduate, said he was 'tired to death of the horrors, the smells, and the sights of war', but was yet 'glad to have got a taste of real war, though, so as to know what it really means'.[33]

There were other Americans at the start of the war who also wanted 'a taste of real war', but as fully-fledged combatants rather than ambulance drivers. Caught up (before anyone knew any better) in the romance of war, a few enlisted in the French army and ended up in the Foreign Legion, but the most romantic of all were the pilots who joined up to fight in the skies, perhaps the only theatre of the Great War which retained some of its romance to the end. Samuel Hynes, the historian of these men who himself was a combat flier in the Second World War, has marvellously explored the experience of these eager and dashing aviators and their adventures (sometimes fatal) in the 'unsubstantial air'. Hynes focuses on seven pioneer American recruits who were the first members of what became the French Air Service's Escadrille (squadron) Lafayette. Six of them were college boys, very similar in background to the AFS volunteers, and they shared many of the motivations to join up. Kiffin Rockwell, an alumnus of Washington and Lee University, a prestigious Virginia liberal arts college, came from a military family and saw the war as 'a great opportunity'. 'If I should be killed in this war,' he wrote from France, 'I will at least die as a man should.' James McConnell (University of Virginia) also saw it as the chance of a lifetime. The North Caroline Sand Hills, he told a friend, 'will be here forever, but the war won't, and so I'm going'. Two others, William Thaw (Yale) and Norman Prince (Harvard), were part-French and clearly felt a special tie to the country. Victor Chapman

(St Paul's School and Harvard) was an art student in Paris who first joined the Foreign Legion before becoming a pilot and Bert Hall, the only non-college man of Hynes's group, had worked as a Paris taxi driver and claimed to have enlisted on the grounds that 'if a country is good enough to live in it is good enough to fight for'.[34]

Initially named the 'Escadrille Américaine', the name was changed to 'Lafayette' after the US government, prompted by the Germans, complained to the French that it contravened American neutrality. In the spring of 1916 the squadron was posted to Bar-le-Duc near Verdun. Here Carroll Dana Winslow, serving with a different unit, encountered them and asserted in a book published the following year that they had simply been motivated by a spirit 'of sincere patriotism to the cause they had made their own'. Winslow reflected, too, on the high casualty rate suffered by airmen. He had dined with Victor Chapman, Norman Prince and Kiffin Rockwell, 'all three since fallen on the "*champ d'honneur*"'. The morning after the dinner, when Winslow's own unit had to move on, one of his colleagues was killed after he took too short a run and his wing caught a tent on take-off. But Winslow yet managed to convey some of the exhilaration of war. Looking over the battlefield at Mort-Homme (north-west of Verdun), 'the sky seemed full of fire-flies – in reality exploding shells. On all sides the guns flashed angrily. Search-lights played about in every direction. It was a most superb spectacle, but it was terrible. It was hell.' Winslow himself emerged unscathed. His squadron was deployed on reconnaissance duties and artillery spotting, which he found boring and uneventful. 'My machine,' he recorded, 'was never once hit by shrapnel nor was it attacked by the enemy.'[35]

Samuel Hynes identifies the 'joy factor' as an important motivation. 'Among military occupations,' he asserts, 'flying was the only one (now that the cavalry had been dismounted) that gave personal pleasure to the individual who was doing it.'[36] James McConnell, who flew with the Lafayette squadron and whose memoir was published posthumously in 1917, remarked on the 'roar of battle – unheard'. 'For us,' he wrote, 'the battle passes in silence, the noise of one's motor deadening all other sounds.' Far below, along a 'brown belt' of trenches, 'myriads of tiny flashes tell where the guns are hidden', but 'those flashes, and the smoke of bursting shells, are all we see of the fighting. It is a weird combination of stillness and havoc, the Verdun conflict viewed from the sky.' In October, when the squadron had been transferred to the Somme, McConnell wrote home that he did not 'get a chance to see much of the biggest battle in the world which is being fought here. We fly so high that ground details are lacking.' But he saw enough to have immense sympathy for the troops suffering under incessant shellfire. 'When one thinks of the poor devils crouching in their inadequate shelters under such a hurricane of flying metal, it increases one's respect for the staying powers of modern man.'[37]

While the Escadrille Lafayette achieved lasting fame as an elite unit, some other American formations had a more chequered existence. In 1914 Sam Hughes, the flamboyant and controversial Canadian Minister of Militia and Defence, proposed a typically ill-thought-out, though ambitious, scheme to enlist Americans into the Canadian Expeditionary Force (CEF). Early in the war he first offered the British a battalion raised from American citizens resident in Canada for over-seas service, and then a corps consisting of 'sixty thousand men from the neighbouring republic'. London reacted coolly, observing that this would violate both the United States Foreign Enlistment Act of 1818 as well as the British Army Act, and the proposal was let lie until the following autumn when Hughes revived it with a new plan for an 'American Legion' to serve with the Canadian forces. By early 1916 a 1,200-strong unit, designated the 97th Overseas Battalion of the CEF, had been assembled in Toronto under the command of the rapidly promoted Colonel Charles Seymour Bullock, an American-born Unitarian minister in Ottawa. Ostensibly operating only in Canada, Bullock's recruiters in fact travelled into the northern USA success-fully soliciting men. The quality of the enlistment was, however, very variable. Numbers of mercenaries joined up, allegedly together with a fugitive general from the Mexican revolution. The unit was plagued with indiscipline and described by the Toronto chief of police as 'the worst behaved battalion in the city'.

Hughes pressed on with his scheme in the face of rising criticism from both Britain and the USA. A plan to use a cap badge combining the maple leaf and George Washington's family coat of arms with the legends 'Canada Overseas' and 'American Legion', was firmly vetoed. American consuls in Canada complained about US flags and other symbols being used at recruiting stations, and in late 1915 two 'English agents' were arrested in Washington for allegedly trying to entice US citizens into the Canadian forces. In May 1915 the battalion was posted to Aldershot Camp in Nova Scotia, and stayed there for over a year, further disrupted by desertions, drunkenness and other disciplinary problems, including an NCO who absconded with the sergeants' mess funds. Eventually in September 1916, the unit, stripped of any insignia which could indicate its American origins, sailed for England, where it was broken up to fill up other Canadian units before the remaining men reached the Western Front. Although a former American Legion medical officer, Captain Bellenden Hutcheson, a native of Illinois, won the Victoria Cross in 1918, the fate of Charles Bullock is more in keeping with that of his ill-starred formation. Bullock reached England and claimed publicly that he had served at the front and been wounded. This may be so, but such records as survive show only that he was treated in England for an accidental gunshot wound to his hand.[38]

THE WAR IN THE UNITED STATES

The fact that the United States was both neutral and, from the very start, a vitally important source of munitions and other supplies for the Allies, meant that over the first two and a half years of the war it became a significant zone of activity where the violent antagonisms of Allied and Central Powers alike were played out in a variety of different ways. Whatever the American public may have thought or hoped, neutrality could not entirely protect the country from the war. The United States was too important, especially in economic terms, to remain in isolation, nor was there any diplomatic or political cordon sanitaire which could wall the country off from the global conflict.

Propaganda was used by both sides. The Germans set up a well-funded 'Propaganda Cabinet' in New York, and a German Information Service. This sponsored a weekly magazine, *The Fatherland*, which under the lively editorship of George Sylvester Viereck claimed a circulation of 80,000 copies. It carried the slogan 'Fair Play for Germany and Austria' on its masthead, and Viereck's intention was 'to place the German side of this unhappy quarrel fairly and squarely before the American people'. Also mobilised was the existing German-American Alliance (the Deutsche-Amerikanischer Nationalbund) which in 1914 boasted 2 million members and branches in forty states. The Alliance produced propaganda pamphlets, sponsored lecture tours and organised rallies to protest against arms shipments to the Allies. During the 1916 presidential election campaign it came out strongly behind Wilson's opponent, Charles Evans Hughes. The Germans had to work hard to counter what Stewart Halsey Ross calls the 'atrocity burden' of the *Lusitania*, the Bryce Report (which detailed German atrocities during the conquest of Belgium in 1914), and the execution of nurse Edith Cavell. Their most brilliant publicist, Bernhard Dernburg, was forced out of the country after intemperately defending the sinking of the *Lusitania*. His successor was the German commercial attaché, Heinrich Albert, who had been working on clandestine economic ways of damaging Allied economic interests in the USA. Among his stratagems was the setting up of a bogus enterprise, the Bridgeport Projectile Company, which would buy up vital machine tools and equipment, hire skilled personnel and negotiate arms contracts (which there was no intention of filling), all aimed at disrupting munitions manufacturing generally and thus supplies to the Allies.[39]

Alerted to unusual financial transactions through intercepted German cables, and suspicious of Viereck's activities, the US Secret Service began monitoring German embassy personnel and German-American 'suspects' in May 1915. On 24 July, while tailing Viereck and Albert, a Secret Service agent, Frank Burke, seized Albert's briefcase on the New York Elevated Railway. The case contained a wealth of documents concerning the planting of German stories in American journals, the financing of *The Fatherland* (which had claimed to be independent), the organising of strikes in American munitions plants and the Bridgeport Projectile Company scheme, among other activities. All this was leaked to the New York newspaper *The World*, which duly responded with a sensational series of articles denouncing German perfidy. A dozen years after the war, Viereck described the publicity as 'a German catastrophe'. 'The loss of the Albert portfolio,' he claimed, perhaps a little extravagantly, 'was like the loss of the Marne.'[40]

The kinds of propaganda and economic activity which the Germans indulged in were broadly mirrored by the Allies. The British distributed pamphlets and fed stories to the American press, with the assistance of such people as Arthur Willert, the brilliant Washington correspondent of *The Times*. The Belgians sent a high-level delegation to the USA in September 1914 to tell the Americans about German atrocities in their country.[41] But the Central Powers indulged in much more aggressive activities. There were wild rumours in late August 1914 that thousands of German reservists in the Detroit area were going to invade Canada. These stories had no foundation, but the threat was sufficient for the Canadians to station secret agents in a number of communities along the American frontier, and for the first two years of the war fears of German- or Irish-American-inspired raids from the United States led the Canadian authorities to keep 16,000 soldiers along the border and a further 30,000 in reserve, ready to repel any direct attack. For their part, the Germans – initially believing that Japan would send troops to the war and despatch them across Canada en route to the Western Front – instructed the German military attaché, Franz von Papen, to prepare plans to attack the Canadian Pacific Railway. There was also a scheme to blow up the Panama Canal should the Japanese use that route, but this (as with the plan for Canada) was shelved pending the arrival of the Japanese, who never came.

In the meantime, aiming to disrupt the transport of war materiel from Canada to Europe, von Papen funded a scheme to bomb the Welland Canal (which links Lakes Ontario and Erie, bypassing the Niagara Falls) and sent saboteurs to attack railways in eastern Canada, but the only result was one half-cock bombing in February 1915, which slightly damaged a railway bridge at Vanceboro, Maine (crossing the St Croix River, and separating the USA from Canada). On 21 June a much more serious bomb in Windsor, Ontario, just across the river from Detroit, Michigan, destroyed a wing of the Peabody Overall Factory, which was manufacturing army uniforms for the British and Canadian governments. A second bomb planted simultaneously at the Windsor Armouries failed to go off. [42]

Although the Windsor attacks were a local initiative, organised by a Detroit German-American businessman called Albert Kalbschmidt, officially sponsored German secret agents were involved in a more extensive sabotage campaign. A German admiralty agent, Franz Rintelen, a reserve naval officer who had worked for a German bank in the USA before the war, was despatched back across the Atlantic to organise the campaign. Rintelen used German- and Irish-American dock workers to plant time-bombs on departing munitions ships. While it is impossible to estimate precisely how successful this was – the British agent Norman Thwaites asserts that thirty-six ships were 'wholly or partially destroyed during the first fifteen months of the war' – when some unexploded devices were discovered in various ports the American authorities immediately increased port security. Rintelin also employed agents provocateurs to foment strikes and labour disputes in munitions factories, and funded 'Labor's National Peace Council' which supported wildcat strikes by dock workers. The German embassy accounts show that $39,800 ($952,000 today) was paid in 1915 to 'an Irish agent' for 'direct strike support'. Rintelen appears to have had a compulsion to boast about his exploits and after doing so to an American female acquaintance, Anne Seward, who promptly passed the information on to the government, he was placed under surveillance. The Bureau of Investigation (which became the FBI in 1935) reported extensively on Rintelen's activities, as well as his impressive (and completely bogus) claim to one of their agents that he had personally ordered the sinking of the *Lusitania*.[43]

Rintelen was recalled by Berlin in August 1915, probably on the advice of von Papen and Bernstorff who had become worried by his insecure behaviour. Although he was travelling with a forged Swiss passport on the Dutch liner *Noordam*, British Naval Intelligence appear to have learned of his journey and when the ship was stopped at Ramsgate, Kent, for blockade control, Rintelen was arrested, interrogated and, after compromising papers were discovered, to avoid being shot as a spy confessed to being a German naval officer. The British Director of Naval Intelligence, Captain Reginald 'Blinker' Hall (he had a nervous twitch), passed evidence of Rintelen's activities to the Americans in order to reinforce the danger which the Germans posed to the USA. As Christopher Andrew has observed, Hall's productive liaison with Edward Bell, a second secretary at the United States embassy in London, was also an early manifestation of what was to become 'the secret Anglo-American intelligence alliance'. Another product of this developing relationship was incriminating evidence about von Papen's activities in copies of documents which the British had seized from an American courier working for the Germans.[44]

German sabotage did not cease with Rintelen's departure (nor that of von Papen, who was expelled in December 1915). In fact the greatest single German attack on the USA during the war occurred during the night of 29 July 1916 at the huge freight terminal on Black Tom Island in New York harbour. A series of enormous explosions destroyed 2 million pounds of munitions stockpiled for dispatch to Europe and great quantities of other commodities. *The New York Times* reported that 'at 2:08 [a.m. on Sunday 30 July] a million people, maybe five millions, were awakened by an explosion that . . . rattled the skyscrapers on the rock foundations of Manhattan' (where plate-glass windows were shattered), and destroyed an estimated $5 million-worth of ammunition and caused $20 million of damage. Half an hour after the first explosion, 'car after car and barge after barge of high explosives ignited'. Thirteen warehouses belonging to the National Storage Company (which had contained 40,000 tons of sugar) were destroyed: 'There remained no vestige of those nearest the base of the explosion. Not a brick to mark where they had stood.' Seven lives were reported lost – mercifully few in the circumstances – though this included a two-month-old child thrown from his bed in Jersey City, and around a hundred people were injured. The event and its aftermath was likened to a battlefield. The firemen fighting the fires had to work under shrapnel and a 'rain of bullets'. Thousands of people were reported to have gathered to watch the spectacle from Battery Park at the south end of Manhattan Island, where they 'acquired a real picture of what the firing line in the European War looks like'.[45]

Sabotage was almost immediately suspected. The *New York Times* rather carefully reported that the police were trying to verify information 'from highly reliable sources that the explosion . . . was the work of alien plotters, acting in this country in the interest of a foreign

Government'. No-one was convicted at the time, but postwar investigations by the Mixed Claims Commission, which was set up to consider American claims against Germany for compensation arising from wartime events (including, for example, the sinking of the *Lusitania*), eventually in 1939 ascribed responsibility for the Black Tom attack to German agents.[46]

The British also ran covert operations in the USA during 1914–17, though these were confined to counter-intelligence and propaganda rather than sabotage. Before the war different British departments, including the Home Office and the India Office, had run agents in North America against Irish and Indian nationalists (who themselves of course shared a common cause against British imperialism) and in addition employed the American detective agency Pinkerton's. There was also a network run on the west coast by William Hopkinson, a fluent Punjabi-speaking official in the Canadian Immigration Department, targeting radical elements in the sizeable Sikh community based along both the Canadian and American Pacific coast. After Hopkinson died in October 1914, some of this work was taken up by Alexander Ross, the British consul-general in San Francisco. From October 1915 he ran an important agent, Vishnu Das Bagai, who managed to gain the confidence of Ram Chandra, the leader of the Ghadar Party, to such an extent that he was put in charge of the party's finances. Ross, however, was restricted in what he could do since the Government of India was extremely anxious to avoid the diplomatic embarrassment which would follow the discovery of Indian-backed espionage operations in the USA. Bagai, nevertheless, was a prolific source of information and considered to have been 'perhaps the most esteemed agent of the Indian empire'.[47]

One problem for the British was that the Americans were quite tolerant of anti-imperialists, seeing themselves as being (or at least having been) in the same tradition, and while the USA remained neutral the American authorities were unlikely to support any legal action against them. The Indian government was so worried about the potential threat from revolutionary subversives, however, that in May 1916 they sent the veteran Indian policeman, Sir Robert Nathan, to Vancouver to renew the intelligence effort against them. Nathan soon identified the New York-based Dr Chandrakanta Chakravarty, who was associated with the German-backed Indian Independence Committee, as 'the chief Indian agent of Germany in America'. In March 1917, Chakravarty was arrested along with a German agent, Erik Sekunna, who (according to Thwaites) eventually cracked and confessed to being part of a scheme to supply German arms for revolutionaries in India. The British had already alerted the Americans in the spring of 1915 to a German operation, funded by von Papen, to supply arms stockpiled in California by ship to Bengal via Mexico. Though the Americans took the line that no breach of their neutrality had taken place, the United States Bureau of Investigation were interested enough to begin investigations which sufficiently disturbed the Germans' plans to abort the whole operation. Once the USA entered the war in April 1917, however, it became a very different matter and between November 1917 and July 1918, with information supplied by Nathan and others, the authorities rounded up and tried nearly a hundred Indian conspirators in California.[48]

On the east coast, Captain Guy Gaunt, the British naval attaché in Washington, built up an intelligence network during the first year of the war, part of which comprised a group of anti-Habsburg Czech nationalists led by Emanuel Voska. Trusted by German-Americans (as fellow citizens of the Central Powers) some of them gained employment as clerks and telephone operators which provided ample scope for intelligence-gathering. But Gaunt, keen though he was (as he testified in his memoirs) as a diplomat, was ill-placed to run clandestine operations of any sort, as discovery would inevitably bring with it serious diplomatic embarrassment at a time when the British government was especially anxious not to upset the Americans unnecessarily. In the autumn of 1915, therefore, the chief of British secret intelligence, Mansfield Cumming, sent agents of his own to the United States. One of these was Sir William Wiseman, a baronet whose title had first been awarded in 1628. Wiseman had been educated at Cambridge University where he won a 'Blue' for boxing against Oxford. He had fought on the Western Front but had been invalided home after being gassed near Ypres in July 1915. Recruited in the familiar ad hoc way the British secret services adopted for many

years – Cumming had served with Wiseman's father in the navy –
Wiseman was despatched with a colleague called Sydney Mansfield to
set up an office in New York.[49]

When they reached the USA they were not welcomed by Gaunt,
who believed he had matters well in hand and was clearly upset at his
role apparently being usurped. But it was both unwise and insecure
for him to continue playing a covert intelligence role and, although
Wiseman returned to England within three weeks (Mansfield stayed a
month longer), he was sent back in January 1916 with Captain Norman
Thwaites as his assistant. Based in New York, they had cover as part of
the British Ministry of Munitions' 'Transport Department'. Thwaites
was another war-casualty recruit to intelligence. Spying was not generally regarded as an appropriate occupation for a British gentleman, and
it was a common pattern to find men disqualified for service on the
battlefield (their definite first choice) ending up in the secret service.
In Thwaites's case he had been wounded in November 1914 (including being shot through the jaw) and gazetted unfit for active service.
Thwaites, however, was actually very well qualified for the intelligence
job. He had been a journalist in the USA before the war, spoke fluent
German and for ten years had been private secretary to the American
newspaper publisher, Joseph Pulitzer (originator of the prizes), so he
was unusually well connected in America.

Although Gaunt grumpily and inaccurately asserted in his memoirs
(published in 1940) that Wiseman only 'played a very small part
under me, and then only at intervals', Wiseman in fact ran British
secret intelligence in the USA for the rest of the war. The office's
initial brief, however, was to focus on counter-espionage, including
'the investigation of suspects about whom the authorities at home
required information'; 'a general watch on the Irish movement in the
United States'; and 'investigation into Hindu Sedition in America'
('conducted jointly with Mr N. [sic] of the India Office'). They were
able to exploit Thwaites's contacts, and got especially helpful unofficial assistance from Thwaites's friend Captain Thomas J. Tunney,
head of the New York Police Department bomb squad and a New
York policeman unusually from an Irish Protestant background (with
a brother, moreover, serving in the Royal Irish Constabulary).[50]

Once established in New York, Wiseman's office was also given some propaganda work. According to his breezy memoirs, Thwaites opportunistically masterminded a diverting publicity coup against the German ambassador. Invited with William Wiseman to a weekend at the Long Island summer house of the Anglophile millionaire industrialist Oscar Lewisohn, he was shown some photographs by a fellow guest of another summer party in the Adirondacks which had been attended by Bernstorff, who by repute had 'a bit of an eye for the ladies'. Among the pictures were several of the ambassador and other guests in swimming costumes. One showed him posing on a diving-board, 'an arm about a lovely companion'; another 'showed the German plenipotentiary in more generous mood, with both arms encompassing the waists of bathing nymphs in ravishing if strictly rationed costume'. Thwaites managed to purloin this photograph long enough to have copies made which were distributed to contacts, including the Russian ambassador, who gleefully displayed it in his office (leading Bernstorff to suspect that the Russians had obtained it in the first place). To the intense embarrassment of the Germans, copies were reproduced in illustrated journals on both sides of the Atlantic. 'As a piece of anti-enemy propaganda,' boasted Thwaites, 'I have no hesitation in saying that this incident was more effective than pages of editorial matter which the British were alleged to inspire in the Press of the United States.' Others were not so impressed or amused. In October 1916 William Wiseman proudly showed Compton Mackenzie (both back in London for briefings) a copy of the picture. Mackenzie reflected that only in Britain or the USA 'could such a photograph have been expected to influence public opinion against the war aims of Germany, and for a moment I felt depressed by the civilisation we were fighting such a great war to preserve'.[51]

Wiseman's greatest achievement was to gain unparalleled access to President Wilson, initially through a contact with his confidential adviser, Colonel House. In December 1916 the British ambassador, Sir Cecil Spring-Rice, used Wiseman to deliver a message to the colonel, upon whom the young Englishman (he was thirty) made an immediate impression. House thought him 'the most imp[ortan]t caller I have had for some time' and the two men began to meet regularly thereafter. The moment was particularly opportune for Wiseman who appeared to offer the Americans a more useful line of communication to London than was provided by Spring-Rice who was ailing and whose Republican sympathies Wilson had found increasingly unattractive. For some time, moreover, Asquith's administration had been under pressure and on 6 December Lloyd George became prime minister. Colonel House's main contact in London, Edward Grey, moreover, was left out of Lloyd George's Cabinet, which seems to have left House especially susceptible to the suggestion that Wiseman would be able to facilitate close communication with the new administration. Wiseman, indeed, so impressed House that the American astonishingly thought that the Englishman, a man with no professional diplomatic experience of any sort, could make a better British ambassador than Spring-Rice. For his part, Wiseman told House 'in the gravest confidence' that he was 'in direct communication with the Foreign Office', and that the embassy was unaware of this. At best this was only half true. Wiseman certainly had a line of direct communication independent of the embassy with his chief, Mansfield Cumming. Since the Foreign Office provided the funds for Cumming's service, Wiseman's claim might not be entirely false, though any implication that he was able to communicate readily with the highest levels of government was almost certainly untrue. House did not know this, overestimated the Englishman's status and assured President Wilson that he thought that Wiseman 'reflects the views of his government'.[52]

Once Wiseman had gained the trust and confidence of both House and Wilson, however, he did become an important conduit of communications between the American and British governments, especially during the months before the USA came into the war. He also provided valuable insights into American attitudes about the war, and the likelihood of their coming in on the Allied side. He and House even drafted a paper, which Wilson approved, summarising American opinion and reminding the British that any decision to enter the conflict would be based primarily on America's own national interest: 'If the United States goes to war with Germany – which she probably will – it will be to uphold American rights and assert her dignity as a nation.'[53] So it was to be, but after the USA came into the war on 6 April 1917,

Wiseman continued to report to British intelligence in London on American political matters and he played a central role in helping to oil the wheels of the Anglo-American wartime partnership. His closeness to House enabled him to have unprecedented access (for a foreigner) to President Wilson. He met the president regularly and even spent a week's vacation with him and House in August 1918. Wiseman's achievement in gaining this access and influence at the very highest levels of the United States administration made him the most successful 'agent of influence' in the history of the British Secret Intelligence Service.[54]

Russia

Grigorii Rasputin, the 'mad monk' of the late Russian empire, was murdered in Petrograd (St Petersburg) on the early morning of Saturday 30 December 1916.[1] The Gothic horror of the event itself, combined with the compelling celebrity of the man, have proved to be an irresistible combination for popular writers, film-makers and novelists alike. But in the real world of wartime Petrograd the killing of Rasputin was a significant waymark on Russia's inexorable (it seemed) slide into chaos and revolution. Rasputin, who was about fifty years old at the beginning of the war, had been born in Siberia and came to prominence as a charismatic holy man and faith healer in the early 1900s. By 1910 he had become an imperial favourite, welcomed especially by the empress for his apparent ability to ease the haemophilia of the tsarevich Alexei, the imperial couple's only son. Rasputin also had a well-deserved reputation for excess, with a prodigious appetite for alcohol and sexual activity, thought by some to be boosted by transcendental and hypnotic gifts. An increasingly powerful and influential outsider, who luxuriated in his peasant-mystic status, he was resented and feared by many at the imperial court. During the war – which Rasputin himself opposed on the sensible grounds that it would cause the deaths of many peasants – rumours circulated that he was actively supporting enemy interests and used his closeness to the tsarina (who was also thought to be pro-German, though this was never substantiated) to influence imperial Church and political appointments in favour of similarly sympathetic individuals. For some, he was not just a monstrous embarrassment to the royal family, but he had also come to represent all that was wrong at the summit of the empire.

Rasputin's death occurred during the crisis winter of 1916/17, which, as Dominic Lieven has argued, 'was decisive not just for the outcome of the First World War but also for the history of twentieth-century Europe'.[2] This crisis resulted in part from the interconnectedness of the domestic and battle fronts. The food shortages and other privations of the civilian population in Russia, Germany and Austria-Hungary, bad enough in 1915–16, were even worse the following winter, so much so that the authorities in Berlin began to believe that the home front could not sustain much more. For the German authorities this, in turn, contributed to the disastrous decision to adopt unrestricted submarine warfare, which was such an important factor bringing the United States into the war and thereby sealing Germany's fate. In Russia, however, the crisis had more immediate domestic consequences, leading to the revolutions of 1917 and the disintegration of the empire itself.

RASPUTIN'S MURDER

The first person in London to have the news confirmed of Rasputin's murder was Mansfield Cumming – 'C' – the head of the British secret service, who got it from his man in the Russian capital, Sir Samuel Hoare. 'Urgent. Private for C:–', read Hoare's telegram of 31 December. 'News correct that Rasputin was killed in Petrograd in private house early morning of Dec. 30'. Hoare's handwritten copy of the telegram survives with the original date '17' crossed out. Since the Russians still used the old Julian calendar (abandoned in the mid-eighteenth century by Britain and after the 1917 revolution by Russia) their 'Old Style' dates were thirteen days behind the calendar used elsewhere in Europe. In his memoirs he said the telegram had been 'coded for greater secrecy' by his wife, Lady Maud (though one cannot help thinking that it would have been even more secret if he had coded it himself). Late the next afternoon Hoare sent 'C' another cable: 'Following is official and absolutely reliable but given me in strict confidence. Body of Rasputin has been found under ice in water near Petrovsky Island Petrograd. Evidence shows that it was the intention of the murderers that body should be discovered.' [3]

Hoare was already writing up a detailed report of the affair and on 2 January 1917 (but still only 20 December 1916 Old Style) he completed it and sent it immediately to London in the care of a king's messenger, Colonel Charles Burn, who, like Hoare, was a Conservative MP. Hoare was acutely conscious of his anomalous position vis-à-vis the embassy as an intelligence officer. While he reported confidentially to Mansfield Cumming in London, he operated openly in Petrograd. In effect, he was not so much a spy as an intelligence liaison officer, but still had to take care to avoid stepping on the sensitive toes of the British diplomats and service attachés who jealously guarded their function to report Russian information back to London. In a covering letter to Cumming's assistant, Colonel Freddie Browning, Hoare said that 'the Embassy will no doubt send some particulars [of Rasputin's death] and it is no business of mine to report upon such an event'. On the other hand Hoare regarded it as 'of such overwhelming importance to Russia that every detail is worth recording. I have,' he continued, 'therefore gone out of my way to find out as much as possible about it.' But, to safeguard his own position, both with the Russians (who might be shocked at the detail of his report) and that of his intelligence mission (which depended on the continued goodwill of the embassy in Moscow and the Foreign Office in London), he told Browning it was 'vitally important that you should only show the account to one or two big people upon whom you can rely'. He said that he had 'purposely included' in his text 'all the details that I could obtain. If it is written in the style of the "Daily Mail", my answer is that the whole question is so sensational that one cannot describe it as one would if it were an ordinary episode of the war.' Perhaps keen to highlight his own success in acquiring the story (and also to enhance the reputation of Mansfield Cumming's comparatively untried organisation), Hoare had his own ideas of which 'big people' might be shown the report. 'I think you will find,' he told Browning, 'that the King would like to see the Report about the Death of Rasputin. I know for a fact that both he and the Queen are particularly interested in the whole affair. I suggest that it might be worth while for C. to take it to him.'⁴

The report itself was in two parts, dated 1 and 2 January respectively. The first certainly began (as Hoare promised) with more than a hint of popular journalism: 'In the early morning of Saturday, December 30th, there was enacted in Petrograd one of those crimes which by their magnitude blurr [sic] the well-defined rules of ethics and by their results change the history of a generation'. Hoare continued in like vein:

GREGORY EPHEMICH NOVICH – for RASPUTIN, 'the rake', was only the nickname that his excesses gained him in his village – had governed Russia since the day, four years ago, when first he showed in the Imperial Palace in Poland, his healing powers over the Tsarevitch. To describe the influence that he possessed, the scandals that surrounded his life, the tragedies that followed in his path, is to rewrite a Dumas romance.

No doubt bearing in mind that all of his readers would already have some knowledge of Rasputin, Hoare went on to describe three previous occasions on which Grigorii had been the target of attempted murder. An 'outraged peasant girl from his native Siberia' had stabbed him. A fellow monk had 'seemed to have him at his mercy in the Petrograd cell of the Metropolitan of Kieff', but Rasputin's 'great strength and the arrival of help saved his life'. Earlier in 1916 in one of Petrograd's best restaurants, 'certain officers of the Chevaliers Gardes would have killed him if his familiars of the secret police had not appeared in time'. Hoare noted that no hint of any of these occurrences ever reached the press, 'indeed to mention his [Rasputin's] name brought a fine of 3000 roubles'. The monk was protected 'day and night' by the secret police. Only 'from time to time' did 'the moujik's [peasant's] uncontrollable appetite for debauch leave him defenceless'. Hoare asserted that a former Guards officer in Moscow ('now relegated to the Gendarmes') had boasted 'that the achievement of his career was the beating he gave Rasputin during some wild orgie [sic]'. Other people had 'seen him madly drunk in the streets and public

places'. 'True to his nickname ['Rasputin' could be translated as 'rake']',
added Hoare, 'it was at an orgie that Rasputin met his death.'⁵

Having sketched the personal background, Hoare briefly outlined
the political context. He reminded his readers that at the start of the
current session of the Russian Duma on 14 November (New Style)
there had been a sensational speech by Professor Pavel Miliukov, leader
of the Constitutional Democrat (or Kadet) Party, when he had fiercely
attacked the prime minister, Boris Stürmer, as incompetent and pro-
German. Miliukov, who had spoken of 'dark forces fighting for
Germany and attempting to destroy popular unity', had explicitly
charged Stürmer of being in collusion with Rasputin. (Hoare had actually sent London a transcript of Miliukov's speech, taken 'from the
Speaker's own notes'.) This was the first time that any Russian parliamentarian had 'dared mention Rasputin by name'. On 29 December
the Duma session had been 'abruptly closed twenty-four hours before
the appointed time'. It had ended, reported Hoare, 'with another
onslaught, less personal, less sensational, but hardly less effective. "The
atmosphere is charged with electricity" – so ran Miliukoff's perora-
tion – "no-one knows where or when the blow will fall" (Applause).'
Here Hoare portentously remarked that 'the following morning [30
December] the blow, the effects of which cannot be gauged, had
already fallen'.

He next described how he himself had got the news. On Saturday
afternoon, 30 December, he had been attending a meeting of the Enemy
Supplies Committee, helping to draw up a Russian black list for the
Allied blockade policy. Several times during the meeting, individuals
had 'left the room and returned with whispered messages to their
neighbours', but Hoare, not suspecting anything was afoot, had paid
no attention. After the meeting broke up, he was chatting to the chairman of the committee, Professor Petr Struve, when a Russian official
arrived 'with the news the Rasputin had been murdered that morning
by the Grand Duke Dmitri Pavlovitch and Prince Youssupoff'.
Demonstrating a touching faith in the Russian press, Struve then sent
out for an evening paper. The *Bourse Gazette*, described by Hoare as
'always a paper of headlines', was brought in. The lead story was
devoted to German peace proposals, and the second to fighting in

Romania. 'Then came a headline: "Death of Gregory Rasputin in Petrograd".' The story on page two of the paper was very short and simply said: 'At six o'clock this morning Gregory Rasputin Novich died after a party in one of the most aristocratic houses in the centre of Petrograd.'

Hoare observed that for someone who had 'only been in Russia a few months the news was almost overwhelming'; to Professor Struve it seemed 'almost incredible'. Naturally there was no further discussion of the blockade and Hoare left to find out everything he could about the affair. Drawing on conversations with 'various people representing different classes and sections of opinion', he pieced together the story as best he could. Rasputin had not been seen since the evening of Friday 29 December, 'when he left his flat in company with an officer in a motor-car'. The gossip was that Count Sumarokoff-Elston ('who is also Prince Youssupoff' – Yusupov) had had a ball that evening 'attended by several of the Grand Dukes in Petrograd'. The following evening Grand Duke Dmitri Pavlovich had hosted another party in his palace, which was reported to have been 'of a most riotous description and did not break up until 7.30 in the morning'.

A range of stories were spreading round the city but it was believed that Rasputin had been killed somewhere between these two parties. 'Some people,' wrote Hoare, 'say that Rasputin was got into a room and told to kill himself. I have heard it said that he did kill himself, I have also heard it stated that he fired the revolver which was given him at 2 o'clock in the morning in self-defence.' The most widely accepted story, however, was 'that he was shot as he was leaving the house in a motor. The motor is supposed to have taken the body to the Islands where it was thrown into the sea or one of the rivers.' There was also general agreement that either Pavlovich or Yusupov had done the deed: 'Many people say that lots were drawn as to who should kill him and that the lot fell on the Grand Duke Dmitri, but that Count Sumarokoff-Elston [Yusupov] undertook the duty.' Yusupov (as Count Elston) had been a great social success in England 'a year or two before the war' when he had been regarded as 'the greatest catch in London'. One of the richest men in Russia, he had since married the Grand Duchess Irene. Whether the murderer was actually Pavlovich or Yusupov, wrote Hoare, 'it seems certain that it was planned and carried out by a number of the greatest people in Petrograd society and that several of the Grand Dukes were present'. Pavlovich and Yusupov had been together 'all the afternoon of December 31st', and when asked they made 'no secret of the fact that Rasputin has been killed. Perhaps,' added Hoare, 'the fact that Rasputin had recently been meddling more than usually in the domestic affairs of the Imperial family, hastened the event.'

Although conceding that the reports of Rasputin's death might prove to be unfounded – as had previously been the case on a number of occasions – Hoare was convinced that the monk had indeed been killed. 'In the first place,' he wrote, perhaps a little extravagantly, 'the whole of Russia regards it as established beyond doubt.' Second, Rasputin's entourage was evidently 'in a state of deep depression and great anxiety. His flat is filled with commotion and lamentation.' But 'far more conclusive' was 'the attitude of the Petrograd press. The "Bourse Gazette" would never have risked its existence for a rumour', and reports in other papers had contained 'numerous indirect and mysterious references to the murder'. Hoare summarised the general feeling in the city as 'most remarkable. All classes,' he asserted, 'speak and act as if some great weight had been taken from their shoulders. Servants, isvostchiks [cab-drivers], working men, all freely discuss the event. Many say that it is better than the greatest Russian victory in the field.'

Reflecting on the probable consequences of the murder, Hoare thought that heads might roll (metaphorically speaking) in the secret police, 'whilst in the course of the next few weeks the most notorious of Rasputin's clientèle will gradually retire into private life'. There might, too, be changes in the Interior Ministry and the Holy Synod, 'where Rasputin's influence was always strongest'. Hoare also considered it 'fortunate for the cause of liberalism in Russia' that (since the perpetrators were aristocrats) 'the crime cannot even be remotely identified with the democratic movement or any revolutionary plot'. Nor, he thought, would 'any regret be felt for the crime except amongst those over whom Rasputin exercised a hypnotic influence, and the unscrupulous intriguers whom he used for his own ends and rewarded with innumerable appointments in the Church and State'. Hoare had no encomium for the dead monk; quite the contrary: 'Of such a man no-one can honestly say "de mortuis nil nisi bonum" [Only say good of the dead]. If one cannot write good about the dead, one can at least say about the death "nothing but good".'

Writing the following day, Hoare was able briefly to supplement his account, thanks to Harold Williams, the London *Daily Chronicle*'s brilliant foreign correspondent, having put him in touch with the magistrates who had been appointed to examine the crime. Hoare reported that he had 'received the definite information that the body of Rasputin has been discovered in the river Nevka, near the Petrovsky Bridge'. Further information confirmed that the monk had been killed in Yusupov's palace, rather than in a motor car or somewhere else, as had variously been suggested. Four secret policemen who had been waiting outside the building had reported 'a certain amount of promiscuous shooting', and that 'early in the morning six men appeared in the courtyard with a body dressed in a "shuba" [fur coat], which they put in a motor that was waiting'.[6]

In an unpublished memoir of his time in Russia, written some years later, Hoare said that the chief of the military police had invited him to come and inspect the corpse. Hoare had declined the offer as he 'was recovering from influenza, and it was one of the black and bleak days that turned the Petrograd winter into perpetual night. I felt I could not face a corpse in a canal.' Although at the time thinking himself 'cowardly', the decision turned out to be very wise as within a very few days a rumour had spread that he (as 'Chief of the British Intelligence Mission') had himself been responsible for the murder. Had he been quickly and prominently on the scene, this might well have fuelled the suspicions.[7] So prevalent, indeed, was the story that he had masterminded the murder that, according to Hoare, the British ambassador, Sir George Buchanan, 'had solemnly to contradict it to the Emperor at his next audience'.[8]

For all its reliance on gossip and hearsay, Hoare's account of Rasputin's end was broadly accurate, though in fact there had been three main conspirators, not just Yusupov and Pavlovich. The ring-leader was the twenty-nine-year-old Prince Felix Yusupov, a member of one of the richest families in Russia. A flamboyant, charming homosexual with a penchant for cross-dressing, Yusupov had spent two years before the war at University College, Oxford. There he had been a member of the extremely exclusive Bullingdon Club, a dining society with a reputation for excess and sometimes debauchery. In 1914 he had married the tsar's niece, Princess Irene Alexandrovna. Like many others close to the centre of power in Russia, Yusupov came to see Rasputin as a deeply malign force, effectively (if not actively) pro-German and thus a dangerous impediment to the successful prosecution of the war. Naively assuming that the situation would be transformed by the removal of Rasputin – 'If he were killed today,' he told Nikolai Maklakov, a Kadet member of the Duma, 'the empress would go to a home for nervous disorders within a fortnight and Nicholas would become a constitutional monarch'[9] – he got Vladimir Purishkevitch, an extreme right-wing member of the Duma, and the Grand Duke Dmitri Pavlovich, a cousin of the tsar and a friend since childhood, to join him. Purishkevitch, for one, was quite open about his intention to at the very least neutralise Rasputin. In November he told Hoare that he 'had determined "to liquidate the affair of Rasputin"'. In his memoirs Hoare said that while it was clear that this meant assassination, he thought it more 'symptomatic of what everyone was thinking and saying rather than the expression of a definitely thought out plan'.[10]

But there was a definite plan. Rasputin was lured to Yusupov's palace, enticed by his renowned hospitality and apparently on the pretext of meeting his famously attractive wife (who was in fact not in Petrograd at all). At the palace Yusupov had prepared a richly furnished basement room where the monk could be entertained in private. A gramophone was played upstairs to give the impression that there was a party elsewhere in the palace. In order to do the deed, cakes and wine were adulterated with lavish quantities of potassium cyanide, enough, it was thought, to despatch him several times over. Yusupov himself went to fetch Rasputin, who, despite some premonitions reported afterwards, seems to have been quite unsuspecting. After he arrived in the basement room there was a black comedy of murderous misadventures. While his co-conspirators remained upstairs, Yusupov served

Rasputin the cake and wine, but the poison appeared to have little effect. Then, with a small Browning pistol, Yusopov shot him in the chest and the monk collapsed to the floor.

Assuming he was now dead, three of the conspirators, one dressed in Rasputin's coat, drove to the monk's apartment to give the impression that he had returned home. Yusupov, meanwhile, discovered that Rasputin, far from being dead, had recovered sufficiently to try to escape. They shot him again – Purishkevitch afterwards claimed responsibility for this – and finally killed him. Then they dumped the body from the Petrovsky bridge over the river Nevka (a tributary of the Neva). A recent, forensic investigation by a former British police officer, Richard Cullen, claims both that Rasputin was tortured before being killed and that members of the British secret service were involved in the affair.[11] The recovered body had certainly been mutilated, but other sources claim this occurred after the murder. As for the involvement of British agents, this is wildly speculative. Cullen claims that Oscar Rayner, a junior member of Hoare's staff and a friend of Yusupov's at Oxford, was present and even fired the fatal shot. There is, however, no reliable evidence whatsoever that Hoare, or the British secret service, were directly linked to the conspiracy. In his secret (and couriered) correspondence with 'C' in London, Hoare conveyed not the slightest indication that any of his staff were connected (even peripherally) with the murder or the murderers. Rayner's involvement, if he was present at all, can only have been as an acquaintance of Yusupov's, and perhaps as an enthusiastic if misguided individual participant in the scheme to rid Russia of a turbulent priest.

As a political technique, assassination – which is such an attractive option to simple-minded people – is almost invariably more exemplary and emblematic than practical or effective. Rarely (if ever), beyond the killing itself, does it produce precisely the desired result. So it was with Rasputin. The empress did not retire 'to a home for nervous disorders', nor did the emperor 'become a constitutional monarch'. Reflecting on the murder fifteen years afterwards, Samuel Hoare noted that in his original report he, too, had made the error of thinking that Rasputin's death 'would liberate the forces of heaven'.

He had been, then, 'too confident' and had not appreciated 'the danger of any sudden shock to the rickety machine of government. Politics had reached such a pass, and public opinion become so morbidly excited, that any startling event was certain to aggravate the dangerous fever from which the country was suffering.' The 'explosion' of the death of Rasputin had shaken 'the crazy structure of government to its very foundations' and 'so far as the conduct of the war was concerned, it would have been better if the murder had never taken place'.[12]

Hoare claimed in his original report that he had written it 'in the style of the "Daily Mail"'. So, how actually did the *Mail* cover the story? If anything, it did so rather more soberly than Hoare. The first mention was in a short article on 2 January 1917, buried halfway down the sixth column on page five, below a rather longer piece reporting a speech by Sir George Buchanan about 'Our Help for Russia'. 'From Our Own Correspondent', it was headlined 'Mystery Monk Again. Another Story of Rasputin's Death'. Telegrams received in Paris (where the story originated) announced Rasputin's death and 'allege that he was killed by Prince Youssoupoff, who is related to the Imperial Family'. This was followed by some biographical details about Yusupov, noting that he was 'frail and weakly in appearance. Those who know him are convinced that if it was he who killed the monk only an overpowering motive could have induced him to do so.' The story concluded with a note that this was 'the third time that the death of Rasputin has been reported'. The next day two further short articles, again emanating from Paris, declared that 'his end was as mysterious as his life', substantially repeated the information of the first article and added both that the monk 'had great influence in very high circles, not least among women, over whom he cast an extraordinary spell', and also that 'Germany knew how to make use of him'.[13]

The first report from Petrograd ('From a Special Correspondent') was not published until 4 January. The *Mail* was a bit stuck as their star man in Russia, Harry Hamilton Fyfe, happened to be away from Petrograd at the time. Having gone to the front line in September, he had just evaded being trapped in Bucharest when the Romanian army collapsed, and only returned to the capital at the end of December. Fyfe was a very experienced journalist who had caught the eye of

Alfred Harmsworth (later Lord Northcliffe) for whom he successfully edited the *Daily Mirror* before joining the *Mail* as a roving reporter in 1907. In August 1914 Northcliffe sent him to France, and in October to Russia where he remained almost continuously for the next three years. In Fyfe's absence the paper had to scrabble around for copy about Rasputin as best it could from unnamed 'special correspondents'. On 4 January they reported that Rasputin's body had been found, and also 'that the whole of Russia breathes more freely on the removal of Rasputin, a most baleful influence recognised as one of the pivots of the Germanophile forces'. Rather primly they added that 'this hideous mediæval nightmare is now dissipated and no purpose would be served by recapitulating its immoral horrors'. Some further details were reported two days later. Six people had allegedly been present for supper at the Yusupov palace. A theory that more than one person took part in the murder was 'borne out by the statement that three wounds were found in his body inflicted by bullets of different calibre'. A 'trail of blood in the neighbourhood of the tragedy' demonstrated that 'the victim was not killed by the first shot, but attempted to escape, till the third bullet laid him low'.[14]

Only when Hamilton Fyfe's own account was published – which was not until 1 February 1917 – did the *Daily Mail* prose match Hoare's. Hamilton Fyfe wrote a long article under a date-line of 'Petrograd, January 2, 1917'. (None of the other *Daily Mail* despatches from Petrograd in December 1916 or January 1917 carried his name.) In it he recounted how he had arrived in the capital from Romania on the evening of Saturday 30 December, the day Rasputin was killed. Within half an hour he had heard about the assassination and, although the news was suppressed by strict censorship (apart from 'a two-line announcement in an evening paper' and a 'veiled reference' in another journal), by Sunday everyone was 'talking about and rejoicing over' the event. 'Even the details of the "removal" of the wretched creature Rasputin were very quickly passing from mouth to mouth.' It was an 'extraordinary crime, which recalls the lurid annals of Byzantine emperors or mediæval Italian princes, and of which the unvarnished account reads like a "penny blood"'. Rasputin, he wrote, had been a regular dinner guest at Yusupov's palace. On 29 December Yusupov and his accomplices, as on previous occasions, had plied the monk with drink. Having 'pumped' him for information about the pro-German party in Russia, the conspirators lost patience and offered him a 'choice between suicide and execution'. He was given a pistol with which to kill himself, but 'he refused, fired at a Grand Duke, missed him, broke a window. At once he was seized, gagged, bound and, after a short interval, despatched.' Without mentioning anyone other than Yusopov, Hamilton Fyfe said that the names of those involved were 'well known in Petrograd, and they will be honoured in the history of Russia as those of Harmodius and Aristogeiton [the 'tyrannicides' of Athens] are honoured in the history of Greece, as that of Charlotte Corday [killer of the revolutionary leader Marat] in the history of France'.

For Hamilton Fyfe, the crucial question following the assassination was the impact it would have on the pro-German party in Russia, the so-called Camarilla. 'All honourable and patriotic Russians,' he said, 'are hoping and praying that the Czar will throw his weight strongly against the clique which has betrayed his and his country's interests.' The nation, asserted Fyfe confidently, 'is determined to carry on the war, and it demands that the methods of carrying it on shall be more vigorous and competent than they ever have been yet.' This over-trenchant opinion echoed Hoare's initial misjudgement that Rasputin's death would transform the situation for the better, especially since he believed that 'all the best minds and hearts in Russia are on the side of the Allies'. Hamilton Fyfe's confident conclusion was backed up by an editorial in the same issue. The men involved in the murder, it declared, were 'devotedly loyal to Russia, to the Alliance, and to the dynasty. Their action,' it continued, 'is the leaven of a benign revolution in which they hope to see the Czar at their head with his splendid Army behind him.'[15] A remarkable common feature about the responses to Rasputin's death is that no-one seems to have thought that murdering him was in any sense a deplorable act. Perhaps the wartime circumstances, in which millions of people had already been killed, had so stupefied everyone that a single killing, however shocking or dramatic, could no longer excite any moral criticism. Or perhaps Rasputin was a special case.

AGENTS OF THE ANGLO-RUSSIAN ALLIANCE

Britain's wartime alliance with Russia was more a marriage of convenience – or even necessity – than one of fondness or mutual regard. For much of the nineteenth century Russia had been one of Britain's most serious imperial rivals and the so-called Great Game played out in central Asia and the Himalayan fastness was, on the British side, designed to protect the vital British imperial position in India and its outliers. By the turn of the twentieth century, while Britain still indisputably possessed the world's single most powerful empire, its relative decline (demonstrated, for example, by the difficulties experienced in defeating a comparative handful of Afrikaner farmers in the Anglo-Boer War of 1899–1902) led to a reassessment of strategic relationships in the early years of the new century. In November 1899 the Russian emperor had – perhaps a bit over-optimistically – asserted that he could alter the course of the war in South Africa simply by ordering his forces in Turkestan to mobilise, thus obliging the British to divert troops to the North-West Frontier. When in 1902 British defence planners calculated that defending India against Russian aggression would require hundreds of thousands of troops (as well as 3 million camels), it was time for the diplomats to come to the assistance of the soldiers. Thus it was that an Anglo-Russian Agreement was signed in 1906, at least temporarily ending the Great Game with Britain and Russia dividing Persia and Afghanistan into agreed 'spheres of influence'.[16]

This arrangement, however, did not constitute any sort of alliance. Indeed, the Liberal politicians who governed the United Kingdom from 1906 until the outbreak of war were politically and temperamentally averse to any close relationship with the Russian imperial autocracy, though Russia's tentative steps towards constitutional democracy from 1905 were welcomed in London. Britain's increasing closeness to France from the Entente Cordiale in 1904, however, brought with it the possibility of closer relations with France's ally, Russia. In the immediate prewar years the implications of alliance politics progressively tied the three countries together. When General Henry Wilson, then British Director of Military Operations, visited France in October 1910 the French General Ferdinand Foch, who was just back from Russia, told him that the Russian army was so ill-prepared that in any war against Germany, France 'must trust to England & not to Russia'.[17] Despite the increasingly close and regular military staff talks between the British and French before the war, there was no move to extend these to the Russians. It was different on the intelligence side, however, no doubt partly because any such contacts could be kept much more secret. In June 1914 the chief of the Russian secret service, who had been visiting Paris, came to London where he met Mansfield Cumming (though no detailed record survives of what was discussed). It seems, however, from the notes in his diary that Cumming had some 'new scheme' in mind 'with Fr. & Russians', though whether this was in conjunction with, or against them, is not clear.[18]

Once war was declared France, Russia and Britain became allies and the whole situation changed. A propaganda and censorship campaign was mounted to portray Russia in as favourable a light as possible. Imperial autocracy was downplayed and the Russians' alleged advance towards parliamentary democracy emphasised. Much was written about the prodigious strength of the 'Russian steamroller' and the stoic endurance of the peasant-soldiers who provided the backbone of the army. Criticisms were suppressed of human rights violations within the empire as well as Russia's oppression of nationalities such as the Poles and the Finns. Among the journalists and academics sent to Russia to promote the new alliance was Bernard Pares, a Trinity Cambridge man, who was Professor of Russian History, Language and Literature at Liverpool University in 1914. He was to remain in Russia in a variety of British official positions until the revolution in 1917.[19]

With the grandiose title 'official correspondent of the British government' to the Russian army, Pares found himself marshalled with a party of foreign journalists including the American Stanley Washburn ('a quite simple and sincere man, and very keen'). Later he became the correspondent of the *Daily Telegraph*, while continuing throughout to promote the alliance in any way he could.[20] Since it was widely believed in Russia that the British were not fully pulling their weight in the alliance, merely acting as paymaster for Russian cannon fodder, in 1915 an Anglo-Russian Bureau was set up under the New Zealand-born English novelist Hugh Walpole with a brief to inform the Russian public about the tremendous sacrifices being made by Britain, though it does not seem to have had very much success.[21]

Pares and his writer colleagues were accompanied by an enormous expansion of British representation on the military, diplomatic and intelligence side. Early in the war General Sir John Hanbury-Williams, a socially very well-connected man who had been military secretary to Sir Alfred Milner (later Lord Milner) in South Africa and subsequently to Earl Grey when he was governor-general of Canada, was personally appointed by Lord Kitchener to head a British military mission at the Stavka (the Russian Army general headquarters). Although a man of considerable charm, and a great raconteur, Hanbury-Williams was an odd appointment. He himself admitted that when he was 'suddenly despatched to Russia', he had 'but a very sketchy idea of the country and its people'. Norman Stone dismisses him as a lightweight whose reports to London displayed 'weakness in spelling, [and] a very shaky knowledge of eastern-European geography'. His chief qualification, it seems, was an effortless ability to converse with members of the imperial royal family, which he did very successfully, assisted by the fact that the emperor spoke excellent English. His appointment, however, put the existing military attaché's nose seriously out of joint. Colonel Alfred 'Flurry' Knox, an able but prickly Ulsterman, had been in post since 1911, spoke fluent Russian and had the reputation of being exceptionally well informed about the Russian army. The War Office argued that Knox was of too junior a rank for such a high-level position, though Knox himself believed that it was his relatively humble social background which disqualified him.[22]

Knox was particularly critical of some of the other missions sent to Russia during the war. He dismissed both the propaganda bureau and the intelligence mission which Mansfield Cumming sent out in the autumn of 1914 as 'joy rides',[23] which made no discernible contribution to understanding or coordination between Britain and Russia. Much of this criticism was simply the result of professional jealousy, but, at least until Samuel Hoare ran it in 1916–17, the intelligence mission had a fairly chequered existence. Cumming had originally sent out Captain Archibald Campbell, an abrasive Scot whom the Director of Military Intelligence described in 1917 as 'an officer of considerable ingenuity, ability and push, but of singularly unattractive personality'. Campbell was accompanied by Lieutenant Stephen Alley, who had been reared in Russia, and was a much more emollient character. Their brief was 'to get in touch with the officers of the Russian General Staff dealing with Secret Service, and so to obtain information from the Russian Intelligence Department about the enemy'. Being in uniform and with an office in the Russian War Ministry, they were hardly a clandestine unit. Their anomalous position, however (and as so often the case with intelligence missions, difficult to fit into established military hierarchies), mystified and irritated Knox, Hanbury-Williams and even the British ambassador, Sir George Buchanan, who all felt that the intelligence mission threatened to undermine their own liaison duties.[24]

In the late spring of 1915 Campbell was withdrawn and replaced by the Tibetan-born Major Cudbert Thornhill of the Indian Army. A striking personality, he was a 'first-class Russian scholar' who spoke Persian and Hindustani ('like a native'), as well as being 'skilled at carpentry and gadget-making' and 'a good shot with rifle, catapult, shot-gun and blow-pipe'.[25] A bad knee kept him from front-line duty. Thornhill repaired relations with both Knox and the embassy, but, for reasons that are unclear, fell out with Cumming in London. When Thornhill was transferred to the embassy as assistant military attaché in 1916 he was replaced by Lieutenant Colonel Sir Samuel Hoare (a baronet who had succeeded his father in 1915).

Hoare, thirty-six years old in 1916, came from a very wealthy banking family and had been a Conservative MP since 1910. He had been commissioned into the Norfolk Yeomany at the beginning of the war, but serious illness prevented him from going to the front and he languished as a regimental recruiting officer during 1915. In the meantime, a talented linguist, he began learning Russian, hoping to find employment perhaps even in the Russian army. Early in 1916 John Baird, a fellow Conservative MP and former diplomat who was working in the Secret Service Bureau, put him in touch with Mansfield Cumming. Recalling in his 1930 memoir his first meeting with

Cumming, Hoare was circumspect in what he could say about him, careful (as Compton Mackenzie was not to be a couple of years later) lest he should be 'charged . . . with disclosing secrets about the holiest of the Intelligence holies'. He described Cumming – though Hoare did not name him, or even use the initial 'C'– as 'the very antithesis of the spy king of popular fiction. Jovial and very human, bluff and plain speaking, outwardly at least, a very simple man. Who,' asked Hoare rhetorically, 'would ever have imagined that this was the chief who conducted the British "Business of Egypt" [espionage] and employed secret agents in every corner of the world?'[26]

Hoare's background in banking was evidently an advantage and he was initially engaged to report both on the general position of the mission as well as economic matters. He did this so satisfactorily that in May 1916 Cumming appointed him to take over from Thornhill, and concentrate particularly on war trade information (including liaison with the Russians on blockade matters), keeping an eye out for openings for British firms provided by the exclusion of enemy companies from the Russian market. In his instructions Hoare was enjoined, 'so far as you can do without risk of causing annoyance to our Ally', to 'obtain information from Russian unofficial sources, taking care that you shall never appear to be doing anything prejudicial to their interests or that could in any way be mistaken for espionage'. Hoare was also put in charge of the Military Control Office, issuing passport visas for travel to the United Kingdom. Since applicants had to be carefully vetted, it was a counter-espionage function, which Frank Stagg, Cumming's assistant in London, remarked was 'no small task in a country like Russia'. Stephen Alley took responsibility for this, which became known as the British Passport Office. This was the inception of what were to become Passport Control officers at British embassies across the world, which between the wars provided cover (and income from the visa fees) for the Secret Intelligence Service and its officers overseas.[27]

Robert Bruce Lockhart, the acting British consul-general in Moscow, had at the start been doubtful about Hoare's appointment. He predicted 'friction and failure', since it was 'hard to understand in what respect his mission could supplement the work which was being done by the other British organisations'. But Hoare succeeded by tact, hard work, learning Russian and pursuing 'his task with unflagging and unobtrusive enthusiasm'. 'Unlike most intelligence officers,' added Bruce Lockhart pointedly, 'he showed a fine discrimination in sifting the truth from the chaff of rumour.'[28]

In the early summer of 1916 extremely high hopes were invested in the possibilities of a visit to Russia by Lord Kitchener. The appointment of Kitchener in August 1914 to be British war minister had, in the short term, been an extremely successful move. Lending both his immense authority as the greatest living imperial proconsul and general, as well as his image drawn by Alfred Leete and used in what was to become the most famous poster of the twentieth century ('Your Country Needs You'), he embodied the national mobilisation of Britain for the war and, warning that it would *not* be 'over by Christmas', helped raise Britain's first-ever mass army. Kitchener, however, as Margot Asquith mordantly observed, was a 'great poster but not a great man'. His immense experience of high command in India and the empire ill-fitted him for the consensual, collective responsibilities of British Cabinet government. With a low opinion of politicians, he found it hard to take his Cabinet colleagues into his confidence, and he could not handle the key notion that political decision-making usually – and desirably – emerged from the give-and-take of debate (which was not conventionally the way of the soldier). On the army side, moreover, unable quite to grasp that the secretary of state for war had no *military* authority, he was inclined to meddle in matters which were rightfully the responsibility of the army commanders. Politically, Kitchener was out of his depth, and militarily he was increasingly sidelined, especially after the appointment of the forceful Sir William Robertson as Chief of the Imperial General Staff in December 1915.

Although at the British end part of the impetus for sending Kitchener to Russia was simply to find something for him to do, at the Russian end Hoare believed that the visit could have a transformative effect on the situation through influencing the tsar in his role as supreme commander of the Russian army. On visits to the Stavka he had been struck at how ineffectual the tsar appeared to be: 'Instead of a leader of men, I found a detached student of affairs,' and there were constant concerns about the poor advice he received from his sycophantic circle of intimates. In his unpublished memoirs (though he slightly toned down this opinion in the published version), Hoare wrote that he and Buchanan 'both believed that Kitchener would be able to influence the Emperor in a way that no one else could, Russian or British . . . Of all the "ifs" of the first War, "If Kitchener had spent some days with the Emperor and the Russian army in June 1916" was the most pregnant with great possibilities.' But of course Kitchener never reached Russia. He was drowned when the cruiser HMS *Hampshire*, on which he was sailing from Scotland, struck a German mine off the Orkney Islands and was lost on 5 June 1916 with only twelve survivors. 'The tragedy of the "Hampshire" was the beginning of the end on the Eastern Front,' wrote Hoare. 'Kitchener with his immense prestige could have stopped the rot.'[29] Whether this was remotely possible or not – the claim has a slight air of desperation about it – other observers were less moved by the tragedy. 'What a business,' Sir Henry Wilson, who had clashed with Kitchener a few times, noted in his diary, 'though in my opinion no loss to the nation.'[30]

The idea of a high-level mission to Russia, however, aiming to bolster the alliance and reinforce the creaking Russian war effort, was not abandoned. In September 1916, David Lloyd George (Kitchener's successor as British war minister), worried about pro-German sentiment in Russia and, keen to sort out the supply of much-needed munitions to the Russian army, proposed an Allied meeting in Petrograd, telling Asquith that 'a person or persons of high standing and influence in this country' should be sent. At a conference in December 1916 at Chantilly, as had been the case a year earlier, the Allies again agreed that they should mount coordinated attacks on each of the main fronts. Lloyd George, who had replaced Asquith as prime minister on 6 December, was a powerful supporter of any strategy which might sidestep Britain's costly commitment to the Western Front. At an Anglo-French conference late in December 1916 he argued that the 'only chance of a really great success in 1917 was completely effective cooperation with Russia'.[31]

So it was that an Allied mission (with British, French and Italian representatives), to be led by Lord Milner, who had been recently elevated to the British War Cabinet, was arranged for early 1917. It was effectively to be the 'last hurrah' of the Entente between Britain, France and Russia. The mission was designed to combine a morale-boosting demonstration of inter-allied unity with practical technical assistance in finance and munitions supply (which was what the Russians were most interested in). Delayed for a fortnight because of Rasputin's murder, in the end a fifty-strong party set off from London on 19 January, and travelling through Murmansk, reached Petrograd ten days later. The 600-mile train journey from Murmansk took four and a half days at an average speed of only eight miles an hour (slower that the sea voyage), which from the start brought home to the visitors the rickety state of Russia's infrastructure upon which her war effort depended.[32]

Once in Petrograd the mission was to discuss strategic plans for the 1917 campaign and explore ways of how best to coordinate the Allied efforts and assist with equipment for the Russian army. As Milner reported afterwards, however, the Russians were only interested in presenting 'an exhaustive list' of all their very considerable wants 'and ask[ing] us to foot the bill'. Henry Wilson, the senior British soldier with the mission, attended meetings of a 'Military Committee' which broadly confined itself to unremarkable platitudes: 1917, it was agreed, 'should be made decisive'; 'we must bring off our attacks together'; and '"Side Shows" must be avoided'. More significantly, over lunches at the British embassy he learned that there was much talk of revolution, even, as he noted in his diary, to the extent of Russian officials speaking openly about 'the advisability of murdering the Tsar & the Empress or the Empress alone & so on. An extraordinary state of affairs,' he thought. On a visit to Moscow, Wilson noticed widespread opposition to the emperor, and painful shortages of bread and coal. 'There will be terrible trouble one day here,' he noted.

Perhaps most symbolic of the whole mission was a gala dinner at the sumptuously appointed Tsarkoe Selo Palace, where both the imperial court and the Allied mission were all dressed up, but really with nowhere to go in either political or military terms. The emperor, recorded Wilson, 'was most affable & talked to every single one of us'. The visitors were 'received in a charming suite of rooms, with Court Officers in quaint uniforms & some servants in marvellous, Catherine [the Great] clothes & feathers in bonnets'. It was, he thought, 'a murderous pity that the Emperor is so weak & so under the Empress' thumb; for according to all the accounts I get he & the Empress are heading straight for ruin.'[33]

Reflecting on the Milner mission in their memoirs long after the revolution, Samuel Hoare and Robert Bruce Lockhart were both acidly dismissive. 'Before the lamp of Tsardom was finally extinguished,' wrote Bruce Lockhart, 'it was to flicker up in one last feeble flame of hope' – the 'inter-Allied delegation.' But 'rarely in the history of great wars can so many important ministers and generals have left their respective countries on so useless an errand'. In his published memoir Hoare described the mission as an 'Allied Noah's Ark' and essentially a waste of time. The Russians needed munitions and 'the military advice of a great soldier like Kitchener or Foch', but 'a large company of British, French and Italian politicians, soldiers and experts was nothing more than an irritating embarrassment to them in their hour of trial'. The Russians, therefore, simply drowned it 'in a series of banquets and ceremonial visits'. In his unpublished version he took a slightly softer line: 'the mission, in spite of all its weaknesses, seemed to provide the last opportunity for making the West face the Russian crisis'. But when it came, Milner, above all, was soon disabused of any hope that good might come of it. He 'relapsed into a state of fatalist depression, unable to understand a world so different from his own, and unwilling to believe that any civilised country could be so badly governed'.[34]

TOWARDS REVOLUTION

Laura Engelstein has argued of Russia that 'in the years leading up to 1917, sexual disarray at the pinnacle of power came to stand for what was wrong with the tsarist regime'. The most notorious example of this was the 'devious and debauched' Grigorii Rasputin, who had subverted the virtues of folk simplicity and holiness. His 'supposed tyranny over the royal family', moreover, 'symbolized the disorder at the heart of the absolute order' of the Russian imperial regime.[35] That being so, it is easy to see why Prince Yusupov and his ultraconservative cronies (as well as Samuel Hoare) thought that Rasputin's removal would have such a therapeutic effect on the Russian body politic. The cancer would be removed and political health would flourish. Setting aside for a moment the problem that Rasputin's assassins were united only in their desire to be rid of the monk, and had no coherent or agreed political programme for Russia beyond a vague (though powerfully held) sense of restoring legitimate authority to the empire, they appeared to have had little, if any, understanding of the extent to which Rasputin was simply a symptom of a deeply dysfunctional regime rather than a prime cause of their country's predicament.

The tsar himself was central to the running of the Russian autocracy. Many people testified to his personal qualities, his honest sincerity and attractive friendliness, but his fitness to govern a sprawling, restless empire is another matter. Samuel Hoare thought that he would have been best suited as a quiet English country squire. George Buchanan asserted that while he had 'many gifts that would have fitted him to play the part of a constitutional Sovereign – a quick intelligence, a cultivated mind, method and industry in his work, and an extraordinary natural charm', he concluded that he had neither 'his father's commanding personality nor the strong character and prompt decision which are so essential to an autocratic ruler'.[36] Buchanan's rather confused analysis – conceding the tsar's capacity to be a constitutional ruler while deploring his *in*capacity as an autocrat – pinpoints part of the Russian conundrum with its uneasy combination of dictatorship and democracy. Following the revolution of 1905, the emperor had reluctantly conceded the introduction of a semi-democratic constitution with a Duma elected through a restricted franchise and with limited powers. But he retained an absolute veto over legislation and ministerial appointments, a power which he exercised frequently and arbitrarily during the war. The tsar's appointment of the Germanophile arch-conservative Boris Stürmer as prime minister in January 1916 was widely condemned by liberals and Allied diplomats alike. Stürmer was 'worse than a mediocrity', thought the French ambassador, Maurice Paleologue. The dismissal in July 1916 of the long-serving, constitutionalist and pro-Allied foreign minister, Sergey Sazonov (and his replacement by Stürmer), was a particular frustration to Sir George Buchanan, who in vain told the tsar of 'the apprehensions which I feel at losing him as a collaborator in the work that still lies before us'.[37] All this was taken to demonstrate the growing influence of the empress, Rasputin and pro-German elements – the so-called 'dark forces' which Miliukov warned the Duma about in November 1916.

The autocratic political power of the tsar was matched on the military side, especially after he assumed the supreme command of the army in August 1915. This was against the advice of his whole Cabinet, and his subsequent absences at the front left a political vacuum in the capital. The assumption of the military command certainly reflected Nicholas's conception of himself as the embodiment of the nation and his desire to align himself with the brave endeavours of his subjects, but it also meant that he was personally and inextricably identified with military reverses and could be blamed for the regular privations and irritations which soldiers inevitably suffered. And while Nicholas the autocrat chose explicitly to sit at the head of his troops, Joshua Sanborn has suggested that the logic of mass conscription and mobilisation (both of which were powerfully accelerated by the war) inevitably undermined the rationale of autocracy. The army became both 'a physical embodiment of the nation and a symbolic brotherhood of citizen-soldiers' with new collective loyalties distinct from the old hierarchies. The Russian 'nation-in-arms', he argues, thus had the capacity to subvert both the tsarist autocracy and, indeed, the communist regime which succeeded it.[38]

At times the Russian army performed extremely well in the war and despite major reverses it also remained remarkably resilient until the winter of 1916/17. The triumphs of the Brusilov offensive resulted not just from excellent leadership and planning, but they also testified to the improvements in Russia's munitions supply by 1916. But these successes were bought at horrendous cost. At the end of July 1916, some eight weeks after the beginning of the offensive, Alfred Knox visited the Russian general's headquarters in Berdichev in northern Ukraine. Knox was told that the Russians estimated the Austro-Hungarian losses since the beginning of the offensive at about '800,000, viz., 320,000 prisoners, 360,000 wounded and 120,000 killed'. Knox reckoned this to be an overestimate, with the real figure being nearer 600,000 in total, but either way the figures were impressive. General Nikolai Dukhonin, Brusilov's 'General Quartermaster', calculated that the Russian losses over the same period had been 450,000. At the beginning of June the Russians had had 400,000 men in reserve, but this figure had now been reduced to 100,000 'and men have been thrown into the fighting with only six weeks' training'. Dukhonin was the first Russian Knox had 'heard to express anxiety regarding the possible exhaustion of our [sic] reserves of men owing to the terrible losses – the result of our feeble technical equipment'.[39] While it was bad enough in July, the extra strain placed on the Russians following the Romanian collapse in the autumn of 1916 further began to stretch the army to breaking point.

As with the battle front, many of Russia's difficulties stemmed from the empire's inadequately staffed and under-resourced infrastructure. Food was a constant concern. Although the production of foodstuffs generally held up quite well, getting them to where they were needed was another thing. All the belligerent powers faced challenges of food production and supply. By 1916 state intervention had become the norm. Both Britain and Germany established central government organisations to meet the structural problems and in both cases private enterprise was integrated into the system and businessmen ran it. But this did not happen in Russia, where the government aimed to supplant the existing market mechanisms with a 'Special Council for Food Supply', staffed by government bureaucrats, members of the legislature and representatives from a range of public organisations set up to bolster the war effort. These included various war industry committees, as well as local government networks. The intention, then, was to cut out the middleman and deal directly with the peasant food producers. Thus grain, for example, could be purchased at a government-fixed price and equitably distributed according to centrally decided priorities. A series of unfortunate circumstances, however, undermined this scheme. Producers proved reluctant to sell at (low) fixed prices, especially at a time when war inflation eroded the value of money. Army pay to soldiers' families, moreover, left peasant households with surplus cash, thus further weakening their need to sell grain. Ironically the war conditions, which permitted the government's intervention in the market, additionally meant that the government had (in Peter Holquist's words) 'nothing to offer . . . but exhortations' to the peasants. This 'then made the state the focus for all dissatisfaction'.[40]

A close study of subsistence riots by Barbara Alpern Engel has revealed that an extremely wide range of people participated in these protests, not just workers, but also 'the wives of workers; the wives and mothers of soldiers; and peasants, male and female', drawing in disparate groups from some sectors of society which had never before taken action into collective demonstrations against merchants, officials, and, ultimately, the government as a whole. One feature of these protests was the extent to which they demonstrated how the 'boundaries separating members of the industrial working class from these other groups had dissolved in the cauldron of war'. Mass mobilisation had a profound impact on the 'home front' and it underpinned a sharp sense of entitlement among 'soldatki' (soldiers' wives). In late 1916 the governor of Tomsk complained that 'soldiers' wives have come to believe that they deserve concessions in everything since their husbands had been sent to the front and were shedding their blood'. The fragility of Russian civil society by the middle of the war is illustrated both by the rapidity with which protests gathered momentum and also the triviality of some of the issues which sparked off disorder. In early June 1916 a thousand-strong crowd of women in the town of Gordeevka in Nizhnii Novgorod province began protesting against the rising prices of necessities such as milk and salt. Within a few hours, according to police estimates, the crowd, which began to attack provisions stores, had grown to be ten-thousand strong. In another incident in Kineshma in Kostroma province a dispute over the price of a spool of thread between a pregnant woman and a single market trader escalated into a protest involving a reported four thousand women.[41]

As living conditions deteriorated in 1916, this general unrest was accompanied by a rise in the popularity of socialist organisations. These networks stiffened and focused the discontent in explicitly political channels. Since trade union activity was restricted, workers began using their membership of War Industries Committees (originally set up to monitor working conditions) to voice their increasingly anti-war opinions and organise political activity. Although at first cautious about direct action – including strikes – by the end of 1916 they had become more militant and began to participate in the general strikes organised from the beginning of 1917.[42]

The revolutionary events in Petrograd in February 1917, which precipitated the abdication of the tsar, began with a mass subsistence demonstration which differed only in scale and location to the wave of similar protests which had developed during 1916. Alpern Engel tellingly identifies an instance in the Don region in August 1916 when Cossacks restrained one of their number from using violence to suppress a food riot involving soldiers' wives. He had, they said, 'no right to raise his sword against women whose husbands were fighting in the army'. The demonstrations of February 1917 were also distinguished by the reluctance of the Cossack imperial guards to put them down by force. To be sure, strikes and protests in factories played an important part in Russia's revolutionary moment, but perhaps, as Peter Holquist suggests, it was 'the Imperial state's failure to deal with food-supply demands [which] ultimately led to the regime's collapse'.[43]

FROM GALLIPOLI TO THE WINTER PALACE

One analysis of Gallipoli, by a historian of the Zion Mule Corps, explicitly links the failure of that campaign with the Russian revolution of 1917. Like many such conjectures associated with the 'war of lost opportunities',[44] this interpretation depends on the dubious assumption that the Gallipoli campaign could have been a success at all. Nevertheless, arguing that the Allied pressure at the Dardanelles, by 'forcing Turkey to withdraw troops from its Russian border' would have ensured 'a much-needed victory' for Russia, this would have raised 'the morale of its troops sufficiently to reduce the danger of mutiny and impending revolution and to ensure that their assault on Germany's eastern front would continue'. But the 'final failure' of the campaign 'sealed the fate of the Russian regime and led indirectly to seventy years of Soviet rule'.[45]

Looking at the history of Russia in 1916 helps us set the revolutionary events of 1917 in their wider chronological and geographical context. Peter Holquist has argued that Russia's 1917 experience cannot be understood in isolation, but should be seen in a broader context, within the intersection of Russia's own 'Time of Troubles', from the revolution of 1905 to the emergence of the Soviet Union by 1921. It was, furthermore, part of an 'overall European [and global] convulsion from 1914 to 1924', which encompassed, not just the 1914–18 war, but the turbulent postwar period, right up to the eventual settlement in the Near and Middle East.[46] Drawing suggestive parallels between the 'revolutionary generation' in Ireland and Russia, Roy Foster traces similar intellectual and cultural developments and argues that in both places 'a sense of dammed-up domestic crisis was released by international war'.[47] Musing on contemporary events from his exile in neutral Switzerland during the summer of 1916, the Russian revolutionary V. I. Lenin asserted that the 'imperialist war of 1914–16' had produced a 'crisis of imperialism'. The 'flames of national revolt,' he wrote, 'have flared up *both* in the colonies and in Europe'. He noted the Indian soldiers' mutiny in Singapore in 1915, as well as 'attempts at rebellion in French Annam [Vietnam] . . . and in the German Cameroons'. In Europe there had been 'a rebellion in Ireland, which the "freedom-loving" English, who did not dare to extend conscription to Ireland, suppressed by executions'. On the Central Powers' side, too, the Austrian government had 'passed the death sentence on the deputies of the Czech Diet "for treason", and [he alleged] shot whole Czech regiments for the same "crime"'. While Lenin welcomed the Irish rising, he thought it both premature and essentially 'petty-bourgeois', occurring 'before the European revolt of the proletariat had *had time* to mature'. Nevertheless, it was, he added, 'only in premature, individual, sporadic and therefore unsuccessful, revolutionary movements that the masses gain experience, acquire knowledge, gather strength, and get to know their real leaders, the socialist proletarians, and in this way prepare for the general onslaught'.[48]

The Russian revolution of 1917, thus, was just one (and perhaps the most extreme) of the violent and opportunistic responses which occurred nearly everywhere to the challenges and demands of the wider conflict. With the progressive intensification of the war, the first

Conclusion: The Potential for Peace in 1916

Towards the end of 1916 various possibilities for a negotiated peace were raised in London, Berlin and Washington. None of them succeeded, but these initiatives were all the product of specific wartime circumstances which persuaded some statesmen at least that the moment was opportune – or even necessary – to contemplate bringing the conflict to an end.

In London the losses incurred on the Somme seem to have been the main factor prompting a remarkable intervention by the senior Conservative, Lord Lansdowne, a former foreign secretary and current member of the Cabinet. On 13 November, in response to a request from the prime minister as to colleagues' 'views as to the terms on which peace might be concluded', he circulated a wide-ranging and lucid discussion of the current situation. While asserting that 'no one for a moment believes that we are going to lose the War', Lansdowne doubted that any sort of clear-cut victory might be possible. He noted Britain's growing economic and supply problems, and glumly reflected on the human cost. Britain, he said, had already suffered over 1.1 million casualties, including 15,000 officers killed. 'We are,' he wrote (perhaps thinking of his second son who had been killed in action in Belgium in October 1914), 'slowly but surely killing off the best of the male population of these islands. The figures representing the casualties of our Allies are not before me. The total must be appalling.' This, he argued, was 'no doubt our duty to bear, but only if it can be shown that the sacrifice will have its reward'. If not, 'the War, with its nameless horrors will have been needlessly prolonged, and the responsibility of those who needlessly prolong such a War is not less than that of those who needlessly provoke it'.

Lansdowne proposed 'a thorough stocktaking' for each ally to ascertain 'which of his desiderata are indispensable', and whether they might not be prepared to consider some sort of compromise peace. The matter was pressing since he thought the likelihood of a definitive victory 'was, to say the least of it, remote'. He was, moreover, not absolutely sure if all 'our Allies are entirely to be depended upon'. Although French soldiers always fought like heroes, civilian opinion in France was less steadfast. Italy 'is always troublesome and exacting', while 'the domestic situation in Russia is far from reassuring'. While he had no 'practical suggestion to offer' as to the basis of any peace negotiation, he urged that 'we ought at any rate not to discourage any movement, no matter where originating, in favour of an interchange of views as to the possibility of a settlement'.[1]

Despite its cool rationality and good sense, Lansdowne's memorandum was quickly rejected as shockingly defeatist. A fortnight earlier in a widely reported interview with an American journalist, Lloyd George, the secretary of state for war, had already committed Britain to a 'fight to the finish'. In what became known as the 'Policy of a Knock-Out Blow', he said he was suspicious of any attempt by President Wilson 'to "butt in" with a proposal to stop the War before we could achieve victory' and before 'the Prussian military despotism' was 'broken beyond repair . . . Peace now or at any time before the final and complete elimination of this menace is unthinkable.' When asked how long the war might continue, Lloyd George reminded his interviewer that it had taken twenty years for 'England' to defeat Napoleon. 'It will not take 20 years to win this war,' he said, 'but whatever time is required, it will be done.'[2]

Lloyd George's pugnacious rejection of negotiation resonated with hardline Conservatives in the British wartime coalition. It added momentum to his bid for power which succeeded when he became prime minister in place of Asquith on 6 December 1916. Once he was in charge there was very little likelihood of the British cooperating in any suggestion of peace talks, and proposals advanced by both the Germans and the Americans (whom the British thought were working in collusion) were summarily rejected in London. The Germans, aware that following his re-election President Wilson was minded to try another peace initiative, and encouraged by the capture of Bucharest on 6 December, thought the moment was opportune for a peace offer and on 12 December the Central Powers issued a 'Peace Note' which combined a confidence in eventual victory with a marked absence of any detailed conditions upon which they might insist. Clearly influenced by the newly installed military leaders in Berlin, Hindenburg and Ludendorff, all that was offered was a willingness to enter into negotiations under conditions 'calculated to assure the existence, honour and freedom of development of their peoples'. It was nevertheless widely (and correctly) assumed that the Germans would insist on retaining some of their conquests (including Alsace-Lorraine) and require restitution of colonies in Africa. Although Berlin actually expected the Allies to reject the approach (which they did), they hoped that the initiative would make a good impression on President Wilson, especially as they were actively considering the introduction of unrestricted submarine warfare.[3]

Wilson, meanwhile, issued a peace note of his own on 18 December 1916, urging the belligerents clearly to state their 'views as to the terms on which the war might be ended'. Once this had happened, Wilson offered to assist any talks that might be arranged. In terms echoing those of Lansdowne, he reflected on the terrible cost of the war:

> If the contest must continue to proceed towards undefined ends by slow attrition until the one group of belligerents or the other is exhausted, if million after million of human lives must continue to be offered up until on the one side or the other there are no more to offer, if resentments must be kindled that can never cool and despairs engendered from which there can be no recovery, hopes of peace and of the willing concert of free peoples will be rendered vain and idle.

But in a passage which gave great offence to the Allies, he also dismissed the war aims of all sides as essentially indistinguishable. 'The objects which the statesmen of the belligerents on both sides have in mind in this war,' he wrote, 'are virtually the same, as stated in general terms to their own people and to the world.' Each side, he asserted, 'desires to make the rights and privileges of weak peoples and small states as secure against aggression or denial in the future as the rights and privileges of the great and powerful states now at war'. Each side also 'wishes itself to be made secure in the future, along with all other nations and peoples, against the recurrence of wars like this and against aggression or selfish interference of any kind'. Patrick Devlin has observed that in an abstract sense, and to a dispassionate reader, there was nothing particularly outrageous about Wilson's analysis. He was not actually 'passing judgement' but merely 'calling attention to the fact that the objects of each side *as stated* were the same'. But, adds Devlin, 'in December 1916 there were not many careful and dispassionate readers among the Allies'.[4]

As had happened before, Wilson's painful and fastidious anxiety to be perfectly even-handed in his efforts at mediation had quite the opposite effect. Although he explicitly said that his intervention had nothing to do with the Central Powers' Peace Note, both London and Paris assumed otherwise. Neither country in any case was at all prepared to negotiate, though the Allied reply to Wilson (sent in January 1917) did contain some fairly detailed war aims. These included the restitution and compensation of Belgium, Serbia and Montenegro; the evacuation of France, Russia and Romania; the freeing of the Italians, Slavs and Romanians from 'foreign domination'; the liberation of subject peoples from the Turks; and a vague reference to the return of 'territory formerly taken from the Allies against the inhabitants' will' (which was understood to include Alsace-Lorraine).[5] Underlying these objectives, and the Central Powers' complete rejection of them, was an assumption on both sides that the war could still be won. For the Allies it was a matter of hanging on, believing that their superior numbers and resources would eventually prevail, but also hoping that the Americans might be drawn into the struggle on their side. For the Central Powers the prospect of victory depended on a shorter-term strategy with the German introduction of unrestricted submarine warfare on 1 February 1917, by which they gambled on bringing the Allies to their knees before the Americans could effectively intervene. In the event the Allies were right and the Central Powers wrong.

While the potential for peace in late 1916 – such as it was – soon evaporated (or was extinguished) and the conflict dragged on for nearly two more years, in the longer term some elements of the events of that year have subsequently been mobilised in the service of reconciliation between and among the former belligerents. An early manifestation of this concerned Gallipoli. In November 1929 the Turkish president (and Gallipoli veteran) Mustafa Kemal (later Kemal Atatürk – 'Father of the Turks') made a statement about the Australian and New Zealand war graves on the peninsula which was evidently intended as a gesture of reassurance about the thousands of Allied remains on the peninsula. He had visited the battlefield and said that the people of both countries 'need have no fear in regard to the graves of the men of Anzac who sleep on the narrow strip of soil that was the scene of their deeds of valor'. Despite their wartime differences, the Turkish people would 'never feel anything but respect for the men of Anzac'. Indeed, 'our soldiers of today and tomorrow ask nothing better than to take your heroic Anzacs as their models of how men ought to fight for the cause they believe in'. In a kind of afterthought he added that 'our people' would also 'honor and respect' the graves of 'other British and Allied dead'. Five years later, on 26 April 1934, the day after the nineteenth anniversary of the first landings at Gallipoli, the *Sydney Morning Herald* published an 'Anzac Day message' from Kemal in which he declared that the fighting 'showed to the world the heroism of all those who shed their blood there. How heartrending for their nations,' he added, 'were the losses that this struggle caused.'[6]

There was a political agenda underpinning these sympathetic and reconciling messages. In order to copper-fasten the new secular republic's orientation towards the West, Kemal was anxious to repair relations with Turkey's former adversaries, not just during the war but from the difficult early days of the state. In 1922–23, Turkey had stood firm against a British threat of renewed war and had managed to negotiate an advantageous final settlement with the wartime Allies. And, as one of Kemal's biographers has observed, 'the fact that he had worsted the British, militarily in Gallipoli and diplomatically in the War of Independence, made it easier to love the old enemy'.[7]

The British reciprocated with conciliatory gestures of their own. The official historian of the campaign described Kemal as having 'an outstanding genius for command' and in 1932 the president was given a presentation copy of the volumes dedicated to him as a 'noble and valiant adversary'. In 1936 a private visit to Turkey by King Edward VIII (sailing in the eastern Mediterranean accompanied by his lover, Mrs Simpson – though this snippet of information was not included in British newspaper reports) 'set the seal on the *rapprochement* with Great Britain'. An account of the king's visit to the British imperial memorials and war graves on Gallipoli was accompanied by a report that there had been some concerns about Turkish attitudes towards the care of the graves by the Imperial War Graves Commission. These, however, had been allayed by an official assurance that the Turkish government would 'continue to maintain the same facilities as in the past in regard to the upkeep and supervision of, and to visits to, the cemeteries'.[8]

In the most famous and quoted of Kemal's statements about Gallipoli, this coolly neutral position was transformed into something very much more positive. Apparently prepared as a message to a party of British battlefield pilgrims in 1934, Kemal eloquently spoke directly to the bereaved mothers:

> Those heroes that shed their blood and lost their lives ... you are now lying in the soil of a friendly country. Therefore rest in peace. There is no difference between the Johnnies and the Mehmets to us where they lie side by side in this country of ours. ... You, the mothers, who sent their sons from faraway countries wipe away your tears; your sons are now lying in our bosom and are in peace. After having lost their lives on this land, they have become our sons as well.[9]

Although (curiously) this powerful and moving expression of comfort and friendship attracted no contemporaneous publicity whatsoever, it has now understandably become the single most predominant text accompanying commemorations of Gallipoli, and, perhaps more than any other single statement, it embodies a natural human desire to extract some positive meaning from the dreadful legacy of the war.

Other Great War locations have been used as sites for reconciliation. On 4 October 1995 the Italian president, Oscar Scalfaro, met his Austrian counterpart, Thomas Klestil, at Gorizia where they jointly dropped a wreath into the Isonzo 'to heal the last wounds lingering in their countries from the fighting'.[10] As early as 1966, at a fiftieth anniversary commemoration of Verdun, President Charles de Gaulle, himself a veteran of the battle, argued that one important lesson concerned the relations between the 'two neighbouring peoples' and their soldiers who had fought so 'courageously and at such great price'. Yet the 'result of their fighting was only pain'. After the 'heartbreaking events' of two great wars, France and Germany, he said, had to act together in a Europe which needed to reorganise itself as the 'main centre of civilisation'.[11]

Nearly thirty years on, President François Mitterrand chose the great Douaumont Ossuary at Verdun as the best place to meet the West German Chancellor, Helmut Kohl, for a 'day of reconciliation' on 22 September 1994. The timing broadly coincided with the eightieth anniversary of the beginning of the First World War, though some commentators believed that the meeting had been 'improvised' after Kohl had been 'left out of the 40th anniversary celebrations' commemorating the Allied landings in Normandy during the Second World War.[12] The meeting, nevertheless, had great symbolic power for the leaders of two countries which had been at war twice within living memory. A memorial tablet testifies that they met 'with one common thought for the dead of the two world wars. They laid wreaths and declared: "We are reconciled. We understand each other. We have become friends."'

In 2014 Douaumont was again used for a reconciliation ceremony. The ossuary, an immense structure which took twelve years to complete between 1920 and 1932, was conceived by the Bishop of Verdun to be a memorial and last resting place for the unidentified dead of the battle. It contains 130,000 remains recovered from the surrounding area. No one has any idea how many are French and how many German. Bereaved relatives could pay to have the names of their dead inscribed in the vault of the monument, and over the years occasional Germans had in vain approached the authorities to see if they could sponsor a memorial plaque. But, on 9 February 2014, for the first time, the name of a German soldier was engraved in the monument. It was, reported a local newspaper, 'a symbol of Franco-German reconciliation'. Appropriately, the German plaque was dedicated together with a French one – 'Ils s'appelaient Peter et Victor'. Peter Freundl was a Bavarian, killed on 25 May 1916; Joseph Victor Manassy had been born in Briey, just thirty miles or so east of where he fell on 2 June 1916.[13]

Common war service was thought to have a reconciling potential in Ireland too. Tom Kettle, the Irish university professor and nationalist politician who fell at Ginchy on the Somme in September 1916, fervently believed that nationalist and Unionist Irishmen could turn away 'from the ashes of dead hatreds' and hoped that 'out of this disastrous war, we may pluck, as France and Belgium have plucked, the precious gift of national unity'. Kettle, an internationalist with a European vision, saw the war as a righteous crusade against the German 'Blood-and-Ironmongers' who had ravished Belgium. But the service of Irishmen at the side of British fellow soldiers could achieve more even than just Irish national unity. 'Used with the wisdom which is sown in tears and blood,' he wrote, 'this tragedy of Europe may be and must be the prologue to the two reconciliations of which all statesmen have dreamed, the reconciliation of Protestant Ulster with Ireland, and the reconciliation of Ireland with Great Britain.'[14]

For all the high hopes of Kettle and many others who thought similarly, this was not to be, or at least not in the short or even medium term. The seeds 'sown in tears and blood' during Ireland's wartime domestic violence (together with the government's response) produced not 'wisdom' but a nasty guerrilla conflict and civil war, the partition of the island into two deeply conservative confessional states and embittered relations all round. The 'unfinished business' of the early 1920s, moreover, contributed to a fresh thirty-year bout of Irish 'Troubles' from 1968 on.

Prompted by a visit to the grave of a fellow Donegal man who had been killed on the Western Front in 1918, an Irish politician, Paddy

Harte, began to reflect on the fate of all those Irishmen – nationalist, Unionist and of no politics at all – who had served and died in the First World War. Together with a Loyalist former paramilitary from Derry/Londonderry, Glenn Barr, they conceived the imaginative idea of taking cross-community groups of young Irish and Ulster people on visits to the Great War battlefields and graveyards of Belgium and France. Thus was born the Journey of Reconciliation Trust, which went on to erect at Mesen (Messines) in Belgium an Irish Peace Tower and an adjacent 'Peace Village', for conferences and community groups. The tower was dedicated on 11 November 1998 by King Albert of the Belgians, Queen Elizabeth II of the United Kingdom and President Mary McAleese of Ireland, who said that the occasion should be seen as a 'redeeming of the memory' of all the Irish who had died in the First World War.[15] This was the first time that the Irish president and the British monarch had joined together in any public ceremony, and it made a powerful statement about the healing of relations between two sometimes antagonistic states. The location, too, was significant, as the political environment was evidently still not quite right for anything quite so shockingly consensual to occur in either Ireland or Great Britain. 'Gallant little Belgium', a suitable neutral territory, once again provided a venue for Allied action, though this time of a distinctly constructive and pacific sort.

These reconciling events do not always pass without controversy. Being powerfully symbolic themselves, and usually attracting great publicity, they can provide opportunities for other political points to be made. In April 1985 at the dedication of the Atatürk Memorial in Canberra, there was a 'loud protest' from some 160 people demonstrating against the current Turkish military regime. According to the *Canberra Times*, they chanted 'Down with fascist military dictatorship', to which some of the larger number of Turkish people present responded with 'Communists' and 'Go home to Russia'. By sharp contrast, an adjacent report of nine Australian Gallipoli veterans visiting Turkey carried the headline 'Former war enemies join in a tearful embrace'. Echoing the words ascribed to Mustafa Kemal, the Turkish president, Kenan Evren (who had led a military coup in 1980), 'told the veterans that soldiers buried at Gallipoli were Turkey's respected guests. "We take care of them and value them as our own martyrs," he said.' [16]

The revival of interest in independent Ireland about the many thousands of Catholic and nationalist Irishmen who joined up to serve in the First World War has provoked some opposition from Irish republicans. The commissioning in 2009 of a brand new war memorial in Killarney, County Kerry, 'to Irish men who fought and died in the British Army' led Republican Sinn Féin (a splinter group opposed to the Northern Ireland peace process) to describe it 'as an insult to the many Irish men who were executed by the same British Army'. Despite the attendance of the Irish president at the dedication ceremony, the republicans asserted that it 'should be boycotted by all nationally minded people'. The carefully choreographed programme of Queen Elizabeth II's first-ever state visit to the Republic of Ireland in May 2011 aimed to precisely balance an appreciation of the apparently diametrically opposed Irish military experiences of 1916. On the first day the queen laid a wreath at the Irish National Garden of Remembrance in Parnell Square, Dublin, which is dedicated 'to the memory of all those who gave their lives in the cause of Irish Freedom'. The next day, again accompanied by President McAleese, she went to the Edwin Lutyens-designed Irish National War Memorial Gardens at Islandbridge, where both heads of state laid wreaths to Irishmen who had died fighting in British uniforms during the First World War. Even this evident order of priority, with the struggle for Irish independence from the United Kingdom clearly in the first place, was insufficient for the mainstream republican party, Sinn Féin, who officially boycotted the visit. [17]

The dedication of the German plaque in the Douaumont Ossuary at Verdun in 2014 also provoked a dissenting voice. A retired local mayor, Yves Jadot, was offended by the whole idea. The gesture, he said, 'betrayed the memory of all the French soldiers who had fought in the battle'. [18] Although today the themes of reconciliation and a commitment to peace predominate in commemorations of the First World War, the sporadic incidence of contrarian opinions does not just (or necessarily even) represent pockets of unreconstructed chauvinism or bigotry. The expression of views which still embody some

of the strong opinions held at the time of the war, as well as the justi-
fications advanced then for fighting, is not just some surviving
historical curiosity, but also reflects the deeply embedded power of
national, communal and personal emotions which today can still
sustain the idea and practice of armed conflict. While war itself remains
as a possible policy option for modern states, no commemoration of
past wars can be entirely pacific. Beneath the wholly admirable expres-
sions of reconciliation and peaceful coexistence which almost
invariably (and rightly) now accompany war commemoration, so
long as states continue to possess armed forces and are evidently
prepared to use them, there will always be some still, small voice
reminding us that on occasion, for some communities and for some
states, war *works*.

For many people the issues of the war, especially those of national
freedom and self-determination, still retain sufficient freshness and
relevance to provoke interventions which run against the prevailing
(and perhaps sometimes starry-eyed) aspirations for peace and reconciliation, however praiseworthy they may be. The nature of war itself,
that is to say the explicit and collective use of lethal violence by one
community against another, incorporates such extreme engagements
that its commemoration can never be a trivial matter, nor wholly free
from reflection about the reasons why men and women may still view
such activity as both appropriate and effective.

In a parliamentary debate in 1922 about the Irish settlement,
Winston Churchill made a famous, and not untypically condescend-
ing, remark about the 'dreary steeples of Fermanagh and Tyrone'. He
recalled that during the late summer of 1914, while Europe was sliding
into war, politicians in the United Kingdom were desperately trying to
find some solution in Ireland which would avoid what seemed to be an
almost inevitable violent conflict between the increasingly well-armed
and belligerent nationalists and Unionists. One option being explored
was that part of north-east Ulster might 'opt out' of the Home Rule
parliament which was about to be established in Dublin. But where
could the line of partition be drawn? Thus, rather than paying attention to the growing international crisis, British and Irish politicians
were grappling with the minutiae of Irish geography, exploring where

the border might run. 'The differences,' wrote Churchill, 'had been narrowed down, not merely to the counties of Fermanagh and Tyrone, but to parishes and groups of parishes . . . And yet, even when the differences had been so narrowed down, the problem appeared to be as insuperable as ever, and neither side would agree to reach any conclusion.' Eight years later, he noted that the 'whole map' of Europe had been changed, 'but as the deluge subsides and the waters fall short we see the dreary steeples of Fermanagh and Tyrone emerging once again. The integrity of their quarrel is one of the few institutions that has been unaltered in the cataclysm which has swept the world.'[19]

The central point here is 'the integrity of their quarrel', the intensity of commitment and engagement which sustained each side, taking them to the brink and beyond of inflicting lethal violence against neighbours and fellow countrymen. In a wider sense, however, Churchill was wrong, though eloquently so (as was often the case). The 'integrity' of the Irish quarrel was not at all 'unaltered in the cataclysm'. It was in fact powerfully intensified, especially by the events of 1916. As in Ireland, so it was for other places. Although, as we have seen, the passage of time, changing international circumstances and the amelioration of communal and national antagonisms has for many people allowed reconciliation to be linked with commemoration, for others, and for a variety of reasons, the wounds of the Great War remain unhealed. The atrocity, suffering and sometimes atavistic hatreds of that conflict cannot be written out of history. Yet, the hope remains that even so the integrity of other aspects of the wartime experience – such things as resilience and endurance, the sense of common human experience in the face of catastrophic circumstances and the often-found impulse to alleviate suffering – might themselves contribute to an appreciation of war in its entirety, not just as an adversarial phenomenon but a collective one as well, and with that understanding illuminate the common humanity of those engaged in it.

In the end it must surely be individual experience which points away from war as a whole. Emilio Lussu, the Sardinian who fought in north Italy in 1916, recalled an occasion when from the Italian trenches he took aim with a rifle on an Austrian officer contentedly smoking a cigarette in the opposing lines. But as he focused on the target, he began to hesitate. 'Could I fire like this, at a few paces,' he asked himself, 'on a man – as if he were a wild boar?'

> I began to think that perhaps I ought not to do so. I reasoned like this: To lead a hundred, even a thousand, men against another hundred, or thousand, was one thing; but to detach one man from the rest and say to him, as it were: 'Don't move, I'm going to shoot you. I'm going to kill you' – that was different. Entirely different. To fight is one thing, but to kill a man is another. And to kill him like that is to murder him.

And so Lussu, the trained and patriotic soldier, put down his rifle and did not fire.[20]

Notes

Abbreviations

AFS   American Field Service
BMH, WS   Bureau of Military History, Ireland, Witness Statement
CUL   Cambridge University Library
IWM   Imperial War Museum
LHCMA   Liddell Hart Centre for Military Archives
NYT   *The New York Times*
TNA   United Kingdom National Archives
YUL   Yale University Library

Introduction

1. Notes for a sermon, 6 Jul 1919 (England papers, in private hands).
2. Strachan, *The First World War*, i, *To Arms*.
3. Jarboe and Fogarty (eds), *Empires in World War I*, p. 1.
4. Gewarth and Manela (eds), *Empires at War*; description from Oxford University Press catalogue.
5. Gallagher, *Decline, Revival and Fall*, p. 86.
6. Tooze, *The Deluge*.

1: Gallipoli

1. There is a very extensive literature on Gallipoli. Among the best for the Allied side are Rhodes James, *Gallipoli*; Broadbent, *Gallipoli: The Fatal Shore*; Prior, *Gallipoli*; Hart, *Gallipoli*; and, for the Turkish, Erickson, *Gallipoli*.
2. The following account is principally drawn from the *Final Report of the Dardanelles Commission*, 1919 [Cmd. 371], especially pp. 53–60.
3. Beecroft to Aspinall-Oglander, 9 Feb 1931 (TNA, CAB 45/241).
4. Williams, 'The evacuation of the Dardanelles', p. 655.

5. Churchill, *World Crisis 1915*, p. 489.
6. *Dardanelles final report*, p. 55.
7. Williams, 'The evacuation of the Dardanelles', p. 656.
8. As in an official Indian government communiqué of 22 Oct 1914 (quoted in Prasad, *The Indian Muslims*, p. 48).
9. Memo by AJB, 19 Nov 1915, TNA, CAB 37/137/36 (quoted in Broadbent, *Gallipoli*, p. 253).
10. Memo by Curzon, 19 Nov 1915, TNA, CAB 37/138/12 (ibid., p. 254).
11. Williams, 'The evacuation of the Dardanelles', p. 664.
12. Bean, *The Story of Anzac*, ii, p. 853. There are good accounts of the evacuation in Bean, pp. 853–86; Hart, *Gallipoli*; and, for Anzac, Cameron, *Gallipoli*.
13. Notes on evacuation, IX Corps War Diary (TNA, WO 95/4276).
14. IX Corps Operation orders, 12 Dec 1915 (TNA, WO 95/4276).
15. Letter by Walter Campbell, 18 Dec 1915 (TS copy) (IWM, Campbell papers 88/65/1).
16. Cameron, *Gallipoli*, pp. 269–72; Notes on evacuation, IX Corps War Diary (TNA WO 95/4276).
17. War diary of 6/South Lancashire Regiment, 19 Dec 1915 (TNA, WO 95/4302); Beckett, *Clem Attlee*, p. 50 (based on Harris, *Attlee*, p. 37); Attlee typescript war memoirs (Lancashire Infantry Museum), p. 14.
18. Kannengiesser, *The Campaign in Gallipoli*, pp. 245–56.
19. Eric Wettern diary, Jan 1916 (IWM, Diary of No 2 Field Company RE, Misc 234, item 3332); Callwell, *The Dardanelles*, p. 306.
20. Letter by Burge, 4 Jan 1916 (TS copy) (IWM, Burge papers, 12138).
21. Report on evacuation of Cape Helles position, by F. J. Davies, Jan 1916 (TNA, WO 158/594).
22. Eric Wettern diary, Jan 1916 (IWM, Diary of No 2 Field Company RE, Misc 234, item 3332).
23. Erickson, *Gallipoli*, p. 180.
24. 1st Royal Dublin Fusiliers war diary, 2 Jan 1916 (TNA, WO 95/4310); Wylly, *Neill's 'Blue Caps'*, p. 63.
25. Fox, *The Royal Inniskilling Fusiliers in the World War*, p. 181.
26. 1st Royal Inniskilling Fusiliers war diary, Jan 1916 (TNA, WO 95/4311).
27. Aspinall-Oglander, *Gallipoli*, ii, pp. 476–78; Facey-Crowther, *Lieutenant Owen Steele*, pp. 123–25.
28. Birdwood, *Khaki and Gown*, pp. 294–95.
29. Report on evacuation of Cape Helles position, by F. J. Davies, Jan 1916; notes enc. with Davies to Aspinall-Oglander, 7 Nov 1931 (TNA, WO 158/594; CAB 45/241).
30. Ibid. (TNA, WO 158/594).
31. Letter by Burge, 10 Jan 1916 (TS copy) (IWM, Burge papers, 12138).
32. Wilson diary (IWM Wilson papers), 1 Feb 1915.
33. Delage, *The Tragedy of the Dardanelles*, p. 256.

34. Heald, *Hero and Humorist*, p. 160.
35. *Sydney Morning Herald*, 1 and 10 Aug; *New Zealand Herald*, 1 Aug 1914.
36. Broadbent, *Gallipoli*, p. 289; Pugsley, *Gallipoli*, p. 368.
37. Chhina, 'Their mercenary calling'; Talbot, *The 14th King George's Own*, p. 82.
38. Davies, *Allanson of the 6th*, p. 51.
39. 'Tea Leaves', *Sydney Morning Herald*, 16 Sep 1916; Bean, *Story of Anzac*, i, p. 215.
40. Cassar, *The French and the Dardanelles*, p. 60. I have drawn on this indispensable study for the following account of French involvement.
41. Jauffret, 'Gallipoli: a French perspective', p. 138.
42. Greenhalgh and Guelton, 'The French on Gallipoli'; Ministère de la Guerre, *Les Armées Françaises*, VIII, i, p. 549; figures for French cemetery from www.anzacsite.gov.au (accessed 30 Oct 2013).
43. Association Nationale. . ., *Dardanelles Orient Levant*, pp. 28, 39, 65–6.
44. Ibid., pp. 66, 39, 70; Eric Wettern diary, Jun–Jul 1915.
45. Erickson, *Gallipoli*, pp. 31–2, 56–7.
46. Broadbent, *Gallipoli*, pp. 99–100.
47. Vedica Kant, 'Çanakkale's children: the politics of remembering the Gallipoli campaign in contemporary Turkey', in Ziino (ed.), *Remembering the First World War*, pp. 157, 160.
48. Sanders, *Five Years in Turkey*, p. 64.
49. Bean, *Story of Anzac*, ii, p. 835.
50. Kannengiesser, *The Campaign in Gallipoli*, pp. 145–46.
51. Erickson, *Gallipoli*, p. 39.
52. Fewster, *Gallipoli: the Turkish Story*, p. 100.
53. Jeffery, *MI6*, pp. 124–25.
54. Aspinall-Oglander, *Gallipoli*, ii, pp. 54, 395, 435; Bean, *Story of Anzac*, ii, pp. 835–36; Chhina, 'Their mercenary calling', p. 369.
55. Mizzi, *Gallipoli: the Malta Connection*, p. 105; details of Camilleri from the CWGC on-line register (www.cwgc.org), accessed 30 Nov 2014.
56. The most reliable biographical source for Patterson is Brian, *Seven Lives of Colonel Patterson*.
57. Sugarman, 'Zion Muleteers'; Patterson, *With the Zionists in Gallipoli*, pp. 40, 95–110.
58. Ibid., pp. 118–19, 106–07.
59. Ibid., pp. v–vi.
60. Bloom, 'Colonel Patterson'; Patterson, *With the Judeans in the Palestine Campaign*, p. 225.
61. Cooper, *The Tenth (Irish) Division*, p. 244.
62. Broadbent, *Gallipoli*, p. 274.
63. Australian and New Zealand war memorials are marvellously covered in Inglis, *Sacred Places* and Maclean and Phillips, *The Sorrow and the Pride*.
64. Macleod, *Reconsidering Gallipoli*, p. 5; Bean, *Story of Anzac*, ii, p. 910.

65. The literature is very extensive. For excellent introductions and guides, see Macleod, *Reconsidering Gallipoli*, and Beaumont, *Broken Nation*.
66. Kent, '*The Anzac Book*'; Bean, *Anzac to Amiens*, p. 181.
67. Thornton, 'Echoes of Gallipoli', p. 118.
68. Mulgan, *The Making of a New Zealander*, pp. 111–12.
69. Quoted in Macleod, *Reconsidering Gallipoli*, p. 90. See also the general discussion in Shefthall, *Altered Memories*.
70. See, for example, Jeffery, 'Ireland and Gallipoli'.
71. Williams, *A Prime Minister Remembers*, p. 38.

2: Verdun

1. Lefebvre, *Verdun: la plus grande bataille de l'histoire*. Good English-language accounts of Verdun include Jankowski, *Verdun*, and Horne, *The Price of Glory*, which I have used extensively for background information.
2. As described in its magazine of war news, *The New York Times Current History of the European War* (henceforward *NYT Current History*), 12 Dec 1914. For *The New York Times* during the war, see Davis, *History of the New York Times*, pp. 331–69.
3. *The New York Times* (henceforward *NYT*), 23 Feb 1916.
4. *NYT*, 24 Feb 1916.
5. *NYT*, 28 Feb, 3 Mar 1916. For the Sayville wireless station, see *NYT*, 23 Apr 1915.
6. *NYT*, 29 Feb, 1 Mar 1916.
7. There is a good introduction to this topic in Nicolas Beaupré, 'Soldier-writers and poets', in Winter (ed.), *Cambridge History of the First World War*, iii, pp. 445–74.
8. Desagneaux, *A French Soldier's War Diary*, pp. 19–31.
9. Quoted in Prost, 'La guerre de 1914', p. 101.
10. Smith, *The Embattled Self*, p. 115.
11. Jean-Charles Jauffret, 'Préface' to Pézard, *Nos autres à Vauquois*, pp. i–xi.
12. Pézard, *Nos autres à Vauquois*, pp. 179–81.
13. Ibid., pp. 288, 290–91.
14. Shanahan, 'Creating the new man', 208–11; Smith, *Embattled Self*, p. 79.
15. *NYT*, 5 Mar 1916.
16. Wedd, *German Students' War Letters*, pp. 275–77.
17. For the evolution of pre-1914 war plans, see Strachan, *The First World War*, i, pp. 163–207.
18. Falkenhayn, *General Headquarters 1914–1916*, pp. 214, 217–18.
19. Horne, *The Price of Glory*, pp. 27–45.
20. Ibid., pp. 132–41.
21. Ousby, *The Road to Verdun*, pp. 100–01.
22. Quoted in Horne, *The Price of Glory*, pp. 188–89.

23. Ibid., p. 339.
24. *NYT*, 26 Feb 1916.
25. *NYT*, 5, 19, 26 Mar 1916.
26. *NYT*, 29 Feb 1916, 'Infantry again a factor'.
27. *NYT*, 4 Apr 1916.
28. Haber, *The Poisonous Cloud*, pp. 86–96.
29. Morrow, 'The war in the air', p. 160.
30. Horne, *The Price of Glory*, p. 205.
31. Ibid., p. 317.
32. Robin Prior, '1916: Impasse', in Winter (ed.), *Cambridge History of the First World War*, i, p. 98.
33. *NYT*, 29 Feb 1916.
34. Binyon, *For Dauntless France*, p. 285.
35. Aitken, *Gallipoli to the Somme*, pp. 57–8.
36. French foreign and imperial recruitment is well covered in Horne, 'Immigrant workers in France'; and Stovall, 'Colour-blind France?'. For the domestic situation generally, see Becker, *The Great War and the French People*.
37. This paragraph draws on McMillan, *Housewife or Harlot*, part 2; quotation from pp. 136–37.
38. McMillan, *Housewife or Harlot*, pp. 106–08.
39. *New Zealand Dictionary of National Biography* (http://www.dnzb.govt.nz/en/biographies/3r31/rout-ettie-annie) (accessed 18 Dec 2013).
40. Horne, *The Path of Glory*, pp. 146–48.
41. Ageron, *Les Algériens musulmans et la France*, pp. 1140–57.
42. Zinoman, *The Colonial Bastille*, pp. 157, 184–8; Smith, 'Opposition to French rule in Vietnam'.
43. Horne, 'Immigrant workers in France', pp. 77–9.
44. Becker, *The Great War and the French People*, p. 142.
45. Horne, 'Immigrant workers in France', pp. 80–1; for Chinese recruiting motivations, see Starling and Lee, *No Labour, No Battle*, p. 299.
46. Inglis, 'Entombing unknown soldiers'; Winter, *Sites of Memory*.
47. *The Times*, 11 and 12 Nov 1920; Jagielski, *Le Soldat inconnu*, pp. 91–124.
48. *The Times*, 10, 11, 12 Nov 1920.
49. Inglis, 'Entombing unknown soldiers', p. 22.
50. *Tomb of the Unknown Warrior* commemorative brochure (http://www.mch.govt.nz/files/booklet_0.pdf (accessed 30 Dec 2013).

3: On the Isonzo

1. Thompson, *The White War*, provides an excellent general account of the fighting on the Italian front.
2. *Manchester Guardian*, 10 and 14 Jan 1916. For Garnett, see Jefferson, *Edward Garnett*.

3. Quoted in Cannadine, *Trevelyan*, p. 78.

4. Hankinson, *Geoffrey Winthrop Young*, pp. 67, 169–70; Lucas, *Outposts of Mercy*, p. 54; Hone, *Life of Henry Tonks*, pp. 119–26; *The Times*, 19 Aug 1915.

5. Trevelyan, *Scenes from Italy's War*, pp. 41–2; Young, *The Grace of Forgetting*, p. 275; Young's 'Italian Journal' quoted in Hankinson, *Geoffrey Winthrop Young*, p. 171.

6. Hankinson, *Geoffrey Winthrop Young*, p. 173

7. 'First British Ambulance Unit for Italy, Occasional News Sheet', no. 4a, 20 Jan 1916 (IWM, Barbour papers, GBB XVIII).

8. Report of the First Crossing of the Isonzo . . . by Ambulances of the Unit, 9 Aug 1916 (ibid.); Young, *The Grace of Forgetting*, pp. 296–301.

9. Monthly Reports for Dec 1916 and Sep 1917 (IWM, Barbour papers, GBB XVIII); Hankinson, *Geoffrey Winthrop Young*; Silvester, *Dancing is My Life*, pp. 24–6.

10. Lucas, *Outposts of Mercy*, p. 16.

11. *Trento*, vol. i no. 1 (Mar 1916) (IWM, Barbour papers, GBB III/2).

12. Lucas, *Outposts of Mercy*, pp. 39–40; http://www.kiplinhall.co.uk/the-families/bridget-talbot (accessed 17 Jan 2014).

13. Gleichen, *Contacts and Contrasts*, pp. 132–255; Hankinson, *Geoffrey Winthrop Young*, p. 174; Barbour diary, 9 Oct 1916 (IWM, GBB XII/4).

14. Lucas, *Outposts of Mercy*, p. 21; Gleichen, *Contacts and Contrasts*, p. 239; Young, *The Grace of Forgetting*, pp. 308–09.

15. Young, *The Grace of Forgetting*, p. 306; Barbour diary, 2 Dec 1916 (IWM, GBB XII/4).

16. Monthly Report for Dec 1916 (IWM, Barbour papers, GBB XVIII).

17. *British Journal of Nursing*, 25 Nov 1916.

18. Gooch, *The Italian Army and the First World War*, p. 64. This book supersedes all previous accounts.

19. Trevelyan, *Scenes from Italy's War*, p. 5.

20. Usefully succinct accounts of the Italian war effort will be found in Rochat, 'The Italian Front', and Gibelli, 'Italy'.

21. This account is primarily based on Gooch, *The Italian Army and the First World War*, pp. 183–86.

22. *The Times*, 12 Aug 1916.

23. Gooch, *The Italian Army and the First World War*, pp. 198, 166–67; Lussu, *Sardinian Brigade*, pp. 13, 26–7.

24. Wilcox, 'Discipline in the Italian army'; Gooch, *The Italian Army and the First World War*, pp. 133–39; Thompson, *The White War*, p. 227.

25. Lussu, *Sardinian Brigade*, pp. 49–50.

26. Wilcox, 'Discipline in the Italian army', p. 84; Gooch, *The Italian Army and the First World War*, pp. 169–71.

27. Taylor, *The Habsburg Monarchy*, p. 2.

28. See the forensic analysis in Clark, *The Sleepwalkers*.

29. The discussion following is primarily drawn from Rothenberg, *The Army of Francis Joseph*, pp. 127–28, 148, 172–200.

30. Spence, 'The Yugoslav role', p. 358.

31. Cornwall, 'Austria-Hungary'.

32. Gál, *In Death's Fortress*.

33. Gleichen, *Contacts and Contrasts*, p. 187.

34. Sondhaus, *In the Service of the Emperor*, pp. 104–05.

35. Ibid., p. 107; *NYT*, 16 Jul; *The Times*, 17 and 28 Aug 1916.

36. Trevelyan, *Scenes from Italy's War*, p. 206.

37. See Schindler, *Isonzo*, pp. 339–47, and Svoljšak, *The Front on Soča*, for guides to some of the surviving war cemeteries and monuments.

38. Mussolini, *My Autobiography*, pp. 58–62.

39. Susmel (eds), *Opera*, p. 151; Massock, *Italy from Within*, p. 334.

40. Trevelyan, *Scenes from Italy's War*, pp. 46–7, 50.

4: 'Ypres on the Liffey'

1. Quotation from the 1916 Proclamation. The best histories of the Rising are: McGarry, *The Rising*; Foy and Barton, *The Easter Rising*; and Townshend, *Easter 1916*.

2. Bureau of Military History, Ireland (BMH), Witness Statement (WS) 1698, pp. 305–07. Róiste deposited a typed transcript of his diary to the BMH on 7 Sep 1957.

3. There is an especially voluminous literature on Casement. Daly, *Roger Casement*, is a good introduction.

4. Dudgeon, *Roger Casement*, p. 426.

5. Andrew, *Defence of the Realm*, pp. 86–7.

6. Casement German diaries, 27 Nov 1914 (quoted in Ó Síocháin, *Roger Casement*, p. 600 n. 59).

7. Ó Síocháin, *Roger Casement*, pp. 408–38; Andrew, *Defence of the Realm*, p. 87; O'Halpin, 'British intelligence', pp. 56–61.

8. Note of interview with Sir E. Blackwell, Home Office, and Thomson to Blackwell, 18 Jul 1916 (TNA, MEPO 2/10664).

9. Jeffery, *The GPO*, pp. 65–6.

10. Howard to Foreign Secretary, 5 May 1916 (TNA, CAB 37/47/34).

11. Foy and Barton, *The Easter Rising*, pp. 205–08, pp. 284–328. For the legality of the trials see Hardiman, '"Shot in cold blood"'.

12. Tom Kettle described this as a 'magnificent lie' and asserted that MacBride had actually been 'looking down the necks of porter bottles all his life' (Lyons, *Enigma of Tom Kettle*, p. 294).

13. Smithson, *The Marriage of Nurse Harding*, p. 104.

14. I argue this point in my essay 'The First World War and the Rising'.

15. Townshend, *Political Violence in Ireland*, p. 302.

16. A. N. Lee, World War I Diary, Mar–May 1916, p. 33 (IWM, 66/121/1).
17. BMH, WS 196, p. 3.
18. [Smyly], 'Experiences of a VAD', p. 839.
19. Wilson diary (IWM), 28 Apr 1916.
20. Jeffery, *The GPO*, p. 89.
21. Ervine, 'The Story of the Irish Rebellion', p. 39.
22. The best general discussion is in Strachan, *The First World War*, ch. 2; Pennell, *A Kingdom United*, provides an especially good study of the United Kingdom.
23. For the general context, see Bartlett, *Ireland*, pp. 363–401, and, for the political debate, Fanning, *Fatal Path*, pp. 30–187.
24. *Hansard (Commons)*, 3 Aug 1914, col. 1824, 1829. For the general impact of the war on Ireland, see Jeffery, *Ireland and the Great War*, and Horne (ed.), *Our War*.
25. *Cork Free Press*, 23 Sep 1914; recruiting pamphlet in the possession of the author; *Newtownards Chronicle*, 12 Sep 1914.
26. Gwynn, *Life of John Redmond*, p. 391.
27. *Irish Times*, 24 Sep 1914.
28. Martin, *The Irish Volunteers*, p. 168.
29. Colvin, *Carson*, pp. 33–4.
30. There is a general discussion of Irish recruitment to the British Army in Jeffery, 'Irish military tradition'.
31. Paseta, *Irish Nationalist Women*, pp. 201–08.
32. BMH, WS 242, pp. 21–3.
33. Proctor, 'Missing in action', p. 547.
34. de Schaepdrijver, 'Belgium', in Horne (ed.), *Companion*, pp. 386–402.
35. Thiel, 'Between recruitment', pp. 41–2.
36. Becker, 'Life in an occupied zone' in Hugh Cecil and Peter Liddle (eds), *Facing Armageddon*, p. 635.
37. Kitchen, *The Silent Dictatorship*, pp. 67–87.
38. *NYT*, 14 Nov 1916; Pirenne, *La Belgique*, pp. 190–91.
39. Whitlock, *Belgium*, ii, pp. 268–9; Thiel, 'Between recruitment', pp. 43–5.
40. Memoir, part 2, p. 150 (IWM, Kirkpatrick papers, 79/50/1).
41. History of Intelligence (B), B.E.F. France, Jan 1917 to Apr 1919 (TNA, WO 106/45); 'Service anglais' to 'Service d'Observation anglais', 21 Jul 1918 (Centre d'Études et de Documentation Guerre et Sociétés contemporaines, Brussels, Dewé papers, vol. 1).
42. Walthère Dewé, 'Notice historique sur le Corps d'Observation Allié' (Dewé papers); Jeffery, *MI6*, pp. 78–81, 86–7.
43. Proctor, *Female Intelligence*, pp. 75–98.
44. *NYT*, 8 Apr; *The Times*, 17 May 1916. Coulson, *Queen of Spies*, provides a popular account of de Bettignies.
45. Andrew, *Defence of the Realm*, pp. 73–5.
46. de Schaepdrijver, 'Belgium', in Horne (ed.), *Companion*, pp. 392–93.
47. Landau, *Spreading the Spy Net*, p. 61.

48. Ervine, *Some Impressions*, p. 280.
49. BMH, WS 1698, pp. 339–30.
50. *Irish Times*, 1 May 1916.
51. McGarry, *The Rising*, p. 256.

5: Jutland and the War at Sea

1. Halpern, 'The war at sea', in Horne (ed.), *Companion to World War I*, pp. 141–55; and Kennedy, 'The war at sea', in Winter (ed.), *Cambridge History of the First World War*, i, pp. 321–48, usefully put the battle in context.
2. Churchill, *The World Crisis*, p. 112.
3. Scheer, *Germany's High Sea Fleet*, pp. 113–16.
4. *The Times*, 7 Mar 1916.
5. Groos, *Der Krieg in der Nordsee*, pp. 136–37.
6. *The Times*, 25 and 26 Apr 1916.
7. Scheer, *Germany's High Sea Fleet*, p. 134.
8. For detail on the battle, see Tarrant, *Jutland*; Marder, *Dreadnought to Scapa Flow*; and Campbell, *Jutland*.
9. Scheer, *Germany's High Sea Fleet*, p. 174.
10. Jeffery, *MI6*, pp. 83–5.
11. Intelligence reports in TNA, ADM 223/637. Casualty figures as quoted in Marder, *Dreadnought to Scapa Flow*, p. 204.
12. Scheer, *Germany's High Sea Fleet*, p. 177.
13. Ibid., pp. 180–84; Marder, *Dreadnought to Scapa Flow*, pp. 235–56.
14. Scheer, *Germany's High Sea Fleet*, pp. 167, 190.
15. Ibid., pp. 103, 168–69, 177.
16. Quoted by Gerald Fienne in the *Observer*, 20 Jul 1919.
17. Hase, *Kiel and Jutland*, p. 6.
18. Kennedy, 'The war at sea', in Winter (ed.), *Cambridge History of the First World War*, i, pp. 343–45. See also the discussion in Kramer, 'Blockade and economic warfare', in ibid., ii, pp. 460–89.
19. This account is principally based on Osborne, *Britain's Economic Blockade of Germany*.
20. *Hansard (Commons)*, 23 Feb 1916, col. 776.
21. There is a useful discussion of these matters in Stig Förster, 'Civil-military relations', in Winter (ed.), *Cambridge History of the First World War*, ii, pp, 91–125.
22. Yaney, *The World of the Manager*, pp. 65–72, 113–84.
23. Denholm (ed.), *Behind the Lines*, pp. 121, 125–27, 134, 136.
24. Chickering, *The Great War*, pp. 209–10; 217, 221, 245–46.
25. Denholm (ed.), *Behind the Lines*, pp. 121, 125–27, 134, 136, 143, 154, 167, 173.
26. Strachan, *The First World War*, i, pp. 748–50.
27. Halpern, *Naval War in the Mediterranean*, pp. 191–205, 243–53.
28. *The Times*, 18 Sep, 30 Oct 1916; Carden, *German Policy Toward Neutral Spain*, pp. 100–60.

29. Jacobson, 'A city living through crisis'.
30. Schatkowski Schilcher, 'The famine of 1915–1918'.
31. Dehne, *On the Far Western Front*, p. 67.
32. Bethell (ed.), *Cambridge History of Latin America*, pp. 302; 534–5; 700; Albert, *South America and the First World War*, pp. 63–72.
33. *London Gazette*, nos 29492 and 29515, 29 Feb and 24 Mar 1916, pp. 2207–12 and 3172–75.
34. Dehne, *On the Far Western Front*, p. 95.
35. Vincent-Smith, 'Britain, Portugal, and the First World War'.
36. Strachan, *First World War*, i, pp. 623–25; Beckett, *The Great War*, pp. 111–12.
37. Barbour diary, 16 Sep, 19 Nov 1916 (IWM, GBB XII/4).
38. Strachan, *The First World War*, i, pp. 455–62.
39. Sexton, 'Anglo-Japanese naval co-operation'.
40. Jellicoe to Beatty, 30 Dec 1916, enc. Notes 'which bear upon the naval content of the war' (Temple Patterson (ed.), *The Jellicoe Papers*, pp. 127–36).
41. Hirama, 'The Anglo-Japanese Alliance', pp. 58–60; Halpern, *The Naval War in the Mediterranean*, p. 344.
42. Marder, *Dreadnought to Scapa Flow*, pp. 203–04.
43. Crane, *Empires of the Dead*, pp. 195–97.
44. 'The German Naval Memorial' (http://www.deutscher-marinebund.de/geschichte_me_English.htm (accessed 14 Apr 2014)); *The Times*, 1 Jun 1936; Lurz, *Kriegerdenkmäler in Deutschland*, pp. 187–88 (I am most grateful to Stefan Goebel for this reference).
45. Marder, *Dreadnought to Scapa Flow*, iii, p. 61; Tarrant, *Jutland*, pp. 102–03.
46. Bingham to Lady Bethell, 7 Jun 1916 (LHCMA, M. J. Bethell papers, folder 2); *The Times*, 15 Jun 1932.

6: The Eastern Front

1. There are good, short accounts of the Eastern Front by Holger Afflerbach, 'The Eastern Front', in Winter (ed.), *Cambridge History of the First World War*, i, pp. 234–65; and Dennis Showalter, 'War in the East and Balkans', in Horne (ed.), *Companion to World War I*, pp. 66–81. Stone, *The Eastern Front*, remains the best book-length treatment.
2. Showalter, 'War in the East and Balkans', p. 73.
3. Stone, *Eastern Front*, pp. 231–32.
4. Brussilov, *A Soldier's Note-Book*, pp. 208–18.
5. Unless otherwise noted, the following account is drawn from Dowling, *The Brusilov Offensive*, and the works cited in n. 1 above.
6. Ulrich Trumpener, 'The Turkish war, 1914–18', in Horne (ed.), *Companion to World War I*, p. 107.
7. See Ashworth, *Trench Warfare*, for an exploration of this phenomenon on the Western Front.

8. Spence, 'The Yugoslav role', p. 360.
9. Anon, *History of* The Times: *The 150th Anniversary and Beyond*, i, p. 241; *The Times*, 9 Feb 1951; quotations from advertisements in Washburn, *Field Notes*.
10. Washburn, *On the Russian Front*, pp. 1–26.
11. Ibid., pp. 29–37; 147–49; 163; 174–75.
12. Washburn, *Field Notes*; *The Russian Campaign*; and *The Russian Offensive*; *The Times*, 16 Sep 1914, 4 May 1915; 'Interview with Mr Stanley Washburn', 19 Nov 1915 (TNA, CAB 31/137/35).
13. Washburn, *The Russian Offensive*, p. v.
14. 'Brusiloff on His Advance', *The Times*, 20 Jun 1916.
15. 'Lutsk from My Balcony', *The Times*, 15 Aug 1916. This article was reproduced almost word for word in *The Russian Offensive*, pp. 42–9.
16. *The Times*, 15 Aug 1916; Blunt, *Lady Muriel*, p. 136.
17. Washburn, *The Russian Offensive*, pp. 171–79; idem., *On the Russian Front*, pp. 203–07 (these accounts differ in some details).
18. Muriel Paget to 'Artie' (her husband), 12 Aug 1916 (quoted in Blunt, *Lady Muriel*, p. 90).
19. Washburn, *The Russian Offensive*, p. 179.
20. Ceaușesu, 'The Romanian army', p. 514.
21. Torrey, *Romania and World War I*, pp. 15–26.
22. Dowling, *The Brusilov Offensive*, pp. 150–53; Stone, *The Eastern Front*, p. 273; Galántai, *Hungary in the First World War*, pp. 186–87; Torrey, *Romania and World War I*, p. 154.
23. Gál, *In Death's Fortress*, pp. 185–95.
24. Torrey, *Romania and World War I*, pp. 121–36.
25. Dowling, *The Brusilov Offensive*, p. 159.
26. McLaren (ed.), *A History of the Scottish Women's Hospitals*, provides an admiring contemporary account.
27. Diary entry for 13 Sep 1916 (Fitzroy, *With the Scottish Nurses in Roumania*, p. 15).
28. Moir letter, 6 Oct; Birkbeck diary, 14 Oct 1916 (all quotations from the excellent collection in Cahill (ed.), *Between the Lines*, chs 2–4).
29. Diary entry for 23 Oct 1916 (Fitzroy, *With the Scottish Nurses in Roumania*, pp. 52–3); Elsie Inglis, 'Three Months on the Eastern Front', *The Englishwoman*, vol. 33 no. 98 (Feb 1917), p. 115.
30. Diary entry for 21 Dec 1916 (Fitzroy, *With the Scottish Nurses in Roumania*, p. 87).
31. Sybil Grey to her mother, n.d. 1916 (quoted in Blunt, *Lady Muriel*, p. 101).
32. Torrey (ed.), *General Henri Berthelot and Romania*, pp. xi–xxv.
33. *The Times*, 29 Sep 1930.
34. 'Report on Destruction of Roumanian Oilfields', 22 Jan 1917 (TNA, CAB 24/6 G.T. 25).
35. Norton-Griffiths to Gwladys, 19 Jan 1917 (quoted in Bridgland and Morgan, *Tunnel-Master and Arsonist*, p. 198).

36. 'Report on the Destruction of Grain and Machinery in Roumania', 27 Jan 1917 (TNA, CAB 24/7 G.T. 140); Perrett and Lord, *The Czar's British Squadron*, pp. 94–5.

37. Birkbeck diary, 18 Dec 1916 (quoted in Cahill (ed.), *Between the Lines*, p. 154).

38. 'Report' as n. 34 above.

39. Kramer, 'Blockade and economic warfare', in Winter (ed.), *Cambridge History of the First World War*, i, p. 477; Jonker and van Zanden, *From Challenge to Joint Industry Leader*, p. 175; Pearton, *Oil and the Romanian State*, pp. 79–84; Stone, *The Eastern Front*, p. 265.

40. Brussilov, *A Soldier's Note-Book*, p. 261.

41. Cahill (ed.), *Between the Lines*, p. 42; 'Report' as n. 34 above.

42. Cruttwell, *A History of the Great War*, p. 293; Moir diary, 6 Dec 1916 (quoted in Cahill (ed.), *Between the Lines*, p. 137); Stone, *The Eastern Front*, pp. 264–65.

43. Afflerbach, 'The Eastern Front', in Winter (ed.), *Cambridge History of the First World War*, i, p. 253.

44. Stibbe, 'Introduction' to idem., *Captivity, Forced Labour*, p. 7; Gatrell, *A Whole Empire Walking*, p. 3.

45. Polonsky, 'The German occupation of Poland', pp. 113–31; Westerhoff, '"A kind of Siberia"'.

46. Liulevicius, *War Land on the Eastern Front*, pp. 54–88. I have used this important work for the details of Ober Ost.

47. Ibid., pp. 76; 113–50.

48. Dowling, *The Brusilov Offensive*, p. 176.

49. Stone, *The Eastern Front*, p. 235.

50. Afflerbach, 'The Eastern Front', in Winter (ed.), *Cambridge History of the First World War*, i, p. 262.

51. Sanborn, 'Unsettling the empire', p. 302.

7: Asia

1. Sokol, *The Revolt of 1916*, pp. 77–8. This pioneering study is the only extended English-language account of the revolt and I have drawn on it for the following narrative.

2. MacDonell, '. . . *And Nothing Long*', p. 175.

3. Sokol, *The Revolt of 1916*, p. 73; Brower, 'Kyrgyz nomads', p. 47.

4. *NYT*, 18 Jun 1916.

5. See Speed, *Prisoners, Diplomats and the Great War*, for the arrangements for monitoring prisoners, as well as the estimates of Russian numbers; Schuyler to Mayre, 5 Apr 1915, quoted in ibid., p. 117. For an overview see Heather Jones, 'Prisoners of war', in Winter (ed.), *Cambridge History of the First World War*, ii, pp. 266–90.

6. Pierce, *Russian Central Asia*, pp. 267–78.

7. Ibid., pp. 273–78; Sokol, *The Revolt of 1916*, pp. 82–96.

8. Iungmeister quoted in Brower, 'Kyrgyz nomads', p. 43.

9. Sokol, *The Revolt of 1916*, pp. 120–24.

10. Ibid., p. 127; Brower, 'Kyrgyz nomads', p. 44; Holquist, 'To count, to extract', p. 121; Pierce, *Russian Central Asia*, p. 293.

11. Pierce, *Russian Central Asia*, pp. 283–86.

12. *NYT*, 25 Aug 1916.

13. Price, *My Three Revolutions*, pp. 46–7

14. Ibid., p. 75; idem, *War and Revolution*, p. 272; *Manchester Guardian*, 28 Nov 1917.

15. Sokol, *The Revolt of 1916*, pp. 129–37.

16. Macartney, 'Chez les Soviets', p. 102.

17. Quoted in Ramnath, *Haj to Utopia*, p. 222.

18. Strachan, *The First World War*, pp. 770–91.

19. Skrine and Nightingale, *Macartney at Kashgar*, pp. 250–54; Hughes, 'The German Mission'.

20. The story was told in weekly parts in *Land and Water*, 6 Jul–9 Nov 1916.

21. Quotations from Buchan, *Greenmantle*, pp. 12, 20, 107, 236, 242, 108, 91; *Times Literary Supplement*, 26 Oct 1916.

22. Crews, *For Prophet and Tsar*, pp. 351–52.

23. *NYT*, 18 Jun 1916.

24. Hardy, *Muslims of British India*, pp. 185–87; Policy of H. M. Government towards Turkey: Position of the Musulmans of India', 16 Mar 1915 (TNA, CAB 37/126/8).

25. Jeffery, '"An English barrack"'; 'Total contribution in men made and casualties suffered by India during the war', 21 Nov 1918 (TNA, CAB 24/70 G.T.6341).

26. Government of India, *India's Contribution*, pp. 78, 118, 121, 137.

27. See, for example, the section 'Asians in Britain/world wars' in the British Library 'Learning' pages: http://www.bl.uk/learning/histcitizen/asians/worldwars/theworldwars.html (accessed 3 Sep 2014).

28 Dodwell, *Cambridge History of India*, vi, p. 481; memo. by Montagu, 15 Oct 1920 (TNA, CAB 24/112 C.P. 1987); Judith Brown, 'War and the colonial relationship: Britain, India and the War of 1914–18', in Ellinwood and Pradhan (eds), *India and World War I*, p. 28; S. D. Pradhan, 'Indian Army and the First World War', in ibid., p. 60; Yong, *The Garrison State*, pp. 115–19, 134–37.

29. DeWitt C. Ellinwood, 'The Indian soldier, the Indian Army and change, 1914–1918', in Ellinwood and Pradhan (eds), *India and World War I*, pp. 189–90, 196; Omissi, *Indian Voices*, pp. 198, 280.

30. Harper and Miller, *Singapore Mutiny*.

31. Bergère, *Sun Yat-sen*, 262; Xu, *China and the Great War*, pp. 81–91.

32. Xu, *China and the Great War*, pp. 92–113.

33. Ibid., pp. 114–30.

34. Xu, *Strangers on the Western Front*, pp. 38–54.

35. Ibid., pp. 80–102; 119–22.
36. Figures extracted from Commonwealth War Graves Commission website, www.cwgc.org (accessed 11 Sep 2014).
37. Summerskill, *China on the Western Front*, p. 163.
38. Quoted in Stovall, 'The color line behind the lines', pp. 746–47.
39. A reliable military history of the campaign is Barker, *The Neglected War*. This is complemented (and in terms of the wider political context superseded) by Townshend, *When God Made Hell*.
40. Falls, *The First World War*, p. 143.
41. Moberly, *The Campaign in Mesopotamia*, ii, pp. 484, 487.
42. Omissi, *The Sepoy and the Raj*, pp. 136–40.
43. Gardner, 'Sepoys and the siege of Kut-al-Amara'.
44 Erickson, *Ordered to Die*, pp. 110–15, pp. 149–51; Townshend, *When God Made Hell*, p. 259.
45. Barker, *The Neglected War*, pp. 166–73; *Daily Mirror*, 22 May 1916; Moberly, *The Campaign in Mesopotamia*, iii, p. 13.
46. The best single account of the fighting on this front is in Allen and Muratoff, *Caucasian Battlefields*, book four.
47. Falls, *The First World War*, p. 228.
48. Allen and Muratoff, *Caucasian Battlefields*, p. 429.
49. *The Times*, 25 Jul 1916.
50. Allen and Muratoff, *Caucasian Battlefields*, p. 439.
51. For this failed enterprise, see Jeffery, *The British Army*, pp. 133–54.
52. Harper, 'Singapore, 1915', pp. 1786–88.
53. Dijk, *The Netherlands Indies*, pp. vii–xiii, 429–31, 453–55, 523–24.
54. Sokol, *The Revolt of 1916*, p. 13.
55. Gull, 'The story of the Chinese Labour Corps', *Far Eastern Review*, 15/4 (Apr 1918) (quoted in Xu, *Strangers on the Western Front*, pp. 53–4).

8: The War in Africa

1. Digre, *Imperialism's New Clothes*.
2. Iliffe, *Modern History of Tanganyika*, p. 240; see also Gallagher, *The Decline, Revival and Fall of the British Empire*, especially pp. 86–99.
3. Hordern, *Military Operations: East Africa*, pp. i, 359–60; *The Times*, 4 Sep 1916.
4. Crowe, *General Smuts' Campaign*, pp. 190–91; Cranworth, *Kenya Chronicles*, p. 230.
5. Ibid., pp. 230–31; Hordern, *Military Operations: East Africa*, p. 360.
6. Fewster, 'A Hull sergeant's Great War diary', entry for 29 Aug 1916.
7. *Morogoro News*, vol. 1, no. 1, 16 Sep 1916; Mwakikagile, *Life in Tanganyika*, pp. 55, 57.
8. Whittall, *With Botha and Smuts*, p. 275.
9. Cranworth, *Kenya Chronicles*, p. 182.

10. Howe, *Race, War and Nationalism*, pp. 95–6; Smith, *Jamaican Volunteers*, pp. 82–9.

11. Gallagher, *The Decline, Revival and Fall of the British Empire*, p. 87.

12. Strachan, *First World War*, pp. 505–09. This book (pp. 495–643) provides the best general account of the war in sub-Saharan Africa. The text has been reprinted (with some corrections) in Strachan, *The First World War in Africa*. Killingray, 'The war in Africa', in Horne (ed.), *Companion to World War I*, pp. 112–26, provides a useful short survey. I have drawn on both these works for the following narrative.

13. Nasson, 'War opinion in South Africa', p. 261.

14. Nasson, *Springboks on the Somme*, pp. 41–55; 210.

15. Osuntokun, *Nigeria in the First World War*, pp. 191–93.

16. Yearwood, '"In a casual way"'.

17. The best single account of the East African campaign is Edward Paice's marvellous *Tip and Run*.

18. Lettow-Vorbeck, *My Reminiscences*, p. 3.

19. Ibid., pp. 67–72.

20. Hyam, *Failure of South African Expansion*, pp. 23–46.

21. Paice, *Tip and Run*, pp. 183–84.

22. Digre, *Imperialism's New Clothes*, pp. 113–14.

23. Molloy to 'Middleton', 7 Apr 1916 (quoted in Bisset, 'Unexplored aspects', p. 59); Paice, *Tip and Run*, p. 184. For his part, von Lettow-Vorbeck noted reports that orders to 'take no prisoners' had been issued on the British side (*My Reminiscences*, pp. 104–05).

24. Whittall, *With Botha and Smuts*, pp. 276–77.

25. Iliffe, *Modern History of Tanganyika*, p. 245; *Bulawayo Chronicle*, quoted in Mosley, *Duel for Kilimanjaro*, p. 223. A search in the *Bulawayo Chronicle* for late 1918 and early 1919 has failed to turn up the original of this quotation.

26. Lettow-Vorbeck, *My Reminiscences*, pp. 320–23.

27. Stiénon, 'L'effondement colonial', pp. 669–70; Matthew G. Stannard, 'Digging in: the Great War and the roots of Belgian empire', in Jarboe and Fogarty (eds), *Empires in World War I*, pp. 26, 29.

28. Page, 'The war of thangata', pp. 87–9.

29. Ibid., pp. 89–100.

30. Lunn, *Memoirs of the Maelstrom*, pp. 39–45.

31. Daly, *Empire on the Nile*, pp. 176–77.

32. Ibid., pp. 177–87.

33. Şaul and Royer, *West African Challenge*, pp. 1–22, 107–08, 230, 267, 311.

34. Plaatje, *Native Life in South Africa*, p. 281.

35. Ibid., pp. 283, 267.

36. Willan, 'South African Native Labour Contingent'.

37. Ibid.; Nasson, *Springboks on the Somme*, pp. 168–69, 246; Jingoes, *A Chief is a Chief*, p. 92–3.

38. Boyd, *An Ice-Cream War,* 1982.
39. As in Paice, *Tip and Run: The Untold Tragedy of the Great War in Africa,* or Samson, *World War I in Africa: The Forgotten Conflict among the European Powers.*
40. Hodges, *The Carrier Corps,* pp. 110–11; idem., 'African manpower statistics', p. 116; Killingray, 'Labour exploitation', p. 485.
41. Echenberg, *Colonial Conscripts,* pp. 42–6.
42. Strachan, *First World War,* p. 497.
43. Major Darnley-Stuart-Stephens, 'Our million black army!', *English Review,* Oct 1916, pp. 353–60.
44. Whittall, *With Botha and Smuts,* pp. 184–86.
45. Briggs, 'German East Africa', pp. 196–99.
46. Pesek, 'The colonial order upside down?'; Holtom, *Two Years' Captivity,* p. 150; Anon., *British Civilian Prisoners,* p. 7; Spanton, *In German Gaols,* pp. 63–4.
47. CWGC website: http://www.cwgc.org/find-a-cemetery/cemetery/142301/ LIVINGSTONE%20CAMP%20MEMORIAL (accessed 30 Jun 2014).
48. Barrett, 'Death and the afterlife', p. 306. The discussion following draws on this important essay.
49. Crane, *Empires of the Dead,* narrates the development of this policy, but does not mention its *non*-application in Africa.
50. Barrett, 'Death and the afterlife', pp. 306–07.
51. Images of the Morogoro military cemetery will be found at http://www. cwgc.org/find-a-cemetery/cemetery/12104/Morogoro%20Cemetery (accessed 2 Jul 2014).

9: The Battle of the Somme

1. Philpott, *Bloody Victory,* pp. 600–02. This is the single most comprehensive account of the whole Somme battle.
2. Russell to Hamilton, 24 Sep 1916, quoted in Macleod, *Reconsidering Gallipoli,* p. 13.
3. Quoted in Watson, *Enduring the Great War,* p. 22.
4. Macleod, *Reconsidering Gallipoli,* p. 13.
5. Pennell, *A Kingdom United.*
6. Middlebrook, *The First Day on the Somme,* p. 263.
7. In, for example, Clark, *The Donkeys.*
8. Denman, *Ireland's Unknown Soldiers,* is the best account of the 16th Division. For recruiting among Belfast Nationalists, see also 6th Connaught Rangers, *The 6th Connaught Rangers* and Grayson, *Belfast Boys.*
9. Edmonds, *Military Operations France and Belgium, 1916,* i, pp. 195–96.
10. Quoted in Denman, *Ireland's Unknown Soldiers,* p. 80. The following battle narrative is largely based on this book, pp. 80–103.
11. Grayson (ed.), *At War with the 16th Irish Division,* p. 127.

12. Jeffery, *Ireland and the Great War*, pp. 10–12, 61.

13. Walker, *Forgotten Soldiers*, pp. 98–102.

14. The most complete account of the first use of tanks is Pidgeon, *The Tanks at Flers*, on which I have depended for the following narrative.

15. Philpott, *Bloody Victory*, p. 361.

16. Miles, *Military Operations France and Belgium, 1916*, ii, p. 323; Pidgeon, *The Tanks at Flers*, p. 169.

17. Ball, *The Guardsmen*, pp. 57–64; Macmillan, *Winds of Change*, p. 88.

18. The Allied dimension of the battle is well covered in Greenhalgh, *Victory through Coalition*, pp. 42–74.

19. Ibid., pp. 65–6; Philpott, *Bloody Victory*, pp. 349–57.

20. Ibid., pp. 350, 383–84.

21. Winter, *Sites of Memory*, p. 10.

22. Information from Accrington Pals' website (www.pals.org.uk, accessed 19 Nov 2014) and Simkins, *Kitchener's Army*, pp. 79–103.

23. Ibid., pp. 85, 92; Lavery, *Life of a Painter*, p. 139.

24. See Sheffield, *Forgotten Victory*, pp. 148–54, for a concise discussion of trench life.

25. Prior and Wilson, *The Somme*, pp. 112–18, in a penetratingly critical chapter, 'Reflections on 1 July'.

26. Beckett, *The Great War*, pp. 223–25; Prior and Wilson, *The Somme*, pp. 55–6, 67–9.

27. Kipling, *The Irish Guards*, p. 28.

28. Casualties from the Brigade War Diary (TNA WO 95/2363), quoted in www.pals.org (accessed 23 Nov 2014).

29. Buchan, *Battle of the Somme: First Phase*, p. 32

30. Facey-Crowther, *Lieutenant Owen Steele*, p. 191.

31. Edmonds, *Military Operations France and Belgium, 1916*, i, p. 436.

32. Ibid.; Philpott, *Bloody Victory*, p. 196; Facey-Crowther, *Lieutenant Owen Steele*, pp. 194–95.

33. The classic account of this is in Falls, *History of the 36th (Ulster) Division*, but see also Orr, *Road to the Somme*, pp. 140–90.

34. Buchan, *Battle of the Somme: First Phase*, p. 33. For a well-founded corrective to this view, see Bowman, *Carson's Army*, pp. 163–75.

35. Nasson, *Springboks on the Somme*, pp. 123–29; Philpott, *Bloody Victory*, pp. 239–41.

36. Information extracted from www.cwgc.org (accessed 25 Nov 2014).

37. Miles, *Military Operations France and Belgium, 1916*, ii, p. 108; Nasson, *Springboks on the Somme*, pp. 129–38.

38. Ibid., pp. 219–36; *The Times*, 11 Oct 1926.

39. Nasson, *Springboks on the Somme*, pp. 237–41.

40. Beaumont, *Broken Nation*, pp. 189–200; 'Faces of our dead: Australians killed at the First World War Battle of Fromelles in 1916 identified', 26 May 2014, on www.news.com.au (accessed, 24 Nov 2014).

41. Bean, *The A.I.F. in France*, p. 862; idem., *The Story of Anzac*, ii, p. 909.
42. Ziino, *A Distant Grief*, pp. 52, 161; Beaumont, *Broken Nation*, pp. 216–17.
43. McGibbon, *New Zealand Battlefields*, pp. 18, 31, 57; *New Zealand Herald*, 10 Oct 1922.
44. Jünger, *Storm of Steel*, pp. 97–8, 100.
45. Sheldon, *German Army on the Somme*, pp. 277–78.
46. Ibid., pp. 293–94; Ebelshauser, *The Passage*, pp. 86, 91.
47. Pidgeon, *The Tanks at Flers*, pp. 132, 172.
48. Max von Gallwitz, *Erleben im Westen 1916–1918* (Berlin, 1932), pp. 109–10 (quoted in Duffy, *Through German Eyes*, pp. 208–09).
49. Kramer, 'Blockade and economic warfare', in Winter (ed,.), *The First World War*, ii, p. 486.
50. Sheldon, *German Army on the Somme*, pp. 273–75.
51. Aitken, *Gallipoli to the Somme*, p. 154.

10: **The Eastern Mediterranean and Balkans**

1. *The Times*, 18 Oct 1916.
2. I have used the accounts in Kitromilides (ed.), *Eleftherios Venizelos*, and Dutton, *The Politics of Diplomacy*, for the general narrative of Allied and Greek relations between 1914 and 1916.
3. Lloyd George to Grey, 7 Feb 1915 (quoted in Dutton, *The Politics of Diplomacy*, 27); Aspinall-Oglander, *Gallipoli*, i, pp. 63–4.
4. Attlee typescript war memoirs (Lancashire Infantry Museum), p. 15; Heald, *Hero and Humorist*, pp. 179–81.
5. Details about Mackenzie's military and intelligence career are drawn from his unexpectedly reliable volumes of memoirs, including *Gallipoli Memories*, *Greek Memories* and *My Life and Times*.
6. Jeffery, *MI6*, pp. 124–26; Falls, *First World War*, p. 120; idem., *Macedonia*, p. 99.
7. Mackenzie, *My Life and Times Octave Five*, pp. 29–49; idem., *Greek Memories*, p. 50.
8. Ibid., p. 343; Falls, *Macedonia*, pp. 124, 131–33; Kitromilides (ed.), *Eleftherios Venizelos*, p. 124.
9. Falls, *Macedonia*, pp. 218–24; *The Times*, 4 Dec 1916.
10. Mackenzie, *Greek Memories*, pp. 473–81; Mackenzie to 'C', 1 Jan 1917 (Mackenzie papers (Harry Ransom Humanities Research Center, University of Texas at Austin), Works I/Aegean Memories folder, fol. 78).
11. Ibid.; Eliot to Mackenzie, 27 Dec 1916 (Mackenzie papers, folder recip. E.); Jeffery, *MI6*, 127–28.
12. Mackenzie, *Extremes Meet*, pp. 21, 23, 60, 70.
13. *Daily Telegraph*, 27 Oct 1932.
14. Jeffery, *MI6*, Mackenzie, *My Life and Times Octave Seven*, pp. 80–100.
15. *The Times*, 13 Jan 1933; Mackenzie, *Ægean Memories*, p. vii.

16. Mitrović, *Serbia's Great War*, p. 102. This is the best single English-language account, and I have drawn on it for the Serbian narrative.

17. Reed, *The War in Eastern Europe*, pp. v–vi.

18. Ibid., pp. 29, 35–6, 43, 87; Yovanovitch, *Les effets économiques et sociaux de la guerre*, pp. 5, 200.

19. Reed, *The War in Eastern Europe*, p. 331.

20. Yovanovitch, *Les effets économiques et sociaux de la guerre*, p. 304.

21. Gordon-Smith, *Through the Serbian Campaign*, pp. 164–74.

22. Sandes, *Autobiography*, p. 9; idem, *An English Woman-Sergeant*, p. 63; MacMahon, 'Captain Flora Sandes'.

23. Sandes, *Autobiography*, p. 12; idem, *An English Woman-Sergeant*, pp. 140–51; *Le Matin*, 7 Aug 1916. The story also appeared in the *New York Times*, 8 Aug 1916. For a stimulating discussion of Sandes' stereotype-challenging experiences, see Lee, 'A nurse and a soldier'.

24. Mitrović, *Serbia's Great War*, pp. 154–64; Tounda-Fergadi, 'The Serbian troops on Corfu', pp. 29–40.

25. Mitrović, *Serbia's Great War*, pp. 245–77.

26. Dutton, *The Politics of Diplomacy*, p. 14.

27. Starling and Lee, *No Labour, No Battle*, pp. 169–72.

28. McIlwain diary (IWM) and 'First to land in Salonika' in *The Mosquito*, Dec 1934 (both quoted in Sandford, *Neither Unionist nor Nationalist*, pp. 178–79).

29. The account which follows is drawn from the British official history, Falls, *Macedonia*, and the best modern English-language account, Wakefield and Moody, *Under the Devil's Eye*.

30. Curtayne, *Francis Ledwidge*, p. 139.

31. Falls, *Macedonia*, pp. 104–05.

32. Hoffmann, *The War of Lost Opportunities*, pp. 123–28.

33. Falls, *Macedonia*, pp. 107–12.

34. Campbell diary (quoted in Johnstone, *Orange, Green and Khaki*, pp. 259–60); Mitchell and Smith, *Medical services*, pp. 187, 194.

35. Thornton, 'Rivalries', pp. 567–68.

36. Bruce, *The Last Crusade*, provides a succinct account of the Suez fighting and the Palestine campaign.

37. Erickson, *Ordered to Die*, p. 155.

38. MacMunn and Falls, *Military Operations Egypt and Palestine*, pp. 23, 247.

39. Khaldidi, 'The Arab experience', p. 647. I have drawn on this essay and Strachan, *The First World War*, chap. 8, for the discussion here.

40. Andrew and Kanya-Forstner, *France Overseas*, pp. 66–7; Antonius, *The Arab Awakening*, pp. 185–90; Abramson, 'Haim Nahnias', p. 23.

41. Melman, 'Re-generation', pp. 130–33.

42. Abramson, 'Haim Nahnias', pp. 18–21; Aaronsohn, *With the Turks*, chs 2, 4 and 11; Jeffery, *MI6*, p. 132.

43. For the McMahon–Husayn correspondence, see Kedourie, *In the Anglo-Arab Labyrinth*.

44. There are good accounts of the Sykes–Picot agreement in Andrew and Kanya-Forstner, *France Overseas*, pp. 87–102, and Barr, *A Line in the Sand*, pp. 7–35.

45. Antonius, *The Arab Awakening*, pp. 227–28.

46. The most reliable accounts of the postwar Franco-British partition of the Middle East are in Andrew and Kanya-Forstner, *France Overseas*, pp. 164–208, and Darwin, *Britain, Egypt and the Middle East*, pp. 143–242.

47. Satia, *Spies in Arabia*, provides a valuable exploration of the cultural context of British imperialism in the Middle East.

11: The USA

1. 12 Sep 1914 (quoted in Thompson, *Woodrow Wilson*, p. 99).

2. Both quoted in Brogan, *Pelican History of the USA*, pp. 481–82.

3. Tumelty, *Woodrow Wilson*, p. 457.

4. 'An appeal to the American people', 18 Aug 14 (Link (ed.), *Papers of Woodrow Wilson*, vol. 30, pp. 393–94).

5. Pacyga, *Chicago*, p. 193.

6. Thompson, *Woodrow Wilson*, pp. 104–05. This book provides an excellent, focused account of Wilson's war policy.

7. Zieger, 'She didn't raise her boy to be a slacker', pp. 9–12.

8. See the discussion in Devlin, *Too Proud to Fight*, pp. 288–89.

9. Baker and Dodd (eds), *The New Democracy*, i, pp. 351–55.

10. Devlin, *Too Proud to Fight*, 283–315; *NYT*, 1 Jul 1915; *Evening Post* quoted in Thompson, *Woodrow Wilson*, p. 115.

11. Link (ed.), *Papers of Woodrow Wilson*, vol. 36, pp. 33, 64, 47, 92.

12. Jensen, *Mobilizing Minerva*, pp. 41–3.

13. The progress of this scheme is covered in great detail in Devlin, *Too Proud to Fight*, pp. 376–492.

14. Ibid., p. 437.

15. Link (ed.), *Papers of Woodrow Wilson*, vol. 37, pp. 113–16.

16. Baker, *Woodrow Wilson*, p. 253.

17. O'Leary to Wilson and reply, 29 Sep 1916 (Link (ed.), *Papers of Woodrow Wilson*, vol. 38, pp. 285–86).

18. Winslow, *With the French Flying Corps*, p. 8.

19. La Motte, *Backwash of War*, 148; [AFS], *History of the American Field Service*, i, p. 18.

20. Letters of 20 Sep; 2, 8, and 27 Oct 1915 ([Derr], *Mademoiselle Miss*, 12, 19–21, 23, 27). Biographical information from http://mademoisellemiss-continued.wordpress.com (accessed 11 Oct 2014).

21. Letters of 16 Jan 1916 and 27 Oct 1915 ([Derr], *Mademoiselle Miss*, 61–7).

22. Hallett, *Containing Trauma*, p. 13.

23. La Motte, *Backwash of War*, iii, pp. 3–4, 15–32, 93–111.

24. Borden, *The Forbidden Zone*, v, pp. 96–102. For Borden, see Conway, *A Woman of Two Wars*.

25. Borden, *The Forbidden Zone*, pp. 117, 145–46, 140–41.

26. Quoted in http://mademoisellemisscontinued.wordpress.com (accessed 12 Oct 2014).

27. Letter of 27 Oct 1915 ([Derr], *Mademoiselle Miss*, 26).

28. Hansen, *Gentlemen Volunteers*, pp. 39–40.

29. [AFS], *History of the American Field Service*, i, p. 18. The following account of the AFS draws on this handsome, detailed and celebratory three-volume history published in 1920.

30. [AFS], *History of the American Field Service*, i, pp. 19–20, 24; iii, p. 440.

31. Ibid., p. 28.

32. Ibid., i, pp. 221–26. Sheahan covered some of the same ground in a memoir, *A Volunteer Poilu* (Boston, 1916).

33 Ibid., i, pp. 420–22, 448–49, 456. For cannibalism, see Seabrook, *Jungle Ways*.

34. Hynes, *The Unsubstantial Air*, pp. 1–12.

35. Winslow, *With the French Flying Corps*, pp. 145, 151, 197.

36. Hynes, *The Unsubstantial Air*, p. 96.

37. McConnell, *Flying for France*, pp. 55, 130.

38. Haycock, 'The American Legion'.

39. Ross, *Propaganda for War*, pp. 91–144, covers German activities.

40. Details of the Albert affair are in McAdoo, *Crowded Years*, pp. 323–30. William McAdoo, as Secretary of the Treasury, was in charge of the Secret Service.

41. Ross, *Propaganda for War*, pp. 48–50, 75–80.

42. Dimmel, 'Sabotage, security, and border-crossing', pp. 407–08; Jennifer D. Keene, 'North America' in Winter (ed.), *Cambridge History*, i, p. 523; Kitchen, 'The German invasion of Canada'.

43. Doerries, *Imperial Challenge*, pp. 176–85; Thwaites, *Velvet and Vinegar*, p. 134; Andrew, *For the President's Eyes Only*, pp. 33–4.

44. Ibid., p. 35; Beesley, *Room 40*, pp. 229–31.

45. *NYT*, 31 Jul, 1 Aug 1916.

46. Ibid., 10 Aug 1916, 16 Jun 1939; Doerries, *Imperial Challenge*, pp. 188–89.

47. Popplewell, *Intelligence and Imperial Defence*, p. 247. For a pioneering overview, see Fraser, 'Germany and Indian revolution'.

48. Popplewell, *Intelligence and Imperial Defence*, pp. 248–52; Thwaites, *Velvet and Vinegar*, pp. 144–49.

49. Jeffery, *MI6*, p. 110; Gaunt, *The Yield of the Years*, p. 172; Spence, 'Englishmen in New York'.

50. Memo. on scope and activities of MI1(c) in New York, 27 Apr 1918 (Wiseman papers, Yale University Library [YUL], box 6, folder 174).

51. Thwaites, *Velvet and Vinegar*, pp. 153–55; Gaunt, *The Yield of the Years*, pp. 192–93; Mackenzie, *Greek Memories*, p. 407.

52. House diary, 17 Dec 1916, 15 Jan 1917; House to Wilson, 26 Jan 1917 (YUL, House papers, diary vols 4–5; box 121, folder 4272).

53. House diary, 23 Feb; 7 Mar (YUL, House papers, diary, vol. 5); 'Relations between the United States and Great Britain', endorsed by House, 8 Mar 1917 (ibid., box 123, folder 4324); and as circulated in Britain in Spring-Rice to Foreign Office, 8 Mar 1917 (British Library, Balfour papers, Add. 49740, fols 96–8).

54. Fowler, *British–American Relations*; Bruce Lockhart, 'Sir William Wiseman Bart, agent of influence'.

12: Russia

1. There is a very extensive literature on Rasputin, which includes much rubbish. De Jonge, *Life and Times*, is encouragingly unsensational (or as unsensational as might reasonably be hoped).

2. Lieven, 'Russia, Europe and World War I', p. 45.

3. Hoare to C, 31 Dec 1916; 1 Jan 1917 (CUL, Templewood papers, II:1, 47 and 48); Hoare, *The Fourth Seal*, p. 133.

4. Hoare to Browning, 1/2 Jan 1917 (ibid., II:1, 49); details of British intelligence organisation and personnel are from Jeffery, *MI6*.

5. 'The death of Rasputin' (CUL, Templewood papers, II:1, 16).

6. Ibid.

7. 'A watchman makes his rounds' (TS memoir) (ibid., II:1, 34). Hoare drew on this text for his published memoirs, *The Fourth Seal*.

8. Hoare, *The Fourth Seal*, p. 157. Buchanan made no mention of this in his memoirs, *My Mission to Russia*.

9. Quoted in De Jonge, *Life and Times*, p. 310.

10. Hoare, *The Fourth Seal*, p. 68.

11. Cullen, *Rasputin*. The argument in this book is disablingly under-referenced. See also Smith, *Six*, pp. 196–201.

12. Hoare, *The Fourth Seal*, pp. 159–60.

13. *Daily Mail*, 2, 3 Jan 1917.

14. Ibid., 4, 6 Jan 1917.

15. Ibid., 1 Feb 1917.

16. Jeffery, 'Kruger's farmers', pp. 190–91. The notion that Britain's strategic reassessment, especially with regard to Russia, was the result of weakness has been challenged in Neilson, *Britain and the Last Tsar*.

17. Wilson diary, 13 Oct 1910 (IWM).

18. Jeffery, *MI6*, pp. 32–3.

19. Neilson, *Britain and the Last Tsar*, pp. 342–33.

20. Pares, *My Russian Memoirs*, pp. 276–77, 343.

21. Hughes, *Inside the Enigma*, p. 56.

22. Ibid., p. 54; Hanbury-Williams, *The Emperor Nicholas II*, p. 1; Stone, *Eastern Front*, p. 151; Neilson, *Strategy and Supply*, pp. 29–33.

23. Quoted in Neilson, 'Joy rides'?, p. 885.

24. Gen. G. M. W. Macdonogh (DMI) to General Sir Henry Wilson, 14 Jan 1917 (IWM, Wilson papers, HHW 3/12/59); Jeffery, *MI6*, pp. 99–104.

25. *The Times*, 13, 16, 23 Aug 1952.

26. Baird to Hoare, 13 Feb (CUL, Templewood papers, II.1.36); Hoare, *The Fourth Seal*, pp. 8–29.

27. Cumming and Frank Stagg (Secret Service Bureau) to Hoare, 11, 12 May; Frank Stagg (Secret Service Bureau) to Hoare, 11 May 1916; 'Instructions to the Agent in charge of the Mission to Petrograd', n.d. (CUL, Templewood papers, II.1.38–41);

28. Bruce Lockhart, *Memoirs of a British Agent*, pp. 137–38.

29. 'A watchman makes his rounds' (TS memoir) (CUL, Templewood papers, II:1, 34).

30. Wilson diary, 6 Jun 1916 (IWM).

31. Lloyd George to Asquith, 28 Sep 1916 (quoted in Neilson, *Strategy and Supply*, pp. 225–26); French, *The Strategy of the Lloyd George Coalition*, p. 45.

32. The best account of the Mission is in Neilson, *Strategy and Supply*, pp. 225–48. Details of the journey from Jeffery, *Sir Henry Wilson*, pp. 184–85.

33. Milner quoted in Neilson, *Strategy and Supply*, p. 236; Wilson diary, 29 Jan–16 Feb 1917 (IWM).

34. Bruce Lockhart, *Memoirs of a British Agent*, p. 162; Hoare, *The Fourth Seal*, pp. 203–4; 'A watchman makes his rounds' (CUL: Templewood papers, II:1, 34).

35. Engelstein, *The Keys to Happiness*, p. 421.

36. Hoare, *The Fourth Seal*, p. 177; Buchanan, *My Mission to Russia*, p. 77.

37. Ibid., p. 17; Paleologue quoted in Warth, *Nicholas II*, p. 220.

38. Sanborn, *Drafting the Russian Nation*, p. 5.

39. Diary entry, 31 Jul 1916 (Knox, *With the Russian Army*, pp. 460–61).

40. Holquist, *Making War, Forging Revolution*, pp. 26–36.

41. Engel, 'Subsistence riots'.

42. Rogger, *Russia*, pp. 257–66.

43. Engel, 'Subsistence riots', p. 712; Holquist, *Making War, Forging Revolution*, p. 36.

44. In the words of General Max Hoffmann. See his 1924 book, *The War of Lost Opportunities*, for an extended discussion of this notion from a German perspective.

45. Sugarman, 'The Zion Muleteers of Gallipoli'.

46. Holquist, 'Violent Russia', p. 630.

47. Foster, *Vivid Faces*, pp. xvi, 68–9.

48. Lenin, 'The discussion on self-determination summed up', in idem., *Collected Works*, pp. 353–58.

Conclusion: The Potential for Peace in 1916

1. Lloyd George, *War Memoirs*, pp. 862–73.
2. Ibid., pp. 853–55. There is a sharply observed and intelligent analysis of the Lansdowne memorandum and its context in Larsen, 'British intelligence and American neutrality', pp. 91–174.
3. Fischer, *Germany's Aims*, pp. 295–309.
4. The Secretary of State to the Ambassadors and Ministers in Belligerent Countries, 18 Dec 1916 (*Papers Relating to the Foreign Relations of the United States, 1916: Supplement, The World War*, Document 132 (https://history.state.gov/historicaldocuments/frus1916Supp/d132) (accessed 1 Feb 2015); Devlin, *Too Proud to Fight*, p. 578.
5. Stevenson, *The First World War and International Politics*, pp. 136–37.
6. *The Mail* (Adelaide, S. Australia), 23 Nov 1929; *Sydney Morning Herald* and *The Times*, 26 Apr 1934.
7. Mango, *Atatürk*, p. 505.
8. Ibid.; Aspinall-Oglander, *Gallipoli*, ii, p. 485; *Adelaide News*, 25 May 1932; *The Times*, 4 and 7 Sep 1936.
9. This is the text as reproduced on the Turkish memorial at Anzac Cove on Gallipoli, and on the Kemal Atatürk Memorial, Anzac Parade, Canberra (among other places). For its provenance, see Jones, 'A note on Atatürk's words' and Davies, 'Anzac Day meanings', pp. 210–17. There is considerable debate about the contemporary political use of the statement. See, for example, Peter Stanley and David Stephens, 'Ataturk's "letter" expresses admirable sentiment but is not necessarily good history' (*Sydney Morning Herald*, 8 Sep 2014).
10. Schindler, *Isonzo*, p. 347.
11. *1916–1966 Cinquantenaire de la bataille de Verdun* (souvenir brochure).
12. *New York Times*, 23 Sep 1984.
13. *L'Est Republicain* (Meuse), 10 Feb 2014.
14. Kettle, *The Ways of War*, pp. 10, 57, 71.
15. Jeffery, *Ireland and the Great War*, pp. 138–43.
16. *Canberra Times*, 26 Apr 1985.
17. Sinn Féin did, however, reverse its stance for Queen Elizabeth's visit to Northern Ireland in June 2012. These matters are discussed in my essay, 'Commemoration and the hazards of Irish politics', in Ziino (ed.), *Remembering the First World War*, pp. 165–85.
18. *L'Est Republicain* (Meuse), 10 Feb 2014.
19. *Hansard* (House of Commons), 16 Feb 1922, col. 1270.
20. Lussu, *Sardinian Brigade*, p. 132.

Bibliography

This bibliography lists secondary sources. Primary sources are given full citations in the reference notes.

Aaronsohn, Alexander, *With the Turks in Palestine* (London, 1917)

Abramson, Glenda, 'Haim Nahnias and the labour battalions: a diary of two years in the First World War', *Jewish Culture and History*, 14/1 (2013), pp. 18–32

[AFS (American Field Service)], *History of the American Field Service in France*, 3 vols (Boston, 1920)

Ageron, Charles-Robert, *Les Algériens musulmans et la France (1871–1919)*, ii (Paris, 1968)

Aitken, Alexander, *Gallipoli to the Somme: Recollections of a New Zealand Infantryman* (London, 1963)

Albert, Bill (with Paul Henderson), *South America and the First World War: The Impact of the War on Brazil, Argentina, Peru and Chile* (Cambridge, 1988)

Allen, W. E. D., and Muratoff, Paul, *Caucasian Battlefields: A History of the Wars on the Turco-Caucasian Border, 1828–1921* (Cambridge, 1953)

Andrew, Christopher, *The Defence of the Realm: The Authorized History of MI5* (London, pbk edn 2010)

—— *For the President's Eyes Only: Secret Intelligence and the American Presidency from Washington to Bush* (London, 1995)

Andrew, Christopher M., and Kanya-Forstner, A. S., *France Overseas: The Great War and the Climax of French Imperial Expansion* (London, 1981)

Anon., *British Civilian Prisoners in German East Africa: A Report by the Government Committee on the Treatment by the Enemy of British Prisoners of War* (London, 1918)

—— *History of* The Times: *The 150th Anniversary and Beyond, 1912–1948*, 2 vols (London, 1952)

Antonius, George, *The Arab Awakening: The Story of the Arab National Movement* (London, 1938)

Ashworth, Tony, *Trench Warfare, 1914–1918: The Live and Let Live System* (London, 1980)

Aspinall-Oglander, C.F., *Military Operations Gallipoli*, 2 vols (London, 1929 and 1932)

Association Nationale pour le Souvenir des Dardanelles et Fronts d'Orient, *Dardanelles Orient Levant 1915–1921: Ce que les Combattants ont écrit* (Paris, 2005)

Baker, Ray Stannard, *Woodrow Wilson: Life and Letters*, vi, *Facing War 1915–1917* (London, n.d. [1937])

—— and Dodd, William E. (eds), *The New Democracy: Presidential Messages, Addresses, and Other Papers (1913–1917) by Woodrow Wilson*, 2 vols (New York, 1926)

Ball, Simon, *The Guardsmen: Harold Macmillan, Three Friends, and the World They Made* (London, 2004)

Barker, A. J., *The Neglected War: Mesopotamia 1914–1918* (London, 1967)

Barr, James, *A Line in the Sand: Britain, France and the Struggle for the Mastery of the Middle East* (London, 2011)

Barrett, Michèle, 'Death and the afterlife: Britain's colonies and dominions', in Sananu Das (ed.), *Race, Empire and First World War Writing* (Cambridge, 2011), pp. 301–20

Bartlett, Thomas, *Ireland: A History* (Cambridge, 2010)

Bean, C. E. W., *Anzac to Amiens* (Canberra, 1946 [1983 reprint]). http://static.awm.gov.au/images/collection/pdf/RCDIG1069802-1-.PDF (accessed 1 Dec. 2014)

——*Official History of Australia in the War of 1914–1918*, i, *The Story of Anzac: from the Outbreak of the War to the End of the First Phase of the Gallipoli Campaign, May 4, 1915* (13th edn, Sydney, 1942)

——*Official History of Australia in the War of 1914–1918*, ii, *The Story of Anzac: from 4 May 1915 to the Evacuation* (13th edn, Sydney, 1944)

——*Official History of Australia in the War of 1914–1918*, iii, *The A.I.F. in France 1916* (13th edn, Sydney, 1942)

Beaumont, Joan, *Broken Nation: Australians in the Great War* (Crows Nest, NSW, 2013)

Becker, Jean-Jacques, *The Great War and the French People* (Leamington Spa, 1985)

Beckett, Francis, *Clem Attlee* (London, 1997)

Beckett, Ian F. W., *The Great War* (2nd edn, Harlow, 2007)

Beesley, Patrick, *Room 40: British Naval Intelligence 1914–1918* (Oxford, 1984)

Bergère, Marie-Claire, *Sun Yat-sen* (Stanford, 1998)

Bethell, Leslie (ed.), *Cambridge History of Latin America*, v, *c. 1870 to 1930* (Cambridge, 1986)

Binyon, Laurence, *For Dauntless France: An Account of Britain's Aid to the French Wounded and Victims of the War* (London, 1918)

Birdwood, Field Marshal Lord, *Khaki and Gown: An Autobiography* (London, 1941)

Bisset, W. M., 'Unexplored aspects of South Africa's First World War history', *Scientia Militaria, South African Journal of Military Studies*, 6/3 1976), pp. 55–61

Bloom, Cecil, 'Colonel Patterson, soldier and Zionist', *Jewish Historical Studies*, 31 (1988–90), pp. 231–48

Blunt, Wilfrid, *Lady Muriel* (London, 1962)

Borden, Mary, *The Forbidden Zone* (London, 1929)

Bowman, Timothy, *Carson's Army: The Ulster Volunteer Force, 1910–22* (Manchester, 2007)

Boyd, William, *An Ice-Cream War* (London, 1982)

Brian, Denis, *The Seven Lives of Colonel Patterson: How an Irish Lion Hunter Led the Jewish Legion to Victory* (Syracuse, NY, 2008)

Bridgland, Tony, and Morgan, Anne, *Tunnel-Master and Arsonist of the Great War: The Norton-Griffiths Story* (Barnsley, 2003)

Briggs, J. H., 'German East Africa during the war', *Journal of the African Society*, 16/63 (Apr. 1917), pp. 193–99

Broadbent, Harvey, *Gallipoli: The Fatal Shore* (Camberwell, Vic., 2005)

Broadberry, Stephen, and Harrison, Mark (eds), *The Economics of World War I* (Cambridge, 2005)

Brogan, Hugh, *The Pelican History of the United States of America* (Harmondsworth, 1986)

Brower, Daniel, 'Kyrgyz nomads and Russian pioneers: colonization and ethnic conflict in the Turkestan revolt of 1916', *Jahrbücher für Geschichte Osteuropas*, new series, 44/1 (1996), pp. 41–53

Bruce, Anthony, *The Last Crusade: The Palestine Campaign in the First World War* (London, 2002)

Bruce Lockhart, John, 'Sir William Wiseman Bart—agent of influence', *RUSI Journal*, 134/2 (Summer 1989), pp. 63–7

Bruce Lockhart, R. H., *Memoirs of a British Agent* (London, 1932)

Brussilov, A. A., *A Soldier's Note-Book, 1914–1918* (London, 1930)

Buchan, John, *The Battle of the Somme: First Phase* (London, n.d. [?1917])
—*Greenmantle* (Pan edn, London, 1947)

Buchanan, Sir George, *My Mission to Russia and Other Diplomatic Memories*, ii (London, 1923)

Cahill, Audrey Fawcett (ed.), *Between the Lines: Letters and Diaries from Elsie Inglis's Russian Unit* (Bishop Auckland, Co. Durham, 1999)

Callwell, Charles, *The Dardanelles* (London, 1919)

Cameron, David W., *Gallipoli: the Final Battles and Evacuation of Anzac* (Newport, NSW, 2011)

Campbell, N. J. M., *Jutland: An Analysis of the Fighting* (London, 1986)

Cannadine, David, *G. M. Trevelyan: A Life in History* (London, 1992)

Carden, Ron M., *German Policy Toward Neutral Spain, 1914–1918* (London, 1987)

Cassar, George H., *The French and the Dardanelles: A Study of Failure in the Conduct of War* (London, 1971)

Ceauşesu, Ilie, 'The Romanian army in World War I', in Béla K. Király and Nándor F. Dreisziger (eds), *East Central European Society in World War I* (Boulder COL, 1985), pp. 513–27

Cecil, Hugh, and Liddle, Peter (eds), *Facing Armageddon: The First World War Experienced* (London, 1996)

Chhina, Rana, 'Their mercenary calling: the Indian Army at Gallipoli, 1915', in Ekins (ed.), *Gallipoli*, pp. 356–98

Chickering, Roger, *The Great War and Urban Life in Germany: Freiburg 1914–1918* (Cambridge, 2007)

Churchill, Winston S., *The World Crisis 1915* (London, 1923)

—*The World Crisis 1916–1918*, part I (London, 1927)

Clark, Alan, *The Donkeys* (London, 1961)

Clark, Christopher, *The Sleepwalkers: How Europe went to War in 1914* (London, 2012)

Colvin, Ian, *The Life of Lord Carson*, iii (London, 1936)

Conway, Jane, *A Woman of Two Wars: The Life of Mary Borden* (n.p., 2010)

Cooper, Bryan, *The Tenth (Irish) Division in Gallipoli* (London, 1918)

Cornwall, Mark, 'Austria-Hungary and "Yugoslavia"', in Horne (ed.), *A Companion to World War I*, pp. 371–85

Coulson, Thomas, *The Queen of Spies: Louise de Bettignies* (London, 1935)

Crane, David, *Empires of the Dead: How One Man's Vision Led to the Creation of WWI's War Graves* (London, 2013)

Cranworth, Lord, *Kenya Chronicles* (London, 1939)

Crews, Robert D., *For Prophet and Tsar: Islam and Empire in Russia and Central Asia* (Cambridge MA, 2006)

Crowe, J. H. V., *General Smuts' Campaign in East Africa* (London, 1918)

Cruttwell, C. R. M. F., *A History of the Great War, 1914–1918* (Oxford, 2nd edn 1936)

Cullen, Richard, *Rasputin: The Role of Britain's Secret Service in His Torture and Murder* (London, 2010)

Curtayne, Alice, *Francis Ledwidge: A Life of the Poet* (Dublin, 1998)

Daly, M. W., *Empire on the Nile: The Anglo-Egyptian Sudan, 1898–1934* (Cambridge, 1986)

Daly, Mary E. (ed.), *Roger Casement in Irish and World History* (Dublin, 2005)

Darwin, John, *Britain, Egypt and the Middle East: Imperial Policy in the Aftermath of War, 1918–1922* (London, 1981)

Davies, George Frederick, 'Anzac Day meanings and memories: New Zealand, Australian and Turkish perspectives on a day of commemoration in the twentieth century' (unpublished PhD thesis, University of Otago, 2009)

Davies, Harry, *Allanson of the 6th: An Account of the Life of Cecil John Lyons Allanson* (Worcester, 1990)

Davis, Elmer, *History of the New York Times, 1851–1921* (New York, 1921)

Decsy, János, 'The Habsburg army on the threshold of total war', in Király and Dreisziger (eds), *East Central European Society*, pp. 280–88

Dehne, Phillip, *On the Far Western Front: Britain's First World War in South America* (Manchester, 2009)

De Jonge, Alex, *The Life and Times of Grigorii Rasputin* (London, 1982)

Delage, Edmond, *The Tragedy of the Dardanelles* (London, 1932)

Denholm, Decie (ed.), *Behind the Lines: One Woman's War 1914–18: The Letters of Caroline Ethel Cooper* (London, 1982)

Denman, Terence, *Ireland's Unknown Soldiers: The 16th (Irish) Division in the Great War* (Dublin, 1992)

[Derr, Norman], *'Mademoiselle Miss': Letters From an American Girl Serving With the Rank of Lieutenant in a French Army Hospital at the Front* (Boston, 1916)

Desagneaux, Henri, *A French Soldier's War Diary, 1914–1918* (Morley, Yorks, 1975)

Devlin, Patrick, *Too Proud to Fight: Woodrow Wilson's Neutrality* (London, 1974)

Digre, Brian, *Imperialism's New Clothes: The Repartition of Tropical Africa, 1914–1919* (New York, 1990)

Dijk, Kees van, *The Netherlands Indies and the Great War, 1914–1918* (Leiden, 2007)

Dimmel, Brandon, 'Sabotage, security and border-crossing culture: the Detroit River during the First World War, 1914–1918', *Histoire Sociale/Social History*, 47/94 (June 2014)

Dodwell, H. H. (ed.), *Cambridge History of India*, VI, *The Indian Empire, 1858–1918* (Cambridge, 1932)

Doerries, Reinhard R., *Imperial Challenge: Ambassador Count Bernstorff and German–American Relations, 1908–1917* (Chapel Hill, NC, 1989)

Dowling, Timothy C., *The Brusilov Offensive* (Bloomington, IN, 2008)

Dudgeon, Jeffrey, *Roger Casement: The Black Diaries* (Belfast, 2002)

Duffy, Christopher, *Through German Eyes: The British and the Somme 1916* (London, 2006)

Dutton, David, *The Politics of Diplomacy: Britain and France in the Balkans in the First World War* (London, 1998)

Ebelshauser, G. A., *The Passage: A Tragedy of the Great War*, ed. Richard Baumgartner (Huntington, WV, 1984)

Echenberg, Myron, *Colonial Conscripts: The Tirailleurs Sénégalais in French West Africa, 1857–1960* (London, 1991)

Edmonds, James E., *Military Operations France and Belgium, 1916*, i (London, 1932)

Ekins, Ashley (ed.), *Gallipoli: A Ridge too Far* (Large print edn: Wollombi, NSW, 2013)

Ellinwood, DeWitt C., and Pradhan, S. D. (eds), *India and World War I* (New Delhi, 1978)

Engel, Barbara Alpern, 'Not by bread alone: subsistence riots in Russia during World War I', *Journal of Modern History*, 69/4 (Dec. 1997), pp. 696–721

Engelstein, Laura, *The Keys to Happiness: Sex and the Search for Modernity in Fin-de-Siècle Russia* (Ithaca NY, 1992)

Erickson, Edward J., *Gallipoli: The Ottoman Campaign* (Barnsley, Yorks, 2010)

—— *Ordered to Die: A History of the Ottoman Army in the First World War* (Westport CON, 2001)

Ervine, St John, *Some Impressions of My Elders* (London, 1923)

—— 'The Story of the Irish Rebellion', *Century Magazine*, 93/1 (Nov. 1916), pp. 22–39

Facey-Crowther, David (ed.), *Lieutenant Owen Steele of the Newfoundland Regiment: Diary and Letters* (Montreal, 2002)

Falkenhayn, Erich von, *General Headquarters 1914–1916 and its Critical Decisions* (London, n.d. [1919])

Falls, Cyril, *The First World War* (London, 1960)

—— *The History of the 36th (Ulster) Division* (Belfast, 1922)

—— *Military Operations Macedonia*, i, *From the Outbreak of War to the Spring of 1917* (London, 1933)

Fanning, Ronan, *Fatal Path: British Government and Irish Revolution, 1910–1922* (London, 2013)

Farmborough, Florence, *Nurse at the Russian Front: A Diary 1914–18 (London, 1974)*

Fewster, Joseph Daniel, 'A Hull sergeant's Great War diary' (ed. Robert B. Sylvester), South African Military History Society, 1999 (http://samilitary-history.org/diaries/zgead1.html) (accessed 4 June 2014)

Fewster, Kevin, Başarm, Vecihi, and Başarm, Hürmüz, *Gallipoli: The Turkish Story* (Crow's Nest, NSW, 2003)

Fischer, Fritz, *Germany's Aims in the First World War* (London, 1967)

Fitzroy, Yvonne, *With the Scottish Nurses in Roumania* (London, 1918)

Foster, R. F., *Vivid Faces: The Revolutionary Generation in Ireland, 1890–1923* (London, 2014)

Fowler, W. B., *British–American Relations 1917–1918: The Role of Sir William Wiseman* (Princeton, 1969)

Fox, Sir Frank, *The Royal Inniskilling Fusiliers in the World War* (London, 1928)

Foy, Michael T., and Barton, Brian, *The Easter Rising* (rev. edn, Stroud, Glos., 2011)

Fraser, Thomas G., 'Germany and Indian revolution, 1914–18', *Journal of Contemporary History*, 12/2 (Apr. 1977), pp. 255–72

French, David, *The Strategy of the Lloyd George Coalition, 1916–1918* (Oxford, 1995)

Gál, Joseph, *In Death's Fortress* (Boulder CO, 1991)

Galántai, József, *Hungary in the First World War* (Budapest, 1989)

Galassi, Francesco, and Harrison, Mark, 'Italy at war, 1915–1918', in Broadberry and Harrison (eds), *The Economics of World War I*, pp. 276–309

Gallagher, John (ed. Anil Seal), *The Decline, Revival and Fall of the British Empire* (Cambridge, 1982)

Gardner, Nikolas, 'Sepoys and the siege of Kut-al-Amara, December 1915–April 1916', *War in History*, 11/3 (2004), pp. 307–26

Gatrell, Peter, *A Whole Empire Walking: Refugees in Russia during World War I* (Bloomington, 1999)

Gaunt, Sir Guy, *The Yield of the Years: A Story of Adventure Afloat and Ashore* (London, 1940)

Gewarth, Robert, and Manela, Erez (eds), *Empires at War 1911–1923* (Oxford, 2014)

Gibelli, Antonio, 'Italy', in Horne (ed.), *A Companion to World War I*, pp. 464–78

Gilbert, Martin (ed.), *The Straits of War: Gallipoli Remembered* (Stroud, Glos., 2000)

Gleichen, Helena, *Contacts and Contrasts* (London, 1940)

Gooch, John, *The Italian Army and the First World War* (Cambridge, 2014)

Gordon-Smith, Gordon, *Through the Serbian Campaign: The Great Retreat of the Serbian Army* (London, 1916)

Government of India, *India's Contribution to the Great War* (Calcutta, 1923)

Grayson, Richard, *Belfast Boys: How Unionists and Nationalists Fought and Died Together in the First World War* (London, 2009)

——(ed.), *At War with the 16th Irish Division 1914–1918: The Staniforth Letters* (Barnsley, 2012)

Greenhalgh, Elizabeth, *Victory through Coalition: Britain and France during the First World War* (Cambridge, 2005)

——and Guelton, Frédéric, 'The French on Gallipoli', in Ekins (ed.), *Gallipoli*, pp. 323–55

Groos, Otto, *Der Krieg in der Nordsee*, v, *Von Januar bis Juni 1916* (Berlin, 1925)

Gwynn, Denis, *The Life of John Redmond* (London, 1932)

Haber, L. F., *The Poisonous Cloud: Chemical Warfare in the First World War* (Oxford, 1986)

Hallett, Christine E., *Containing Trauma: Nursing Work in the First World War* (Manchester, 2009)

Halpern, Paul G., *The Naval War in the Mediterranean 1914–1918* (London, 1987)

Hamilton, Ian, *Gallipoli Diary*, 2 vols (London, 1920)

Hanbury-Williams, John, *The Emperor Nicholas II as I Knew Him* (London, 1922)

Hankinson, Alan, *Geoffrey Winthrop Young: Poet, Educator, Mountaineer* (London, 1995)

Hansen, Arlen J., *Gentlemen Volunteers: The Story of the American Ambulance Drivers in the First World War* (New York, 1996)

Hardiman, Adrian, '"Shot in cold blood": military law and Irish perceptions in the suppression of the 1916 rebellion', in Gabriel Doherty and Dermot Keogh (eds), *1916: The Long Revolution* (Cork, 2007), pp. 225–49

Hardy, Peter, *The Muslims of British India* (Cambridge, 1972)

Harper, R. W. E., and Miller, Harry, *Singapore Mutiny* (Singapore, 1984)

Harper, Tim, 'Singapore, 1915, and the birth of the Asian underground', *Modern Asian Studies* 47/6 (Nov. 2013), pp. 1782–1811

Harris, Kenneth, *Attlee* (London, 1982)

Hart, Peter, *Gallipoli* (London, 2011)

Hase, Georg von, *Kiel and Jutland* (London, n.d. [1921])

Haycock, Ronald G., 'The American Legion in the Canadian Expeditionary Force, 1914–1917: a study in failure', *Military Affairs*, 43/3 (Oct. 1979), pp. 115–19

[Heald, Ivan], *Ivan Heald: Hero and Humorist* (London, 1917)

Higonnet, Margaret R., *Nurses at the Front: Writing the Wounds of the Great War* (Boston, 2001)

Hirama, Yoichi, 'The Anglo-Japanese Alliance and the First World War', in Ian Gow and Yoichi Hirama (eds), *The History of Anglo-Japanese Relations, 1600–2000*, iii, *The Military Dimension* (Basingstoke, 2003), pp. 51–70

Hoare, Samuel, *The Fourth Seal: The End of a Russian Chapter* (London, 1930)

Hodges, Geoffrey, *The Carrier Corps: Military Labor in the East African Campaign, 1914–1918* (New York, 1986)

Hodges, G. W. T., 'African manpower statistics for the British forces in East Africa, 1914–1918', *Journal of African History*, 19/1 (1978), pp. 101–16

Hoffmann, Max, *The War of Lost Opportunities* (London, 1924)

Holquist, Peter, *Making War, Forging Revolution: Russia's Continuum of Crisis, 1914–1921* (Cambridge MA, 2002)

—— 'To count, to extract, and to exterminate: population statistics and population politics in late imperial and soviet Russia', in Ronald Grigor Suny and Terry Martin (eds), *A State of Nations: Empire and Nation-Making in the Age of Lenin and Stalin* (Oxford, 2001), pp. 111–44

——'Violent Russia, deadly Marxism? Russia in the epoch of violence, 1905–21', in *Kritika: Explorations in Russian and Eurasian History*, 4/3 (2003), pp. 627–52

Holtom, E. C. H., *Two Years' Captivity in German East Africa* (London, n.d. [1918])

Hone, Joseph, *The Life of Henry Tonks* (London, 1939)

Hordern, *Military Operations: East Africa*, i, *August 1914–September 1916* (London, 1941)

Horne, Alastair, *The Price of Glory: Verdun 1916* (London, 1962)

Horne, John, 'Immigrant workers in France during World War I', *French Historical Studies*, 14/1 (Spring, 1985), pp. 57–88

——(ed.), *A Companion to World War I* (pbk edn, Chichester, 2012)

——(ed.), *Our War: Ireland and the Great War* (Dublin, 2008)

Howe, Glenford, *Race, War and Nationalism: A Social History of West Indians in the First World War* (Kingston, Jamaica, 2002)

Hughes, Michael, *Inside the Enigma: British Officials in Russia, 1900–1939* (London, 1997)

Hughes, Thomas L., 'The German Mission to Afghanistan, 1915–1916', *German Studies Review*, 25/3 (Oct. 2002), pp. 447–76

Hyam, Ronald, *The Failure of South African Expansion, 1908–1948* (London, 1972)

Hynes, Samuel, *The Unsubstantial Air: American Fliers in the First World War* (New York, 2014)

Iliffe, John, *A Modern History of Tanganyika* (Cambridge, 1979)

Inglis, K. S., 'Entombing unknown soldiers: from London and Paris to Baghdad', *History and Memory*, 5/2 (Fall–Winter, 1993), pp. 7–31

—— *Sacred Places: War memorials in the Australian Landscape* (Carlton South, Vic., 1998)

Jacobson, Abigail, 'A city living through crisis: Jerusalem during World War I', *British Journal of Middle Eastern Studies*, 36/1 (Apr. 2009), pp. 73–92

Jagielski, Jean-François, *Le Soldat inconnu: invention et postérité d'un symbole* (Paris, 2005)

Jankowski, Paul, *Verdun: The Longest Battle of the Great War* (Oxford, 2013)

Jarboe, Andrew Tait, and Fogarty, Richard S. (eds), *Empires in World War I: Shifting Frontiers and Imperial Dynamics in a Global Conflict* (London, 2014)

Jauffret, Jean-Charles, 'Gallipoli: a French perspective', in Gilbert (ed.), *The Straits of War*, pp. 137–51

Jefferson, George, *Edward Garnett: A Life in Literature* (London, 1982)

Jeffery, Keith, *The British Army and the Crisis of Empire* (Manchester, 1984)

—— '"An English barrack in the oriental seas"? India in the aftermath of the First World War', *Modern Asian Studies*, 15/3 (July, 1981), pp. 369–86

—— *Field Marshal Sir Henry Wilson: A Political Soldier* pbk edn: (Oxford, 2008)

—— 'The First World War and the Rising: mode, moment and memory', in Gabriel Doherty and Dermot Keogh (eds), *1916: The Long Revolution* (Cork, 2007), pp. 86–101

—— *The GPO and the Easter Rising* (Dublin, 2006)

—— 'Ireland and Gallipoli', in Jenny Macleod (ed.), *Gallipoli: Making History* (London, 2004), pp. 98–109

—— *Ireland and the Great War* (Cambridge, 2000)

—— 'The Irish military tradition and the British empire', in Keith Jeffery (ed.), *'An Irish empire'? Aspects of Ireland and the British Empire* (Manchester, 1996), pp. 94–122

—— 'Kruger's farmers, Strathcona's Horse, Sir George Clarke's camels and the Kaiser's battleships: the impact of the South African War on imperial defence', in Donal Lowry (ed.), *The South African War Reappraised* (Manchester, 2000), pp. 188–202

—— *MI6: The History of the Secret Intelligence Service, 1909–1949* (pbk edn: London, 2011)

Jensen, Kimberly, *Mobilizing Minerva: American Women in the First World War* (Urbana ILL, 2008)

Jingoes, Stimela Jason, *A Chief is a Chief by the People* (London, 1975)

Johnstone, Tom, *Orange, Green and Khaki: The Story of the Irish Regiments in the Great War, 1914–18* (Dublin, 1992)

Jones, Adrian, 'A note on Atatürk's words about Gallipoli', *History Australia*, 2/1 (2004), 10-1-10-8

Jonker, Joost, and van Zanden, Jon Luiten, *From Challenge to Joint Industry Leader, 1890–1939: A History of Royal Dutch Shell*, i (Oxford, 2007)

Jünger, Ernst, *Storm of Steel* (Penguin edn: London, 2004)

Kannengiesser Pasha, Hans, *The Campaign in Gallipoli* (London, 1928)

Kedourie, Elie, *In the Anglo-Arab Labyrinth: The McMahon–Husayn Correspondence and Its Interpretations 1914–1939* (Cambridge, 1976)

Kent, D. A., '*The Anzac Book* and the Anzac legend: C. E. W. Bean as editor and image-maker', *Historical Studies*, 21/84 (Apr. 1985), pp. 376–90

Kettle, Thomas, *The Ways of War* (Dublin, 1917)

Khaldidi, Rashid, 'The Arab experience of the war', in Hugh Cecil and Peter Liddle (eds), *Facing Armageddon: The First World War Experienced* (London, 1996), pp. 642–55

Killingray, David, 'Labour exploitation for military campaigns in British colonial Africa 1870–1945', *Journal of Contemporary History*, 24/3 (July 1989), pp. 483–501

Kipling, Rudyard, *The Irish Guards in the Great War: The Second Battalion* (Spellmount edn, Staplehurst, 1997)

Király, Béla K., and Dreisziger, Nándor F., (eds), *East Central European Society in World War I* (Boulder CO, 1985)

Kitchen, Martin, 'The German invasion of Canada in the First World War', *International History Review*, 7/2 (May 1985), pp. 245–60

—— *The Silent Dictatorship: The Politics of the German High Command under Hindenburg and Ludendorff, 1916–1918* (London, 1976)

Kitromilides, Paschalis M. (ed.), *Eleftherios Venizelos: The Trials of Statesmanship* (Edinburgh, 2006)

Knox, Alfred, *With the Russian Army 1914–1917*, ii (London, 1921)

La Motte, Ellen N., *The Backwash of War: The Human Wreckage of the Battlefield as Witnessed by an American Hospital Nurse* (New York, 1916; London 1919; new edn, New York, 1934)

Landau, Henry, *Spreading the Spy Net: The Story of a British Spy Director* (London, n.d. [1938])

Larsen, Daniel, 'British intelligence and American neutrality during the First World War' (unpublished PhD dissertation, University of Cambridge, 2014)

Lavery, John, *The Life of a Painter* (London, 1940)

Lee, Janet, 'A nurse and a soldier: gender, class and national identity in the First World War adventures of Grace McDougall and Flora Sandes', *Women's History Review*, 15/1 (Mar. 2006), pp. 83–103

Lefebvre, Jacques-Henri, *Verdun: la plus grande bataille de l'histoire racontée par les survivants* (Chamery, France, n.d. [2005])

Lenin, V. I., *Collected Works*, xxii, *December 1915–July 1916* (Moscow, 1964)

Lettow-Vorbeck, General von, *My Reminiscences of East Africa* (2nd edn, London, n.d. [1922])

Lieven, Dominic, 'Russia, Europe and World War I', in Acton, Edward, Cherniaev, Vldimir Iu., and Rosenberg, William G. (eds), *Critical Companion to the Russian Revolution 1914–1921* (London, 1997), pp. 37–47

Link, Arthur S. (ed.), *The Papers of Woodrow Wilson*, 69 vols (Princeton, 1966–94)

Liulevicius, Vejas Gabriel, *War Land on the Eastern Front: Culture, National Identity, and German Occupation in World War I* (Cambridge, 2000)

Llewellyn Smith, Michael, 'Venizelos's diplomacy, 1910–23: from Balkan alliance to Greek-Turkish settlement', in Kitromilides (ed.), *Eleftherios Venizelos*, pp. 134–92

Lloyd George, David, *War Memoirs*, ii (London, 1933)

Lucas, E. V., *Outposts of Mercy: The Records of a Visit in November and December 1916 to the Various Units of the British Red Cross in Italy* (London, 1917)

Lunn, Joe, *Memoirs of the Maelstrom: A Senegalese Oral History of the First World War* (Oxford, 1999)

Lurz, Meinhold, *Kriegerdenkmäler in Deutschland*, Band 5 (Heidelberg, 1986)

Lussu, Emilio, *Sardinian Brigade* (Prion edn, London, 2000)

Lyons, J. B., *The Enigma of Tom Kettle: Irish Patriot, Essayist, Poet, British Soldier, 1880–1916* (Dublin, 1983)

McAdoo, William G., *Crowded Years* (Boston, 1931)

Macartney, George, 'Chez les Soviets en Asie centrale', *Journal of the Central Asian Society*, 16/1 (1929), pp. 99–102

McConnell, James R., *Flying for France: With the American Escadrille at Verdun* (Garden City NY, 1917)

MacDonell, Ranald, '... *And Nothing Long*' (London, 1938)

McGarry, Fearghal, *The Rising: Easter 1916* (Oxford, 2010)

McGibbon, Ian, *New Zealand Battlefields and Memorials of the Western Front* (Auckland, 2001)

Mackenzie, Compton, *Ægean Memories* (London, 1940)

——*Extremes Meet* (London, 1928)

——*Gallipoli Memories* (London, 1929)

——*Greek Memories* (University Publications of America edn, [Frederick, MD], 1987)

——*My Life and Times: Octave Five, 1915–1923* and *Octave Seven: 1931–1938* (London, 1966 and 1968)

McLaren, Eva Shaw (ed.), *A History of the Scottish Women's Hospitals* (London, 1919)

Maclean, Chris, and Phillips, Jock, *The Sorrow and the Pride: New Zealand War Memorials* (Wellington, 1990)

Macleod, Jenny, *Reconsidering Gallipoli* (Manchester, 2004)

MacMahon, Bryan, 'Captain Flora Sandes of the Serbian Army', *Irish Sword*, 25/102 (Winter, 2007), pp. 419–36

Macmillan, Harold, *Winds of Change 1914–1939* (London, 1966)

McMillan, James F., *Housewife or Harlot: The Place of Women in French Society 1870–1940* (Brighton, 1981)

MacMunn, Sir George, and Falls, Cyril, *Military Operations Egypt and Palestine*, i, *From the Outbreak of War with Germany to June 1917* (London, 1928)

Mango, Andrew, *Atatürk* (pbk edn, London, 2001)

Marder, Arthur J., *From the Dreadnought to Scapa Flow: The Royal Navy in the Fisher Era, 1904–1919*, iii, *Jutland and After* (London, 1966)

Martin, F. X., *The Irish Volunteers, 1913–1915* (Dublin, 1963)

Massock, Richard G., *Italy from Within* (London, 1943)

Melman, Billie, 'Re-generation: nation and the construction of gender in peace and war – Palestine Jews, 1900–1918', in eadem (ed.), *Borderlines: Genders and Identities in War and Peace, 1870–1930* (London, 1998), pp. 121–40

Middlebrook, Martin, *The First Day on the Somme* (Penguin edn, London, 2001)

Miles, Wilfrid, *Military Operations France and Belgium, 1916*, ii (London, 1938)

Ministère de la Guerre, *Les Armées Françaises dans la Grande Guerre*, Tome VIII, i, *La campagne d'Orient, jusqu'à l'intervention de la Roumanie (février 1915–août 1916* (Paris, 1924)

Mitchell, T. J., and Smith, G. M., *Medical Services: Casualties and Medical Statistics of the Great War* (London, 1933)

Mitrović, Andrej, *Serbia's Great War 1914–1918* (London, 2007)

Mizzi, John A., *Gallipoli: the Malta Connection* (Luqa, Malta, 1991)

Moberly, F. J., *The Campaign in Mesopotamia, 1914–1918*, ii and iii (London, 1924 and 1925)

Morrow Jr, John H., 'The war in the air', in John Horne (ed.), *A Companion to World War I* (pbk edn, Oxford, 2012)

Mosley, Leonard, *Duel for Kilimanjaro: An Account of the East African Campaign, 1914–1918* (London, n.d. [1963])

Mulgan, Alan, *The Making of a New Zealander* (Wellington, 1958)

Mussolini, Benito, *My Autobiography* (rev. edn, London, 1939)

Mwakikagile, Godfrey, *Life in Tanganyika in the Fifties* ([Grand Rapids MI], 2006)

Nasson, Bill, *Springboks on the Somme: South Africa in the Great War 1914–1918* (Johannesburg, 2007)

—— 'War opinion in South Africa, 1914', *Journal of Imperial and Commonwealth History*, 23/2 (1995), pp. 248–76

Neiberg, Michael S., *Fighting the Great War: A Global History* (Cambridge MA, 2005)

Neilson, Keith, *Britain and the Last Tsar: British Policy and Russia, 1894–1917* (Oxford, 1995)

—— '"Joy rides"? British intelligence and propaganda in Russia, 1914–1917', *Historical Journal*, 24/4 (1981), pp. 885–906

—— *Strategy and Supply: the Anglo-Russian Alliance, 1914–17*, (London, 1984)

O'Halpin, Eunan, 'British intelligence in Ireland, 1914–1921', in Christopher Andrew and David Dilks (eds), *The Missing Dimension: Governments and Intelligence Communities in the Twentieth Century* (London, 1983), pp. 54–77

Omissi, David, *Indian Voices of the Great War: Soldiers' Letters, 1914–1918* (Basingstoke, 1999)

—— *The Sepoy and the Raj: The Indian Army, 1860–1940* (Manchester, 1994)

Orr, Philip, *The Road to the Somme: Men of the Ulster Division Tell their Story* (Belfast, 1987)

Osborne, Eric W., *Britain's Economic Blockade of Germany 1914–1919* (London, 2004)

Ó Síocháin, Séamas, *Roger Casement: Imperialist, Rebel, Revolutionary* (Dublin, 2007)

Osuntokun, Akinjide, *Nigeria in the First World War* (London, 1979)

Ousby, Ian, *The Road to Verdun: France, Nationalism and the First World War* (London, 2002)

Pacyga, Dominic A., *Chicago: A Biography* (Chicago, 2009)

Page, Melvin E., 'The war of thangata: Nyasaland and the East African campaign, 1914–1918', *Journal of African History*, 19/1 (1978), pp. 87–100

Paice, Edward, *Tip and Run: The Untold Tragedy of the Great War in Africa* (London, 2007)

Pares, Bernard, *My Russian Memoirs* (London, 1931)

Paseta, Senia, *Irish Nationalist Women, 1900–1918* (Cambridge, 2013)

Patterson, J. H., *With the Judeans in the Palestine Campaign* (London, 1922)

—— *With the Zionists in Gallipoli* (London, 1916)

Pearton, Maurice, *Oil and the Romanian State* (Oxford, 1971)

Pennell, Catriona, *A Kingdom United: Popular Responses to the Outbreak of the First World War in Britain and Ireland* (Oxford, 2012)

Perrett, Bryan, and Lord, Anthony, *The Czar's British Squadron* (London, 1981)

Pesek, Michael, 'The colonial order upside down? British and Germans in East African prisoner-of-war camps during World War I', in Ulrike Lindner et al. (eds), *Hybrid Cultures — Nervous States: Britain and Germany in a (Post) Colonial World* (Amsterdam, 2010), pp. 23–41

Pézard, André, *Nos autres à Vauquois 1915–1916* (new edn, Nancy, 1992)

Philpott, William, *Bloody Victory: The Sacrifice on the Somme* (Abacus edn, London, 2010)

Pidgeon, Trevor, *The Tanks at Flers: An Account of the First Use of Tanks in War at the Battle of Flers-Courcelette, The Somme, 15th September 1916*, 2 vols (Cobham, 1995)

Pierce, Richard A., *Russian Central Asia, 1867–1917: A Study in Colonial Rule* (Berkeley CA, 1960)

Pirenne, Henri, *La Belgique et la guerre mondiale* (Paris, n.d. [1928])

Plaatje, Sol. T., *Native Life in South Africa* (London 2nd edn, n.d. [1916])

Polonsky, Antony, 'The German occupation of Poland during the First and Second World Wars: a comparison', in Roy A. Prete and A. Hamish Ion (eds), *Armies of Occupation* (Waterloo ONT, 1984), pp. 97–142

Popplewell, Richard J., *Intelligence and Imperial Defence: British Intelligence and the Defence of the Indian Empire, 1904–1924* (London, 1995)

Prasad, Yuvaraj Deva, *The Indian Muslims and World War I* (New Delhi, 1985)

Price, M. Philips, *My Three Revolutions* (London, 1969)

—— *War and Revolution in Asiatic Russia* (London, 1918)

Prior, Robin, *Gallipoli: The End of the Myth* (New Haven, 2009)

—— and Wilson, Trevor, *The Somme* (Sydney, 2005)

Proctor, Tammy M., 'Missing in action: Belgian civilians and the First World War', in *Revue Belge d'Histoire Contemporaine*, 35/4 (2005), pp. 547–69

—— *Female Intelligence: Women and Espionage in the First World War* (New York, 2003)

Prost, Antoine, 'La guerre de 1914 n'est pas perdue', in *Le Mouvement Social*, no. 199 (2002), pp. 95–119

Pugsley, Christopher, *Gallipoli: The New Zealand story* (Auckland, 1990)

Ramnath, Maia, *Haj to Utopia: How the Ghadar Movement Charted Global Radicalisation and Attempted to Overthrow the British Empire* (Stanford CA, 2011)

Ramsey, Bruce, *Unsanctioned Voice: Garet Garrett, Journalist of the Old Right* (Caldwell ID, 2008)

Reed, John, *The War in Eastern Europe* (New York, 1916)

Rhodes James, Robert, *Gallipoli* (London, 1965)

Rochat, 'The Italian Front, 1915–18', in Horne (ed.), *A Companion to World War I*, pp. 82–96

Rogger, Hans, *Russia in the Age of Modernisation and Revolution, 1881–1917* (London, 1983)

Ross, Stewart Halsey, *Propaganda for War: How the United States was Conditioned to Fight the Great War of 1914–1918* (Progressive Press edn, Joshua Tree CA, 2009)

Rothenberg, Gunther E., *The Army of Francis Joseph* (West Lafayette IN, 1976)

Samson, Anne, *World War I in Africa: The Forgotten Conflict among the European Powers* (London, 2013)

Sanborn, Joshua A., *Drafting the Russian Nation: Military Conscription, Total War, and Mass Politics, 1905–1925* (DeKalb ILL, 2003)

—— 'Unsettling the empire: violent migrations and social disaster in Russia during World War I', *Journal of Modern History*, 77/2 (June, 2005), pp. 290–324

Sanders, Liman von, *Five Years in Turkey* (Annapolis MD, 1927)

Sandes, Flora, *An English Woman-Sergeant in the Serbian Army* (London, 1916)

—— *Autobiography of a Woman Soldier: A Brief Record of Adventure with the Serbian Army, 1916–1919* (London, 1927)

Sandford, Stephen, *Neither Unionist nor Nationalist: The 10th (Irish) Division in the Great War* (Salins, Co. Kildare, 2015)

Satia, Priya, *Spies in Arabia: The Great War and the Cultural Foundations of Britain's Covert Empire in the Middle East* (New York, 2008)

Şaul, Mahir, and Royer, Patrick, *West African Challenge to Empire: Culture and History in the Volta-Bani Anticolonial War* (Oxford, 2001)

Schatkowski Schilcher, Linda, 'The famine of 1915–1918 in Greater Syria', in John P. Spagnolo (ed.), *Problems of the Modern Middle East in Historical Perspective: Essays in Honour of Albert Hourani* (Reading, 1992), pp. 230–58

Scheer, Admiral, *Germany's High Sea Fleet in the World War* (London, 1920)

Schindler, John R., *Isonzo: The Forgotten Sacrifice of the Great War* (London, 2001)

Seabrook, William B., *Jungle Ways* (London, 1931)

Sexton, Timothy D., 'Anglo-Japanese naval cooperation, 1914–1918', *Naval War College Review*, 53/1 (Winter, 2000), pp. 62–92

Sheffield, Gary, *Forgotten Victory: The First World War: Myths and Realities* (Review edn, London, 2002)

Shefthall, Mark David, *Altered Memories of the Great War: Divergent Narratives of Britain, Australia, New Zealand and Canada* (London, 2009)

Silvester, Victor, *Dancing is My Life: An Autobiography* (London, 1958)

Simkins, Peter, *Kitchener's Army: The Raising of the New Armies, 1914–1916* (Manchester, 1988)

6th Connaught Rangers Research Project, *The 6th Connaught Rangers: Belfast Nationalists and the Great War* (2nd edn, Belfast, 2011)

Skrine, C. P., and Nightingale, Pamela, *Macartney at Kashgar: New Light on British, Chinese and Russian Activities in Sinkiang, 1890–1918* (London, 1973)

Smith, Leonard V., *The Embattled Self: French Soldiers' Testimony of the Great War* (Ithaca, NY, 2007)

—— Audoin-Rouzeau, Stéphane, and Becker, Annette, *France and the Great War 1914–1918* (Cambridge, 2003)

Smith, Michael, *Six: A History of Britain's Secret Intelligence Service Part 1: Murder and Mayhem, 1909–1939* (London, 2010)

Smith, Ralph, 'Opposition to French rule in Vietnam', *Past & Present*, 54 (1972), pp. 104–112

Smith, Richard, *Jamaican Volunteers in the First World War: Race, Masculinity and the Development of National Consciousness* (Manchester, 2004)

Smithson, Annie M. P., *The Marriage of Nurse Harding* (Dublin, 1935)

[Smyly, Vivienne], 'Experiences of a VAD', *Blackwoods Magazine*, 200 (July–Dec. 1916), pp. 814–40

Sokol, Edward Dennis, *The Revolt of 1916 in Russian Central Asia* (Baltimore, 1954)

Sondhaus, Lawrence, *In the Service of the Emperor: Italians in the Austrian Armed Forces 1814–1918* (Boulder CO, 1990)

Spanton, Ernest F., *In German Gaols: A Narrative of Two Years' Captivity in German East Africa* (London, 1917)

Speed III, Richard B., *Prisoners, Diplomats and the Great War: A Study in the Diplomacy of Captivity* (Westport CON, 1990)

Spence, Richard B., 'Englishmen in New York: the SIS American Station, 1915–21', *Intelligence and National Security*, 19/3 (Autumn, 2001), pp. 511–37

—— 'The Yugoslav role in the Austro-Hungarian army, 1914–18', in Király and Dreisziger (eds), *East Central European Society*, pp. 354–65

Starling, John, and Lee, Ivor, *No Labour, No Battle: Military Labour during the First World War* (Stroud, Glos., 2009)

Stevenson, David, *The First World War and International Politics* (Oxford, 1988)

Stibbe, Matthew (ed.), *Captivity, Forced Labour and Forced Migration in Europe During the First World War* (London, 2009)

Stiénon, Charles, 'L'effondement colonial de l'Allemagne', *Revue des deux mondes*, (Apr. 1917), pp. 645–84

Stone, Norman, *The Eastern Front, 1914–1917* (London, 1975)

Stovall, Tyler, 'Colour-blind France? Colonial workers during the First World War', *Race and Class*, 35/2 (Oct.–Dec. 1993), pp. 35–55

—— 'The color line behind the lines: racial violence in France during the Great War', *American Historical Review*, 103/3 (June 1998), pp. 737–69

Strachan, Hew, *The First World War*, i, *To Arms* (Oxford, 2001)

—— *The First World War in Africa* (Oxford, 2004)

Sugarman, Martin, 'The Zion Muleteers of Gallipoli', (https://www.jewishvirtuallibrary.org/jsource/History/gallipoli.html) (accessed 27 Oct. 2013)

Summerskill, Michael, *China on the Western Front: Britain's Chinese Work Force in the First World War* (London, 1982)

Susmel, Edoardo and Duilio (eds), *Opera Omnia di Benito Mussolini*, xxix (Florence, 1959)

Svoljšak, Petra, *The Front on Soča* (Ljubljana, 2002)

Talbot, F. E. G., *The 14th King George's Own: The 1st Battalion (K.G.O.) (Ferozepore Sikhs), the 11th Sikh Regiment* (London, 1937)

Tarrant, V. E., *Jutland: The German Perspective* (London, 1995)

Taylor, A. J. P., *The Habsburg Monarchy 1815–1918* (London, 1941)

Temple Patterson, A. (ed.), *The Jellicoe Papers*, ii, *1916–1935* (London, 1968)

Thiel, Jens, 'Between recruitment and forced labour: the radicalization of German labour policy in occupied Belgium and northern France', *First World War Studies*, 4/1 (2013)

Thompson, Elizabeth, *Colonial Citizens: Republican Rights, Paternal Privilege, and Gender in French Syria and Lebanon* (New York, 2000)

Thompson, John A., *Woodrow Wilson* (Harlow, 2002)

Thompson, Mark, *The White War: Life and Death on the Italian Front, 1915–1919* (London, 2008)

Thornton, A. P., 'Rivalries in the Mediterranean, the Middle East and Egypt', in F. H. Hinsley (ed.), *New Cambridge Modern History*, xi, *Material Progress and World-wide Problems, 1870–98* (Cambridge, 1970), pp. 567–92

Thornton, Leonard, 'Echoes of Gallipoli', in Gilbert (ed.), *The Straits of War*, pp. 109–21

Thwaites, Norman, *Velvet and Vinegar* (London, 1932)

Tooze, Adam, *The Deluge: The Great War and the Remaking of Global Order, 1916–1931* (London, 2014)

Torrey, Glenn E., *Romania and World War I: A Collection of Studies* (Oxford, 1998)

—(ed.), *General Henri Berthelot and Romania: Mémoires et Correspondence 1916–1919* (New York, 1987)

Tounda-Fergadi, Areti, 'The Serbian troops on Corfu: the problem of transporting them to Thessaloniki and Greek public opinion on the affair', in *Proceedings of the Fifth Greek–Serbian Symposium, 9–12 October 1987* (Thessaloniki, 1991), pp. 29–44

Townshend, Charles, *Easter 1916: The Irish Rebellion* (London, 2005)

—*Political Violence in Ireland: Government and Resistance since 1848* (Oxford, 1983)

—*When God Made Hell: The British Invasion of Mesopotamia and the Creation of Iraq 1914–1921* (London, 2010)

Trevelyan, G. M., *Scenes from Italy's War* (London, 1919)

Tumelty, Joseph P., *Woodrow Wilson as I Know Him* (New York, 1924)

Vanthemsche, Guy, *Belgium and the Congo, 1885–1980* (Cambridge, 2012)

Vassal, Joseph, *Uncensored Letters from the Dardanelles* (London, 1916)

Vincent-Smith, John, 'Britain, Portugal, and the First World War, 1914–16', *European Studies Review* 4/3 (1974), pp. 207–38

Wakefield, Alan, and Moody, Simon, *Under the Devil's Eye: The British Military Experience in Macedonia, 1915–1918* (Barnsley, 2011)

Walker, Stephen, *Forgotten Soldiers: The Irishmen Shot at Dawn* (Dublin, 2007)

Warth, Trobert D., *Nicholas II: The Life and Reign of Russia's Last Monarch* (Westport CON, 1997)

Washburn, Stanley, *Field Notes from the Russian Front* (London, n.d. [1915])

—*On the Russian Front in World War 1: Memoirs of an American War Correspondent* (New York, 1982)

—*The Russian Campaign: April to August, 1915* (London, n.d. [1915])

—*The Russian Offensive* (London, 1917)

Watson, Alexander, *Enduring the Great War: Combat, Morale and Collapse in the German and British Armies, 1914–1918* (Cambridge, 2008)

Wedd, A. F. (ed.), *German Students' War Letters* (London, 1929)

Westerhoff, Christian, '"A kind of Siberia": German labour and occupation policies in Poland and Lithuania during the First World War', in *First World War Studies*, 4/1 (2013), pp. 51–63

Whitlock, Brand, *Belgium under the German Occupation: A Personal Narrative*, 2 vols (London, 1919)

Whittall, William, *With Botha and Smuts in Africa* (London, 1917)

Wilcox, Vanda, 'Discipline in the Italian army, 1915–1918', in Pierre Purseigle (ed.), *Warfare and Belligerence: Perspectives in First World War Studies* (Leiden, 2005), pp. 73–100

Willan, B. P., 'The South African Native Labour Contingent, 1916–1918', in *Journal of African History*, 19/1 (1978), pp. 61–86

Williams, Francis, *A Prime Minister Remembers* (London, 1961)

Williams, Orlo, 'The evacuation of the Dardanelles', *National Review*, 74/443 (Jan. 1920), pp. 652–68

Winslow, Carroll Dana, *With the French Flying Corps* (New York, 1917)

Winter, Jay, *Sites of Memory, Sites of Mourning* (Cambridge, 1995)

— (ed.), *The Cambridge History of the First World War*, 3 vols: i, *Global War*; ii, *The State*; iii, *Civil Society* (Cambridge, 2014)

Wylly, H. C., *Neill's 'Blue Caps'*, iii, *1914–1922* (Aldershot, n.d. [?1924])

Xu, Guoqi, *China and the Great War* (Cambridge, 2005)

— *Strangers on the Western Front: Chinese Workers on the Western Front* (Cambridge MA, 2011)

Yaney, George, *The World of the Manager: Food Administration in Berlin During World War I* (New York, 1994)

Yearwood, Peter J., '"In a casual way with a blue pencil": British policy and the partition of Kamerun, 1914–1919', *Canadian Journal of African Studies*, 27/2 (1993), pp. 218–44

Yong, Tan Tai, *The Garrison State: The Military Government and Society in Colonial Punjab, 1849–1947* (New Delhi, 2005)

Young, Geoffrey Winthrop, *The Grace of Forgetting* (London, 1953)

Yovanovitch, Draglioub, *Les effets économiques et sociaux de la guerre en Serbie* (Paris, n.d. [1930])

Zieger, Susan, 'She didn't raise her boy to be a slacker: motherhood, conscription, and the culture of the First World War', *Feminist Studies*, 22/1 (Spring, 1996), pp. 6–39

Ziino, Bart, *A Distant Grief: Australians, War Graves and the Great War* (Crawley WA, 2007)

—(ed.), *Remembering the First World War* (Abingdon, 2015)

Zinoman, Peter, *The Colonial Bastille: A History of Imprisonment in Vietnam, 1862–1940* (Berkeley CA, 2001)

Acknowledgements

Like all historical projects, this book depends on the hard work and willing assistance of a host of friends, fellow historians and other dedicated professionals. In the first place I must thank my colleagues and students in the School of History and Anthropology at Queen's University Belfast who provide such a stimulating and supportive environment in which to work. Among them I must give special mention to Stewart Aveyard, Paul Corthorn, Peter Gray, David Hayton, Andrew Holmes, Fearghal McGarry, Sean O'Connell and Alex Titov, as well as Frances Mercer, whose unflappable efficiency and good humour is a lesson to us all. My PhD students Emily Robinson and Stephen Sandford kept me on my intellectual toes. I am grateful to the School for granting me research leave for the academic year 2013–14, and to Trinity College Cambridge for electing me to a Visiting Fellow Commonership during this period, which combined space, time and opportunity for research and reflection when I wrote most of the book. The Trinity College community made me one of their own and I would especially like to thank Boyd Hilton, Dominic Lieven, David McKitterick, and, above all Anil Seal, for their collegial companionship and conversation. Among others in Cambridge who helped me along the way were Andrew Arsan, Eugenio Biagini, Eamon Duffy, Howard Hughes and William O'Reilly. Friends who provided hospitality included Chris and Jenny Andrew, Lindsay Duguid and

John Murray-Browne, Edwin and Hilary Green, Robin Smyth and Francesca Conti, and David and June Gould who marvellously put up with us for three months while we looked for a new home in Belfast and I endeavoured to complete the book.

I owe an enormous debt to the custodians of libraries and archives which provide much of the vital raw material upon which historians depend. For many years I have found the Cambridge University Library to be both a scholarly haven and an unparalleled treasure trove of information and inspiration. Closer to home, the wonderful new library of Queen's University (and especially the inter-library loan staff) has been an essential resource. My thanks also go to the staff of those other archives and repositories mentioned in the reference notes.

Many individuals have helped in a variety of ways, providing information, support and often going out of their way to chase up fugitive references that I may only imperfectly have communicated to them. These include Tom Bartlett, Sophie De Schaepdrijver, Stefan Goebel, John Gooch, John Horne, Yvonne McEwan, Laurie Milner, Jock Phillips, Mark Seaman and Peter Stanley. What particularly distinguishes them is the willingness with which they were generously prepared to share their knowledge, an inclination to which we all should aspire.

Bill Hamilton has been a constant and cheerful ally, and the staff at my publishers, Bloomsbury – especially Michael Fishwick, Anna Simpson, Greg Heinimann and Kate Johnson – have been exemplary in every way.

Finally, I have to thank my immediate family: Ben and Alex for help at crucial moments and Sally Visick (as always) for constant support.

K.J., February 2015

Index

A Note on the Type

The text of this book is set in Linotype Stempel Garamond, a version of Garamond adapted and first used by the Stempel foundry in 1924. It is one of several versions of Garamond based on the designs of Claude Garamond. It is thought that Garamond based his font on Bembo, cut in 1495 by Francesco Griffo in collaboration with the Italian printer Aldus Manutius. Garamond types were first used in books printed in Paris around 1532. Many of the present-day versions of this type are based on the *Typi Academiae* of Jean Jannon cut in Sedan in 1615.

Claude Garamond was born in Paris in 1480. He learned how to cut type from his father and by the age of fifteen he was able to fashion steel punches the size of a pica with great precision. At the age of sixty he was commissioned by King Francis I to design a Greek alphabet, and for this he was given the honourable title of royal type founder. He died in 1561.